Martin Heidegger and the Question of Literature

Toward a
Postmodern Literary Hermeneutics

Edited by WILLIAM V. SPANOS

Indiana University Press
BLOOMINGTON • LONDON

3 1940

First cloth edition published by Indiana University Press 1979

Copyright © 1976 by *boundary 2*

Library of Congress Cataloging in Publication Data
Main entry under title:
Martin Heidegger and the question of literature.
  (Studies in Phenomenology and existential philosophy)
  Includes bibliographical references.
  1. Heidegger, Martin, 1889-1976 — Addresses, essays, lectures. 2. Hermeneutics—Addresses, essays, lectures. 3. Literature—Philosophy—Addresses, essays, lectures. I. Spanos, William V.
B3279.H49M285 801'.9 79-84261 ISBN 0-253-17575-5

1 2 3 4 5 83 82 81 80 79

For Margaret,
carefully

CONTENTS

**Martin Heidegger
and the
Question of Literature**

MARTIN HEIDEGGER AND THE QUESTION OF LITERATURE:

A Preface

Conscience manifests itself as the call of care: the caller is Dasein, which, in its throwness (in its Being-already-in), is anxious about its potentiality-for-Being. The one to whom the appeal is made is this very same Dasein, summoned to its ownmost potentiality-for-Being (ahead of itself...). Dasein is falling into the "they" (in Being-already-alongside the world of its concern), and it is summoned out of this falling by the appeal. The call of conscience . . . has its ontological possibility in the fact that Dasein, in the very basis of its Being, is care.

—Martin Heidegger, *Being and Time*

You see I can't get away from the old measure of care.

—Charles Olson, "Letter 5,"
The Maximus Poems

Martin Heidegger's philosophical thought has been a guiding presence on the European continent for half a century, having influenced virtually every area of the human sciences from psychology to art in what must be called a revolutionary way. And, yet, a meaningful understanding of the enormous importance of his thinking, especially of his unmethodical methodological impulse, which informs the more immediately appealing "existential analytic" in *Being and Time (Sein und Zeit,* 1927) and his later ontological meditations in such texts as *Holzwege* (1936-46), *Vorträge und Aufsätze* (1936-53), *Gelassenheit* (1944-55), and *Unterwegs zur Sprache* (1950-59), is still limited in the United States and England to a small community of philosophers who have responded to the crisis of the human sciences. This is the case despite the important ground broken by the American schools of theology, above all by Union Theological Seminary during the postwar (Tillichean) period, and, more recently, by publishers such as Harper and Row and Northwestern University Press, which have made translations of this work and commentary on it available to Anglo-American scholars.

It is true, of course, that along with the recent emergence of a sense of the crisis of knowledge, Heidegger's presence is now coming to be felt, however tentatively, by some American scholars professing the other humanities, especially literary studies. But this Heidegger, by and large, is the one appropriated, by way of Friedrich Nietzsche, by the French philosopher Jacques Derrida and the Belgian literary critic Paul de Man and their followers — critics such as J. Hillis Miller, Joseph N. Riddel, Eugenio Donato, Samuel Weber, among others. He is, in other words, the deconstructed Heidegger, "saved" from the metaphysics that, according to them, it was his project to de-center and surpass, but which he failed to accomplish. He is the "post-Structuralist" Heidegger, who, finally, points the way to deconstructive literary criticism, the free-play of a de-centered *écriture* against the logocentric *parole.* However viable this appropriation of Heideggerian thought may be — and the essays by Joseph N. Riddel, Frances C. Ferguson, Donald G. Marshall, and Stanley Corngold suggest that it is indeed viable — the fact remains that Heidegger's work itself has not "spoken" to American literary critics directly. It is, therefore, the purpose of this "gathering" of essays not only to introduce Heidegger's destructive hermeneutic thinking as it pertains to the question of literary interpretation and criticism to the serious writers, readers, interpreters, and critics of literature in the English-speaking world, but also to suggest, by way of example, some of the significant aspects of the problematic distinction — not yet made explicit, as far as I know — between the phenomenological Heidegger and the post-Structuralist Heidegger, that is, between the "destructive" and "deconstructive" possibilities for literary hermeneutics that his thought has opened up.

But the purposes of this gathering go deeper than merely to

introduce to the Anglo-American literary community another provocative voice contributing to the current dialogue on the philosophy of literature. Heidegger's *Destruktion* of what he has called the Western onto-theo-logical tradition as it developed from his masterpiece *Being and Time* to his later meditations on poetic language as the saying of being was, despite the well-known problematic "turn" *(Kehre)* after *Being and Time,* a continuing explorative effort to overcome what Husserl, before him, called the "crisis of European thought," generated by the hardening of ontological inquiry. For in fulfilling its informing imperative to perceive *meta-ta-physica* (from after or beyond or above things-as-they-are) or, to use the significantly analogous rhetoric valorized by Modernist literary criticism, to spatialize temporality, the metaphysical tradition "comes to its end" in the modern period—the time of the world picture *(Weltbild),* as Heidegger aptly calls our de-temporalized age of technology in the essay that introduces this volume. More specifically, in fulfilling its historical mission in the triumph of technological method, that is, in succeeding by way of re-presentation *(Vorstellung)* to Enframe *(ge-stellen) physis* and thus virtually to transform the earth *(die Erde)* into standing reserve *(Bestand),* metaphysics finally succeeds in imposing its will to power over being or rather the *be-ing* of being.[1] To adapt Michel Foucault's useful rhetoric to Heidegger's project, in initially assuming the privileged status of the en-compassing eye in the pursuit of truth, metaphysics finally becomes in the modern period a self-generating, in-clusive, and monolithic *discourse* that does not simply *over-look* the "truth" of temporal process but, in fact, *super-vises* panoptically, as it were, the difference generated by the temporality of being and thus coerces the "text" of existence into an abiding Identity or Presence.[2] Metaphysics as discourse or, in Gadamer's term, as method, thus comes "full circle." It "achieves" the re-collective — and recuperative — dream of Western philosophers from Plato through Augustine to Descartes, Hegel, and Bentham: the forgetting of being *(die Seinsvergessenheit)* — and the "accomplishment" of what Heidegger, alluding to the logocentric myth inscribed in all the supplements of the ontotheological tradition, refers to as Western man's "spirit of revenge" against the "transience of [fallen] time."[3]

In thus remembering the be-ing of being that a recollective panoptic metaphysics "forgets" or, to use another important Heideggerian metaphor, in dis-covering the be-ing of being from the oblivion in which a fulfilled metaphysics and its calculative measure has buried it, Heidegger's destructive/projective thought appears more and more, we are beginning to recognize, like a Copernician Revolution. It is in this sense that his paradoxical hermeneutic project "to surpass" *(überwinden)* the metaphysical tradition by way of a demystification of the *logos* and retrieval or repetition *(Wiederholung)* of ontological beginnings (not as "absolute origin" but in the sense of "in-the-midst," of "occasion," as it were) can be called postmodern.

As such, it seems to me — and, in various degrees of explicitness, to all the other contributors to this volume — Heidegger's thought, especially on human understanding and linguistic interpretation, constitutes a remarkable parallel in recent philosophical inquiry to the essential formal activity of contemporary, or what is now coming to be called, however problematically, "postmodern," literature. I am referring, of course — to name only the most obvious — to fiction such as Samuel Beckett's *Watt,* Jorge Luis Borges' *Ficciones,* John Barth's *Lost in the Funhouse,* Thomas Pynchon's *Gravity's Rainbow,* Donald Barthelme's *The Dead Father;* to plays such as Beckett's *Waiting for Godot,* Eugène Ionesco's *Victims of Duty,* Jean Genet's *The Blacks,* Harold Pinter's *The Homecoming,* Tom Stoppard's *Rosencrantz and Guildenstern Are Dead;* and to poetry such as Wallace Stevens's "An Ordinary Evening in New Haven," William Carlos Williams's *Paterson,* Charles Olson's *The Maximus Poems,* Robert Creeley's *Pieces,* Edward Dorn's *Gunslinger,* and A. R. Ammons's *Tape for the Turn of the Year.* For, like Heidegger's destructive hermeneutics, this is, in the phrase Wallace Stevens appropriates from Simone Weil, a "decreative" literature.[4] It is a literature, in other words, that simultaneously destroys the received forms (and their rhetorics) inherited from the Tradition — forms that are recognized as agencies of the general will to power deeply inscribed in the Western mind — and, in the process, dis-closes or opens up projective possibilities for a "new" poetics, a poetics of and for our *occasion.*

As in the case of Heidegger's thought, the emergent "measure" of this "postmodern" poetics is not, as it is in the poetics of the tradition, modeled on a music that has its ultimate source in a centered universe. It is not, for example, the stately, ceremonial, and predictable measure of the Elizabethan poet Sir John Davies:

> Dancing, bright Lady, then began to be,
> When the first seeds, whereof the world did spring,
> The fire, air, earth, and water did agree,
> By Love's persuasions nature's mighty king,
> To leave their first disorder'd combating,
>   And in a dance such measure to observe
>   As all the world their motions should preserve.
>
> ("Orchestra")

Nor is it the nostalgic and distancing "Byzantine" measure of the Modern poet W. B. Yeats — the ego-centric measure, that is, of the *polis* of Art that becomes the *supplément* of the old logocentric measure of the *Civitas Dei:*

Once out of nature I shall never take
My bodily form from any natural thing,
But such a form as Grecian goldsmiths make
Of hammered gold and gold enamelling
To keep a drowsy Emperor awake;
Or set upon a golden bough to sing
To lords and ladies of Byzantium
Of what is past, or passing, or to come.

("Sailing to Byzantium")

It is, rather, the de-centered and generous measure enacted in the following passage from Charles Olson's *The Maximus Poems* — a measure that, like Heidegger's (as the allusion to Heraclitus suggests), "owes" much to the pre-Socratics:

I have had to learn the simplest things
last. Which made for difficulties.
Even at sea I was slow, to get the hand out, or to cross
a wet deck.
        The sea was not, finally, my trade.
But even my trade, at it, I stood estranged
from that which was most familiar . . . .

I have made dialogues,
have discussed ancient texts,
have thrown what light I could, offered
what pleasures
doceat allows

        But the known?
This, I have had to be given,
a life, love, and from one man
the world.

        Tokens.
        But sitting here
        I look out as a wind
        and water man, testing
        and missing
        some proof. . . .

        It is undone business
        I speak of, this morning,
        with the sea
        stretching out
        from my feet

("Maximus, to himself")

xiii

In a phrase of Robert Creeley's that echoes Wallace Stevens, its measure is "the measure of its occasion."[5] That is, as the etymology suggests — from *occasus* ("the setting of the sun"), which, with the word "case," ultimately derives from the ablative form of *cadere* ("to fall," "to drop," as of the setting of heavenly bodies, and "to fall," "to perish," "to die") — it is, whether it takes the form of the *periplus* of Olson's poetry or the "free-play" of Beckett's prose, the ec-centric measure of mortality or, in Heidegger's rhetoric, of "dwelling" in the context of mortality:

> Poetry is presumably a high and special kind of measuring. But there is more. Perhaps we have to pronounce the sentence, "Poetry is a *measuring,*" with a different stress. *"Poetry* is a measuring." In poetry there takes place what all measuring is in the ground of its being. Hence it is necessary to pay heed to the basic act of measuring. That consists in man's first of all taking the measure which then is applied in every measuring act. In poetry the taking of measure occurs. To write poetry is measure-taking, understood in the strict sense of the word, by which man first receives the measure for the breadth of his being. Man exists as a mortal. He is called mortal because he can die. To be able to die means: to be capable of death as death. Only man dies — and indeed continually, so long as he stays on this earth, so long as he dwells. His dwelling, however, rests on the poetic. Hölderlin sees the nature of the "poetic" in the taking of the measure by which the measure-taking of human being is accomplished.[6]

As such, it is the primordial measure of the West, of the *Abendland* — a *westering* measure, as it were — gradually forgotten since Homer and Heraclitus (according to both Heidegger and Olson, postmodern thinker and poet) in the hardening process that has characterized the history of the ontotheological tradition. (Derrida, it should be pointed out, does not subscribe to this projective "step back" to the pre-Socratics, claiming that they — and thus Heidegger — are "within the lineage of the logos" insofar as they posit the "original and essential link" between *logos* and *phone* [voice].[7] This is, of course, the basis of a crucial difference between a Derridean deconstructive and a Heideggerian destructive interpretive stance toward literary texts, the problematics of which are clearly suggested in the following essays.) For another etymological root of "occasion" is, of course, the cognate *occidere* (which "means" both "to fall," especially "to set" or "to wester," as in the case of the "movement" of the sun, and "to die," "to perish") from the present participle of which *(occidens)* the English word "occident" derives.[8]

Given, therefore, the continuing authority of the formalist interpretive orientation of the New Criticism in literary studies and broader semiotic contexts — an authority in the process of being, not superseded as it is misleadingly claimed, but theoretically shored up by Structuralist poetics[9] — Heidegger's project, as these essays variously suggest, has much to teach contemporary literary critics who are responding positively to the crisis of criticism. What it offers is not simply an interpretation of understanding and a rhetoric capable of suggesting what the New Criticism is driven by its enclosed horizon, by the blindness of its insight, as it were, to condemn as manifestations of the "fallacy of imitative form": the experiments in open, or, as I prefer to call them, "dis-closive" or "de-structive," forms of much of the most dynamic and powerful contemporary writing; forms whose mastered irony assigns us as readers to ourselves and activates rather than nullifies consciousness of being-in-the-world as our *case*. As these essays suggest, Heidegger's project also, and perhaps even more importantly, points to modalities of literary hermeneutics capable, in their willingness to remain "in uncertainties, mysteries, doubts, without any irritable reading after fact and reason,"[10] of leading criticism out of the impasse into which the will to power of the metaphysical tradition has driven it. Indeed it promises a re-vitalization of the literary tradition, which, in having become reified, has transformed the originary explorative and/or playful activity of understanding into a secondary or derivative and finally coercive methodological confirmation of unexamined formal and ontological logocentric presuppositions. In Ezra Pound's misunderstood formulation of the postmodern imperative, these essays suggest that Heidegger's destructive/projective hermeneutics promises to "make it [the tradition] new."

For explicitly or implicitly most of the contributors to this volume — whether Heideggerian or Derridean in approach — feel that Western literature or, at least, Western literary criticism, if it has not already come to its end, is moving toward closure as it comes increasingly, like Western philosophy, to assert its will to power over the being of the "text," that is, to fulfill the formalist imperatives of its determining *logos,* the imperatives of a hermeneutics in which Form (Being) is ontologically prior to temporality, Identity to difference, the Word to words. Like Heidegger, therefore, they feel that the time has long since come to call into question — to dis-cover — what Heideggerians call the unexamined privileged status of "metaphysical" or "spatial" presuppositions and Derrideans, the "nostalgic" and "recuperative" logocentric assumptions that silently guide traditional hermeneutics. For they recognize, each in their own way, that these unjustified "givens" have increasingly informed the reading and interpretation of literary texts and the "text" of Western literary history in behalf of the certainty of Identity ever since Aristotle, on the model of his *Metaphysics,* affirmed the plot — the beginning, middle, and determining end *(telos)* — as the primary constitutive element ("the soul, as it were") of the highest form of poetic discourse, and repose — the annulment of the kinetics of anxiety about difference *(catharsis)* — as the end of these recuperative teleological formal strategies.

Put positively, these essayists feel that such an interrogation of the ontological priority of form over temporality — and its innocent rhetoric of closure — in the hermeneutic process, will suggest "new" hermeneutic modalities that are capable of dis-closing and preserving the mystery of the Earth, or in Derrida's brilliant adaptation, the *différance,* which is contained or closed off and annulled within the logocentric circle.[11] For this, it is becoming increasingly clear, is the essential imperative of the de-centered world that, to adapt Heidegger's seminal rhetoric from *Being and Time,* the breaking of the Western epistemological hammer has left postmodern man heir to.

The following essays certainly go far in clarifying the "crisis of criticism" and in dis-closing the disabling lack of logocentric interpretive methodology. In thus interrogating the "tradition," they also suggest, however tentatively, at least two broad ways, "grounded" in a care-ful (as opposed to dis-interested or objective) phenomenological intentionality, by which its logocentrism may be surpassed: the Heideggerian De-struction that retrieves the infinitely open-ended *Seinsfrage,* and the Derridean De-construction that activates the Nietzschean free-play in the void of absence. It must be emphasized that the essays that represent these modalities do not by any means constitute completely developed postmodern hermeneutic strategies. As I understand the examples included in this volume, each has its particular limitation. On the one hand, the Heideggerian destructive mode, as the Derrideans insistently remind us, is always in danger of recuperating the metaphysical *logos* in its tendency to read texts temporally. On the other, the Derridean deconstructive mode, as the Heideggerians insistently imply, is always threatening to recuperate the *logos* of Modernist aestheticism in its tendency to read texts spatially. That is to say, these essays are or should be approached as being "on the way," "forwardings," to borrow, perhaps presumptuously, a phrase the American poet Charles Olson uses to define his own de-centered postmodern voyage of exploration — *his periplus* — in the first of *The Maximus Poems,* "I, Maximus, to You":

(o my lady of good voyage
in whose arm, whose left arm rests
no boy but a carefully carved wood, a painted face, a schooner!
a delicate mast, or bow-spirit for

forwarding
("I, Maximus of Gloucester, to You")

As such, they should, like Heidegger's hermeneutic phenomenology, contribute in a significant way to the emergent postmodern dialogue on poetics, hermeneutics, and literary history that the closure of the Western literary tradition has made a necessity of our time.

This preface, it must be borne in mind, is not intended as an authoritative summary statement of the essential "truth" that informs the apparent diversity of the essays gathered in this volume on Heidegger and the question of literature. Seen as summary — as prefaces to scholarly books usually are — it becomes, in fact, a postface, a vicious re-view that is thus inevitably and necessarily guilty of *over-looking* precisely those differences that make this text the *explorative* — and provocative — process it essentially is. It is intended, rather, to *interest* the reader whose understanding of the crisis of literary criticism is not explicit. It is intended, that is, as a plunge in the midst: not to inform, but simply to provide a point of departure for an access *into* the "open" hermeneutic circle. As such, it is, of course, itself subject to destruction. It will be seen (I put this word under erasure here), in other words, that these essays themselves play freely around the preface, always interrogating its assertions, always breaking open its abstractions to disclose what has been left unsaid, always, "finally" dis-covering other possibilities concealed inside its bounding line. To adapt a phrase from Ben Jonson, it will be seen by the engaged reader that they "stirre the mould about the 'root' of the Question . . ." that the preface — and the text at large — poses.

This volume of essays had its origins in the fall of 1973, when I was on a sabbatical leave in Lyons, France, working on a book on hermeneutics. I then suggested to my co-editor, Robert Kroetsch, that we follow up several recent numbers of *boundary 2* devoted in large part to seminal efforts to define the "post-modernism" of postmodern literature with a special issue exploring the implications of Heidegger's post-metaphysical thought for literary studies. Although I was certain of the need for such an inquiry, I was far from sure at that time that I would be able to find American philosophers who could address themselves to immediate literary issues or, further, literary critics who could (or would) address themselves to immediate philosophical issues in the light of the crisis of literary criticism. The search for such authors was, in fact, a long, but happily successful one, because it culminated in a gathering of a richly diverse community of articulate and deeply committed students of Heideggerian thinking who were also aware of the resulting volume's seminal significance for other areas of the human sciences. As editor, I wish to thank all my colleagues who contributed to this project for their generosity in the face of severe pressures I imposed on them while the issue was in the making. I attribute this generosity before the emerging text — this *Gelassenheit,* to appropriate, to en-own, Heidegger's beautiful and good word — not to academic exigencies but to the dignity and worth of the questions this explorative text asks.

I was also far from certain at the time I proposed it that such an interdisciplinary project would find a receptive audience within a literary community nurtured by the New Criticism, especially by its dogmatic commitment to the autonomy of the work of art, which, in one of its aspects, insisted on the sequestration of literary texts from the alien ambience of philosophical thought. With the publication of this issue (vol. IV, 2) in the winter of 1976, I was pleasantly surprised by the powerful impact (if modest in numbers) that it immediately made, thus corroborating my intuition of the felt need in the literary community of precisely what this volume had to offer. I thus also lamented the limited print run we had decided on. When it became clear that the growing demand for the issue was in excess of our supply, I made inquiries at Indiana University Press about the possibility of reprinting it in a hardback format. The response was prompt and enthusiastic. I want, therefore, to acknowledge my gratitude to the Press for its faith in the importance of the issue the text confronts.

I want especially to thank William Overstreet for his acute sense of decorum as copy editor; Marian Madden, whose organizational genius kept a wayward vessel more or less on course; and, above all, Paul Bové, my former student, who, in the process, has become my teacher, and Robert Kroetsch, my co-editor and dear friend, whose support, as always, involved a lot more than the mere expense of valuable time and energy he could have better devoted to his writing.

Finally, in another context — and once more — I want to express my deepest gratitude to my wife, Margaret, above all, for her maddening — and always generative — resistance.

WILLIAM V. SPANOS

SUNY-Binghampton
January 30, 1979

1   Martin Heidegger, "The Question of Technology," *The Question of Technology and Other Essays,* trans. with Introduction by William Lovitt (New York: Harper Colophon Books, 1977), pp. 14-17.

2   Michel Foucault, *Discipline and Punish: The Birth of the Prison,* trans. Alan Sheridan (New York: Pantheon Books, 1977), 195-227. Originally titled *Surveillir et Punir: Naissance de la prison* (Paris: Editions Gallimard, 1975).

3   Martin Heidegger, "Who Is Nietzsche's Zarathustra?" *The New Nietzsche: Contemporary Styles of Interpretation,* ed. David B. Allison (New York: Dell, 1977), p. 73.

4   Wallace Stevens, "The Relations between Poetry and Painting," *The Necessary Angel: Essays on Reality and the Imagination* (New York: Vintage Books, 1951), p. 174.

5   William V. Spanos, "Talking with Robert Creeley," tr., *Robert Creeley: A Gathering,* a special issue of *boundary 2* (Vol. VI, 3; VII, 1 Spring/Fall 1978) ed. William V. Spanos, pp. 19-20. See also Wallace Stevens, "An Ordinary Evening in New Haven," *Collected Poems* (New York: Alfred A. Knopf, 1964): "The Poem is the cry of its occasion,/ Part of the res itself and not about it" (p. 473).

6   Martin Heidegger, ". . . Poetically Man Dwells . . .'," *Poetry, Language, Thought,* trans. Albert Hofstadter (New York: Harper & Row, 1971), pp. 221-22. See also "Building Dwelling Thinking," pp. 146-61.

7   Jacques Derrida, *Of Grammatology,* trans. Gayatri Spivak (Baltimore: The Johns Hopkins University Press, 1976), p. 10.

8   See William V. Spanos, "Postmodern Literature and The Hermeneutic Crisis," *Union Seminary Quarterly Review,* Vol. XXXIV, No. 2 (Winter 1979).

9   See Robert Scholes, *Structuralism in Literature: An Introduction* (New Haven: Yale University Press, 1974); and Jonathan Culler, *Structuralist Poetics: Structuralism, Linguistics and the Study of Literature* (Ithaca: Cornell University Press, 1975).

10 *Letters of John Keats,* ed. M. B. Forman (London: Oxford University Press, 1935): letter to George and Thomas Keats, December 21, 1817, p. 72.

11 Jacques Derrida, "Différance," *Speech and Phenomenon and Other Essays on Husserl's Theory of Signs,* trans. David B. Allison (Evanston: Northwestern University Press, 1973): "The verb 'to differ' [*différer*] seems to differ from itself. On the one hand, it indicates difference as distinction, inequality, or discernibility; on the other, it expresses the interposition of delay, the interval of a *spacing* and *temporalizing,* that puts off until 'later' what is presently denied, the possible that is presently impossible. . . . In the one case "to differ" signifies nonidentity; in the other case it signifies the order of the *same.* Yet there must be a common, although entirely differant [*différante*], root within the sphere that relates the two movements of differing to one another. We provisionally give the name *differance* to this *sameness* which is not *identical:* by the silent writing of its *a,* it has the desired advantage of referring to differing, *both* as spacing/ temporalizing and as the movement that structures every dissociation" (pp. 129-30).

Martin Heidegger
and the
Question of Literature

The Age of the World View*

Martin Heidegger
translated by Marjorie Grene

Metaphysics reflects on the nature of the existent and on the nature of truth. Metaphysics lays the foundation of an age by giving it the basis of its essential form through a particular analysis of the existent and a particular conception of truth. This basis dominates all the phenomena which distinguish the age. Conversely, it must be possible to recognize the metaphysical basis in these phenomena through sufficient reflection on them. Reflection is the courage to question as deeply as possible the truth of our own presuppositions and the exact place of our own aims.

Among the essential phenomena of modern times we must count science. A phenomenon with the same degree of importance is mechanical

*This translation first appeared in *Measure,* 2 (1951), 269-84. Heidegger's original is included as "Die Zeit des Weltbildes" in *Holzwege* (Frankfurt am Main: V. Klostermann, 1963), pp. 69-89.

technique. This should not be misinterpreted, however, as a mere application of modern mathematical natural science to practice. Mechanical technique is itself an independent transformation of practice such that it of itself demands the application of mathematical natural science. Mechanical technique remains the most visible product to date of the essence of modern technology, which is identical with the essence of modern metaphysics.

A third equally important phenomenon of modern times consists in the process by which art comes within the horizon of aesthetics: the work of art becomes the object of an experience; as a result, art is viewed as the expression of the life of man.

A fourth modern phenomenon is exhibited in the fact that human activity is understood and accomplished as culture. Culture thus becomes the realization of the highest values through the cultivation of the highest goods of man. It is part of the essence of culture, as such cultivation, to cultivate itself and so become "culture politics."

A fifth phenomenon of modern times is the transition to godlessness. This expression does not mean the mere displacement of the gods — coarse atheism. The transition to godlessness is a twofold process: on the one hand the world view becomes Christianized in so far as the cause of the world is conceived as the infinite, the unconditioned, the absolute; on the other hand Christendom transforms its Christianity into a world view (the Christian world view) and so adapts itself to modern times. The transition to godlessness is the state of indecision about God and the gods. Christianity has contributed most to its development. But the transition to godlessness is far from excluding religiosity; on the contrary, it is through religiosity that the relation to the gods becomes, for the first time, a religious experience. When it has come to that, the gods have fled. The resulting void is filled by the historical and psychological investigation of the myth.

On what conception of the existent and on what interpretation of truth do these phenomena rest?

We limit our question to the first phenomenon, to science.

Wherein lies the essence of modern science?

On what conception of the existent and of truth does this essence rest? If we succeed in reaching, finally, the metaphysical foundation on which modern science is grounded, then it must be possible to perceive the very essence of modern times.

When we use the word science today, it means something which differs essentially from the *doctrina* and *scientia* of the Middle Ages, but also from the Greek *episteme*. Greek science was never exact — precisely for the reason that it could not by its nature be exact and did not need to be exact. There is therefore no sense whatever in supposing that modern science is more exact than that of antiquity. Nor can we say that Galileo's doctrine of freely falling bodies is true, and that Aristotle, who teaches that light bodies strive upward, is wrong; for the Greek conception of the nature of body and place and their relation to one another rests on a different explanation of the existent, and therefore requires a correspondingly different kind of viewing and questioning of natural processes. No one would think of maintaining that Shakespeare's poetry is more advanced than that of Aeschylus. But it is even more impossible to say that the modern apprehension of the existent is more correct than the Greek. Thus if we want to understand the essence of modern science, we must first of all free ourselves of the habit of contrasting the newer science with the older simply by applying the standard of gradual progress.

The essence of what we now call science is research. What is the essence of research?

It is the fact that knowledge establishes itself as a procedure in a realm of the existent, of nature or of history. Procedure means here not only method, a way of proceeding — for every procedure needs a sphere in which it can move — but, more precisely, the opening of such a sphere; this is the basic procedure of research. It is accomplished through the projection of a definite ground plan of natural processes in a sphere of the existent, for example, in nature. The projection indicates the way in which the cognitive procedure must adhere to the sphere it has opened up for itself. This adherence is the discipline of research. Through the projection of the ground plan and the condition of exactitude the method secures for itself its proper area within the sphere of being. A glance at the earliest, and normative, modern science, mathematical physics, reveals what is meant. In so far as modern atomic physics is still physics, the essential aspect — the only one we are concerned with here — is applicable.

Modern physics is called mathematical because it distinctively applies a very definite mathematics. But it can proceed mathematically in this way only because it is in a deeper sense already mathematical. *Ta mathemata* means for the Greeks that which man knows prior to his observation of the existent and his acquaintance with things: of bodies — the corporeal; of plants — the vegetative; of animals — the animate; of man — the human. Numbers, too, belong to this category of the already known, that is, the "mathematical." If we find three apples on the table, we recognize that there are three of them. But the number three, threeness, we know already. This means that number is something "mathematical." Only because numbers represent, as it were, the most obvious of things always known beforehand, and hence the best known in the class of the mathematicals, was "mathematical" forthwith reserved as the name of things of the nature of number. But the essence of the mathematical is by no means determined by the numberable. Physics is in general the knowledge of nature, then in particular the knowledge of the substantially corporeal in its motion; for this appears immediately and universally, even if in different ways, in all natural phenomena. If, then, physics explicitly takes on a mathematical form, this means that something is emphatically

3

defined in advance as the already known. This definition means nothing less than the demarcation of what nature is to mean for the knowledge of nature that is sought, that is, the self-sufficient kinetic relation of points of mass connected in space and time. On this blueprint of nature that is assumed to be already known, the following conditions — among others — are entered. Motion means change of place. No motion or direction of motion is preferred to another. Every place is like every other. No point of time is superior to any other. Every force is determined only by — *is* only — its consequences in motion, that is to say, by the magnitude of change of place in the unit of time. Every event must be read into this blueprint of nature. It is only within the framework of this blueprint that a natural event becomes visible as such. This design of nature therefore contains its verification in the fact that for every step of its investigation physical research depends on it in advance. The character of dependence, the discipline of research, is in each case derived from the "ground plan." The discipline of mathematical natural science is exactitude. All events, if they are to be perceived as natural events at all, must here be determined in advance as spatiotemporal kinetic magnitudes. Such determination is carried out through measurement with the help of number and calculation. But mathematical science is not exact because it makes exact calculations; rather it must make such calculations because its way of adhering to its sphere has the character of exactitude. On the other hand, all humanistic disciplines, in fact, all sciences of living things, must, precisely in order to remain disciplines, necessarily be inexact. To be sure, the living can also be apprehended as a spatiotemporal kinetic magnitude — but then it is no longer understood as living. The inexactitude of the historical disciplines is not a shortcoming, but only the fulfillment of a demand essential to their kind of research. Of course, the delineation and the fixation of the object area of the historical disciplines remains not only different from but, as a task, much more difficult than the realization of the discipline of exact science.

Science becomes research through the projection and through the verification of the projection in the discipline of the procedure. But projection and discipline develop into what they are only in the procedure. This is the mark of the second essential characteristic of research. If the projected area is to become objective, then we must make it accessible in all the complexity of its layers and interlacings. Therefore the procedure must have its vision free for the mutability of the given. Only within the orbit of the ever-otherwise of change is the plenitude of the particular, of the facts, revealed. But the facts must become objective. The procedure must therefore represent the changeable in its change, bring it to a standstill, and nevertheless let the motion be as motion. The permanent in the facts and the permanence of their change as such are the rule. The permanence of change in the necessity of its course is the law. Only within the boundaries of rule and law are facts revealed as the facts they are. The investigation of facts in the sphere of nature is in itself the establishment and preservation of rule and law. The procedure through which an object area is apprehended has the character of clarification. It always remains twofold. It founds an unknown by means of a known, and at the same time preserves this known through that unknown. Clarification is carried out in investigation. This occurs in natural science — according to the type of field investigated and the aim of the clarification — by means of experiment. However, natural science does not become research through experiment; on the contrary, experiment becomes possible where, and only where, natural knowledge has already been transformed into research. It is because, and only because, modern physics is essentially mathematical that it can be experimental. But because neither the medieval *doctrina* nor the Greek *episteme* is science in the sense of research, they leave no room for experiment. It was indeed Aristotle who first understood what *empeiria* (*experientia*) means: the observation of the things themselves, of their properties and alterations under changing conditions and therewith the knowledge of the way in which things as a rule behave. But an observation which is aimed at this kind of knowledge, the *experimentum*, remains essentially different from the research experiment which belongs to science as research — essentially different even when the ancient and medieval observations work with number and measurement, and when the observation makes use of particular contrivances and instruments. For in this the decisive feature of the experiment is entirely lacking. This begins when a law is taken as a point of departure. To set up an experiment means to assume a situation where it becomes possible to trace a definite nexus of motions in the necessity of its course, that is, to control its calculation in advance. But the determination of the law occurs with a view to the ground plan of the object area. The latter gives the measure and fixes in advance the representation of the situation. Such representation, in which and with which the experiment starts, is no capricious imagining. That is why Newton said: *hypotheses non fingo*, the bases are not arbitrarily invented. They are developed out of the ground plan of nature and are written into it. The experiment is that procedure which in its arrangement and execution is borne and guided by the law basic to it, in order to produce the facts which confirm the law or deny confirmation. The more exactly the ground plan of nature has been projected, the more exact will be the possibility of the experiment. The much cited medieval schoolman Roger Bacon can therefore never be the forerunner of the modern experimental research scientist, but he remains simply the successor of Aristotle. For in the interval Christianity has assigned the genuine possession of truth to faith, to the acceptance of Holy Writ and church doctrine. The highest knowledge and doctrine is theology as the exegesis of the divine word of revelation which is set down in the Scriptures and is proclaimed through the Church. Knowledge is here not research, but the correct understanding of the authoritative word and

5

the authorities proclaiming it. Therefore, in the acquisition of knowledge in the Middle Ages the exposition of the sayings and doctrines of the various authorities takes precedence. The *componere scripta ex sermones*, the *argumentum ex verbo* is decisive and is at the same time the reason why the Platonic and Aristotelian philosophy transmitted to the Middle Ages had to become scholastic dialectic. If Roger Bacon here demands the *experimentum* — and he does demand it — he does not mean the experiment of science as research; but he requires, instead of the *argumentum ex verbo*, the *argumentum ex re*, and instead of the exposition of doctrines, the observation of the things themselves, that is, Aristotelian *empeiria*.

The modern research experiment, however, is not only an observation more exact in degree and scope, but the radically different procedure of the confirmation of a law in the framework and in the service of an exact projection of nature. In the historical disciplines the critique of sources corresponds to the experiment in scientific research. Let this name designate here the whole process of finding, sifting, confirming, evaluating, preserving, and interpreting sources. Historical explanation grounded on the critique of sources does not, indeed, reduce the facts to laws and rules. But neither is it limited to the mere reporting of facts. In the historical disciplines just as in the natural sciences the procedure aims at representing the permanent and making history an object. But history can become objective only if it is past. The permanent in history, that with reference to which historical explanation assesses the unique and the diverse in history, is that-which-has-always-already-happened-once, the comparable. In the constant comparison of everything with everything the intelligible is figured out and is indicated as the ground plan of history. The sphere of historical research extends only as far as historical explanation reaches; the unique, the infrequent, the simple — in short, the great — in history is never self-evident and therefore remains inexplicable. Historical research does not deny greatness in history but explains it as the exception. In this explanation greatness is measured against the common and the average. Nor is there any other historical explanation so long as explanation means reduction to the intelligible, and so long as history remains research, that is, explanation. It is because history as research projects and objectifies the past in the sense of a nexus of events which can be explained and surveyed that it requires the critique of sources as the instrument of objectification. In the measure in which history approaches the journalistic, the standards of this critique are altered.

Every science is, as research, founded on the projection of a limited object area and is therefore necessarily specialized science. But, in the development of the projection, every specialized science must, through its procedure, separate itself into definite fields of investigation. But this separation or specialization is by no means only the unavoidable concomitant of the increasing vastness of the results of research. It is not a necessary evil, but the necessary essence of science as research. Specialization is not the consequence, but the cause of the progress of all research. In its procedure the latter does not fall apart into arbitrary investigations in which it loses itself; for modern science is determined by a third basic procedure: busy-ness.

By this we understand, first of all, the phenomenon that a science, whether a natural science or a humanistic discipline, today attains the prestige of a science only when it has become capable of being institutionalized. However, research is not busy-ness because its work is carried on in institutes; but the institutes are necessary because science as research has acquired the character of busy-ness. The procedure through which the particular object areas are mastered does not simply pile up results. Rather, with the help of its results, it always organizes itself for a new procedure. The whole of physics up to the present is contained in the mechanical apparatus which physics needs in order to smash the atom. Similarly, in historical research, the available sources can be used for the purpose of explanation only after the sources themselves have been substantiated on the basis of historical explanation. In these processes the procedure of science is circumscribed by its results. The procedure is adjusted more and more to the possibilities of the method which it has itself laid bare. This necessity of accepting its own results as determining the ways and means of the advancing method is essential to the business character of research. This, however, is what forces upon research its institutional character.

It is only in busy-ness that the projection of the object area is incorporated in the existent. All arrangements which facilitate coordination of procedures according to plan, which facilitate the checking and communication of results and regulate the exchange of talents, are measures which are by no means merely the external consequence of the fact that research work is spreading and expanding. Rather, it is a symptom, coming from far back and largely not yet understood, that modern science is beginning to enter upon the decisive phase of its history. Only now is it taking possession of its own real nature.

What is really happening in the expansion and consolidation of the institutional character of the sciences? Nothing less than that the procedure is granted definitive precedence over Being (nature and history), which research makes objective. On the basis of this business character, the sciences provide themselves with the appropriate coherence and unity. For this reason an institutionally conducted historical or archaeological research project more closely resembles physical research that is similarly organized than it does a discipline of its own humanistic faculty which has remained in the area of mere scholarship. The decisive development of the modern business character of science therefore forms men of a different stamp. The scholar disappears. He is replaced by the research man who is engaged in research projects. This, rather than the pursuit of scholarship, gives his work its keen atmosphere. The research man no longer needs a library at home. Besides, he is always moving about. He does business at meetings and gets information at congresses. He contracts to work for commissions from publishers, who now help to determine what books must be written.

The research worker forces himself automatically into the orbit of the technologist in the form essential to his work. Only in this way does he remain effective and thus, in the sense of his age, real. Alongside him, for some time and in a few places there will continue an increasingly thin and empty romanticism of scholarship and of the university. The effective character of the university as a unifier — and hence its reality — does not consist, however, in a spiritual force which proceeds from it because it is nourished by it and preserved in it, that is, the original interrelation of the intellectual disciplines. The university is real as an organization only in a unique, because administratively self-sufficient, form which makes possible and visible the tendency of the sciences to separate into specialties, and the specific unity of these businesslike pursuits. Because the power that is of the essence of modern science takes effect immediately and unequivocally in its busy-nesses, it is only their peculiar research which can designate and organize the inner unity appropriate to them.

The real system of sciences rests on the consistency of its methods and on the attitude with respect to the objectification of Being. The advantage demanded of this system is not that it should offer an abstract and rigid unity of relations among the object areas, but rather the greatest possible ability to switch its research — freedom of research, yet regulated mobility of transference and integration of activities with respect to whatever tasks happen to be of paramount importance. The more exclusively science becomes specialized for the complete pursuit and mastery of its work, and the more realistically these business activities are shifted to separate research institutes and professional schools, the more irrevocably the sciences move toward the fulfillment of their modern destiny. But the more unconditionally science and researchers take seriously their modern nature, the more unequivocally and the more immediately they can offer themselves for the common good, and the more unreservedly they must subordinate themselves and enter the public ambiguity of every socially useful work.

Modern science is at once founded on and specialized in the Plan of definite object areas. This Plan develops in a procedure adequate to it, certified through its discipline. Each procedure is organized as busy-ness. Plan and discipline, procedure and busy-ness, mutually postulating one another, constitute the essence of modern science, transform it into research.

We are reflecting on the nature of modern science in order to find its metaphysical basis. What conception of the existent and what concept of truth cause science to become research?

8

Understanding as research holds the existent to account on the question of how and how far it can be put at the disposal of available "representation." Research has the existent at its disposal if it can either calculate it in advance, in its future course, or calculate it afterwards as past. Nature — in advance calculation, history, in retrospection, calculation — is, as it were, held at bay. Nature and history become the object of expository representation, while the latter counts on nature and reckons with history. Only what thus becomes an object *is*, is recognized as existent. Science as research occurs only when it is in this objectification that the being of the existent is sought.

This objectification of the existent takes place in a re-presentation which aims at presenting whatever exists to itself in such a way that the calculating person can be secure, that is, certain of the existent. Science as research is produced when and only when truth has been transformed into such certainty of representation. In the metaphysics of Descartes the existent was defined for the first time as objectivity of representation, and truth as certainty of representation. The title of his chief work is *Mediationes de prima philosophia*, Meditations on First Philosophy. *Prote philosophia* is the designation coined by Aristotle for what was later called metaphysics. The whole of modern metaphysics, including Nietzsche, remains within the conception of the existent and of truth initiated by Descartes.

Now, if science as research is an essential phenomenon of modern times, then whatever constitutes the metaphysical basis of research must determine, first and far in advance, the nature of modern times as such. We can see the essence of modern times in the fact that man sets himself free from the medieval bonds, by freeing himself to himself. Nevertheless, this correct characterization remains superficial. It leads to those errors which prevent our grasping the real basis of modern times, and from this, determining its full significance. It is certain that as a consequence of the liberation of man the modern age has produced subjectivism and individualism. But it is just as certain that no age before this has created a comparable objectivism, and that in no previous age did the nonindividual in the form of the collective come into its own. The essential point here is the necessary interplay between subjectivism and objectivism. It is precisely this mutual conditioning which points in turn to deeper processes.

What is decisive is not that man frees himself to himself out of his previous commitments, but that the essence of man as such changes in that man becomes a subject. To be sure, we must understand this word *subjectum* as the translation of the Greek *hypokeimenon*. The word designates what lies before us, that which gathers everything to itself to become its basis. This metaphysical meaning of the concept of subject has at first no specific relation to man and none at all to the I.

But when man becomes the first and real *subjectum*, then man becomes that existent, in which all that exists is grounded in the character of its existence and its truth. Man becomes the center to which the existent as such is related. But this is possible only if the conception of the existent as a whole is transformed. Where does this transformation appear? What accordingly, is the essence of modern times?

When we reflect on modern times, we ask about the modern "world view." We characterize it by a contrast with the medieval and the ancient world view. But why, in the analysis of a historical period, do we ask about the world view? Does every age of history have its world view, and precisely in the sense that in each case it is concerned about its own particular world view? Or is it characteristic only of the modern type of representation to ask about the world view?

What is a world view? Obviously a view, or picture of the world. But what does world mean here? And what does view or picture mean? World stands here as the designation of the existent as a whole. The name is not limited to the cosmos, to nature. History also is part of the world. But even nature and history, as they interpenetrate and affect one another, do not exhaust the world. In this term the foundation of the world is included, regardless of how its relation to the world is conceived.

Hence the world view would be, as it were, a painting of the existent as a whole. Yet world view means more. We mean by this the world itself, the existent as a whole, as it is for us normative and binding. View or picture means here not a copy, but the notion reflected in the idiom: we are "in the picture" with respect to something. This means the matter is present to us in so far as, in its actuality, it matters to us. To "put oneself in the picture about something" means to represent to oneself the existent itself with respect to its state and as so presented to keep it constantly before one. But one decisive aspect of the essence of the view or picture is still lacking. "We are in the picture" with respect to something does not mean only that the existent is simply presented to us, but that, in everything that belongs to it and constitutes it as a system, it stands before us. "To be in the picture" connotes having the know-how, being equipped and oriented toward the matter in question. Where the world becomes a view, the existent as a whole is posited as that with respect to which a man orients himself, which therefore he wishes to bring and have before himself and thus in a decisive sense re-present to himself. World view, properly understood, therefore means, not a view of the world, but the world understood as view. The existent as a whole is now so understood that it is existent when and only when and in the degree to which it is held at bay by the person who represents and establishes it. Where a world view arises, an essential decision takes place about the existent as a whole. The being of the existent is sought and found in the representational character of the existent.

But wherever the existent is *not* conceived of in this sense, the world cannot change into a view; there can be no world view. The fact that the existent becomes existent as representation makes the age in which this happens a new one over against the preceding one. The phrases "world view of modern times" and "modern world view" say the same thing twice and suppose something which could never before exist, namely, a medieval and an ancient world view. The world view does not change from a previous medieval to a modern one, but this fact — that the world as such becomes a view — is the distinguishing mark of modern times. For the Middle Ages, on the other hand, the existent is the *ens creatum*, that which is created by the personal Creator-God as highest cause. To be existent here means to belong to a definite level in the order of created things, and thus caused to correspond to the cause of creation (*analogia entis*). But here the being of the existent never consists in the fact that it is brought before man as what is objective, is present and alone existent within the area susceptible to his skills and at his disposal.

The modern conception of the existent is even farther from the Greek nature. One of the oldest expressions of Greek thought about the being of the existent reads: *To gar auto noein estin te kai einai*. This statement of Parmenides means that the perception of the existent belongs to being, because it is demanded and determined by it. The existent is what rises and opens itself, that which being present comes upon man as the one who is present, that is, upon the one who opens himself to what is present by perceiving it. The existent does not become existent through the fact that only man faces it in the sense of subjective perception. Rather is it man who is faced by the existent, who is gathered into its presence by the self-disclosing. To be faced by the existent, to be drawn into its disclosure and included and so borne by it, to be harassed by its contradictions and marked by its conflict — that is the essence of man in the great age of Greece. Therefore, Greek man, in order to fulfill his nature, must collect (*legein*), the self-disclosing in its disclosure and save it (*sozein*), catch it up and preserve it, and remain exposed to all sundering confusion (*aletheuein*). The Greek man *is* as he who perceives the existent, wherefore in Greece the world cannot become a view. On the other hand, the fact that for Plato the existent character of the existent is determined as *eidos* (appearance, view) is the presupposition, coming far in advance and for a long time acting secretly and indirectly, for the eventual transformation of the world to a view.

Quite different, in contrast to the Greek perception, is the modern representation, significance of which is best expressed by the word *representatio*. To re-present here means to bring what is present before one as something confronting oneself, to relate it to oneself, the person representing it, and to force it back into this relation to oneself as the normative area. Where this kind of thing happens, man "gets into the picture" with respect to the existent. But in so far as man thus puts himself in the picture, he puts himself into the setting, that is, into the open horizon of the universally and openly represented. Therefore man

11

posits himself as the setting, in which the existent must from now on represent itself, present itself, that is, be a view or picture. Man becomes the representative of the existent in the sense of the objective.

But what is new in this process by no means consists in the fact that now the viewpoint of man in the midst of the existent is simply different over and against that of medieval and ancient man. What is decisive is that man himself takes this viewpoint as produced by himself, maintains it voluntarily as that taken by himself, and as the basis of a possible development of humanity. Now, for the first time, there is such a thing as a viewpoint of man. Man takes on himself the manner in which he is to stand to the existent as the objective. That type of being-a-man begins which uses the sphere of human powers as the place for measuring and accomplishing the mastery of the existent as a whole. The age which is determined by this event is not only for retrospective reflection a new one as against the preceding one, but it asserts itself specifically as the new one. To be new is peculiar to the world which has become a view.

If, therefore, the view-character of the world has been made clear as the fact that the existent is represented, then in order to grasp fully the modern nature of representation we must feel out the original power of speech in the banal word and concept "represent": to place as present before and near one. Thus the existent assumes the position of object and only in this role does it receive the seal of being. That the world becomes a view is one and the same process with that by which man, within the existent, becomes a *subjectum*.

Only because and in so far as man as such has essentially become subject must there consequently arise for him the express question: whether it is as the I limited to his own whim and let loose for his own caprice or as the We of society, whether it is as man as individual or as community, whether it is man as personality in society or as mere group member in the corporate body, whether it is as state and nation and people or as the universal humanity of modern man that man wants to and must be the subject which *as* a modern being he *already is*. Only where man is already essentially subject does there exist the possibility of slipping into the monstrosity of subjectivism in the sense of individualism. But only where man *remains* subject does the open battle against individualism and for the community as the goal of all achievement and usefulness have a meaning.

The interweaving of both processes — that the world becomes a view and man a *subjectum*, which is decisive for the essence of modern times — at the same time throws a light on the basic process of modern history, which at first sight seems almost absurd. To wit: the more completely and thoroughly the conquered world stands at our disposal, the more objective the object seems to be, the more subjectively — that is, the more prominently — does the *subjectum* rise up, and the more inevitably do contemplation and explanation of the world and doctrine about the world turn into a doctrine of man, into anthropology. It is no wonder that humanism arises only when the world becomes a view. But as little as a world view was possible in the great age of Greece, so little could a humanism come into effect then. Humanism in the strict historical sense is therefore nothing but a moral-aesthetic anthropology. This term does not mean here natural scientific investigation of man. Nor does it mean the doctrine established within Christian theology about man as created, fallen, and redeemed. It designates that philosophical interpretation of man which explains and evaluates the existent as a whole from the viewpoint of and in relation to man.

The increasingly exclusive rooting of world analysis in anthropology which set in at the end of the eighteenth century finds its expression in the fact that the basic attitude of man to the existent as a whole is determined as world view (*Weltanschauung*). Since then this term has come into common usage. As soon as the world becomes a view or picture, the attitude of man is conceived as a world view. To be sure, the phrase world view suggests the erroneous notion that it is a matter simply of an inactive contemplation of the world. It has therefore been correctly emphasized as early as the nineteenth century that world view also means — and means above all — a view of life. That nevertheless the phrase world view is asserted as the name for the attitude of man in that midst of the existent demonstrates how decisively the world became a view, as soon as man brought his life as subject into the forefront of the frame of reference. This means that the existent holds as existent only in so far as and to the extent that it is drawn into and back to this life, that it is lived through or experienced and becomes experience. As discordant as every humanism must remain to the Greek spirit, just so impossible was a medieval world view, so absurd is a catholic one. As necessarily and fittingly as everything must become experience for modern man, the more limitlessly he penetrates into the configuration of his essence, so certainly could the Greeks at the Olympian festival never have experiences.

The basic process of modern times is the conquest of the world as picture. The word "view" now means the product of representational building. In it man fights for the position in which he can be that existent which sets the standard for all existence and forms the directive for it. Because this position is secure and itself organized and expressed as world view, the modern relation to the existent in its decisive development becomes a debate between world views — and not between world views at random, but only between those which have already taken extreme basic positions of man with the last decisiveness. For this battle of world views, and in accord with the significance of this battle, man brings into play the unlimited power of calculation, planning, and cultivation of all things. Science as research is an indispensable form of this adjustment in the world, one of the paths on which the modern age races to the fulfillment of its nature with a velocity unknown to the participants. It is only with this battle of world views that the modern age enters the definitive and probably the most persistent segment of its history.

It is a sign of this process that everywhere, in the most varied forms and disguises, the gigantic makes its appearance. In this connection the gigantic also announces itself in the direction of the ever smaller. Think of the numbers of atomic physics. The gigantic presses forward in a form which appears precisely to make it vanish: in the destruction of great distances by the airplane, in the unlimited power of representation of foreign and remote worlds, made present by the turn of a hand, through the radio. But we think too superficially if we suppose that the gigantic is simply the endlessly extended emptiness of the merely quantitative. We think too rashly if we believe that the gigantic in the form of the continuously novel springs only from the blind desire to exaggerate and to surpass. We do not think at all if we suppose we have interpreted this phenomenon of the gigantic with the catchword Americanism.

The gigantic is, rather, that through which the quantitative becomes a peculiar quality and thus a distinctive type of greatness. Every historical period differs from others not only in its greatness; it has also in each case its own concept of greatness. But as soon as the gigantic in planning and calculation and organization and affirmation shifts from the quantitative to a peculiar quality, the gigantic and that which can apparently be completely and continually calculated becomes, precisely because of this, the incalculable. This remains the invisible shadow which is cast over all things everywhere when man has become *subjectum* and the world a view.

Through this shadow the modern world projects itself into a space withdrawn from representation and so grants to the incalculable its proper determination and its historical uniqueness. But this shadow points to something else which it is denied to us of today to know. Yet man will not be able even to experience and consider this forbidden reality so long as he wastes his time in the mere negation of his age. The flight to tradition, which combines humility and arrogance, is powerless, taken by itself, for anything except blindness and self-deception over against the historical moment.

To know, that is, to preserve in its truth, this incalculable, will be possible for man only in creative questioning and shaping of the power of true reflection. It sets the man of the future in that in-between area, in which he belongs to being and yet remains a stranger to the existent. Hölderlin knew of it. His poem which bears the superscription "To the Germans" closes:

> Wohl ist enge begrenzt unsere Lebenszeit,
> Unserer Jahre Zahl sehen und zählen wir,
> Doch die Jahre der Völker,
> Sah ein sterbliches Auge sie?

Wenn die Seele dir auch über die eigene Zeit
Sich die sehnende schwingt, trauernd verweilest du
Dann am kalten Gestade
Bei den Deinen und kennst sie nie.

Narrowly bounded is our time to live,
We see and count the number of our years,
But were the years of nations
Seen by a mortal eye?

And if your soul over your own time
Swings, the longing one, mourning you linger
On the cold shore then
Among your own and know it not.

Enownment

Albert Hofstadter

> To think is to confine yourself to a
> single thought that one day stands
> still like a star in the world's sky.
> — *Poetry, Language, Thought*

Martin Heidegger's life work as a thinker has been a struggle to attain a single thought.

By this thought he has worked to take the measure of man's Being. By it he has sought to illuminate man's nature and world, his personal and social existence, his art and poetry, his language, his past and present and future.

This thought becomes more and more articulate in the sequence of the writings. It is most stringently spoken of in the lecture *On Time and Being*. That is fitting, since the second part of *Being and Time* was supposed to be a reversal, a *Kehre*, although perhaps the turn itself took a surprising turn. While there are only hints of the possibility of the thought's later form in that early book, it is brought out as clearly as its nature permits only in the later writings — like *Identity and Difference, On Time and Being*, and the essays in *Poetry, Language, Thought*.

17

The poem *The Thinker as Poet* was written in 1947 and published in 1954. Its original title is *Aus der Erfahrung des Denkens, From the Experience of Thinking*. This poem does not name the single thought, although it does name Being. It says many things about Being: about Being's relation to the world, to man, to thought, destiny, and language. It speaks of the call of Being to man, man's thinking of Being, Being's topology, the source of singing, thinking, and poetry in Being, and the truth of Being. But it does not give a specific name to the single thought. It speaks of it only in its singleness.

Out of the experience of a lifetime of thinking, Martin Heidegger reflects upon that experience and finds its meaning in the struggle to attain a single thought.

We are interested in that thought. It has something to do with Being: it thinks Being. Being is presence, presencing; it is the letting-presence which lets beings be, as they presence, whether present or absent. This thought of Being Heidegger found initiated by the pre-Socratic thinkers of Greece. It could be called the matter of thought, that which thinking is called upon to think. But just to think Being as presence, *Anwesen*, and letting-presence, *Anwesenlassen*, is not yet to think it in its truth. It is only first to approach it as the matter of thought.

In mutual belonging with it is time. Time too is presencing: enduring, remaining, *as* presencing, *anwesen*. Neither time nor Being is a being that absences and presences, yet the absencing and presencing of beings is what is thought as their timing Being. Time, too, is the matter of thought, which thinking is called upon to think. But to think time as presencing, again, is not yet to think it in its truth, but only first to approach it as the matter of thought.

Being and time, both, have been the matter of thought from the beginning, before philosophy and throughout the history of philosophy. What does thinking think when it seeks to apprehend Being and time? One could speak of the mystery of Being — which is also the mystery of time — as Heidegger does toward the close of *The End of Philosophy*.

> It is one thing just to use the earth, another to receive
> the blessing of the earth and to become at home in the
> law of this reception in order to shepherd the mystery
> of Being and watch over the inviolability of the possible.
> (EP, 109)[1]

The image of man as the shepherd of Being pervades Heidegger's writings. What man shepherds is the mystery of Being. To do this he must be able to receive the blessing of the earth, to become at home in the law of this reception. Instead of willfully using the earth, as he has done since the days of classical antiquity and at an accelerating pace since the first

Industrial Revolution, he is to receive its blessing. The imagery moves from imposing to receiving, taking to being granted, wresting to being blessed.

The single thought had to do with the mystery of Being, the mystery of time. Thinking is confining oneself to this thought that one day stands still in the world's sky. After the search and the struggle for the mystery, if fortune nods her head, one looks up one auspicious night and sees a certain star in the sky and knows that this star, this one thought, is the thought that enlightens.

It is not any indiscriminately encountered thought. It is a unique thought, one that stands still while all the others shift and change, light up and become extinguished once again. It is a steadfast thought, staying throughout, to which one can confine oneself with confidence, just because it stays firm and stays all. It is the trustworthy thought, just as it is the thought that is worthy of being thought.

How does it stay all? An early thinker, Heraclitus, said:

Wisdom is one thing: to know the *gnome* — the thought-
token — by which all things are guided through all.

The star that stays is the pole star. Wanderers tell the directions from it, sailors steer by it, the sky of solstices, equinoxes, and seasons turns about it, and man knows when and where he is only as he takes sight of it, keeping it firmly and constantly in view. So it leads and directs all. Knowing it or not knowing it, men are guided by it. Those who know it see the guidance. The shepherds in the night can tell when and where they and their flocks are, too.

What is this thought? What is the name of the mystery of Being and of time? What is the guidance it gives? How shall we come to view it? How shall we tell when we have seen it? To such questions as these, once asked by a young student, a Mr. Buchner, Heidegger replied in a letter dated 18 June 1950:

Everything here is the path of a responding that examines as it listens. Any path risks going astray, leading astray. To follow such paths takes practice in going. Practice needs craft. Stay on the path, in genuine need, and learn the craft of thinking, unswerving, yet erring. (PLT, 186)

This answer does not yet name the thought. Nor does it give criteria for checking off the traits of the thought in order to determine whether it agrees with antecedently given specifications. It admonishes the student only to stay on the path that swings around the thought of the mystery of Being and time. When the student grows older, perhaps he will then genuinely have become old.

> To be old means: to stop in time at
> that place where the unique
> thought of a thought train has
> swung into its joint. (PLT, 10)

But the letter was appended in publication to a lecture bearing the title *The Thing* given earlier that month on June 6 at the Bavarian Academy of Fine Arts. In it Heidegger not only names the thought but also shows how it guides errant man in regard to *things*. By means of this thought the thing — any thing — is grasped as own to man and man is grasped as own to it. In the thing thought by it, earth, sky, mortals, divinities all become own to and with one another. By way of the light this thought brings into the gloomy thicket of the world, the things of the world are able to stand out as what they are, gatherers into ownment, and man is first able to descry them there and to come out toward them, joining with them in the freedom of the clearing they have opened, entering into their gathering.

Even if one cannot offer specifications beforehand for checking the characteristics and the validity of the thought by means of some methodological computation, nevertheless the freedom into which one steps vouches for something by its very openness.

It is a matter of experience — the experience of (a lifetime of) thinking.

II

How are Being and time to be thought? They are the matter of thinking, to be sure. But what is this matter of thinking?

The early Greeks, Heraclitus, Anaximander, Parmenides, first thought Being and time as presencing. This presencing was thought as a coming out into openness, an unconcealment, deconcealment. Even Aristotle, for whom potentiality and actuality were the chief thoughts, could not help thinking actuality as a coming out into openness, an unconcealing, deconcealing, a becoming manifest and overt of what was beforehand hidden and concealed as potentiality. The Greek name for unconcealment is *aletheia*, which is at the same time a name for truth.

But the truth that is taken into view here is not the truth of ordinary thought. It is not just correctness, the agreement between thought and being, concept and thing, statement and fact. It is the truth that lies at the foundation of any possibility of such a truth of correctness. For one cannot tell whether statement agrees with fact, concept with thing, or thought with being, unless first the fact, thing, or being becomes manifest, evident, comes out into the open, and is given as a datum. This openness of evidence is the basis of truth as correctness. The nature of

20

truth lies in openness, unconcealment, *aletheia, die Entbergung, die Unverborgenheit*, unhiddenness.

If Being is presencing and time is presencing, then this presencing must be thought by way of de-concealing, un-concealing. What presences does so by coming out into the open and staying there; its staying is its presencing. As it leaves, it becomes absent, absences; but in its absencing it stays, as absent, and this is its presencing as having been. Both the beings that presence and the beings that absence are, and persist, in their way of staying in the open that has been deconcealed. Being, as presencing, is being and staying unconcealed. Time, as presencing, is coming into the open, staying, departing, yet remaining in the unconcealment in just that way. Being and time are both thinkable only by way of *aletheia*.

From his early writings, Heidegger already began to see the meaning of Being and of time by way of the nature of truth as *aletheia*. This vision of truth, lying at the core of *Being and Time*, has remained with him throughout. In a lecture of 1958, published in 1960, "Hegel and the Greeks," he says (following a charge that Hegel failed to assess properly the nature of truth and its relation to thought, Greek and subsequent):

> Thus we discover, looking toward *aletheia*, that with it our thinking is appealed to by something which drew thinking to itself *before* the beginning of "philosophy" and throughout its whole history. *Aletheia* forestalled the history of philosophy, but in such a way that it withholds itself from philosophical definability as that which demands to be discussed by means of thinking. *Aletheia* is the trustworthy that has not been thought, *the* matter of thinking. Thus, then, *aletheia* remains for us that which is first and above all to be thought — we are to think it as released from regard to the notions, furnished by metaphysics, of "truth" as correctness and of "Being" in the sense of actuality.[2]

From this, as from the almost countless statements about truth scattered through the writings, and as from the equally manifold uses of the notions of concealment and unconcealment, hiddenness and overtness, the closed and the open, it is plain that the clue to the mystery of Being and of time lies for Heidegger in truth as *aletheia*.

It is the same with the idea of freedom — the third of the great concepts in the philosophical tradition, along with Being and truth. In Heidegger's view, freedom can be truly understood only by way of *aletheia*. In the essay *Die Technik* (whose earlier version is the lecture by the same name, also dated as having been given on 6 June 1950 at the Bavarian Academy of Fine Arts) we read:

21

The essential nature of freedom is *originally* not coördinate with the will nor with the causality of human volition at all. Freedom governs the free in the sense of the cleared or illuminated, that is, of the unconcealed. It is the happening of unconcealing, that is, of truth, with which freedom stands in closest and most intimate affinity. All deconcealing belongs within a sheltering, hiding, and concealing. But what is hidden and always conceals itself is that which liberates, the mystery. All deconcealing comes out of the free, goes into the free, and brings into the free. The freedom of the free consists neither in the arbitrary will's being unbound nor in being bound by mere laws. Freedom is the clearing concealer, in which clearing there flutters the veil which covers all that presences of truth and lets the veil appear as covering. Freedom is the domain of the destiny which, in each instance, brings a deconcealment on the latter's way. (V&A, 32f.; T&K, 24f.)

So, now, the clue to the meaning of Being and of time is the same as the clue to the meaning of freedom, and this clue is the thought of truth as *aletheia*. But what is deconcealed is first concealed. Presupposed in deconcealment is necessarily the concealment out of which what is concealed is brought and liberated. And what liberates is, as we now hear, precisely the mystery which always conceals itself.

This mystery which liberates is the trustworthy that has not been thought, *the* matter of thinking; and the truth of man's Being consists above all in shepherding this mystery — the mystery of Being, time, truth, and freedom. If any thought is the polar thought, then this mystery is it.

Thinking is called upon to perform a unique task, thoroughly paradoxical. It must think what by its very nature appears to be incapable of being reached by thought, the mystery that conceals itself, withholding itself from thought in the very act of liberating everything that is brought into the clearing of truth. Thinking must think what retracts itself from the very clearing which it brings about. Thinking can do this only by holding back on its own account. Of all the dangers that threaten thinking,

The evil and thus keenest danger is
thinking itself. It must think
against itself, which it can only
seldom do. (PLT, 8)

We are back to our question. What is the thought of the mystery of Being and of time? The clue is to be found in the thought of truth as *aletheia*, which is also the clue to the same mystery of freedom. But the clue is not the thought. For the thought of truth as deconcealment includes within itself the thought of the mystery of concealment without specifically thinking that thought. The word "truth" rather names the mystery as a mystery than thinks it:

> What this name names is not the crude key that unlocks
> every riddle of thought; rather, *aletheia* is the riddle
> itself — the matter of thought. (W, 268)

The word "truth" names the clue to the mystery but still leaves untraveled the pathway into it.

Is there such a pathway? Can there be any meaning to the idea that man, as thinking being, can do more than name the fact that in the constitution of truth as the presencing of Being and time and the liberating of freedom there persists the self-withholding giver/giving of this truth? Can thinking think *against* itself in such a way as to envision its way into the darkness of the concealment out of which the clearing of truth emerges?

III

What we are in search of is what conceals itself in unconcealment. If we could think this, then we would be thinking Being in its truth, time in its truth, freedom in its truth. If there is any sense in asking questions like "What is Being?," "What is time?," "What is freedom?," and "What is truth?," then, if there is any answer at all, it would have to be given in some such form as "Being is such-and-such," "Time is such and such," and so forth. A statement of this nature would bring into view Being *as* such-and-such, time, freedom, and truth as the same. Is there then such a such-and-such?

At one point in the lecture *On Time and Being* Heidegger says that "the sole purpose of this lecture aims at bringing into view Being itself as *das Ereignis*" (T&B, 20; SD, 22). For the moment let us leave this noun untranslated. As a noun it is presumably the name of something, and what it names would presumably be just the such-and-such desiderated. The lecture, in its own peculiar way, says, "Being is *das Ereignis*." Heidegger is careful to point out immediately that in the context of the lecture this German word does not mean what it ordinarily does. He specifies that the word "as" in the expression "Being as *das Ereignis*" is also to be interpreted in a special way suitable to the special sense of *das Ereignis*.

Leaving *das Ereignis* temporarily untranslated allows us to keep it as a mystery. The mystery deepens when, toward the end of the lecture, Heidegger uses the corresponding verb *ereignen* to answer the question, "What remains to be said?" The reply is, "Only this: *Das Ereignis ereignet.*" The such-and-such such-and-suches. Saying this, he says, we say the same from the same to the same.

> To all appearances this says nothing. It says nothing indeed, as long as we hear what is said as a mere propositional statement and submit it to examination by logic. But suppose we take what is said as clue for reflection and consider that this same is not even something new but is the oldest of the old in Western thought: the immemorially ancient that conceals itself in the name *a-letheia*?

> From what is prompted or initially said by this earliest of all the *leitmotifs* of thought there speaks an obligation that binds all thinking, provided that thinking complies with the bidding of what is to be thought. (T&B, 24; SD, 24f.)

What primordially has hidden itself in the name *aletheia* must be what conceals itself in unconcealment. The word *das Ereignis* names the thought which we seek, Heidegger's single orienting thought.

This earliest of *leitmotifs* of thought fore-speaks something which provides an obligation that binds all thinking that tries to think *the* matter of thought. If we are to try to think *the* matter of thought, then we are bound to think *das Ereignis* and, indeed, to think it in such a way that we grasp the truth that *das Ereignis ereignet. Das Ereignis* is the mystery which liberates, the trustworthy that has not been thought, the self-concealing which brings all into the clear, Being, time, truth, freedom. Not only Being *as das Ereignis.* The word is introduced by definition as

> what determines both, time and Being, in their own, that is, in their belonging together. (T&B, 19; SD, 20)

And this is repeated more intensively:

> What lets both matters belong to one another, what not only brings the two into their own but keeps and holds them in their belonging together . . . is *das Ereignis.*[3] (T&B, 19; SD, 20)

There are two important facets of the meaning of *das Ereignis* to which we shall have to attend. The first is already stated in these defining statements. Heidegger places emphasis upon what is *own* to time and Being. And, specifically, their own is their belonging together. *Das Ereignis* lets time and Being belong to one another. It not only brings them into their own — that is, their belonging together — but keeps and holds them in that mutual belonging.

As what determines, lets, brings, keeps, and holds, it could be said, in some suitable sense, to be quite active. But we cannot think of it as some special being which is active, as, for instance, a symphony conductor is active in bringing and keeping the orchestra members together into their musical belonging. A close analogy might be the music which does this, bringing the conductor in as well as keeping him in his own. Not the ghost of Beethoven still lingering, but the *Eroica* itself. Still, that is only one analogy and should not be allowed to fixate our thinking. It is but one of innumerable analogies, others being, for instance, friendship or enmity.

The mutual belonging of what belongs together is a theme which runs through Heidegger's thinking. It turns up again at a decisive juncture of *Identity and Difference*, published in 1957. Here too it appears in a statement determining the use of the term *das Ereignis*. In this context it is especially the belonging together of man and Being which occupies Heidegger's attention. Metaphysics would think of this belonging together as if man were something given on the one hand and Being something given on the other hand. Their belonging together would then be conceived as a kind of coördination of the two. But that is not how Heidegger thinks. Man is man only in his belonging together with Being, and Being is Being only in its belonging together with man. They are not given antecedently to the belonging. First of all there is the belonging to one another; and only as a result of this is it possible to see that the essential natures of man and Being, as metaphysics conceives them, have their source in this mutual belonging.

Man is a being. But man's distinctive feature lies in the fact that as the thinking being, unlike stone, tree, or eagle, he is placed before Being, open to Being, that he remains referred to Being and thus co-responds to Being. Indeed, Heidegger goes so far as to say that strictly speaking man *is* this relation of co-respondence, and, he adds, "he is only this." The "only" signifies not a limitation but an excess, an overmeasure (I&D, 31, 94).

Being is presence. But Being does not presence to man incidentally or exceptionally. Being presences and stays only by making its claim on man as it concerns him, goes to him.

For it is only man who, open for Being, lets Being arrive
as presence.

The two belong to one another as what they are, man and Being. This is not an idealism. Being is not posited first and only by man. On the contrary, Being and man are *übereignet* — made over, assigned — to each other. They belong together (I&D, 31, 95).

25

This mutual belonging, which has to be thought prior to any metaphysical or representational conception of man and Being as co-related, and by virtue of which man is man and Being is Being — this belonging is the matter of thought which has yet to be thought. In order to reach this thought we have to go to the belonging together itself. We have to experience it. It is a matter of experience, as well as of thinking. Heidegger speaks of the going to the experience as a leap, a *Sprung* (hinting at a leap to the origin, *Ursprung*), and declares that it is only the leap into the domain of the belonging together of man and Being that attunes and determines the experience of thinking.

In the present epoch, according to Heidegger's diagnosis, the belonging together of man and Being occurs in the form of a mutual challenge. Being challenges man through technology and man challenges Being to let beings appear as calculable. This reciprocal challenge he calls *das Ge-Stell* — the frame, the framework, the whole set-up and setting-up in the context of which all beings, whether men or things, are calculable. The significance of this mutual challenge, as a disclosure of Being to man which is its self-hiding and as man's opening of himself to Being which is a complete forgetting of it, lies beyond this essay's sphere. I mention it only because, by its central position today, it is where we are said to stand. When we become aware of it, we become dismayed, startled that (and how) man is delivered over to be owned by Being and Being is appropriated to human being: strange ownership, strange appropriation.

> It is imperative to experience simply this *Eignen* (suiting, fitting), in which man and Being are *ge-eignet* (suited, fitted, en-owned) to one another, that is, to enter into that which we call *das Ereignis*. (I&D, 35, 100)

The importance of *das Ereignis* as the matter of thought which is the mystery of Being and time, the nature and source of truth and freedom, is expressly underlined in *Identity and Difference*. I use these expressions "nature" and "source" only with great hesitation, since they are essentially misleading here, corresponding to the language of metaphysics which Heidegger believes it indispensable to leave behind. What has to be stressed, in any event, is the central and dominating significance of the thought of *das Ereignis* as the object of thinking's search, the pole star in the sky to which thinking looks in its attempt to fulfill the task of the shepherding of Being. Thus we are told, in successive paragraphs, the following:

> *Das Ereignis* is the realm, vibrating within itself, through which man and Being reach one another in their nature, achieve what is natural to them by losing those characteristics which metaphysics conferred on them.

To think *das Ereignis* as *Er-eignis* means to be a builder in the building of this realm that vibrates within itself. Thinking receives the building equipment for this self-suspended structure (or: this structure that hovers within itself, intrinsically) from language. For language is the most delicate, but also (and therefore) the most susceptible vibration, holding everything, in the hovering structure of *das Ereignis*. Inasmuch as our nature is given over to (*vereignet*) language, we dwell in *das Ereignis*.
. . . .

Das Ereignis appropriates, gives man and Being over to their essential Together. In the *Ge-Stell*, the frame, we catch sight of a first, distressing flash of *das Ereignis*. This frame constitutes the essential nature of the modern technical world. (I&D, 37f, 100ff.)

In a word, *das Ereignis* is the letting-belong-together, *das Zusammengehörenlassen*, in and through and by which man and Being belong together. It is the self-suspended, self-hovering *Bau*, building-structure, *Bereich*, realm or domain, within which language vibrates and holds all together. We recall from the essay "Building Dwelling Thinking" that building and dwelling are in truth Being, that man's Being is his building and dwelling, and that the thinking which also belongs to his Being is the thinking involved in his building and dwelling. Building and thinking

are, each in its own way, inescapable for dwelling. The two, however, are also insufficient for dwelling so long as each busies itself with its own affairs in separation instead of listening to one another. They are able to listen if both — building and thinking — belong to dwelling, if they remain within their limits and realize that the one as much as the other comes from the workshop of long experience and incessant practice. (PLT, 160f.)

With regard to language we remember also the remark in the essay "Language" that to discuss language, to place it (*erörtern*)

means to bring to its place of Being not so much language as ourselves: our own gathering into *das Ereignis*. (PLT, 190)

So *das Ereignis* is that which lets both Being and time belong to one another. It is the letting-belong-together of Being and time. But, too,

27

it is the letting-belong-together of Being and man, of building and dwelling and thinking. Language is a potent agent in this letting-belong-together: it is the delicate, susceptible vibration that holds everything in the hovering structure of the letting-belong-together.

That is the first significant facet of the meaning of *das Ereignis*, namely, its being the letting-belong-together by which Being, time, man, building, dwelling, thinking — in the end, all beings as well as the fundamental matters of thought like Being and time, which are not beings — belong together.

We can see this part of the meaning of *das Ereignis* announced in the word itself. We have already had abundant illustration of the operation of the root portion of the word, *eig-*, as it now stands, in words like *eigen*, own; *vereignen*, deliver over as own to; *zueignen*, dedicate or appropriate; *eignen*, to own, suit, or fit; *eigentlich*, true, essential, proper. It appears in other shapes too, which Heidegger uses on occasion, as for instance *Eigentum*, property, and *eigentümlich*, peculiar. Belonging together is being own to one another, in the specific manner of the specific belonging. Man and Being belong to one another in the way in which man and Being today challenge one another through the technical nature of contemporary civilization. They belong to one another always by the fact that Being presences to man and man lets Being arrive as presence. Building and dwelling belong to thinking, and thinking to building and dwelling in a different way. Language belongs to all things in its own special universal way, and all things belong to it in their special ways.

At a time when he had not yet come to name *das Ereignis* as the thought of the mystery of Being, Heidegger was already thinking this belonging together and the letting-belong-together which is now called by that name. So in the essay "The Origin of the Work of Art," the most important and incisive phrase in the entire piece is "the intimacy of simple belonging to one another" (PLT, 49). In the work of art, world and earth strive, as opponents, raising each other into the self-assertion of their own natures.

> The more the struggle overdoes itself on its own part, the more inflexibly do the opponents let themselves go into the intimacy of simple belonging to one another. . . . It is because the struggle arrives at its high point in the simplicity of intimacy that the unity of the work comes about in the fighting of the battle. . . . The repose of the work that rests in itself thus has its presencing in the intimacy of striving. (UK, 51f; PLT, 49f.)

Only later, in an "Addendum" to this essay written in 1956, does Heidegger identify *das Ereignis* as the real thought that enables us to comprehend the nature of art by way of its relation to Being and truth.

> Art is considered neither an area of cultural achievement
> nor an appearance of spirit; it belongs to *das Ereignis* by
> way of which the "meaning of Being" (see *Being and
> Time*) can alone be defined.   (PLT, 86)

At the center of *das Ereignis* is *own*.

If we were to give the most literal possible translation of *das Ereignis* it would have to consist of *en-, -own-,* and *-ment: enownment.* Enownment is the letting-be-own-to-one-another of whatever is granted belonging-together. It is the letting be married of any two or more — Being and time, Being and man, earth and world, earth and sky and mortals and divinities (the fourfold), bridge and river, automobile and speedway, buying and selling commodities, management and labor — which can only be by means of belonging to one another. Enownment is not their belonging, but what lets their belonging be. *Sein* is not *Seiendheit.*

Heidegger is not the man to speak of love — for his own reasons, whatever they may be. So it is we, rather, who have to say also that enownment is what lets love be. And as Nietzsche celebrated those who were his most active opponents as those dearest to him, so also it must be said that enownment is what lets conflict, with all its hatred, opposition, and destruction, be. Heidegger has no God. Enownment is the god beyond God. It is that Being, or that Non-Being, which is beyond all beings, even beyond all divine beings, which grants both Being and Non-Being and all the dimensions of time, without being and being itself. In *On Time and Being* he presents enownment as the source which gives Being and gives time, as gifts are given. It sends the destiny of Being and extends time, expropriating itself so that man can stand in appropriation — enownment — with Being within time. Enownment is the mystery which withdraws itself in letting Being and time appear. It dedicates Being as presence and time as the realm of the open while, and through, keeping itself back. We can say *"das Ereignis ereignet,"* "enownment enowns," but this does not mean that there is some being, named Enownment, who or which is doing something, as a king might grant gifts to his subjects. It hovers; it does not act. It is hovering in the very act of my writing this and your reading it.

IV

The second important facet of the meaning of enownment is also reflected by the root portion of the word, *eig-*, seen from a different vantage point. For *eig-* is in fact the result of an auditory-etymological conflation. As Heidegger points out, *ereignen* orignally meant *eräugen. Äugen* is a verb form whose noun form is *Auge*, eye. *Eräugen* is, as it were, to en-eye.

The word *Ereignis* is taken from natural language. Originally *er-eignen* means: *er-äugen*, that is to say, *er-blicken*, to see or catch sight of, to call to oneself in looking, *an-eignen*, to en-own, ap-propriate.[4] (I&D, 100f.)

Other interpretations of the etymology are possible. The earlier word, *eräugen*, bears the sense "to place before the eyes, to show," and hence also, "to show itself, *sich zeigen*." The present word *ereignen* in its ordinary sense of "to happen" develops naturally out of this notion of manifestation and self-manifestation. The connection is that which is designated by a word like *show, show up*: something that happens shows, it shows up, turns up, shows itself. Someone who has been missing or absent shows up. Showing is a metaphor for happening and thus can come to mean happening literally. It is perhaps surprising that Heidegger did not make more specific use of this connection, precisely in view of the present aspect of the meaning of enownment which is under consideration.

Enownment is not just the belonging together of the beings (and non-beings) that belong together. It is the letting be of that mutual belonging, the letting be of the mutuality of belonging. If the first facet of its meaning lays stress on the belonging, the second stresses the letting-be. For one can ask about enownment *how* it comes about — how *das Ereignis ereignet*. The *how* is not something distinct from the enownment, added to it, so that it may be brought into being. The enownment is itself the letting-be of the mutuality of ownness of all that is and is not. Our question is only, "How are we to think the letting-be?"

If *own* is at the center of enownment, nevertheless *en-* is at the beginning and *-ment* is at the end, and the beginning and the end are one: *letting-be*. God creates. The god beyond God lets be. God lets light be. The god beyond God lets be . . . . what?

It is imperative, Heidegger thinks, not only to think *das Eigensein des Seienden*, the being-own or ownness of beings, in thinking enownment, but before and above all, *das Ereignen*, enowning, *enownment*. And the meaning of enowning, *Ereignen*, is evident specifically in the working of language. (God *said*, Let there be light. And there was light.) Saying, *die Sage*, which is able to let-be-heard, which (by a peculiar coincidence in German, in which *gehörenlassen* means not only to let be heard but also to let belong) is able to let-belong, is showing.

Die Sage ist Zeigen. (UZS, 257; OWL, 126)

Etymologically the German for to say, *sagen* — from which Heidegger derives the noun *die Sage*, which is not to be interpreted as saga, but as saying in a special and fundamental sense, a sense in which saying is the silence in which language allows of being spoken and heard — belongs also to a word group bearing the meanings to let see, to show. Heidegger is etymologically accurate in making saying showing. But showing too is understood in a special and fundamental sense, in which, without itself appearing or being a being that appears, it is what lets what appears appear. What presences — what is essential — in language is this saying as showing (UZS, 254; OWL, 121).

This Saying is not to be understood as mere human saying, as speaking or being silent in a human way. It is therefore natural to capitalize its name. It has to be thought of as the Saying of language itself. It is explicitly introduced by Heidegger as the name for the whole being of language, the multiform saying that pervades the entire structure of language (UZS, 253; OWL, 122f). Human saying is made possible because humans dwell within this Saying of Language.

As Being and man belong to one another mutually, so that man needs Being for the presencing of what presences, and Being needs man so that it may presence and grant presencing to beings, so Saying and man belong to one another mutually. For, while man needs Saying in order to be able to listen and speak, Saying needs man's listening and speaking in order that it may do what it has to do. As the ultimate nature of Being is enownment, so too the ultimate nature of Saying is enownment, granting Saying its nature. Because Saying is enownment, one can ask also about it, whether

> Saying is itself the bringer of rest, which grants the repose of the belonging-together of that which belongs within the structure of language? (UZS, 256; OWL, 125)

Language, as Saying, is enownment, because it is showing, *Zeigen.*

> In everything that speaks to us, that touches us by being spoken and spoken about, in everything that gives itself to us in speaking, or waits for us as unspoken, but also in the speaking that is done by *us*, there is at work the showing that lets what presences appear, what absences disappear. Saying is in no way the linguistic expression added on to what is appearing; rather, all appearing and disappearing is grounded in the showing Saying. (UZS, 257; OWL, 126)

The essential nature of language is showing. The essential nature of Saying is showing. What is this showing? What does Saying do when it shows?

> It liberates what presences into its specific presencing, de-liberates what absences into its specific absencing.

Saying pervades, ordains, disposes the free of the clearing which all appearing must seek out, all disappearing must leave behind, the place into which every presence and absence must show itself, into which it must say itself. (UZS, 257; OWL, 126)

The connection of Saying's showing with freedom is essential. The freedom of the clearing in which what appears appears, what disappears disappears, what presences presences and what absences absences — this freedom is the same freedom we have met with earlier. It stands in closest affinity with the happening of truth — unconcealing. Appearing is the unconcealing of what has been concealed. What disappears returns to its concealment, yet remains revealed precisely as concealed. We are alerted once more to the mystery which, being hidden and always concealing itself, is nevertheless that which liberates. But what liberates is the Saying which is showing. The mystery lies in the Saying which is showing.

What is this mystery that quickens within the showing Saying? We can only name it, says Heidegger, because it will not endure any discussion, any argument. For it is the locale of all places and of all time-play-spaces. An ancient word is available for naming it:

What quickens in the showing of Saying is *das Eignen.*

Das Eignen — how, now, shall we read this? Of course, it is *owning.* But *das Eignen* is *das Äugen*, and so it must be *showing* as coming out to be seen or as letting be seen or as seeing or being seen or both. Appearing is owning and owning is appearing. The sameness of appearing and owning immediately strikes the eye here.

What appears can appear only as it owns and is owned. What is to own and be owned can do so only by appearing. What quickens within Saying's showing is that which lets be the appearing of mutual belonging, the belonging of mutual appearing, the truth and Being of all that is, the presencing together of Being, time, man, things, places and times, earth and sky and mortals and divinities. And so once more Heidegger defines the words *Ereignen, Ereignis,* enowning, enownment. *Das Eignen,* the letting-own-show,

brings what presences and what absences each into its own; each shows itself, as it is, in this own; each stays in it in its own way. (UZS, 258; OWL, 127)

This letting-own-show is what quickens within Saying's showing. It is the bringer. It quickens Saying as the show in its showing. Let it be called, says Heidegger, *das Ereignen,* the enowning. Enowning, we now realize, can be what it is only as the showing that quickens language's Saying, and therefore as bringer of what presences and absences each into its own, what liberates the present and de-liberates the absent. The intimacy of simple belonging to one another can come about only by an enowning which, as enowning, is the bringer of appearing and disappearing.

It is imperative — this needs to be repeated — not only to think the being-own of beings when we think enownment, but before and above all, the enowning itself. This enowning

> yields the free of the clearing in which what presences
> can stay, from which what absences can escape and keep
> its staying in this escape. (UZS, 258; OWL, 127)

Enowning yields and brings. It yields the free and it brings its presences and absences. What is it that does the yielding and bringing in this enowning? It is the enownment itself, and nothing but that.

Enownment thus is two things that are one and the same. It is the letting-belong-together, the letting-be-own-to-one-another of all that belong together, and it is the yielder of the free, the clearing in which those that belong together are able to be together. It is the original and originary letting-belong out of which presencing and absencing as showing, appearing, disappearing, staying in presence or in absence, come to be. It lets all this come to be.

One thinks, in thinking of coming-to-be, of the Greek *physis*, not in the Aristotelian sense, but in the sense that Heidegger believes he can find in the pre-Aristotelian thinkers, as for instance in Heraclitus. The original sense of *physis* (the Roman *natura*, our *nature*) is Being, but Being as *das sich verbergende Entbergen*, the deconcealing that conceals itself.

> Self-deconcealing is coming forth into unhiddenness, and
> this means to hide, to shelter unhiddenness as such in
> the essential being: unhiddenness is called *a-letheia* —
> truth, as we translate it, is primordial, and this means
> that it is essentially not a character of human knowledge
> and statement. Truth, also, is not mere value or an
> "Idea" toward whose realization man — the reason is not
> very clear — ought to strive. Truth, rather, as
> self-deconcealing, belongs to Being itself: *physis* is
> *aletheia*, deconcealment, and therefore *kryptesthai
> philei*, it loves to hide itself. (W, 371)

Enownment, the letting-be-shown-own, names the mystery that loves to hide itself in showing all that is to be shown; and the mystery is

33

that it is the letting-be of the mutual belonging of all — beings and non-beings — which need one another.

V

How can we speak of this letting-be? How are we to think it? The questions do not ask for a discussion, disputation, argument. They are intended only to initiate a search for an appropriate way of thinking and speaking about that which is the yielder and the bringer, the locale and hovering structure, of all the beings and nonbeings that fit into the opened sphere of belonging.

How are we to think our way into and through that sphere? The answer to this question is not to be given here. It is given only by the actual effort of the thinking itself. Heidegger has not outlined his own path or the paths that could or must be followed. We must say on our own responsibility what path opens before us.

Life and history follow the paths that are opened to them through the enownment which the opening of Being and time provides for them. Within life, every stratum and dimension partakes of the ownment that enownment opens. Perception, for instance, is an ownment between man, Being, and time, in which the world opens up for man in his seeing, hearing, touching, smelling, tasting. In perception, what is other to the individual human being appears as enowned in its otherness. The house we see over there is seen as the dwelling place, whose entrance beckons or repels, which harbors within it the family, the hidden place of love and hate, conflict and healing. Saying, in uttering "house," has allowed this structure of enownment to appear and has opened up the possibility of ourselves grasping it and even entering into it to partake of the mode of life-presencing and -absencing which it makes accessible. These brief sentences must do as example for the whole of a path of thinking that has hardly begun to become plain as the way in which thinking is challenged to proceed now and for the present epoch.

Every shape of experience familiar to man is a shape of a limited enownment. As earth, sky, mortals, and divinities constitute the encompassing fourfold which saying first opens for humans and within which all four are own to and with each other, the encompassing enownment within which human history happens, so every stratum and strand of history is thinkable in its truth as a way of staying within some finite form of this mutual ownness. The social order, for instance, is an order of enownment. In it, women and men, children and adults, classes, castes, creeds, and colors all presence together, finding, making, receiving statuses, entering into groups, associations, and institutions, under norms — ranging from statutory laws, rules, and regulations to customs and mores, rites and rituals, ceremonies and conventions — which make explicit what the saying that constitutes the social order says. That saying opens up the realm of the social order within which each individual presences in the encompassing and pervading mode of being-own which characterizes his community. The community is the *com+munus,* in which gifts, obligations, services, and duties are exchanged, that is, in which each one is granted the opportunity to be (presence) among the entitled ones. It is the Ge-*mein*-de, that is, the collectivity of all those who are *mine* to and with the individual, his own, the ones for whom he too is own. The opening of that clearing of earth-world, mortals-divinities, which is a human society is the opening of a sphere of enownment in which the heroes and villains of bygone days remain in their absence and in which the historic events of the past and the actualities and possibilities of the present and future take shape as a destiny which the group takes upon itself as its own. The myths and legends by which it imagines itself in its world express its sense of how all belongs to all. The material means of which it disposes — clothing, utensils, machines, vehicles, foodstuffs — all bear its imprint and lend their imprint to it, the two, the culture and its material, belonging to one another in a mutually constitutive ownness. This socio-cultural Being is constantly opening up, constantly vibrating as a clearing in the total world-fourfold, in and through the enownment that lets it be and that it lets be. In it, man and Being and time are together in their mutual belonging in the specific, limited, finite, tragedy-ridden configuration of being-own characteristic of the society and the epoch. If we are to reach the real meaning of the group's life and history, it can only be by way of thinking of the enownment in which this life and history take shape in presencing.

What has been said here should be taken as a mere hint at the possibilities of thinking which are made accessible to us by the concept of the opening of the own. Heidegger has set his eyes toward one direction of these possibilities — the one described in the present essay under the heading of "enownment" as the source which gives Being and gives time, which sends Being's destiny and out-reaches the time for it, which expropriates itself so that man can enter appropriation. Hegel's entire thought was an exploration of the systematic context discernible in his day, uttered in the language of enownment which saying allowed at the time: the enownment of the dialectical unity of opposites. Modern existentialism has attempted over and over, from Kierkegaard to Jaspers, Marcel, Buber, and Sartre, to enter into the thinking of enownment, even if it did not yet know how to name its thought. In Sartre's case, particularly, enownment beckoned as an unreachable and untrustable illusion, a haunting ghostly shape forever eluding him. Therefore he had to declare that man is essentially incapable of living in enownment.

The meaning of politics in the Marxian and post-Marxian age can be understood in its essential character only, again, in terms of the thought of the enownment that lets contemporary communities presence in their character. Heidegger has attempted to name this mode of enownment by way of *das Gestell*, but there is little actual concrete political analysis in his writing; and indeed the whole task remains to be done as a real project.

What is true of the socio-cultural order, of philosophical thinking, and of politics, is true also of the meaning of literature and the arts. Heidegger has had more to say about these, perhaps, than about any other of the dimensions of culture. But his thinking here has in fact only reached so far as to begin to name the basic thought. The essays in *Poetry, Language, Thought*, and essays of a similar nature outside that volume, offer as yet only impressionistic touches of a picture that calls for painting and repainting.

Once the thought of enownment has come to stand still in the world's sky, new journeys begin to announce their possibilities, guided by the vision.[5]

University of California, Santa Cruz

NOTES

1   The abbreviated bibliographical references in the text are to the following works, all by Heidegger:

EP   *The End of Philosophy.* Trans. Joan Stambaugh. New York: Harper and Row, 1973.

I&D   *Identity and Difference.* Trans. and introd. Joan Stambaugh. New York: Harper and Row, 1969.

OWL   *On The Way To Language.* Trans. Peter D. Hertz. New York: Harper and Row, 1971.

PLT   *Poetry, Language, Thought.* Trans. and introd. Albert Hofstadter New York: Harper and Row, 1971.

SD   *Zur Sache des Denkens.* Tübingen: Max Niemeyer Verlag, 1969.

T&B   *On Time and Being.* Trans. Joan Stambaugh. New York: Harper and Row, 1972.

T&K   *Die Technik und die Kehre.* Pfullingen: Neske, 1962.

UK   *Der Ursprung des Kunstwerkes.* Mit einer Einführung von Hans-Georg Gadamer. Stuttgart: Reclam, 1960.

UZS   *Unterwegs zur Sprache.* Pfullingen: Neske, 1959.

V&A   *Vorträge und Aufsätze.* Pfullingen: Neske, 1954.

W   *Wegmarken.* Frankfurt am Main: Vittorio Klostermann, 1967.

2   This statement expresses Heidegger's evaluation of philosophy, as he understands it historically, as something to be surpassed by returning to the thinking that already preceded it in ancient Greece and by carrying on from there. I shall not attend to this part of his view here. What philosophy is, has been, and can be, remains for me an open question. I do not hesitate to think of Heidegger as a philosopher, despite his disclaimer of that name. Indeed his thinking appears to me to fall within that great tradition, alternative to the Aristotelian thinking of Being, in which the clue to Being is sought not in Being itself but beyond Being, as in Plato's The Good (which was not a being) and in Plotinus' The One (which was not a being). On this point, Etienne Gilson's *Being and Some Philosophers* remains enlightening even if it does not yet reach to the time of Heidegger's vision. Heidegger would not see himself in this way, of course, but when does anyone see himself as others see him?

Moreover, in my view, Hegel's concept of Spirit, when rightly understood, represents a halfway stage between philosophies of Being and philosophies transcending or alternative to Being. It therefore has a certain affinity to the latter, just as Heidegger's thought does. It is an essential affinity and it holds despite all criticism that Heidegger may wish to make of Hegel.

3 The portion of the text which I have omitted, ". . . *der Verhalt beider Sachen, der Sach-Verhalt . . . ,*" is virtually untranslatable. Joan Stambaugh renders it "the way the two matters stand, the matter at stake." It contains - more than a pun - a metamorphosis of the word *Sachverhalt,* which ordinarily means the facts of the case, the circumstances, state of affairs, etc. One could say: the fact of the matters of Being and time, their situation, their factual circumstances, that which gives them the hold they have on one another and as fact, that which lets them hold together as belonging together in fact. We could venture: the matter-hold, on the analogy of the wrestler's hold, imagining Being and time as holding to each other, where *das Ereignis* is that which lets this matter-hold be. More simply — bearing in mind that *sich verhalten* also means, in the case of a thing (a matter, *Sache*) to be, and in the case of a person, to behave, to conduct oneself, to take up and hold an attitude (toward) — we could say that this *Sach-verhalt* is what Being and time *are,* how they conduct themselves, in their belonging together.

4 The references to German etymology are omitted in the English translation of this passage. See I&D, 36.

5 The research for this study was done under a Senior Fellowship from the National Endowment for the Humanities and with the aid of funds from the Research Committee of the University of California at Santa Cruz, for which grateful acknowledgment is here made.

Art and Truth in Raging Discord:
Heidegger and Nietzsche on the Will to Power

David Farrell Krell

"Very early in my life I took the question of the relation of *art* to *truth* seriously: even now I stand in holy dread in the face of this discord." — Friedrich Nietzsche in 1888 on the occasion of a critical reappraisal of *The Birth of Tragedy* (1871).[1]

In that book's "Foreword to Richard Wagner," Nietzsche had expressed his conviction that "art is the supreme task and authentic metaphysical activity of man's life. . . ."[2]

In the body of the text he had defined this supreme task: " — to redeem the eye from its vision of horrid night, and with the healing balm of semblance [*Schein*] to rescue the subject from the convulsions of an agitated will" (SI, 108).

Again in 1888 Nietzsche noted the hither side of this discord in a phrase Camus later found at the center of his thought on artistic creation: "We have *art* in order *not to perish from the truth*" (WM, 822).

And why should truth harm men?
Because "the truth is ugly" (ibid.).
This by way of *prelude*.

*

This paper raises the question of the relation between art and truth in three thinkers

Plato
Nietzsche
Heidegger.

But the texts it examines determine its optics: Heidegger's lectures on "Will to Power as Art" and "Will to Power as Knowledge," delivered in Freiburg during the winter semester of 1936-37 and the summer semester of 1939, invoke Nietzsche's pronouncements on art, which in turn invite Heidegger's study of certain Platonic texts.

The discord between art and truth appears as a fortunate or beneficial division in Plato's philosophy;

with Nietzsche that division becomes "a dreadfully raging discord";

finally, Heidegger rethinks the discord between art and truth — transferring it to the essence of truth itself.

I

From Nietzsche's unpublished notes (WM, 797) Heidegger extracts five propositions on art, formulated as follows (NI, 90):

1. Art is the most transparent and familiar form of will to power.
2. Art must be grasped in terms of the artist.
3. According to the expanded concept of the artist, art is the basic occurrence of all being; being is, insofar as it is, a self-creating; it is something created.
4. Art is the exceptional countermovement against nihilism.
5. Art is worth more than "the truth."

These five theses elaborate what Nietzsche says most simply when he designates art as "the greatest stimulant to life" (WM, 808). In a more diffuse formulation:

Art must be viewed as the creative production of the artist (not in terms of the purely receptive/reactive aesthetics of enjoyment) who participates in the life-enhancing will to power at work everywhere in the fundamentally creative cosmos and who therefore struggles against the life-negation of moralists and metaphysicians — whose atavistic "truth" is no more than a symptom of *décadence, ressentiment,* and impotence to power. Yet his struggle against these others must be by way of indirection, since the artist's creative life must be ruled by a yes-saying response to the chaos of Becoming. This yes-saying response is productive frenzy, and it constitutes "the grand style." The achievement of art in the grand style shatters the subject-object relation, fusing worker and work. It is the artist's self-production.

The essence of creation in the grand style is, according to Heidegger, "the frenzied production of the beautiful in the work" (NI, 135). But because Nietzsche does not interpret the essence of creation (*Schaffen*) in terms of the work of art — he speaks instead of the artist's "aesthetic behavior" — the joint production in the grand style of the art work and the artist is not adequately determined in his thought (NI, 138). Here Heidegger makes hidden reference to his own starting point in *Der Ursprung des Kunstwerkes* ("The Origin of the Work of Art").[3]

In that essay Heidegger begins with the originating circle of art and artist. Art is the work of the artist who becomes what he is only through the work of art (H, 7-8; English ed., 17-18). In the Nietzsche lecture Heidegger speaks of *Schaffen,* but the circle is the same. Creation is the pathos of the artist who becomes what he is only through the work of creation. But Heidegger complains that Nietzsche's analyses of "aesthetic behavior"

especially when they try to ground creativity in a physiology that is in turn grounded in the metaphysics of life-enhancing will to power, by reference to its erotic/sexual stirrings, the excitement of its play of forms, the sensuality of Protean shapes, the remarkable similarity to nervous conditions and morbid symptoms

exert a centrifugal force on reflection on the matrix of the artist and the art work. A silence obtrudes which Heidegger's own interpretation dares to break, since it too pursues the question of art with Zarathustran dedication. "Precisely because the grand style is a gift-giving, yes-saying will toward Being, it reveals its essential nature only when a decision has been made, indeed through the grand style itself, about what the Being of beings means" (NI, 158). Nietzsche identifies the grand style as the "classical," yet this identification fails to penetrate the circle of art and artist in the work, and so fails to determine the grand style as such. "Nietzsche never expressed himself otherwise about it; for every great thinker *thinks* always one jump more originally than he directly *speaks.* Our interpretation must therefore try to say what is unsaid in his" (NI, 158).

II

Heidegger brings the issues of will to power as art and truth into the sphere of his fundamental questioning of metaphysics (*Grundfragen der Metaphysik*), whose predominant question is that of the truth of Being (*die Wahrheitsfrage*). He seeks enlightenment concerning Nietzsche's understanding of art in the grand style through his understanding of "truth." But the question of *the essence of truth* is precisely the one Heidegger cannot find in Nietzsche. "It is of decisive significance to know that Nietzsche did not pose the authentic question of truth, the question of the essence of the true and the truth of essence, and thereby the question of the necessary possibility of its essential transformation — and that Nietzsche therefore never unfolded the domain of this question" (NI, 175). The "unsaid" of Nietzsche's philosophy is precisely the *Wahrheitsfrage*.

However, no one knew better than Nietzsche that the prevailing interpretation of "truth" in philosophy devolved from Plato. From his experience of nihilism Nietzsche came to understand his life's task as — overturning Platonism.

For Platonism truth resides in supersensuous being (*to on*). Yet if the truth of Platonism is in fact a nihilistic flight from the sensuous, and if this flight is the fundamental event of occidental history, then Nietzsche's project becomes that of "rescuing and giving form to the sensuous" (NI, 189). Inasmuch as philosophy and science strive to know the true — which remains supersensuous and eidetic — Nietzsche rejects them.

Art is worth more than truth.

For Plato, on the other hand, truth is clearly worth more than art.[4] Yet in the Dialogues the relation between art and truth cannot be called a discord, although a division does obtain between them. In the *Republic* (Bks. III and X) Plato interprets art as *mimesis* and criticizes it because of its distance from the Ideas (*eidei*). *Porro ara pou tou alethous he mimetike estin*: "Art is far away from the truth" (*Rep.* 598 b; NI, 216). But not hopelessly far. In the *Symposium* eros appears as that process whereby beauty — which is what most brightly shines — calls men away from the sensuous world (*me on*) to the realm of permanent being (*to on*) (NI, 195; 226). The *Phaedrus* takes up this calling most explicitly. Beauty awakens us from forgetfulness of Being and grants us a view on the Ideas. But its action is most mysterious. If Being is supersensuous, and if the sensuous is nonbeing, how can essential beauty shine through sensuous appearance? How can beauty conduct the soul from *me on* (the *eidolon*) to *to on* (the *eidos*)?

In Plato there is a division between the sensuous and supersensuous, the transient and the permanent, and hence a division between art and philosophy —

> Yet this division, a discord only in the broadest sense, is for Plato not a dreadfully raging discord but a beneficial one. Beauty lifts us beyond the sensuous and carries us back into the true. Accord prevails over the division

because beauty, as what shines, the sensuous, has in
advance secured its essential nature in the truth of Being
as supersensuous. (NI, 230)

If there is a distance and a division between *to on* and *me on* it belongs to
the essence of Platonism that it eliminate all discord and close the distance
by an unseen maneuver. Nietzsche exposes this maneuver and lets the
discord rage.

III

Nietzsche's reversal of Platonism and exposure of its concealed
maneuver takes the form of a tracing back (*Rückführung*) of the Platonic
to on and *me on* — that is, of the "true" and "merely apparent" realms of
being — to perspectival relations of *value*. Decisive for Nietzsche's thought
is, first, that he decides to interrogate the origins of the Platonic division,
and second, how he conducts the interrogation (NI, 539 ff.). Although the
second is determined in advance by the metaphysical tradition in ways
Nietzsche himself could not discern, the first signals nothing less than the
end of metaphysics.

For Plato *to on* is what endures in presence, what persists and
lasts. Being is permanence (*Beständigkeit*). For Nietzsche "true Being" is a
fiction necessary for securing and preserving human life; it is an attempt to
freeze the flow of Becoming and impose order on a chaotic manifold. Such
imposition is the securing of permanence — illusory permanence — or
permanentizing (*Bestandsicherung*). Will to power expresses the final
possibility of Idealism and brings the Platonic projection of Being to an
end by bringing its covert maneuver to light: Nietzsche's genealogical
critique on the basis of will to power exposes ontological *Beständigkeit* as
anthropological *Bestandsicherung*, which is to say, it brings to light the
fictitious but necessary character of the Platonic realm of permanent(ized)
Being. Platonic permanence betrays the concealed dominance of that
conception of *time* according to which metaphysics has interpreted the
Being of beings. Nietzsche's unmasking of permanence as a projection of
the permanentizing perspective of human existence necessitates a new
exploration of the way temporality conjoins man and world. By referring
to Nietzsche's fundamentally new comprehension of metaphysics as the
permanentizing of beings into Being, Heidegger points toward Nietzsche's
central role in compelling the question of *Being and Time*.

If the essence of truth is *Bestandsicherung* then *to on* is merely
what is taken to be permanent and fast. Of course, this taking to be
permanent by will to power is not an intuition of *eidos* in the Platonic
manner. Far rather, *Bestandsicherung* is the delirious embrace of the
eidolon or illusory image which idealistic reflection takes to be *eidos*. In

this sense Nietzsche may be said to have overturned Platonism — by inverting the divided-line sketched in Plato's *Republic* (509 d ff.):

Nietzsche identifies true knowledge (*episteme*) as mere imaging (*eikasia*).

Instead of progressing up the divided-line from the merely apparent realm to true Being, Platonic dialectic unwittingly regresses to mere shadowplay and image; inasmuch as metaphysics plants its feet on the floating ground of the eidoletic *eidei* it may be said to be standing on its head. By exposing the genuine character of the Ideas to be illusory fixations Nietzsche overturns Platonism and sets it upright.

Or? Perhaps it would be more correct to say that, far from overturning the divided-line, Nietzsche completes its advance by identifying the state of mind that corresponds to the highest reality, the Good, a state of mind Plato himself was never able to define, as value-judgments (*Werturteile*) executed by perspectival will to power. Actually Nietzsche does both. He advances beyond dianoietic knowledge of the Ideas to an intuition of their essential nature. They are valuative projections of and by will to power

and particularly that negative/reactive will to power that maintains the moral prejudice of the exclusivity of opposites on this side of Good and Evil.

But how can Nietzsche complete the Platonic advance, or overturn it, which here amounts to the same thing? Upon what ground does Nietzsche (correctly) see the illusory nature of all knowledge? "For only if truth is essentially correctness can it according to Nietzsche's interpretation be incorrectness and illusion" (NI, 548). In fact, Nietzsche's is the uttermost transformation of metaphysically conceived truth, which is to say

correctness
adaequatio
correspondentia
homoiosis

because it destroys the horizon upon which the correct and incorrect can be determined. We cannot know the *Bestand* of *Bestandsicherung*; neither can we ground the meaning of *Sicherung*. Nietzsche says that life requires imposition of structures within the chaos of Becoming in order to secure itself. What "life" means is a problem: Nietzsche uses the word to mean human, animal, and vegetable life, and even Becoming as a whole. The issue of "perspectival valuation" in life's self-securing remains perplexing so long as "life" hovers in this ambiguity. Nor does the "chaos of Becoming" disspell the confusion: in Nietzsche's pronouncements on truth the relation of life to chaos remains hopelessly obscure. One might say that "chaos" is the last name conceivable for the Being of beings in the manner of metaphysics, the final and most desperate appellation of being as a whole, because its inadequacy does not simply result from oversight or incapacity on the thinker's part to determine (correctly) what is true.

Neither in *Bestand* nor in *Sicherung* does the horizon upon which man and world meet take recognizable or cognizable form. What the horizon could be Nietzsche cannot say — unless it is precisely what the grand style in each case must create for itself. Heidegger insists that the new horizon can appear only in "a *more original, essential form* of human Being (in *Da-sein*)."[5]

IV

We are now in a position to return to our central question, which asks how the beneficent division of art and truth in Plato's philosophy becomes for Nietzsche a dreadfully raging discord. If Nietzsche is to overturn the Platonic value-structure the division or dichotomy of art and truth may change in one of two ways:

either the discord between art and truth must disappear altogether when Platonism is overturned (NI, 218)

or, if the dichotomy of art and truth is indeed a friendly one for Plato, so much so that art is absorbed into his philosophical project, the overturning of Platonism must vigorously reassert the discord — this time as "raging discord" (*erregende Zwiespalt*) (NI, 231).

Heidegger argues that for both Plato and Nietzsche art and truth are events that disclose the Being of beings. "Beauty and truth are both related to Being, both indeed by way of unveiling the Being of beings" (NI, 231). No matter what sort of dichotomy between art and truth subsists, whether harmonious or furious, each sustains a relation to the way beings show themselves to be. "Accordingly, the essence of will to power must yield a belonging-together that at the same time becomes a discord" (NI, 231). What this curious relation of art and truth might be is extremely difficult to say, but in Heidegger's view one thing is sure: Nietzsche's attempt to rescue the sensuous world from the deprecations of Platonistic metaphysics cannot succeed if it merely reverses the latter's value-scheme, if it exalts semblance (art) at the expense of being (truth). So long as Nietzsche's revaluation of all values embraces the truth of art and scorns the art of truth the Platonic structure persists. To insist that according to the principle of will to power art stands over truth, truth under art, is not to escape metaphysical modes of thought. "Inasmuch as this Over and Under determines the structural form of Platonism, he [Nietzsche] remains essentially within it" (NI, 233).

The will to truth petrifies Becoming, holds it fast as "Being," and so maintains itself, whereas the will to art in the grand style opens itself to the manifold possibilities of Becoming by transfiguring it in frenzied creativity, and so enhances itself. From the point of view of the enhancement of life the latter is of greater worth. But with the expression of "worth" the structure of Platonism — and even its secret maneuver — survives.

> The true world is that of Becoming; the apparent world that which is stable and permanent. The true and apparent worlds have exchanged places, ranks, and forms. But in this exchange and reversal just that *distinction* between a true and apparent world is maintained. (NI, 617)

"Semblance" is held to be of greater value than "truth." Yet "truth" is an illusion, so that it is a question simply of two types of illusion or appearance. One is claimed from the point of view of life-enhancement to be of more worth than the other. The groundlessness of this claim Heidegger calls "the uttermost position of the metaphysical conception of truth" (NI, 622). Not only must "truth" stand aside, however, but also semblance
since without the first as a standard (of correctness) the second cannot be (correctly) ascertained.

What then remains? Having experienced the loss of the horizon upon which truth and illusion can be distinguished, has Nietzsche not radically dismantled the Over and Under of Platonism and instigated the raging discord between art and truth?

That Nietzsche did not simply reverse the Over and Under of *to on* and *me on, eidos* and *eidolon*, the supersensuous and the sensuous, or at least that he knew such a reversal would not decisively leave behind the nihilism entrenched in the Platonistic mode of thought, Heidegger attests toward the close of his lecture on "Will to Power as Art." Here he cites Nietzsche's six theses entitled, "How the 'True World' Finally Became a Fable" (1888). As they recount a succinct comic history of metaphysics these fragments address a kind of ultimatum to metaphysicians. Most important for our discussion is the final thesis:

> 6. We have done away with the 'true world': which world remains? The apparent one perhaps? But no! *Along with the true world we have also done away with the world of appearances*! (SII, 963)

Nietzsche appears to realize full well that Dionysian loyalty

> to the earth
> to Becoming rather than Being

> to semblance rather than essence
> to art rather than "the truth"

hovers in a groundless region where truth and semblance come to the same. Yet if that is the case Nietzsche's exaltation of art and denunciation of truth reverberate within the very Platonic value-structure they seek to escape. "When we recall *that* and *how* Nietzsche wants to ground art in the life of the body through his physiological aesthetics we see an affirmation of the sensuous world — but not its dismantling" (NI, 241). The irony of course is that any decision to ground art in identifiable physiological traits necessarily adopts a stance toward the supersensuous: it covertly appeals to something "permanent."

How can the Platonic division between supersensuous permanent Being and sensuous nonbeing, hence the subordination of art to truth, be overcome? Nietzsche recognizes that it is insufficient to overturn Platonism in the way one overturns an hourglass

> or the divided-line.

Heidegger calls Nietzsche's way of overturning the Platonic value-scheme

> "a new interpretation of sensuousness and the raging discord between art and truth" (NI, 243 ff.).

In Nietzsche's view living beings struggle against forces that mean their defeat and death by subjecting them to rhythm and form. The ceaselessly striving will to power of creative frenzy most successfully achieves this for man. The artist's subjugation of multiple alien forces opens a raging discord between art and truth

> inasmuch as "truth" means capitulation of will and escape from the arena of sensuous multiplicity to the security of a permanent(ized) One. From within this raging discord Nietzsche can assert, "Being, the true, is mere appearance, error" (NI, 246).

Precisely because the discord between will to power as art and as the search for truth is a violent one Nietzsche leaves the dimension of perspectival life undetermined. What is he to do? To "determine" the dimension that reveals to him the raging discord between art and truth means — at least in terms of traditional metaphysical thought — to bring it to a ground. But the will to ground, the will to yoke Becoming in Being, is the Platonic will. To resolve the discord would mean the forfeiture of the task of overcoming Platonism and would be a betrayal of Dionysus. Not to resolve it means to leave the entire project of a philosophy of will to power and revaluation of all values in crippling suspense. The only way to advance the Nietzschean project, Heidegger insists, is to surpass its critique of truth as negative will to power to a meditation on the essence of truth as disclosure.

Truth, that is, the true as the permanent, is a form of
appearance which justifies itself as a necessary condition
of self-assertive life. However, upon deeper reflection it
becomes clear that all apparition and all semblance are
possible only if something shows itself and comes into
prominence. (NI, 247)

For Nietzsche truth is the making-fast or tying down of
appearances: in the perspective of life all determination (*Festmachen*) is in
fact fixation (*Verfestigung*) (NI, 246-47). Nietzschean truth comes to its
sole truth: the will to truth (as correctness) is the cardinal deception.
Truth is error because it is lie. Why does the will to truth lie? Because
truth is ugly and life cannot bear the horrid testimony of its eye.

A philosopher recuperates differently and with different
means: he recuperates, for example, with nihilism. Belief
that there is no truth at all, the nihilistic belief, is a great
relaxation for one who, as a warrior of knowledge,
ceaselessly struggles with ugly truths. For truth is ugly.
(WM, 598)

Of course the only lastingly effective therapy is art in the grand style. But
Heidegger notes that if truth is ugly, so much so that man cannot bear it
but must either recreate it in Dionysian frenzy or flee from it to the
metaphysical realm, then Becoming must somehow *disclose* its ugliness:
somehow in spite of all metaphysico-moral screens Nietzschean
man knows why he must fear his knowing. In order not to succumb to his
knowing he transfigures the sensuous world in the creative fulguration of
art in the grand style. *"Art is, as transfiguration, more enhancing to life
than truth, as fixation on an apparition"* (NI, 250). Truth is necessary for
the maintenance of life, but at some critical point in its epiphany becomes
destructive of it. Nietzsche stands at that critical juncture and pleas for art
and creativity; Heidegger occupies the same point and urges meditation on
Dasein's disclosedness — and that means on the essence of truth.
But thought on the essence of truth demands attention to the
work of art, so that Heidegger's thought from hence — at least partly as a
result of its encounter with Nietzsche — will strive to rethink the raging
discord between art and truth.

V

The third of his Frankfurt lectures on art, and hence the final
part of "The Origin of the Work of Art," Heidegger entitled "Truth and
Art." There he defined art — poetry in the sense of essential *poiesis* — as
"the becoming and happening of truth" (H, 59; Eng. ed., 71). How had it

fallen out with truth — that Heidegger had to ascribe to it a "becoming"?

Two earlier statements in his essay relate Heidegger's interpretation of art and truth to the Nietzsche-material just considered.

1. *Das Sein des Seienden [im Werk der Kunst] kommt in das Ständige seines Scheinens.* ("The Being of the being [in the work of art] comes into the steadiness of its shining.") (H, 25; Eng. ed., 36)

2. *So wäre denn das Wesen der Kunst dieses: das Sich-ins-Werk-Setzen der Wahrheit des Seienden.* ("Thus the essence of art would be this: the truth of beings setting itself to work.") (H, 25; Eng. ed., 36)

The first proposition invites a critical question. Can the *Ständige des Scheinens* here named be identified with the *Beständigkeit* of the Platonic Ideas, of *to on*, and is it therefore exposed to the Nietzschean critique of *Beständigkeit* as *Bestandsicherung* (see Section III above)? The second invites a more neutral question. What is the character of the *Setzen* that takes place in the work of art?

To the first we must reply that the *Ständige*, far from indicating permanence of presence, suggests the double character of presence and absence. What comes to appear in Van Gogh's "Shoes of the Peasant" for example is insight into the *world* of the peasant; yet this insight is steeped in shadow almost from the start by a turn in which *earth* becomes the prevailing force. The background of the painting is "an undetermined space" — even "nothing." The opening of the shoes depicted there is "dark." These are woman's shoes. They are heavy — like the peasant woman's steps through the wintry field. As she goes in them the shoes sink into the obscure realm of pure dependability. In short, everything about the painting calls the shoes back to the earth: theirs is no eternal truth but one of numbered seasons.

> The world of "Antigone" is gone

> > So now the light goes out
> > for the house of Oedipus . . .

as is the world of Paestum. "The works are no longer the works they were" (H, 30; Eng. ed., 41). The art trade sells *objets* because it cannot hold on to works.

What comes to stand in the shining of the work of art stands in the moment of time, and that means it falls. Not that its shining is mere semblance, which is the obverse of metaphysically conceived truth, but that the art work originates in a region where

> Being and Becoming
> Being and Semblance
> > converge.[6]

That may not be ugly but it does induce a certain anxiety.

What sort of *Setzen* is at play in the work of art? It is neither a "positing" of an idea nor the establishment or expression of some supercelestial truth. "Truth becomes present only as the conflict between clearing and concealing in the opposition of world and earth" (H, 51; Eng. ed., 62). Being *comes* to stand in the work; the truth of being *sets* itself to *work*. The emphasis is on movement and struggle.

Heidegger transfers the raging discord between art and truth to the event of truth (Ereignis-Enteignis) itself, whether it come to pass in the work of art or the labor of thinking.

He calls it the *Urstreit*: primal conflict (H, 43; Eng. ed., 55).

The struggle is not so much between two projects in which postmetaphysical man may engage (the frenzied creation of art in the grand style or impotent flight to a realm of secure Ideas) as between

> arrival-departure
> approach-withdrawal
> presence-absence

in the truth of Being (unconcealment) itself.

It is wholly through Heidegger's eyes that recent French commentators can portray Nietzsche's fundamental experience of Being as (in Jean Granier's words) *la duplicité de l'être.*

For Heidegger Being itself is through *Moira* duplicitous in the literal sense: twofold in its nominal-participial nature. Moreover, its unfolding is finite, limited by its need of mortals. As mortals shatter against death and so first open themselves to the unconcealment of beings, as the revelation of Being remains essentially lethal, so does the clearing of Being find and lose itself among the thickening shades.

For Heidegger it is not Zarathustran struggle between the spirit of gravity and affirmation of life — although if thinking is thanking it cannot be a stranger to the Nietzschean problematic; it is rather the duplicity of all self-showing or manifestation, which in its very showing remains reticent and keeps to itself, a duplicity that no decision or legislation of man, no set of new tablets, can resolve.

*

Thinking can respond to the event of primal conflict only by learning *Gelassenheit*
> *releasement*
> *not-willing*

willing neither art nor truth nor any discord between them but heeding thoughtfully the generative opposition willy nilly of disclosure and concealment in both truth and art. Such thoughtful attention requires at least two traits manifested by James Joyce's Leopold Bloom, "the distinguished phenomenologist," about whom there is "a touch of the artist."[7]

In *Twilight of the Idols* a man possessed of both phenomenological acuity and artistic creativity offers a first lesson in *Gelassenheit* and an exhibition of *thinking* in the grand style:

> *Seeing* must be learned, *thinking* must be learned, *speaking* and *writing* must be learned. . . . To learn how to see: to get the eye accustomed to calmness and patience, to letting things emerge unto it. . . . To learn how to see is close to what the unphilosophic way of speaking calls "a strong will." The most essential aspect of a strong will is precisely *not* to will, to be *able* to postpone decision. . . .
>
> To learn how to think . . . as a kind of dancing. . . . To be able to dance with the feet, with concepts, with words and — need I add — with the pen. (SII, 987-89)

This by way of *gigue*.

Universität Freiburg-im-Breisgau

NOTES

1   Cited from Nietzsche's *Nachlass* (Grossoktav ed., XIV, 368) in M. Heidegger, *Nietzsche* 2 vols. (Pfullingen: G. Neske Verlag, 1961), I, 88; 167. The two lecture courses cited throughout this paper ("Will to Power as Art" and "Will to Power as Knowledge") appear in Volume One. References in the text appear as: (NI, 88; 167). I am now preparing for the Harper and Row Heidegger series a four-volume English translation of Heidegger's *Nietzsche* material; the first volume, due to appear in 1977, contains the lectures mentioned. Much of the material in the present piece derives from my unpublished doctoral dissertation, "Nietzsche and the Task of Thinking: Martin Heidegger's Reading of Nietzsche" (Ann Arbor, 1971), Chapter Two.

2   Friedrich Nietzsche, *Werke,* 3 vols. ed. by Karl Schlechta, 6th ed. (Munich: Carl Hanser Verlag, 1969), I, 20. References in the text appear as: (SI, 20). References to *The Will to Power* are from the Gast Förster edition, issued in the Kröner series, which Heidegger assigned as the textbook for his courses; the references appear in the text as: (WM, with aphorism number). See the English edition by W. Kaufmann (New York: Vintage-Random House, 1968).

3   Heidegger had delivered an abbreviated form of this lecture in Freiburg on 13 November 1935, repeating it in Zurich in January 1936. Over the next few months he expanded it and delivered the new version in Frankfurt during the autumn. This expansion took place *while the first Nietzsche course was in session*. The text of "The Origin of the Art Work" that we have today bears closely on the question of Nietzsche's ideas on art, just as these at least partly shape Heidegger's single most important pronouncement on that subject. See M. Heidegger, "Der Ursprung des Kunstwerkes," in *Holzwege* (Frankfurt am Main: Vittorio Klostermann Verlag, 1950), pp. 7-68, which we cite in the text as: (H, with page number). See the English translation in M. Heidegger, *Poetry, Language, Thought*, translated by Albert Hofstadter (New York: Harper & Row, 1971), pp. 17-87.

4   We should note that for all three thinkers "art" means primarily *poiesis*, poesy, *Dichtkunst*. See NI, 193.

5   NI, 574; on *Bestand* see *Sein und Zeit*, Section 44.

6   See M. Heidegger, *Einführung in die Metaphysik* (Tübingen: Max Niemeyer Verlag, 1953), pp. 71 ff. See the English translation, M. Heidegger, *An Introduction to Metaphysics*, translated by Ralph Manheim (Garden City, N.Y.: Doubleday-Anchor, 1961), Chapter Four, parts one and two. Nietzsche's pervasive influence in this text appears most directly in Chapter One, but it haunts the entire work.

7   James Joyce, *Ulysses* (New York: Modern Library, 1961), pp. 343 and 235.

The Owl and the Poet:
Heidegger's Critique of Hegel

David Couzens Hoy

In the epilogue to the essay "The Origin of the Work of Art," Heidegger chooses a text of Hegel's to summarize his own reflections on the situation and nature of art in modern times. This choice is not arbitrary. On the contrary, it emphasizes the centrality of Hegel's thought for Heidegger's attempt to criticize and rethink the history of thought. Reflecting on the role of art in the course of history, Hegel makes the famous but often misinterpreted remark that "art no longer counts for us as the highest manner in which truth obtains existence for itself." He maintains that "art is and remains for us, on the side of its highest vocation, something past."[1]

Heidegger grants that the so-called death of art may in fact be occurring. The death of art is not an isolated phenomenon — to see art as isolated is already to adopt an "aesthetic" attitude toward it, to stand at a disinterested distance and reduce art to art for art's sake alone. The death of art is tied to the death of metaphysics and the triumph of technology in the modern era. Heidegger himself, however, opposes to this emergent nihilism the possibility of a new beginning. This new beginning could also be called a new poetics, for it is generated through *Dichtung*, which is not merely one form of art, the writing of poems, but the essence of all art.[2] Furthermore, poetry, in this larger sense of *Dichtung*, has not only aesthetic but also ontological import, for it is revelatory of the truth of being: "Dichtung ist das stiftende Nennen des Seins und des Wesens aller Dinge."[3] In apparent contrast to Hegel, then, Heidegger views art not as that which is no longer an essential carrier of the meaning of history, but as that which will potentially allow history to overcome the present impasse, to move beyond *Ge-stell*, the uncreative domination of technology, to *Geviert* and the sudden, new beginning.[4]

Paradoxically enough, Hegel appears to understand his role as philosopher in a less prophetic way than Heidegger. The owl of Minerva, symbolizing Hegel's self-understanding, is a figure of the dusk, not of the dawn:

> One word more about giving instruction as to what the world ought to be. Philosophy in any case always comes on the scene too late to give it. As the thought of the world, it appears only when actuality is already there cut and dried after its process of formation has been completed. . . . When philosophy paints its grey in grey, then has a shape of life grown old. By philosophy's grey in grey it cannot be rejuvenated but only understood. The owl of Minerva spreads its wings only with the falling of the dusk.[5]

In assigning philosophic vision to the grey in grey of an aging form of life, Hegel declines to posit a totally new world. Nor is this difference in mood between Hegel and Heidegger explained by the fact that Heidegger often attributes the possibility of founding the new beginning to the poet and not to the philosopher, who only awaits the poet's essential word. The resignation suggested in Hegel's owl of Minerva passage could not generate Heidegger's image of the philosopher awaiting a new call of being. The possibility of being completely superseded is not tolerated by philosophical comprehension that believes itself absolute.

The contrast in the thinking of Heidegger and Hegel is not merely aesthetic. The difference is neither simply one of taste, nor is it limited to one aspect of their philosophies, their analyses of the nature of art. The issue at stake is rather one permeating their entire thinking: it concerns the historical nature of thought and the very possibility of history. Given the contrasting positions, a philosophical dialogue should be possible, and Heidegger himself begins this dialogue in several of his later essays.

I. The Historicity of Art

Although the epilogue to "The Origin of the Work of Art" is quite short — only two and a half pages in *Holzwege* — it tries to give a thumbnail sketch of the history of metaphysics. While such laconism is in some ways absurd, the text is so closely related to other texts — especially those in which Heidegger's central concern is with Hegel — that a coherent and intriguing view of the relation of philosophy and art in history is readily obtainable.

At the end of the main body of the essay Heidegger raises the question about the place of our own time in history. Are we at the beginning of a new period of art and of history, he asks, or are we merely lingering in a worn-out inspiration?[6] Is art for us today capable of revelation and truth, or is it essentially connected with the past?

The epilogue raises these problems again in relation to Hegel's account of the connection of art and the historical world spirit. Heidegger is aware, of course, of the ambiguity in Hegel's claim that art is past. The thesis that spirit has passed art by as a locus of truth is not disproved by pointing out that there have been developments in art since Hegel's time. In this sense the term "death of art" is a misnomer. Art certainly continues to occur, but how it signifies may well change from the way it previously signified (for instance, in the Romanesque period, where art and religion are entwined). Indeed, art may even cease to signify, and this event is itself significant.

The essence of phenomena is not unhistorical and there can be such changes in the manner of signifying. Hegel in the *Phenomenology* sees each successive form of consciousness as having its own truth criterion or *Maßstab*, and Heidegger maintains that there has been change in the nature of truth throughout the history of philosophy. In fact, Heidegger is suggesting another sense of understanding Hegel's dictum that art has become something past for us. Art can be past not in the sense that it is over, but in the sense that much of its value for us comes from its belonging to the past, to an inherited tradition comprising the history of art.

What exactly does Heidegger mean by the pastness of art? Hegel's word describing art in German is *ein Vergangenes*. Heidegger also uses this word (*Holzwege*, 65), but one must remember that the "past" receives a special analysis in *Being and Time*. There Heidegger restricts the term *Vergangenheit* to the historical being of present-to-hand things and derives this sense of "pastness" from a more primordial sense in which the existence of human beings is past as *Gewesenheit*.[7] When the purely antiquarian historian forgets the meaning of his research for the present — and the future — and simply loses himself in an aesthetic contemplation of the past for the past's sake alone, then he is objectifying the past (as *Vergangenheit*) and treating it like a thing that is merely no longer present-to-hand (*vorhanden*).[8] The past, however, includes human beings, and individuals cannot treat their pasts (or the pasts of others) in that way. The meaning of the past can still change with present or future actions. Thus, Heidegger can even say that the past (as *Gewesenheit*) is still operant in the present, and indeed, even "arises from the future" (SZ, 326).

To say that art for us has the character of the past as *Vergangenheit* is to imply that we have reduced art to a specific temporal dimension. The greatness of art is now inseparable from the historical aura surrounding it. Art now belongs in the museum. Even modern art, as Karsten Harries shows, takes some of its character from being the first to do something new.[9] In this regard, one can notice how the *act* of producing the artwork becomes more important than the final result itself — a large, yellow, but otherwise blank canvas in the museum may be surprising at first, but does not provide the opportunity for study or wonderment as does, say, a Vermeer. Other happenings, such as wrapping up a skyscraper, and then unwrapping it shortly thereafter, may be an interesting technological act, showing wonderful "free play of the imagination," but it also acts to destroy the very notion of art as object or product. This use of technology to parody technology is thus an invaluable antidote to the obsession with progress. Nevertheless, its effect depends on surprise, and its temporal character is very much that of a succession of "nows" rapidly retreating into the past as it searches for new kinds of things to wrap.

Heidegger's analysis of art involves a useful interpretation both of Hegel's death of art thesis and of the temporality of art. That art gradually dies does not mean that it will cease altogether, but rather that its essence changes.[10] Karsten Harries describes this change for Hegel as involving a shift from an ontological to an aesthetic conception of beauty.[11] In the aesthetic mode art is contemplated for its own sake and is viewed independently of its other possible functions. In religious art, for instance, the artwork is closely connected to other beliefs about the world — beliefs which in the aesthetic mode of perception are bracketed in such a way that they are known and understood, but not necessarily shared. The temporal nature of religious art, such as that of the Romanesque period, should also be described differently. It clearly is connected to the past insofar as it often depicts the life of Christ or the saints, yet there is no concern about anachronism — the settings are not Roman but contemporary. The art deals more with future expectations. It announces rather than simply depicts, and the early Romanesque sculptors are clearly concerned with the expressive and evocative portrayal of their themes, perhaps even moreso than with mimetic or realistic reconstruction of ideal forms (as is more typical in Gothic sculpture). While this Romanesque art may appear formally quite primitive, it is in fact quite refined and rich in regional variation. The art could be more adequately described as a new beginning, a rediscovery of the origins of art and of artistic technique. Heidegger's own statement about the difference between primitive or unhistorical art and a genuinely historical beginning is controversial, but it is worth repeating in this regard:

A genuine beginning, as a leap [*Sprung*], is always a
head start [*Vorsprung*], in which everything to come is
already leaped over [*übersprungen*], even if as something
disguised. A genuine beginning, however, has nothing of
the neophyte character of the primitive. The primitive,
because it lacks the bestowing, grounding leap and head
start, is always futureless.[12]

The German text plays with the movements and meanings of the root
word *Sprung*, which is also contained in the title of the essay — "The
Origin," *Ursprung*, "of the Work of Art." While this particular passage
does not explain the fascination of the primitive, nor take into account the
influence primitive art has had on modern art (e.g., on Picasso), it does
point out an important difference in the temporality of the two art forms.

The genuine beginnings Heidegger is discussing are not merely
those of periods in art history. Art can also function as the foundation and
beginnings of history as such: "Whenever art happens — that is, whenever
there is a beginning — a thrust enters history, history either begins or starts
over again."[13] While this definition of art may appear to be a normative
one, it clearly shows an ontological conception of art, and a refusal to
reduce art to the merely aesthetic.

If Heidegger's interpretation of the death of art thesis is in many
respects similar to, or indeed only an explication of, Hegel's, in what ways
does it differ? Heidegger links the historical change in the essence of art to
the change in the essence of truth. In Heidegger's historical overview Hegel
occupies a place in this philosophical change — a place that now needs to
be surpassed. In order to grasp the meaning of Heidegger's epilogue on art,
then, it is necessary to understand his critique of Hegel's notion of truth.

II. The Historicity of Truth

Two important texts clarifying Heidegger's understanding of
Hegel are the essay "Hegel and the Greeks" and the second essay in
Identity and Difference, entitled "The Onto-theo-logical Constitution of
Metaphysics."[14] The latter results from a seminar given in 1956/57 and a
lecture given in 1957, while the former is a lecture originally delivered in
1958. Other texts, of course, also discuss Hegel to some extent, as do the
"Letter on Humanism" and *Being and Time*. The two texts mentioned
above, however, complement "The Origin of the Work of Art" and clarify
not only the epilogue but also its often overlooked *Zusatz*, written in 1956
and published in 1960.[15]

In the *Zusatz* Heidegger points out a possible misinterpretation of
his statements about the truth of the artwork, and again begins his
self-interpretation with a reference to Hegel (and to his own essay "Hegel
and the Greeks"). Heidegger wishes to avoid any suggestion that the truth

of art involves the positing of something completely determinate by a particular subject. He is aware, however, that a statement like "art is the fixing in place[*feststellen*]of a self-establishing truth in the figure" possibly implies a willed creation, as by the poet, of a discursive truth. Yet the truth of art cannot be so determinate and "fixed" (*fest*); art is more a continuous act of appearing, a letting-happen.

Heidegger attempts to clarify his view with reference to the Greek word *thesis* (in German *stellen*), which involves immediate manifestation. In the German idealist tradition, however, "thesis" has precisely the sense of being something posited by a subject. So Heidegger must distinguish his term from Hegel's. Hegel is correct, Heidegger believes, in seeing the thesis as untrue because it is not yet mediated by the antithesis.

How can Heidegger affirm the correctness of Hegel's insistence that mediation is essential to truth and then fall back on the immediacy of *thesis* in explicating his own notion of truth? The *Zusatz* does not explain this point, and Heidegger offers clarification only by citing the entire essay "Hegel and the Greeks." Reflecting on this latter essay, one infers that Hegel's notion of truth is correct as far as it goes, but also that it does not go far enough, even for its own purposes. Heidegger's procedure here in criticizing Hegel is thus dialectical, if by "dialectical" one means the discovery that the criterion for knowledge avowed by a particular consciousness is not adequate to or does not satisfactorily explain the knowledge it actually has.

When discussing Hegel, Heidegger in fact uses the language of dialectical method — speaking of thesis, antithesis, and synthesis, and thereby distorting Hegel's actual procedure. Hegel's treatment of the Greeks, Heidegger argues, posits their philosophical beginnings as the thesis that remains incomplete without the antithesis and synthesis (WM, 271).[16] Heidegger maintains that by viewing the Greek notions of truth and being from the perspective of the end of a philosophical tradition, Hegel misconstrues these beginnings and is "historically incorrect" (WM, 268).

To hear Heidegger accuse another philosopher of inaccurate historical scholarship is an interesting twist, since this charge is raised so often against Heidegger himself. Indeed, this accusation involves methodological problems of which Heidegger is well aware. Heidegger thinks Hegel distorts the Greek view by seeing it from a later philosophical perspective, yet Heidegger's own view is also perspectival. Is Heidegger's philosophical interest more valid simply because it is more recent? Of course not, and appropriate criticism should be based on an immanent reading of the Greeks. For both Hegel and Heidegger, however, the notion of a purely immanent reading is an illusion. Both philosophers insist on the historicity of thought, and on the contribution to the meaning of texts made by the tradition of their reception. In "Hegel and the Greeks"

Heidegger gives the classical argument for the determination of thought by history:

> Nun bewegen sich aber schon jede historische Aussage und deren Begründung in einem Verhältnis zur Geschichte. Vor dem Entscheid über die historische Richtigkeit des Vorstellens bedarf es daher der Besinnung darauf, ob und wie die Geschichte erfahren wird, von woher sie in ihrem Grundzügen bestimmt ist. (WM, 268)

> (Now every historical assertion and its justification, however, already moves within a relation to history. Before the decision about the historiographical correctness of the manner of conceiving, there must be reflection on whether and how history is experienced, and from whence it is determined in its basic features.)

As important as Heidegger's reading of the Greeks is, then, it also needs to be complemented by an argument that Hegel's method, on its own terms, is inadequate to the interpretive task and therefore that Hegel's results are inconsistent.[17]

Although Heidegger follows this procedure, he still does not claim absolute certainty for his own historical judgment. He thus remains a consistent and thoroughgoing historicist:

> Freilich kann auch eine solche Prüfung niemals sich selbst als der Gerichtshof gebärden, der schlechthin über das Wesen der Geschichte und ein mögliches Verhältnis zu ihr entscheidet; denn diese Prüfung hat ihre Grenze, die sich so umschreiben läßt: Je denkender, d.h. von seiner Sprache beanspruchter ein Denken ist, je maßgebender wird für es das Ungedachte und gar das ihm Undenkbare. (WM, 268)

> (Admittedly, even such an examination can itself never serve as the tribunal that decides in an absolute manner about the essence of history and a possible relation to it. For this examination has its limit, which can be defined as follows: the more ratiocinative an act of thinking is, that is to say, the more it is claimed by or caught up in its language, the more decisive for it will be the unthought and even that which for it is unthinkable.)

This belief that thought is conditioned by something unthought or unthinkable is, of course, unconfirmable. Heidegger is not, however, thereby condemned to an irrational, completely relativist brand of historicism. The reminder that one's own judgments are not absolutely certain does not entail that there are no good reasons for them.

How, then, does Hegel's historical place condition his perception of the Greeks? The very fact that Hegel has a historical vision in which the Greeks have a particular position is, of course, a factor to take into account, especially since Hegel's notion of history is itself a new development in history — one that appears antithetical to Greek thought. Heidegger himself, though, rejects Hegel's theory of history as the dialectical development of the consciousness of freedom:

> Allen richtigen oder unrichtigen historischen Aussagen voraus geht, daß Hegel das Wesen der Geschichte aus dem Wesen des Seins im Sinne der absoluten Subjektivität erfahren hat. Es gibt bis zur Stunde keine Erfahrung der Geschichte, die, philosophisch gesehen, dieser Geschichtserfahrung entsprechen könnte. (WM, 269)

> (Prior to all correct or incorrect historiographical assertions is the fact that Hegel experienced the essence of history from the essence of being in the sense of absolute subjectivity. Up until now there has been no experience of history that, philosophically speaking, could correspond to this historical attitude.)

Heidegger does not argue the point that there has been no experience of history confirming the Hegelian theory, and it remains merely a statement of opinion. The opinion is widely shared, but the Hegelian reply is easily imaginable. When Heidegger says the Hegelian historical experience is not confirmed or confirmable, he does not explain what evidence would count as confirmation. Nor does Heidegger's own picture of history include such a theory of evidence, and his statement is equally telling against his own historical speculations. Since Hegel and the Hegelian tradition (including Marx, Lukács, and others) offer interpretations of historical data, and since these accounts have in fact been found appealing by some people, Heidegger's claim that there has been no such experience of historical development is gainsaid.

Heidegger perhaps guards against this line of reply by saying that "philosophically speaking" there has been no confirming experience. What this phrase means is unclear, but Heidegger has advanced arguments of a different sort against Hegel. These arguments challenge Hegel's notion of history on the basis of the way this notion is grounded in Hegel's understanding of being as absolute subjectivity.

With this point Heidegger comes to the heart of his criticism of Hegel. Before testing his analysis both as an interpretation of Hegel and as an argument against Hegel's view of philosophy, two common charges against Heidegger's own philosophy should be mentioned. In dealing with Hegel, Heidegger is at the same time indirectly defending and clarifying his own views.

The first charge has a long history, including Carnap's diatribe against Heidegger, and concerns the apparent abstractness and even meaninglessness of Heidegger's notion of being. Hegel's analysis of being is an important precedent in this regard, for he too maintains that being is abstract and the poorest of concepts despite its apparent richness.

The second charge against which Heidegger is defending himself while at the same time criticizing Hegel develops from their differences on the concept of being. Heidegger maintains that his own attempt to free being from any trace of subjectivism is itself not to be charged with subjectivism. For instance, it might seem that there is implicit subjectivism in Heidegger's emphasis on the poet as the subject who sees into the real meaning of being and thus founds the new historical beginnings. Heidegger must reply that it is not the poet per se who is responsible for this disclosure.[18] Heidegger himself, in "Hegel and the Greeks," makes this point in more general terms. He mentions as a possible misinterpretation of his notion of the unconcealment (*Unverborgenheit*) of being that unconcealment must be unconcealment "for somebody," and is therefore subjective (WM, 270). Heidegger maintains that this interpretation still persists in thinking of man as a subject, and therefore falls back into the philosophical antinomies Heidegger's language intends to avoid. Must "for somebody," he asks, necessarily mean "posited or determined *by* somebody"? The Greeks, he thinks, would not have made this subjectivizing inference. Hegel, on the other hand, does infer it, at least insofar as he sees subjectivity or spirit in all manifestations of being. Heidegger's self-defense, then, turns on his interpretation of Hegel, and that must now be examined more closely.

III. Dialectic and the History of Being

Hegel's error in interpreting the Greek notion of being, Heidegger argues, stems from his inability to think of being except in relation to subjectivity. The Greeks, however, did not have a conception of the subject in the same way. Therefore, Heidegger believes, Hegel cannot grasp the true essence of the Greeks' understanding of being (WM, 269).

Leaving aside the question of the validity of Heidegger's own often-criticized interpretation of the Greeks, one sees that this argument is clearly grounded in a different attitude toward the history of thought. Hegel begins the history of philosophy with the Greeks' explicit language and concepts. Heidegger, on the other hand, believes that the explicit theorizing of philosophy occurs only in response to a claim by or concern with something that remains inexplicit and inadequately conceptualized by philosophy. His analysis of the Greek notion of *aletheia* develops the point that "unser Denken von etwas angesprochen wird, was *vor* dem Beginn der 'Philosophie' und durch ihre ganze Geschichte hindurch das Denken schon zu sich eingeholt hat" (WM, 272). (Our thinking is claimed by something that *before* the beginning of "philosophy" and throughout its entire history already comprehends this thinking.) Thus, whereas Hegel attributes inadequacy to the Greeks, and sees his own thought as no longer inadequate because completely self-certain, Heidegger maintains that the inadequacy of the Greeks' thought is also our own inadequacy (WM, 272).

In *Identity and Difference* Heidegger also discusses this difference in attitudes toward the history of philosophy. Heidegger rejects Hegel's basic dialectical principle of *Aufhebung*, which is the movement wherein the negation of a position does not completely cancel it, but preserves its essential truth in making a step forward to a greater or more complete truth. Instead of this step forward, Heidegger wants a step backward (*Schritt zurück*) (ID, 49ff.). His goal is to rediscover the skipped (*übersprungen*) region from which we derive our idea of truth.

Truth, for Heidegger, is thus not a primitive term, but follows from an understanding of prior conditions. These conditions are what philosophy aims to reveal, what it wishes to get back to, but this stepping back is not a going back in time — for instance, to before Plato and Aristotle. Rather, it is a getting away from the ordinary involvement with things and a getting back to the very essence of what a thing is — and for modern man this means seeing through the technological way of thinking to the essence of technology itself.

In the German idealist tradition truth is understood ultimately as self-certainty. Yet for Heidegger the question about what is involved in establishing something as a certainty or truth does not deal with the more fundamental question about how that of which we are certain itself even comes to be. While the idealist tradition does not separate these questions, Heidegger thinks they are clearly distinct, and he believes the Greek notion of *aletheia* indicates this. If *aletheia* is most fundamentally disclosure (*Entbergung*), then the idealist concept of truth as correctness and certainty depends on *aletheia*, but *aletheia* does not depend on truth.[19] In other words, the question of how the subject can ascertain his judgments is a later question than the one as to the conditions for the existence or nonexistence of states of affairs. Instead of thinking of the absolute subject as the origin of the disclosure of being, Heidegger suggests this disclosure be considered as the place wherein the very notion of a subject first comes to be (WM, 268).

Is this question about being so general as to be meaningless? Hegel thinks of being as indeterminate generality, and therefore as the concept in its "most empty emptiness" (ID, 56). Heidegger in one sense agrees that being, if so conceived, is indeed an empty concept. He appeals to Hegel's own example about the man who wants to buy "fruit," but finds only apples, pears, peaches, etc., and thus cannot obtain what he seeks (ID, 66). For Heidegger this indicates the limitations of Hegel's logic and his conceptualization of being. Being appears in a light, says Heidegger, that comes from the illumination of Hegel's thought. Yet this thought is historically formed, and being in fact only appears in a determinate, epochal historical form (e.g., as logos, *idea*, substance, objectivity, will, will to power, etc.). The inquiry into the meaning of being is thus not abstract and formal, but rather, historical and concrete.

Is the procedure of this inquiry actually so different, however, from Hegel's own method of inquiry into the history of thought? Heidegger uses different words and spellings in an attempt to make a difference. Thus, the word "historical" in German is spelled with a "t" (*Geschichte, geschichtlich*) whenever Heidegger is referring to the ordinary, "Hegelian" way of thinking about history as a progression in a series of moments, and with a "k" (*Geschick* — often translated as "mittence" — and *geschicklich*) when speaking of his own later analyses. The word *Geschick* indicates that the meaning and course of history is not determined by man himself, but rather that history is "sent" to man and grounds human self-consciousness.[20]

This attempt to outstrip Hegel's thought is complemented by explicit rejection of other concepts. The attack on *Aufhebung* has already been mentioned, and Heidegger likewise avoids speaking of lawlike *necessity* in history. This creates a problem, as he is well aware, since he must explain how his history of being could have a continuity (*Durchgängigkeit*), an all-pervading character (ID, 67-68). He posits such an initial issue or "perdurance" (*Austrag*) lying at the beginnings of philosophy and governing the history of philosophy even while being covered-up and forgotten (ID, 68). While this ontological cover-up is the thread running through the history of being, its status is difficult to investigate and clarify: "Yet it remains difficult to say how this all-pervasiveness [*Durchgängigkeit*] is to be thought, if it is neither something universal, valid in all cases, nor a law guaranteeing the necessity of a process in the sense of the dialectical" (ID, 67-68). The claim in "The Origin of the Work of Art" (pp. 77-78) that history is grounded in art and therefore only moves by a leap (*Sprung*) makes continuity seem almost impossible.

In view of these difficulties it is not surprising that Heidegger often expresses his speculations about history in a subjunctive mood or as a "possibility." With the rejection of history as a dialectical progression of self-consciousness goes a disavowal of any absolute certainty about achieving the philosophical goal of the *Schritt zurück*. At the end of *Identity and Difference*, therefore, Heidegger admits that the step back may in fact never escape modern metaphysical-technological thinking (ID, 72-73). Such a philosophy can only explore its possibilities in the subjunctive, and this tone of the later writings contrasts with the ontological ambitions toward a positive theory marking the more assertory tone of *Being and Time* (which is subjunctive only insofar as it remains incomplete). Heidegger appears to have actually experienced the consequences of his potentially relativistic claim in *Being and Time* that "higher than actuality stands *possibility*" (SZ, 38). The step back and the attempt to think history as originating from a now-forgotten *Austrag* is only a possibility, he admits in *Identity and Difference* (p. 68). The subjunctive mood of Heidegger's historicism thus makes it impossible for him to state precisely his predictions about the aftermath of the overcoming of our technological metaphysics. In fact, the overcoming of metaphysics is not something that occurs by projecting a standpoint outside of metaphysics — Heidegger's "overcoming" (*Überwindung*) is indeed much like Hegel's *Aufhebung* in that it does not simply negate something, but rather goes beyond it by seeing more deeply and essentially into it, thus transforming it from within.[21] Heidegger is forced into a poetic mode, one that is constantly forced to take back its language so that it is not frozen into mere terminology (see ID, 74-75).

IV. Hegel and Heidegger: Identity in Difference?

Strangely enough, the philosopher to whom Heidegger is most akin in this philosophical mood is Hegel — although not the Hegel who is terminologically frozen into later Hegelianism. Heidegger's interpretation is itself influenced by the Hegelian tradition insofar as he thinks of dialectic as a *method* aiming at unity through the synthesis of opposites.[22] Heidegger speaks of dialectic as "die Methode" which believes itself identical with "die Seele des Seins," and he even sees modern science, with its emphasis on the method of total computability and its search for a unitary basis of matter, as still manifesting Hegelian dialectic (WM, 260).

To dispel these metaphysical illusions Heidegger insists that the original issue of philosophy is the difference between being and beings, and that this difference is never overcome. The difference is, rather, constantly at issue and continually generating new understandings of this difference: "Speaking in terms of the difference, this means: perdurance [*Austrag*] is a circling, the circling of Being and beings around each other" (ID, 69). The hermeneutic circle of human understanding and interpretation analyzed in *Being and Time* thus reappears at the more fundamental level of the question of being.

Heidegger's circular movement in *Differenz* is not, however, so far removed from Hegel's dialectical movement. Hans-Georg Gadamer, whose own philosophical hermeneutic can be said to mediate between Heidegger and Hegel, challenges Heidegger's reading of Hegel's notion of the absolute. Gadamer raises the question whether Heidegger does not go too far in characterizing Hegel's dialectical self-transparency (*Selbstdurch-sichtigkeit*) as result rather than as the whole process itself. Seen as a continual, self-renewing process, dialectic does not culminate so much in a final, totally determinate synthesis as in an "unresolved tension."[23] Dialectic, according to Gadamer, is not only reason's grasp of the whole — the moment Heidegger emphasizes — but also the maintenance of contradictions in their tension and opposition. This latter moment achieves a unity of the contradictions, but only by preserving their difference. Heidegger's own notion of the *Differenz* constituting the unifying *Austrag* of history is thus quite close to Hegel's actual philosophical practice.

Gadamer does not hesitate, therefore, to claim that in important respects Heidegger's thought is as dialectical as Hegel's. Most significantly, Heidegger's notion of the history of metaphysics as unified by the growing oblivion of being (*Seinsvergessenheit*) is equally as encompassing as Hegel's absolute and his notion of reason in history.[24] Furthermore, since what has been forgotten in the "forgetting of being" is posited as returning again and thus casting new light on the whole of the preceding process, it serves the dialectical function of allowing one to see the actuality behind the apparent arbitrariness of the present. This seeming negation through forgetting that then returns with even greater significance again shows more proximity to Hegelian *Aufhebung* than Heidegger would like to acknowledge. In fact, it undercuts his claim that history and the step back depends upon a leap. As Gadamer remarks, is not the step back inevitably *mediated*, in the Hegelian sense of the term, by metaphysics? Certainly Heidegger's own subjunctive hesitancy about the very possibility of success for the step back indicates that the leap always gets entangled in the thicket of present philosophical language.

Gadamer's observations encourage further reservations about Heidegger's critique of Hegel. In the essay "Hegel's Concept of Experience,"[25] Heidegger himself indicates parallels between his own thought and Hegel's. In fact, he translates dialectical terms from the *Phenomenology* into terms used in *Being and Time*. Natural consciousness, which for Hegel is consciousness wherein the subject is directly concerned with an object, is said to be ontic, as opposed to ontological, consciousness (HCE, 105). This natural consciousness, furthermore, is identified with modern technology, with its claim to absoluteness through "its irresistible transformation of everything into an object for a subject" (HCE, 62-63). When the subject becomes aware of itself in the act of beholding the object, when it grasps the object qua object (or objectivity per se), consciousness becomes ontological (HCE, 106-108). The ontic, natural consciousness is itself pre-ontological because it contains the conditions for objectivity implicitly in its knowledge.

From these definitions emerges the basic concept of the historicity of being and of thought as understood by both Heidegger and Hegel, for it follows that as the ontic changes, so does the ontological (HCE, 106). This is the basic principle of change in the movement of the

Phenomenology: as thinking gradually becomes aware of its basis, the emergence of the basis alters the basis itself. Thinking, the ontological, always comes too late — like the owl of Minerva — since the change that thinking itself produces remains still to be thought. Or in Heidegger's terms, thinking is measured by the as yet unthought and even unthinkable (see WM, 268).

In this essay Heidegger's characterization of Hegel's dialectical movement is closer to the *Phenomenology* not only in spirit but also in its explicit statement. In contrast to the essays previously discussed, Heidegger here rejects the attempt to explain dialectic in terms of thesis, antithesis, and synthesis (HCE, 117). He likewise rejects discussion of whether dialectic is merely a method, or whether it describes a real process. He does, however, suggest that dialectic is more than an arbitrary, conceptual schematization into which experience is stuffed and crammed. Rather, Heidegger believes that Hegel in fact truly understands the nature of experience: "Hegel does not conceive experience dialectically; he thinks of dialectic in terms of the nature of experience" (HCE, 119).

Of course, "experience" is a negative concept for both Hegel and Heidegger. It means that a subject stands over against an object in the attempt to obtain knowledge of that object. Both thinkers wish to overcome the subject-object antinomy, and it has been seen that Heidegger interprets Hegel as an idealist who resolves the antinomy in favor of subjectivity, albeit absolute subjectivity. Yet the question must be raised whether Heidegger does justice to Hegel's own self-understanding in this regard. Hegel himself has as little use for subject-object language as Heidegger and is equally concerned with overcoming the traditional metaphysics of experience usually associated with Kant's transcendental enterprise. In discussing Kant, Hegel says that the terms "subjective" and "objective" are only "convenient expressions in current use," and he in fact goes on to argue against the ultimate value of the distinction.[26]

Hegel does not want his philosophy confused with a transcendental idealism that begins and ends with the truth of the *cogito*. In fact, recent interpretations[27] of the *Phenomenology* find that Hegel changes his conception of the book in the course of writing it and moves away from the merely epistemological and transcendental concern with experience characterizing the "Introduction" — the only section Heidegger explicates in "Hegel's Concept of Experience." Similarly, Heidegger's *Kehre*, the break between the earlier and later writings, is said to involve the disavowal of a "transcendental self-interpretation" whereby the question of being depends upon its understanding in *Dasein*.[28] Heidegger certainly shares Hegel's reservations about transcendental, purely critical philosophy and admits that Hegel's dialectic is not this kind of thinking (WM, 259).

Is Hegel still caught in subjectivity in that he, as a philosopher, claims insight into the absolute and into the meaning of history? Does he attribute a role to the individual in creating or understanding history that Heidegger would not? Certainly Hegel's "world-historical individuals" — figures like Napoleon — are essential to the movement of history. As is often pointed out, however, although their willing may be constitutive of what happens, history itself does not develop as they will it.

Perhaps the individual poet for Heidegger has more constitutive force than Hegel's historical agents. Yet it is always difficult to identify in the ordinary, historical world — in the ontic realm — particular individuals or occurrences that could satisfy Heidegger's ontological claim that a totally new world is created through poetry. This difficulty is not merely ontic but also philosophical, in that Heidegger cannot specify how a true manifestation of being could ever be recognized as such. His subjunctive tone in this regard makes clear that we must wait not only to find out the truth of Hegel's claim about the death of art but also to find out whether Heidegger's pathway is the right one. In fact, one wonders whether the wait for Heidegger's *Geviert* is not an indefinite one. Does not such a postulation of the "end of history" function merely as a regulative principle, one that serves as a critical measure for the present but is itself not actually capable of instantiation?[29]

Heidegger would not be content with this construal of his project as mainly critical and regulative. Yet this conclusion is forced on one insofar as Heidegger appears to have given thinking an impossible task. How could rational thinking with constitutive ambitions overcome the claims that poetry is the founding force of history and that the mystery of being has been lost precisely through "Hegelian" obsessions with reason, method, and scientific completeness? On the other hand, if thinking does at least have real critical force, then its pathway becomes worthy of being explored.

By a curious twist it appears that Heidegger's critique of Hegel has the consequence that what must be criticized most is not Hegel's thought but the interpretation of it that also misleads Heidegger. Or at least Heidegger's thinking confrontation with Hegel must itself be rethought. Hegel's famous owl of Minerva passage does not show the self-certain, self-satisfied thinker of the absolute Heidegger often portrays. Rather, it expresses an attitude shared with Heidegger toward the relation of philosophy and history — a mood of resignation, indicating a desire for a critical, realistic grasp of the present accompanied at the same time by a refusal to project in detail a more ideal state of affairs in the future. Both thinkers find themselves in the twilight of an age, painting the "grey in grey" that comes too late. Even Heidegger is unwilling to claim that the owl of Minerva has yet been superseded by a new poet.

Barnard College
Columbia University

NOTES

1   G. W. F. Hegel, *Vorlesungen über die Ästhetik*; quoted by Martin Heidegger, "The Origin of the Work of Art," *Poetry, Language, Thought*, trans. Albert Hofstadter (New York: Harper & Row, 1971), p. 80.

2   "The Origin of the Work of Art," p. 72.

3   Heidegger, *Erläuterung zu Hölderlins Dichtung*, 4th ed. (Frankfurt: Vittorio Klostermann, 1971), p. 43; quoted by Karsten Harries, "Das befreite Nichts," in *Durchblicke: Festschrift für Martin Heidegger zum 80. Geburtstag* (Frankfurt: Vittorio Klostermann, 1970), pp. 51-52.

4   For a particularly enlightening discussion of this point, see Werner Marx, "The World in Another Beginning: Poetic Dwelling and the Role of the Poet," in *On Heidegger and Language*, ed. Joseph J. Kockelmans (Evanston: Northwestern Univ. Press, 1972), pp. 235-59, esp. p. 257.

5   *Hegel's Philosophy of Right*, trans. T.M. Knox (London: Oxford Univ. Press, 1967), pp. 12-13.

6   "The Origin of the Work of Art," p. 78.

7   Heidegger, *Sein und Zeit* (Tübingen: Max Niemeyer, 1963), pp. 326-28 and 380-81. Although the English translation of *Being and Time* by John Macquarrie and Edward Robinson (New York: Harper & Row, 1962) will be used, pages will be cited from SZ since the translators give the German pagination in the margins.

8   SZ, pp. 396-97; for further discussion see my article "History, Historicity, and Historiography in *Being and Time*," in *Heidegger and Modern Philosophy: Critical Essays*, ed. Michael Murray (New Haven and London: Yale Univ. Press, 1978), pp. 329-53.

9   See Harries, "Das befreite Nichts"; also his book *The Meaning of Modern Art: A Philosophical Interpretation* (Evanston: Northwestern Univ. Press, 1968).

10 See H.-G. Gadamer, *Hegels Dialektik: Fünf hermeneutische Studien* (Tübingen: J.C.B. Mohr, 1971), p. 84.

11 Karsten Harries, "Hegel on the Future of Art," *The Review of Metaphysics*, 27 (1974), 677-96.

12 "The Origin of the Work of Art," p. 76; the German words have been added to the translation.

13 "The Origin of the Work of Art," p. 77.

14 Heidegger, "Hegel und die Griechen," reprinted in Heidegger's *Wegmarken* (Frankfurt: Vittorio Klostermann, 1967), pp. 255-72; cited as: WM (translations are my own). "The Onto-theo-logical Constitution of Metaphysics," *Identity and Difference*, trans. Joan Stambaugh (New York: Harper & Row, 1969); cited as: ID.

15   See Hofstadter's translation, pp. 82-87; for the German see the Reclam edition (Stuttgart: 1960) containing an introduction by H.-G. Gadamer.

16   Hegel's actual feelings about the Greeks, however, are much more rich and ambiguous than this formulation suggests. Clearly the discussion of Antigone in the *Phenomenology* shows that the Greek conception of existence contained its own antitheses in ways still problematic for modern moral and social life.

17   Heidegger himself should not object, of course, if a similar procedure is used to criticize his own readings (although the insistence of his being only "on the way toward" something may remove the very basis for criticism, or even for comprehension).

18   Heidegger remarks in his commentary on the line of poetry "Kein ding sei wo das wort gebricht" that the origin of the thing to be named is obscure — it is certainly not created by the poet in any case, but is granted to him. (See *Unterwegs zur Sprache*, p. 226, or Joan Stambaugh's translation in *On the Way to Language* (New York: Harper & Row, 1959), pp. 145-46.) Heidegger appears to have overlooked a problem with this account of poetic inspiration that, however, Werner Marx has discovered: "If the works of the poets find access to Saying — that is, to Saying in the form it has in withdrawal — and if they are to transform it into an essence of Saying which can be called 'the poetic,' then the power of affecting the granting nonhuman sphere would be attributed to the human sphere of the poem after all, which was itself granted as such by Saying: the power of affecting the 'granting' sphere would be attributed to the 'granted' sphere" (p. 248).

19   See WM, 270; compare SZ, 213-14.

20   See *Hegels Dialektik*, p. 91.

21   Heidegger, "Overcoming Metaphysics," *The End of Philosophy*, trans. Joan Stambaugh (New York: Harper & Row, 1973), p. 85; compare the translator's note on "overcoming," p. 84.

22   See Walter Kaufmann's criticisms of this misleading and overly systematic interpretation of Hegel in *Hegel: A Reinterpretation* (Garden City: Doubleday Anchor, 1965), p. 154.

23   *Hegels Dialektik*, pp. 91-92.

24   *Hegels Dialektik*, p. 91.

25   Heidegger, *Hegel's Concept of Experience* (New York: Harper & Row, 1970); cited as: HCE.

26   *Hegel's Logic*, trans. William Wallace (Oxford: Clarendon Press, 1975), Section 48, p. 68.

27   Hans Friedrich Fulda, *Das Problem einer Einleitung in Hegels Wissenschaft der Logik* (Frankfurt: V. Klostermann, 1965), and O. Pöggeler, "Die Komposition der *Phänomenologie des Geistes*," in *Hegel-Studien*, Beiheft 3 (Bonn: Bouvier, 1966), 27-74. But Werner Marx, in his book *Hegel's Phenomenology of Spirit*, trans. Peter Heath (New York: Harper & Row, 1975), remarks in his

discussion of this recent literature that "it was questioned even by the older Hegelian scholars whether Hegel had adhered to this intention, or whether — as I.H. Fichte thought — the First Part had been composed from the standpoint of a transcendental philosophy, while the Second Part — as Haym saw it — had been conceived in terms of a philosophy of history and *Realphilosophie* " (pp. x-xi).

28 Gadamer (*Hegels Dialektik,* p. 86) finds this *Kehre* similar to Hegel's movement beyond subjective spirit, beyond consciousness and self-consciousness.

29 Kant's reflections on history, and his postulation of the perfect constitution toward the achievement of which history necessarily progresses, generate such regulative principles. The end or goal is something for which we can hope, but not something we can know. See, for instance, "An Old Question Raised Again: Is the Human Race Constantly Progressing?" in Kant, *On History*, ed. Lewis White Beck (New York: Library of Liberal Arts, 1963), p. 150.

The Postmodernity of Heidegger

Richard E. Palmer

I. Heidegger as Postmodern?

Why discuss the "postmodernity" of Heidegger? There is good reason: for many American readers Heidegger appears as regressive, as a mystic or a crank. His interpretations of poetic texts are often taken as ideosyncratic exercises which would merit no attention at all were they not by a man whose major accomplishments were "in philosophy." His imitators and literary disciples do not come off as well; their efforts are viewed by establishmentarians as bypassing the rigors of exegesis for abstruse musings about "the happening of Truth" and "the e-mergence of Being." Hermeneutics is mistaken to be a new and wrong way to go about the task of interpreting texts, a "dangerous tendency" that may tempt the unwary student away from the text and into strictly hypothetical musings about the nature of language which do not rightly deserve the name either of philosophy or of literary interpretation.[1]

Others, more continentally inclined, hold that French structuralist thought has "superseded" Heidegger's views on language, and that his poetical and "expressionistic" exegeses have little to do with the disciplined procedures and fine distinctions one finds in structuralism. The

71

range of disciplines touched by the implications of structuralism would seem to be much greater than what could be affected by reflections on poems by Hölderlin, Trakl, or Rilke, which can only be properly appreciated in the German original in any case. Moreover, Jacques Derrida has assertedly shown the entrapment of Heidegger in metaphysics, in that he seems to assume a fixed origin that could be recovered through hermeneutical reflection; whereas the more radical view is that language contains within itself the resources for endless variations and depths of meaning, and that there is no fixed, original, and "real" meaning that can be recovered.[2]

Is it really proper, therefore, to refer to Heidegger as a "postmodern" thinker at all? Such a question already contains within itself the problem of defining the "postmodern" or perhaps the assumption that one already can define this elastic and suggestive term. Does it move toward a "New Gnosticism" — an unmediated contact with a "universal consciousness," as Hassan has recently argued?[3] Or is postmodernity really a matter of venturing with Derrida to the other side of that rupture which occurred in the late nineteenth century in which structure was perceived as an interpretive creation of language without anchor in any logos or firm principle outside of language itself — i.e. beyond "metaphysics"?[4] Is perhaps language-centeredness and an awareness of interpretive matrix without subject or object the essence of the postmodern? What happens to the arcadian, technophobic rejection of modernity?[5] Or the movement to a more radical psychology as evidenced in the impact of existentialism and phenomenology and more recently the move to a transpersonal psychology?[6]

The attempt to fit Heidegger to one of these prior definitions of postmodern would be misguided and insulting. It would wrongly subordinate the contribution of Heidegger to the issue of the definition of the postmodern, when the more significant question is rather Heidegger's contribution to the postmodern. By asking *what Heidegger contributes to a "postmodern interpretive self-awareness,"* however, one can leave in abeyance (1) the problem of defining the postmodern (since what is at issue is Heidegger's contribution to a new interpretive awareness, however defined) and (2) the question of whether Heidegger may properly be classified as "postmodern" (since he could contribute to a postmodern interpretive self-awareness whether or not he were classified as a "postmodern" thinker). The real issue, of course, is not one of categories and classifications but rather the character of Heidegger's contribution.

A major problem in the American reception of Heidegger's contribution is the need to make clear its radicality. Heidegger's significance does not lie in contributing a new technique or method to literary interpretation; this makes it very easy to pass off Heidegger's explications as one style among others. Rather, Heidegger calls into question the underlying view of language, the model of knowing and interpretation, the character and goals of thinking, and the definitions of truth that literary critics are assuming as axiomatic. It is not permissable, therefore, to pass Heidegger off as a mystic or a crank; his arguments regarding language, interpretation, and truth must be met by a direct defense of the conceptions of language, interpretation, and truth one presupposes. It is our general thesis that Heidegger's contribution to literary interpretation lies not so much in providing a style or "approach" that can be taken over (or rejected) by journeyman interpreters of literature who refuse to inspect their own presuppositions; rather, it involves a fundamental, reflexive criticism of the interpretive mindset — the presuppositions about interpretation itself — that are at work in the interpreter's interaction with a poem, play, or novel. Heidegger's contribution lies, in other words, in the direction of a new hermeneutical self-awareness.[7]

II. The Problem of Beginnings

But where does one begin in trying to articulate the hermeneutical significance — the significance for a new interpretive self-awareness — of Heidegger's thought? This dilemma is itself illustrative of the problem, for Heidegger confronts us with a thinking so radical that it resists being taken up into our (modern) conceptualities; it resists all easy integration, so foreign is it to prevailing ways of thought. Four possible avenues of approach suggest themselves, of which we shall choose the fourth.

The first approach would be to list the "beyonds" that one finds in Heidegger and to explicate the significance of each. For instance, Heidegger takes thinking resolutely *beyond humanism*; as he explains in his famous "Letter on Humanism," the very concept is freighted with prior conceptions of man as "rational animal" possessing language, and with a conception of man in relation to the world, which Heidegger rejects.[8] Heidegger's thought is *beyond metaphysics*; that is, beyond every logos-centered conception that there is a reality-substratum, a *Hinterwelt* (world behind our world) that is the foundation for our fleeting phenomenal world.[9] It is *beyond the conceptualities of transcendental philosophy*; Heidegger discovered that even his innovative vocabulary in *Being and Time* still pulled his thought back into the modes of transcendental philosophy.[10] It is *beyond the modes of calculative thinking;* for Heidegger makes a clear distinction between a kind of thinking that merely calculates with what already is and another kind of thinking that brings things into being.[11] It is *beyond the will to power*; Heidegger criticizes technological thinking as expressing the inner thrust of a desire for mastery. It is *beyond modern subjecticity*; that is, it does not make the willing, feeling, evaluating subject the center of reference for thought.[12] It is *beyond presentational thinking;*[13] Heidegger raises profound questions as to the ground for modern conceptualities. And it is, in ways fairly difficult to articulate, *beyond phenomenology*.[14] These "beyonds" tend to form a chain and to hinge on each other: the profundity of what being "beyond humanism" means only emerges when one understands the way in which Heidegger moves "beyond metaphysics" and "beyond subjecticity," the way in which the later Heidegger moves into a language-oriented thought centered in *"Ereignis"* (the event of coming into one's own), and his critique of technological thinking itself.[15] This approach of listing the negations, the "beyonds," would have the advantage that it clarifies his critique of modernity. Thus it would be one way of articulating the "postmodernity" of Heidegger.

A second approach could set forth and explain a series of "redefinitions" that Heidegger's thought demands: of time, truth, language, being, history, art, thinking, experience, understanding, interpretation, communication, etc. As with the series of "beyonds," these radical new conceptions form a chain (or hermeneutical circle), so that going into any one term in depth will involve the others. This would be a thematic approach, and would involve the corpus of his works, for the subject of *time* is discussed as the temporality of being in *Being and Time* and elsewhere;[16] *truth* in a half-dozen major essays;[17] *art* especially in his "Origin of the Work of Art";[18] and *language* throughout the later works, such as the famous "Letter on Humanism"[19] and *On the Way to Language*.[20] Again the issue of postmodernity arises, in that the prevailing "modern" conceptions are again and again placed in the radical context of Heidegger's post-metaphysical, post-subjectist quest for the meaning of being. The issue would seem to be not whether Heidegger is postmodern or not but rather the acceptance of Heidegger as a *version* of postmodernity.

A third sort of approach could take its bearings from a clarification of Heidegger's relation to Nietzsche. It would require some elucidation of Nietzsche's contribution to modern and postmodern thought and then demonstration of the way in which Heidegger builds on Nietzsche.[21] This would involve three major parts:

— What Heidegger holds in common with Nietzsche: a lifelong radical stance, with global rejection of modernity; a grounding in philology (both are humanists, which has significance in understanding Heidegger's difference from Husserl, whose academic grounding was in mathematics and logic); a rejection of Cartesian subject-centered consciousness-centered philosophy (again in contrast to Husserl); a sense of man as the historically self-creating and self-transcending being; decentrism and the project of going definitively beyond metaphysics (which links Heidegger and Nietzsche with contemporary structuralist and post-structuralist thinking).

— Heidegger's critique of Nietzsche. Heidegger is not the slavish disciple of Nietzsche but rather admires Nietzsche as a *"thinker"* (in Heidegger's special sense of the word as one who creatively articulates matters). Heidegger argues in the "Letter on Humanism" that Nietzsche does not go beyond metaphysics but remains trapped by his antithesis to it;[22] he goes perceptively into Nietzsche's philosophy of art as the highest manifestation of the will to power;[23] he finds that Nietzsche falls back into a conception of truth that relies on correspondence and thus implies the very metaphysics from which he is trying to free himself;[24] and finally Heidegger rejects Nietzsche's biologism and the self-assertion of the will-to-power as only the culmination of Western philosophies of will that trace themselves back to the human subject (Descartes, Leibnitz, Kant, Schelling, Schopenhauer; i.e., a philosophy of will is still a philosophy of consciousness and subjectivity), and thus argues that Nietzsche does not overcome metaphysics but is, on the contrary, the last great metaphysical thinker of the West.[25]

    — Elements in Heidegger not present in Nietzsche. The themes of time and being play little role in Nietzsche compared to their centrality in Heidegger. The energetic Dionysianism of Nietzsche becomes an orphic serenity in Heidegger, although one still senses a common commitment to "life" as a force deeper than logic: the way in which the "little reason" of the mind is surpassed by the "great reason" of the body in Nietzsche[26] is paralleled in Heidegger's *Being and Time* by the way in which the fabric of the lifeworld in pre-articulated understanding is antecedent to every articulated understanding in interpretation.[27] The priority of the life-force in Nietzsche becomes in Heidegger the priority of the "call of being," and thus the importance of an attitude of "listening" and receptivity. Although the "sacred" is certainly not missing in Nietzsche, in Heidegger the feeling for the "near," the call of "destiny," the demand that man wait ("only wait") in *Gelassenheit*,[28] and the image of man as "shepherd of being" (as he is called in the "Letter on Humanism") all provide the starkest contrast (at least externally) with Zarathustra. The definition of being as *"physis,"*[29] truth as *"aletheia,"*[30] and language as the house in which being dwells and emerges; the reverent openness to poetry; the focus on the centrality of language as the site for the eventing of being — all contrast with Nietzsche. Another way of putting this is to recall that Heidegger's thinking is oriented to the recovery of a forgotten concept of being — an ontological problematic — and it circles round the "ontological difference"; Nietzsche's thought, on the other hand, takes as its goal a new, higher man. For this purpose, Nietzsche seeks to break free from the thought-forms of modernity and thus be able to articulate the nature and conditions for the overman. Preoccupied with nihilism, Nietzsche seeks to define a mode of existence that is positive and creative — both beyond nihilism and beyond the chains of "good and evil." The radicality of such thinking is certainly suited to the purposes of Heidegger, who wants to think the problem of "being" in a way that breaks free of the context of metaphysics. But Heidegger's quest has been more narrowly focussed than Nietzsche's, for his lifelong project has remained the quest for the meaning of being. Heidegger ventures to believe that the word "being" might contain within its meaning "the spiritual destiny of the West."[31] The significance of this for the question of postmodernity lies in its tendency to define the problem of modernity in ontological terms: the transition from "modern" to "postmodern" is the transition from the metaphysical definitions of truth and being to the postmetaphysical conceptions of *aletheia* and *physis* (or *Ereignis*). Postmodern thinking would be thinking that takes its bearings from a postmetaphysical conception of being.

The fourth approach is hermeneutical, both in theme and method. It will select a half dozen texts and through careful unfolding of their meaning attempt to capture a sense of Heidegger on the path of thought. In this way it will try to bring the reader closer to the texture of Heidegger's thought and suggest the contribution his reflections can make to a postmodern interpretive self-awareness.

III. Six Texts of Heidegger

From the many sides of Heidegger's contribution to modern or postmodern thought, we choose six texts that have special hermeneutical significance. One is from *Being and Time* and the others from various later writings. Each contains a principal idea or theme which is distinctly Heideggerian and a part of what he contributes to a postmodern interpretive self-awareness. This selection of passages is not intended as exhaustive but as a beginning.

1. *The hermeneutical and apophantic "as."*

The "as" makes up the structure of the expressability of what is understood — it constitutes the interpretation (*Auslegung*). Circumspective and interpreting intercourse with what is at hand in one's world — which "sees" this *as* dish, door, carriage, bridge — does not necessarily also need the circumspectively interpreted thing to be laid out in a determining assertion. All prepredicative simple seeing of what is at hand is in itself already understanding-interpretation. . . . The leveling of the original "as" of circumspective interpretation to the "as" as the determination of something merely on hand is the advantage of assertion. Only so does it gain the possibility of a mere pointing designation.

So the assertion cannot deny its ancestry in an understanding interpretation. The original "as" of circumspectively understanding interpretation (*hermeneia*) we call the *existential-hermeneutical* "as" in contrast with the *apophantic* "as" of assertion.[32]

The key to this passage is the assertion that all prepredicative simple seeing is already interpretive. In the same section ("Understanding and Interpretation"), Heidegger goes to some trouble to explain that this prepredicative seeing already contains within it a prior way of *having* what is seen, and thus a prior *view* of the thing seen, and is directed by a prior *conceptuality* in the very process of the seeing. Only on the foundation of this implicit understanding (or preunderstanding) does seeing take place, and only on the basis of such interpretive seeing can there be an interpretive articulation in words. Thus, "interpretation is never a presuppositionless grasp of a pregiven thing."[33] Rather, "All interpretation is grounded in understanding."[34]

The priority of understanding over its articulated form in interpretation (*Auslegung*) parallels and is the basis for the priority of interpretation over specific assertions. Assertions are therefore a "derivative" mode.[35] That is, they could not exist at all without the prior context of understanding. Heidegger then makes a distinction between two kinds of interpretation: that which arises out of a direct, prereflective, immediate, and yet interpretive intercourse with the world and that which merely points to something through constructing a proposition. The latter steps out of the original full and complex relationship into another kind of relationship which merely points. The former sees the dish or door in a familiar way, a way that does not have to bring that relationship to articulation, although it sees the door "as" door; this is the way of the "existential-hermeneutical *as*." The latter, however, does not relate to the door except in a way that points; it refrains from any kind of relationship other than that of true or false designation. This is the "apophantic *as*." Both see the door "as" door, but in radically different ways.

The significance of this basic distinction for interpretive self-awareness lies first in the reflexivity about interpretive relationship which it involves, and secondly, in the ontological status that is accorded to understanding. Understanding is grounded in the fabric of relationships we have as we exist. To exist, we understand; and understanding is a basic mode of existing. Understanding is a way of describing what being is and does; yet one can understand in a shallowly related way or with a depth rooted in the prereflexive and never fully articulated realm out of which all meanings, and all "as" 's come. Thus, the interpreter who is fully reflexive realizes that his seeing (and hearing) is rooted in prior ways of having, viewing, and conceiving, on the character and depth of which will depend what he sees. The "as" may already, in its shallow form as "apophantic *as*," wall him away from seeing something as it might appear in the existential-hermeneutical relationship.

Certain aspects of the formulation of this distinction reflect the stage of earlier Heideggerian thinking. The impetus and decision between the two forms of relation to the world seem implicitly to lie in the human subject, and thus the discussion has the appearance of speaking about the

77

subjectivity of a subject although its actual purpose is the explication of ontological structures. Language is not seen as the "house of being" but more as a medium which "already hides within itself a developed conceptuality."[36] Yet there is within this early formulation a critical reflexivity which is the foundation of genuine interpretive self-awareness. Also in this formulation, the depth of what is hidden and can never be rendered explicit is reflected, giving interpretation a foundation not in the process of pointing and designating but in the impenetrable flesh of existence. This has the advantage of retaining the sense of the depths and mystery of life and furnishes a formidable barrier to the presumptions of technological rationalists. Logic is also assigned a derivative place as the mere manipulation of propositions, and is not accorded honor and centrality.[37] Existence, not a metaphysical logos, is made the ground for interpretation. Already the basis is laid for a philosophy that rests on a sense of the reality of what is "concealed," a philosophy which attempts to go "beyond metaphysics." Already Heidegger can deal satirically with assertions of "objective validity" and with "value theory" as confused and unclear about their own foundations.[38]

One feels in the critical attack on conceptions of objectivity, of language, of understanding and interpretation, a definitive leap beyond the context of presuppositions of modern thought. Heidegger, in *Being and Time*, clearly felt the global character of his new standpoint as placing everything in a different light. It is clear from his tone that he feels himself to be a postmodern thinker. This sense of outsideness and aheadness has remained with him through his life.

2. The "step back."

> For Hegel, the conversation with the earlier history of philosophy has the character of *Aufhebung*, that is, of the mediating concept in the sense of an absolute foundation.
>
> For us, the character of the conversation with the history of thinking is no longer *Aufhebung*, but the step back.
>
> *Aufhebung* leads to the heightening and gathering area of truth posited as absolute, truth in the sense of the completely developed certainty of self-knowing knowledge.
>
> The step back points to the realm which until now has been skipped over, and from which the essence of truth becomes first of all worthy of thought. . . .
>
> The term "step back" suggests various misinterpretations. "Step back" does not mean an isolated step of thought, but rather means the manner in

which thinking moves, a long path. Since the step back determines the character of our conversation with the history of Western thinking, our thinking in a way leads us away from what has been thought so far in philosophy. Thinking recedes before its matter, Being, and thus brings what is thought into a confrontation in which we behold the whole of this history — behold it with respect to what constitutes the source of this entire thinking, because it alone establishes and prepares for this thinking in the area of its abode. . . . We speak of the difference between Being and beings. The step back goes from what is unthought, from the difference as such, into what gives us thought, which is the forgottenness of the difference. The forgottenness here to be thought is the veiling of the difference as such, thought in terms of *lethe* (concealment). . . .

The difference between beings and Being is the area within which metaphysics, Western thinking in its entire nature, can be what it is. The step back thus moves out of metaphysics into the essential nature of metaphysics.[39]

This text brings a number of themes together: the "step back," the forgottenness of "being," the status of the ontological difference, and the effort to move beyond metaphysics. It occurs as the third in a series of three contrasts between Hegel's thought and his own, and it helps make clear the relationship of the ontological difference to the effort to overcome metaphysics.

The "step back" is, as Heidegger says, not a particular move of thought but a movement of thinking in which he seeks to leap (or step) out of metaphysical thinking — that is, a thinking that is grounded in a fixed logos — and to find a standpoint that can think the ontological difference between Being and beings *as* a difference. As in *Being and Time*, the ground of thought is not sought in absolute thought but in what one might call a "groundless" ground — the ontological difference as such. Instead of moving "upward" as is implied in the word *Aufhebung*, Heidegger moves downward toward what is unthought, what is concealed.

Such a quest has its consequences for interpretation. In the first place, there is no absolute truth that can be the object of the philosophical quest, and truth is not a matter of thought but of something prior to thought. The "step back" is a step outside a whole form of thinking, away from the body of Western thought. What Heidegger is seeking is not some accidental fact that has nothing to do with interpretation and interpretive awareness; it is rather an effort to uncover a fundamental turn in language reference, in what is meant by "being."

Finally, the nature of Heidegger's quest poses peculiar difficulties in that it does not have a goal lying in a direction clearly indicated in advance. Like Hegel, he seeks to enter into the force of earlier thinking, but with the difference that "we do not seek that force in what has already been thought: we seek it in something that has not been thought, and from which what has been thought receives its essential space."[40] The oblivion or forgottenness from which Being is being rescued is not present in the manifest content of what earlier thinkers have thought but instead in what was hidden from them. It is a combination of blindness and insight; interpretation has to penetrate to what the earlier thinker himself was blind to, but which was the essential determination of his thinking. Interpretation is not destructive but deconstructive; it seeks for what is behind the manifest content of thought. Again, this is a general characteristic of the hermeneutical — it discloses the hidden — which is a central trait of the Heideggerian path. The quest is the harder when one doesn't know what one is looking for, and this is the case with Heidegger, since his thought does not have a specific goal known in advance but rather seeks to recover a lost sense of Being.

3. *The unsaid in the said.*

> *Heidegger* (about Heraclitus): We have said we are not going to interpret a text metaphysically that is itself not yet metaphysical. Is the no-longer-metaphysical already contained in the not-yet-metaphysical?
> *Eugen Fink:* That would be Heraclitus interpreted through Heidegger.
> *Heidegger*: The important thing here is not interpreting Heraclitus through Heidegger but working out the impulse behind your interpretation. We are both agreed that when we would speak with a thinker, we must pay attention to the unspoken in the spoken. The question is only which way leads to this and of what kind is the foundation for such an interpretive step.[41]

In this text, dating from 1966, Heidegger again takes as his theme the overcoming of metaphysics. This time he is in dialogue with Fink about Heraclitus and attempting to interpret him without projecting a subsequent ontology onto him or seeing him through the eyes of Parmenides or Plato.

Heraclitus, standing at the beginning of Greek philosophy, offers the possibility of recovering another conception of being prior to the fateful turn in Plato toward a metaphysical conception of Being as ground, as logos, and truth as correspondence. At the end of the Heraclitus seminar, Heidegger is explicit about the importance of his task: "What if there be in the Greeks something unthought, and what if precisely this unthought thing be what determines their thinking and what is thought down through history?"[42] To which Fink asks: "But how do we gain the viewpoint for this unthought? Perhaps this viewpoint will be generated only out of our late situation."[43] Heidegger's reply, tentative as always, is a suggestion that *"aletheia* as unconcealment moves in the direction of what a 'clearing' is":

> For me it was a matter of experiencing unconcealment as clearing. That is the thing that is unthought in the whole history of thought. In Hegel there existed the need for a pacification through what was thought. For me on the other hand there was the pressure of the unthought in the thought.[44]

Heidegger is here speaking retrospectively, now in his late seventies, and singles out the word *"aletheia"* — "There is nothing in the whole of Greek philosophy about *aletheia as aletheia*. . . . This has nothing to do with "truth" but means unconcealment."[45]

Aletheia — disclosure — is the regular Greek word for truth, but Heidegger's point here is not truth but the process of emergence from concealment. About the nature of this emergence *as* emergence, Heidegger finds little in Greek philosophy. It remained unthought, and perhaps precisely this unthought emergence process more adequately describes being than the conception of being in terms of a principle, idea, or causal ground; this latter would tend to make the difference between Being and beings the difference between a static, unchanging principle, a kind of inner logos, and the world of change and becoming. In other words, it would constitute the basis for metaphysics.

4. *Truth as poetic.*

> Truth, as the clearing and also the covering up of what-is, happens in being *gedichtet* — composed like a poem. *All art* is, as the letting-happen of the arrival of the truth of what-is as such, *by nature poetry*. The nature of art, by which both artist and work are governed, is the self-setting of truth into a work. . . . Language first brings a being into the open as a being. Where no language *is* (*west*), as in the being of stone, plant, or animal, there is also no realm of openness of the extant thing (*des Seienden*) and consequently none for the nonextantness and the empty. Language for the first time names the extant thing, and such naming brings the thing to word and appearance for the first

time. This naming names the thing *to* its being and *from* it. Such "saying" (*Sagen*) is a kind of projecting of the light in which the thing is to be taken, the light wherein is announced what the thing will come into the open *as*. . . .

The founding-projecting (*entwerfende*) Saying is poetry: the Saying of world and of earth, the Saying of the *Spielraum* (arena) of its struggle and therewith of the place in which the gods will be near or remote. Poetry is the Saying of the unconcealment of the extant thing.[46]

Poetry, then, as the saying of the unconcealment, is a defining of the unconcealment. It can define the light in which a thing is seen in such a way that the gods are near, or such that the gods remain far away. The concept of truth, then, is not a matter of correspondence to an already perceived nature of a thing; it is a matter of placing that thing in the light of understanding for the first time. Saying does not have unlimited rights to distort the meaning of a thing when it takes it from the inarticulate depths of "earth" up into the openness of "world." Thus the loving struggle between earth and world, realms of darkness and light, hiddenness and disclosure. "Saying" is the bridge between the hiddenness of earth and the disclosedness of world, and this projective saying is the essence or nature of poetry.

The significance of this view of language, poetry, and truth is that it gives poetry an ontological function, and it makes language not the unproblematical medium in which a thing already understood is conveyed to another person who will understand it because he already has perceived it in some universally same way, but rather the projective "saying-structure" that presents things to us *in a certain light*, a clearing. It is also not accidental that Heidegger mentions the gods, since again it is language which can hold things in nearness to the divine or in remoteness from all sacredness. The moment of "translation" is made into the essential function of language and not the moment of communicating the thing translated once it has been placed in a certain light. It is of course evident that language does convey meaning to others, but the more significant and founding function is its articulation — its "saying" — of meaning, its placing the thing known in a certain light.

This emphasis on the first transition, on "saying," is of highest importance in overcoming the shallow technological view of language as mere vehicle of communication, as if language were a mere vehicle in the way a truck is a vehicle for carrying fruit. For interpretive self-awareness, it urges a view of language as a shaping, projecting, light-shedding structure in which every extant thing is "announced" in a certain way as it is "seen." Heidegger had already said something similar but in less poetic terms in *Being and Time* when he noted that language always contains within itself a certain conceptuality, an already shaped way of seeing.[47] One might describe the project of Heidegger as an effort to show the way in which metaphysics operates as a hidden shaper of our seeing, such that it is our fate, the fate of the West, to exist within the horizon of technology. Language itself contains other possibilities and could reveal the world in a quite different way, but it requires the work of thinker and poet to bring this about.

Truth contains both the realm of clearness (the clearing) and also the realm of concealment of what is. Truth discloses *in a certain light*. Art, as the letting happen of truth, as the placing of *a* truth (disclosure) in the medium of a work — letting it shine through earth's gifts of shininess in metal, colorfulness in color, timbre in sound, and in structures of tension and interrelationships — is *poetical*: it constructs, builds, articulates, lets emerge. As Heidegger says elsewhere, "Poetically man dwells on this earth."[48] He is continually bringing things into the open.

Ontologically stated, what a thing *is*, it is through the openness of language. Being is inseparable from the operation by which language causes earth to shine forth "in a certain light." Language is therefore the "house of being":[49] it is there that being will be found; being resides in language; being, as the process by which language brings things into the open, is linguistic in its nature.

5. *"Nearness" versus objectivity.*

> What and how the jug *is* as this jug-thing, is something we can never learn — let alone think properly — by looking at the outward appearance, the *idea*. That is why Plato, who conceives of the presence of what is present in terms of the outward appearance, had no more understanding of the nature of the thing than did Aristotle and all subsequent thinkers. Rather, Plato experienced (decisively, indeed, for the sequel) everything present as an object of making. Instead of "object" — as that which stands before, over against, opposite us — we use the more precise expression "what stands forth. . . ."
>
> Science's knowledge, which is compelling within its own sphere, the sphere of objects, already had annihilated things as things long before the atom bomb exploded. The bomb's explosion is only the grossest of all gross confirmations of the long-since-accomplished annihilation of the thing: the confirmation that the thing as a thing remains nil. The thingness of the thing remains concealed, forgotten. The nature of the thing never comes to light, that is, it never gets a hearing. This

is the meaning of our talk about the annihilation of the thing. . . .

Today everything present is equally near and equally far. The distanceless prevails. But no abridging or abolishing of distances brings nearness. What is nearness? To discover the nature of nearness, we gave thought to the jug near by. We have sought the nature of nearness and found the nature of the jug as a thing. But in this discovery we also catch sight of the nature of nearness. The thing things. In thinging, it stays earth and sky, divinities and mortals. Staying, the thing brings the four, in their remoteness, near to one another. This bringing-near is nearing. Nearing is the presencing of nearness. . . .

Mortals are who they are as mortals, present in the shelter of Being. They are the presencing relation to Being as Being.

Metaphysics, by contrast, thinks of man as *animal*, as a living being. Even when *ratio* pervades *animalitas*, man's being remains defined by life and life-experience. Rational living beings must first *become* mortals.[50]

In this essay, "The Thing," Heidegger differentiates sharply between object and thing. The object is not near but in a distanceless region lacking all nearness. The scientific revolution has robbed things of their thinghood, has brought about the annihilation of "things." Here, more than in other essays, Heidegger is explicit about the consequences of the scientific stance as a way of seeing. Heidegger is not attacking science as useless to accomplish what it seeks; he is trying to make very clear the starkness of the kind of relationship scientific objectivity involves. It is *a* way of seeing and *a* way of relating, one might say a way of "being-toward" things. It reduces things to objects and strips them of their depth and suggestiveness: "The nature of the thing never comes to light, that is, it never gets a hearing."

This text is also of hermeneutical interest in that it relates this contrast of object and thing to metaphysics and the thinking of man as a mortal. Metaphysics looks for "causes" and "grounds," but "the inexplicable and unfathomable character of the world's worlding lies in this, that causes and grounds remain unsuitable for the world's worlding."[51] They also remain unsuitable for explaining man as mortal being. Heidegger is suggesting a medium of relating to the world in which things no longer appear in the same "light" as they do in metaphysical seeing. In this new light they are no longer man's objects, the objects of man's judging consciousness, but things that step forth in their being through the saying of language. For this reason one must learn to listen carefully to language.

A way of stating this contrasting mode of relating is by reference to the *Kehre* — reversal — in Heidegger. This turn, this transformation, did not abandon the quest for the meaning of being but it altered the mode of receptivity to it. It attempted to affirm the priority of being and the interpretive obligation to listen, respond, allow being to be. This is a departure from all humanism and from the "metaphysical" perspective; and it is a "step back" from metaphysical thinking. Typical of post-*Kehre* Heidegger is the assertion that things do not appear as things by virtue of human making:

> When and in what way do things appear as things? They do not appear *by means of* human making. But neither do they appear without the vigilance of mortals. The first step toward such vigilance is the step back from the thinking that merely represents — that is, explains — to the thinking that responds and recalls.
>
> The step back from the one thinking to the other is no mere shift of attitude. It can never be any such thing for this reason alone: that all attitudes, including the ways in which they shift, remain committed to the precincts of representational thinking. The step back does, indeed, depart from the sphere of mere attitudes. The step back takes up its residence in a co-responding which, appealed to in the world's being by the world's being, answers within itself to that appeal.[52]

The step back is given an added dimension: it is the step back from "representational thinking" as such. It is placed in the post-*Kehre* context of man not as center of the universe but as the shepherd of being, the responder who responds to the appeal of the world's being.

6. *Man's hermeneutical relation to beings: man as messenger.*

> *Heidegger*: In the source of appearance, something comes toward man that holds the two-fold of presence and present beings.
> *Japanese*: That two-fold has always already offered itself to man, although its nature remained veiled.
> *Heidegger*: Man, to the extent he is man, listens to this message. . . . Man is used for hearing the message.
> *Japanese*: This you called a while ago: man stands in a relation.

Heidegger: And the relation is called hermeneutical because it brings the tidings of that message.

Japanese: This message makes the claim on man that he respond to it . . .

Heidegger: . . . to listen and belong to it as man.

Japanese: And this is what you call *being* human, if you still admit the word 'being."

Heidegger: Man is the message-bearer of the message which the two-fold's unconcealment speaks to him.

. . . .

Japanese: I believe I now see more clearly the full import of the fact that hermeneutics and language belong together.

Heidegger: The full import in what direction?

Japanese: Toward a transformation of thinking — a transformation which, however, cannot be established as readily as a ship can alter its course, and even less can be established as the consequence of an accumulation of the results of philosophical research.

Heidegger: The transformation occurs as a passage . . .

Japanese: . . . in which one site is left behind in favor of another . . .

Heidegger: . . . and that requires that the sites be placed in discussion.

Japanese: One site is metaphysics.

Heidegger: And the other? We leave it without a name.[53]

In this famous passage from the later works, Heidegger returns to the hermeneutical phenomenon to explain his effort to "overcome metaphysics" ("neither a destruction nor even a denial of metaphysics"[54]), and to try to "place" his thinking. The goal of his early thought under the impetus of phenomenology was to rethink the question of the being of beings (*das Sein des Seienden*) "no longer in the way of metaphysics but in such a way that Being itself comes to appear. Being itself — this says: the presence of the present being, i.e. the twofoldness of both out of their unity. This is the thing to whose nature men are responsible."[55] It was this quest for the meaning of being that led him to the hermeneutical phenomenon and the growing sense that "language is the dominant and sustaining element in the relation of the being of man to the twofold. Language determines the hermeneutical relation."[56] The term hermeneutical goes with the language-centeredness of the relationship of man to the two-fold.

But more than this, the hermeneutical (being a term not so

freighted with metaphysical tradition) also suggests "a transformation of thinking" by which man moves from one "site" to another — the first being that which has been the clearing for Western man since Plato, and the other which — "We leave it without a name." This namelessness is significant not only because it attempts to avoid the over-simplification that comes with slogans but also because in a deeper sense the roots of Heidegger's thought remain in the nameless, the unsaid, the unthought. One could almost say that the thrust of Heidegger's thought is to preserve the significance of this area of indeterminacy for interpretation: interpretation is not simply the manipulation of what is already manifest, it is pre-eminently the bringing of a certain light to bear on what is.

One finds in this late text the overwhelming priority of the Saying over the human process of interpretation. The dialogue is one between the two-fold, into which man fits himself as the consciously hermeneutical being. This priority of being over the human being, so typical of post-*Kehre* Heidegger, offers the starkest contrast to the hubris of modern ego-centric thought. The step back from metaphysical thinking is also a step back from representational thought as such and also from any representable (rational logos) center for such thought. The problem is that of penetrating, or retaining a sense of being guided by, what is indefinable, a stillness prior to all articulate sound.

> *Japanese*: Are we not attempting the impossible?
> *Heidegger*: Indeed — so long as man has not yet been given the pure gift of the messenger's course that the message needs which grants to man the unconcealment of the two-fold.
> *Japanese*: To call forth this messenger's course, and still more to go forward on it, seems to me incomparably more difficult than to discuss the nature of *Iki*.
> *Heidegger*: Surely. For something would have to come about by which that vast distance in which the nature of Saying assumes its radiance, opened itself to the messenger's course and shone upon it.
> *Japanese*: A stilling would have to come about that quiets the breath of the vastness into the structure of Saying which calls out to the messenger.
> *Heidegger*: The veiled relation of message and messenger's course *plays* everywhere.[57]

IV. The Postmodern Contribution of Heidegger

The "postmodernity" of Heidegger is of a special kind, for his is a thought and a path that resists categories, so that he himself wishes to leave it in the nameless. Yet he has left some suggestive articulations of that path of thought: the step back from metaphysical thinking, the search for the unthought within the thought, the between-character of man's existence, the importance of co-responding to the Saying of language, and so on. The "turn" in Heidegger's thought suggests a principle and an issue of highest importance for a postmodern interpretive awareness, for it attacks the conception of man as the king and center of the world of interpretations, the inventor and user of language, the holder of tremendous technological power. Heidegger's critique of the abstractness, distancelessness, and one-dimensionality of scientific objectivity is not unique in twentieth century thought, but his vivid articulation of that critique in terms of metaphysics cuts a level deeper than most merely sociological criticism. And his presentation of "nearness" as a way of being toward things comprises an important alternative possibility and image of what is lost. When one has explored in some detail the way in which Heidegger's thinking moves beyond objectivity, beyond "humanism," beyond technological rationality, beyond traditional concepts of language, truth, and thinking as such, one cannot escape the sense that this is a path resolutely outside and beyond the general horizons of modern thought. In fact, an understanding in depth simply of what Heidegger meant by the "overcoming (*Uberwindung*) of metaphysics" already points to a new "site" for thinking, and toward a postmodern interpretive awareness.

MacMurray College

NOTES

1   See Campbell Tatham, "High-Altitude Hermeneutics," in *Diacritics* 3 (Summer 1973), 23.

2   See Jacques Derrida, "Structure, Sign, and Play in the Discourse of the Human Sciences," in Richard Macksey and Eugenio Donato, eds., *The Languages of Criticism and the Sciences of Man: The Structuralist Controversy* (Baltimore: The Johns Hopkins University Press, 1970), pp. 247-48. Of interest in this regard is the recent book by Joseph N. Riddel, *The Inverted Bell: Modernism and the Counterpoetics of William Carlos Williams* (Baton Rouge: Louisiana State University Press, 1974), and the review of it by J. Hillis Miller, who discusses the contrast between Derrida and Heidegger on origins, "Deconstructing the Deconstructers," *Diacritics* 5 (Summer 1975), 24-31.

3   See "The New Gnosticism: Speculations on an Aspect of the Postmodern Mind," essay No. 6 in his *Paracriticisms* (Urbana: University of Illinois Press, 1975).

4   See the Derrida article cited above.

5   See Hassan, *Paracriticisms*, pp. 124-26, as well as the final essay, "Models of Transformation: Ideology, Utopia, and Fantasy in America," pp. 151-76.

6   I have in mind especially "third force" psychology, the work of Rollo May, R.

D. Laing, Maslow, Erikson, Rogers, and others, as well as the more radical Jacques Lacan, and the "fourth force" psychology that explores mystical experiences, bliss, awe, wonder, synergy, and compassion. I have in manuscript an essay, "Some Versions of Postmodern," in which I suggest ten non-Heideggerian versions of postmodern; one section is devoted to psychology and postmodernity.

7   This theme is explored in my paper, "Heidegger's Contribution to a Postmodern Interpretive Self-Awareness," presented at the annual meeting of the Heidegger Circle, May 17, 1975. The meeting was hosted by the Center for Advanced Research in Phenomenology at Wilfrid Laurier University, Waterloo, Canada, whose director, Professor José Huertas-Jourda, will edit the proceedings for possible publication. The three parts of my paper were: "The Postmodern Turn," "Nietzsche's Negations," and "Heidegger's Contribution."

8   See the "Humanismusbrief" in *Platons Lehre von der Wahrheit: Mit einem Brief uber den "Humanismus"* (Bern: A. Francke, 1947), pp. 53-119.

9   Among other writings, this point is made especially clear in the essay, "The Onto-theo-logical Constitution of Metaphysics," in *Identity and Difference* (New York: Harper & Row, 1969).

10   See Heidegger's letter to Father William J. Richardson, published as the preface to his book, *Heidegger: Through Phenomenology to Thought* (The Hague: Martinus Nijhoff, 1963), p. xix, and the "Letter on Humanism."

11   See the famous Epilogue to *Was ist Metaphysik?*, in which Heidegger discusses *"das wesentliche Denken"* (Frankfurt: Vittorio Klostermann, 1949), the opening essays in *Vorträge und Aufsätze* (Pfullingen: Günther Neske, 1954), and the discussion of Text No. 5 below.

12   This is especially clear in "Die Zeit des Weltbildes," *Holzwege* (Frankfurt: Vittorio Klostermann, 1950), pp. 69-104.

13   See *Holzwege*, pp. 69-104, as well as the discussion of the "step back" later in this essay.

14   See *Heidegger: Through Phenomenology to Thought*, p. 623. Father Richardson's argument is that "the method characteristic of Heidegger II is the process of thought, of Heidegger I the process of phenomenology." A paper with the title "Heidegger and Phenomenology" by Walter Biemel was presented to the Heidegger Circle meeting in May, 1975, and will undoubtedly be published shortly, either in the proceedings of the meeting or elsewhere.

15   See "Die Frage nach der Technik," in *Vorträge und Aufsätze*, pp. 13-44.

16   In the introduction to *Was is Metaphysik?*, written in 1949, Heidegger calls time the "first name" (*Vorname*) of Being. In *On Time and Being* (New York: Harper & Row, 1972), time is the "realm of the open," is what "gives" Being; in this latter essay Heidegger proposes to go back to "what determines both time and Being" — the *Ereignis*, "the event or process of coming into one's own" (translated by Joan Stambaugh as "the event of Appropriation").

17   See pre-eminently *Vom Wesen der Wahrheit*, (Frankfurt: Vittorio

Klostermann, 1943), translated in *Existence and Being*, ed. Werner Brock (Chicago: Regnery, 1949), pp. 292-324, and *Platons Lehre von der Wahrheit*, cited above.

18   Translated by Albert Hofstadter in *Poetry, Language, Thought* (New York: Harper & Row, 1971), pp. 17-87. Subsequent references to this book will be abbreviated as: PLT.

19   "Language is the house of Being," p. 53 in *Platons Lehre von der Wahrheit*, cited above.

20   Trans. Peter D. Hertz (New York: Harper & Row, 1971).

21   This was the general strategy I followed in my paper cited in note 7 above.

22   *Platons Lehre von der Wahrheit*, p. 85.

23   *Nietzsche* (Pfullingen: Günther Neske, 1961), I, 11-254.

24   Also at greater length in "Nietzsches Metaphysik," *Nietzsche*, II, 257-333.

25   "With Nietzsche's metaphysics, philosophy is completed. That means: It has gone through the sphere of prefigured possibilities. Completed metaphysics, which is the ground for the planetary manner of thinking, gives the scaffolding for an order of the earth which will supposedly last for a long time. The order no longer needs philosophy because philosophy is already its foundation. But with the end of philosophy, thinking is not also at its end, but in transition to another beginning." *The End of Philosophy*, trans. Joan Stambaugh (New York: Harper & Row, 1973), pp. 95-96; *Vorträge und Aufsätze*, p. 83.

26   See "On the Despisers of the Body," in Book I of *Thus Spoke Zarathustra*: "Your little reason, which you call 'Geist,' is the tool and plaything of your great reason (the body)." *Werke*, ed. Karl Schlechta (Munich: Hanser, 1966), II, 300.

27   See especially Sections 31 and 32 in *Being and Time*.

28   Translated as *Discourse on Thinking* by John M. Anderson and E. Hans Freund (New York: Harper & Row, 1966). See especially the second part, "Conversation on a Country Path."

29   E.g., as discussed in *An Introduction to Metaphysics* (Garden City: Anchor Books, 1961), pp. 11-14.

30   See note 17 above.

31   As in *Introduction to Metaphysics*, p. 31: "Is 'being' a mere word and its meaning a vapor or is it the spiritual destiny of the Western world? . . . From a metaphysical point of view, Russia and America are the same; the same dreary technological frenzy, the same unrestricted organization of the average man. . . . The spiritual decline of the earth is so far advanced that the nations are in danger of losing the last bit of spiritual energy that makes it possible to see the decline (taken in relation to the history of 'being'), and to appraise it as such. . . . For the darkening of the world, the flight of the gods, the destruction of the earth, the transformation of men into a mass, the hatred

and suspicion of everything free and creative, have assumed such proportions throughout the earth that such childish categories as pessimism and optimism have long since become absurd."

32 *Sein und Zeit,* 10th ed. (Tübingen: M. Niemeyer Verlag, 1963), pp. 149 and 158. My translation. When the primary footnote reference is to the German, the translation is my own. Subsequent references abbreviated as: SZ.

33 SZ, p. 150: "Auslegung ist nie ein voraussetzungsloses Erfassen eines Vorgegebenen."

34 SZ, p. 153: "Alle Auslegung gründet im Verstehen."

35 As indicated in the heading of Section 33 of SZ: "Assertion as derivative (*abkünftiger*) mode of interpretation."

36 SZ, p. 157: "die Sprache je schon eine ausgebildete Begrifflichkeit in sich birgt."

37 SZ, pp. 158-60.

38 SZ, pp. 154-56.

39 *Identity and Difference,* pp. 49-51. I follow the Stambaugh translation, in general, although I render *Vergessenheit* as "forgottenness" rather than "oblivion." Subsequent references abbreviated as: ID.

40 ID, p. 48.

41 Martin Heidegger, Eugen Fink, *Heraklit: Seminar Wintersemester 1966/67* (Frankfurt: Vittorio Klostermann, 1970), p. 111. Subsequent references abbreviated as: H.

42 H, p. 259.

43 H, p. 259.

44 H, p. 260.

45 H, p. 259.

46 *Der Ursprung des Kunstwerkes,* introd. Hans-Georg Gadamer (Stuttgart: Reclam, 1965), pp. 82-83. See the excellent English translation by Albert Hofstadter in PLT, pp. 72-74.

47 See note 37 above. Also: "Alles vorprädikative schlichte Sehen des Zuhandenen ist an ihm selbst schon verstehend-auslegend . . ." (SZ, p. 149).

48 *Vorträge und Aufsätze,* pp. 187-204; PLT, pp. 213-29.

49 *Platons Lehre von der Wahrheit,* p. 53. (This is from the first page of the "Humanismusbrief.")

50 PLT, pp. 168, 170, 177, 179.

51   PLT, p. 180.

52   PLT, pp. 181-82.

53   "A Dialogue on Language between a Japanese and an Inquirer," *On the Way to Language*, trans. Peter D. Hertz (New York: Harper & Row, 1971), pp. 40, 42. Subsequent references abbreviated as: OWL.

54   OWL, p. 20.

55   OWL, p. 30; *Unterwegs zur Sprache* (Pfullingen: Günther Neske, 1959), p. 122. My translation.

56   OWL, p. 30; *Unterwegs zur Sprache*, p. 122.

57   OWL, p. 53.

Heidegger: A Photographic Essay

Donald Bell

Sein und Zeit:
Implications for Poetics

Stanley Corngold

The effect upon poetics of *Sein und Zeit* during the fifty years of its history now has a history of its own. Explicit references to literature in *Sein und Zeit* are in fact very few. For this reason Beda Allemann speaks of an "essential absence of connection between *Sein und Zeit* and the phenomenon of literature as such (and not merely as pre-ontological evidence)."[1] But he goes on to note that "apparently nothing stands in the way of interpreting the results of the existential analytic for the sake of a theory of literature" (HH, 89). Continental and, of late, American criticism bears him out. Indeed, to judge from the rigor and inner coherence of much poetic speculation based on *Sein und Zeit,* one would now be reluctant to speak of an "essential" absence of connection between *Sein und Zeit* and literature.

In the work of Staiger, Pfeiffer, Blanchot, Bense, de Man, and Derrida, to name a few, *Sein und Zeit* has shaped theoretical and practical poetics in decisive ways, and it has done so despite an important objection. This objection is based not on the inexplicitness of Heidegger's poetics in *Sein und Zeit* but on the ontological bearing of that enterprise. *Sein und Zeit* defines the structures which constitute human existence.

These "existentials" are put forward as part of an analysis of the understanding of Being which informs the question of Being. The existentials are not meant to organize our experience of some particular entity or to serve as the leading ideas of an ontic discipline, such as the study of literature.

But this argument, while it rightly invokes caution, is not strong enough to debar literary speculation based on *Sein und Zeit*. Taken strictly, it amounts to the assertion that in *Sein und Zeit* ontological discourse and ontic discourse — ontic implying empirical discourse — are informed by absolutely separate intents. But this assertion is not right. When Heidegger writes, for example, "The history of the signification of the ontical concept of 'care' permits us to see . . . basic structures of Dasein,"[2] he describes a relation not of polarity but of hermeneutic circularity. The ontological perspective emerges in and through the ontic conception. The presence of a number of such moments of reciprocal disclosure between the ontological phenomenon and the ontical concept is not accidental. It is based on the fact that "the roots of the existential analytic, on its part, are ultimately . . . *ontical*" (BT, 34). "The task of an existential analytic of Dasein has been delineated in advance, as regards both its possibility and its necessity, in Dasein's ontical constitution" (BT, 33). This is not to question, even within this circular relation, the priority of the ontological project. The existential analytic in *Sein und Zeit* produces a zone of clarity in which literary language can become transparent to its possibilities of ontological disclosure. But such an analysis would also profile legitimate ontical features of literature. Indeed, as we shall see, Heidegger guides this analysis.

He suggests an important place for literature within the existential analytic. The "deposition" he selects from "the history of the signification of the ontical concept of 'care' " is a literary text, a fable by the Latin writer Hyginus. In this document, Heidegger asserts, his interpretation of human existence as care has been "sketched out beforehand in elemental ways" (BT, 242). True, what is decisive about this document is its character as a self-interpretation of *Dasein* and not as a literary text. But its literary character is not therefore irrelevant. Allemann writes, "In *Sein und Zeit* there is not the slightest indication that literature would be particularly conducive to such a self-interpretation. Rather, in its bearing on the interpretation of Dasein, literature is grouped together with philosophical psychology, anthropology, ethics, 'political science,' biography and the writing of history (SZ, 16)" (HH, 88). This argument is not telling. Heidegger justifies his choice of the Hyginus fable as follows: ". . . A deposition which comes from [*Dasein's*] history and goes back to it, and which, moreover, is *prior* to any scientific knowledge, will have especial weight, even though its importance is never purely ontological" (BT, 241-42). A deposition prior to scientific knowledge could not have come out of the canonical texts of just any of the disciplines named above (although history or biography could still have come into question). Moreover, Heidegger's note describing how he came to discover the Hyginus-fable takes pains to mention that "the fable of *Cura* . . . was taken over from Herder by Goethe and worked up for the second part of his *Faust*" (BT, 492). He is undoubtedly conjuring with the authority of Goethe's insight into the literary value of the work as a warrant for its "pre-ontological" importance.[3]

But there is another crucially important statement in *Sein und Zeit* which argues further and more decisively for the privilege of "poetic discourse." "In 'poetical' discourse," writes Heidegger, "the communication of the existential possibilities of one's state-of-mind can become an aim in itself, and this amounts to a disclosing of existence."[4] The critic Schrimpf, who also finds an absence of connection between *Sein und Zeit* and poetics, altogether omits mentioning this sentence.[5] Allemann alludes to it, but glosses it so as to diminish its force:

> If within the existential analytic, literature nonetheless thus acquires a certain importance as the self-expression of Dasein, it should be further noted that Heidegger's concept of existence itself does not possess characteristics derived, say, from the psychology of the artist as the "creative" human being, as is the case with central concepts (life, *évolution créatrice*) in the thought of Dilthey and Bergson. (HH, 88)

This of course is true. Heidegger attributes to mood a power to disclose the totality of *Dasein's* being-in-the-world — a power more fundamental than the large emotions attributed by Dilthey to the artistic personality. He perceives with considerable originality that the poetic character of language could be the measure with which language realizes the possibilities of the disclosure reserved to mood.

We shall be exploring this sentence as constituting a vital moment within an epoch of German poetics. Allemann's comment makes a helpful distinction, but it should not diminish the force of Heidegger's statement. The poetics of *Lebensphilosophie*, in the hands of Dilthey and the George circle, is rooted in an ethic of experience and expressiveness. It could not inspire, except by calculated negation, Heidegger's existential analytic of everyday *Dasein*. But Heidegger's description of the goal of poetic discourse is, on the other hand, perfectly consistent with the existential analytic and has implications extending throughout the entire root system of *Sein und Zeit*. Can it therefore be the case, as Allemann concludes, that "state-of-mind and understanding as constitutive modes of Da-sein's being . . . are initially indifferent with respect to the phenomenon of artistic existence"? (HH, 88). We have noted that Heidegger speaks differently in according to poetic discourse the possibility of truth precisely by its power of taking hold of and communicating the existential possibilities of states-of-mind. "The phenomenon of artistic existence" would arise as the concern for turning moods back to their source, wresting from them their fallen character of revealing only by way of "an evasive turning-away" from existence (BT, 175).

Finally, in light of the central role of the "basic state of mind" of anxiety in *Sein und Zeit*, it would not follow that "an existentialistic poetics (*Literaturwissenschaft*) basing itself on Heidegger is possible only on the strength of the anthropological misunderstanding" (HH, 89). In paying heed to literature as a disclosure by mood of existential possibility, the literary theoretician proceeds in basic accord with Heidegger's project in *Sein und Zeit*. For Heidegger will justify his study of anxiety in the existential analytic by the same concern.

> Like any ontological Interpretation whatsoever, this analytic can only, so to speak, "listen in" to some previously disclosed entity as regards its Being. And it will attach itself to Dasein's distinctive and most far-reaching possibilities of disclosure [as principally contained within the mood of anxiety], in order to get information about this entity from these. (BT, 179)

When Heidegger's notion of poetic discourse is taken as a center, poetics and ontology participate in *Sein und Zeit* in a circle of reciprocal disclosure. The relation between particular and general in this work is then formally comparable with the intimate relation of empirical aesthetics and critical thought in Kant's *The Critique of Judgment*. Here, too, "the poetic art" (but also formal gardens and pure arabesques) are held in the play of reciprocal illumination with "something . . . connected with the ground of freedom."[6]

Heidegger's assertion linking poetry, mood, and truth is important in several ways. Because it has obvious implications for poetics, it helps define a system of assertions in *Sein und Zeit* inspiring reflection on literary language. Its terms moreover profile an earlier Romantic tradition of poetic speculation. When their implications are spelled out, they articulate a stage in Heidegger's poetics which differs instructively from the poetics of subsequent texts. Therefore, to assert as does Schrimpf, that in *Sein und Zeit* "poetry as poetry is not yet *in any way* expressly thematized" or that "the *first evidence* of the contribution of what is specifically poetic to the self-interpretation of thought . . . is *The Origin of the Work of Art*"[7] (italics mine), is mere polemical overstatement. It dangerously dismisses the implications for poetics of the fruitful complex of mood, temporality, and interpretation on behalf of the problematical effort of Heidegger's later *Erläuterungen* to displace all philologically-based literary study. Heidegger's poetics are then absorbed in his un-exemplary, "self-imposing" effort at dialogical thinking, and subsequent literary study is left to court exhaustion through the technologies of linguistics and sociology.

The key term in Heidegger's account of poetic discourse is "*Befindlichkeit*" (state-of-mind), which Heidegger also refers to by its ontic counterpart, "*Stimmung*" (mood). The term mood acquires its main force from its place within the ordonnance of *Sein und Zeit*. But the fact that it figures here in the context of a poetics invokes a diachronic line of force, the "pathic" tradition in aesthetics.

Western aesthetics has been seen as the history of a dichotomy defined in innumerable ways. One opposes the terms "an aesthetics of measure and symmetry, *consonantia* or *proportio*, the *unum-multum*, the aesthetics of sapience, the play of the faculties, totality, form, . . . " to "emotions of pity and fear and their catharsis, enthusiasm, the sublime, . . . empathy, expressiveness. . . ."[8] Heidegger belongs to this second sequence, recognizable as the tradition which, from Greek times, has stressed the feeling dimension of literature. Whatever else may originate or define it, literary communication is, at least in one of its moments, essentially feeling. The location of the term of feeling varies, but recurs. Plato, in *Ion*, stresses the manic state-of-mind of the poet. Aristotle stresses the feeling object imitated by the tragic poet, "incidents embodying pity and fear," as well as the feelings aroused and purged in the spectator.[9] Kant defines the state of mind arising from the perception of form as a *Gefühl*, a sentiment; for Kant the poem is essentially form, but the analogy for form is a feeling — of the harmonious interplay of imagination and understanding.

But if, in poetics, feeling is admitted, it is at once modified; indeed, for Dilthey, in his more radical style, it is "metamorphosed."[10] Aesthetic tradition distinguishes between actual feelings and the feelings constituting art, which are fictive — feelings whose motive is not personally interesting. Poetics must then stress the power of literature to reveal, by means of signs having the character of feelings, something different from lived experience. Volkelt speaks of the literary work as *gefühlsanalog*, as analogous to feeling, but ideal, as other than feeling.[11] Literature generates the distinction between the fictive and the lived at the level of feeling; this can be seen in Aristotle. The purgation of tragedy is linked to the fact that what it communicates is not so much feelings (which have an historical existence) as the possibility of feelings; with this distinction Aristotle grounds the superiority of poetry to history.

The distinction between feeling as sensation-bound and feeling as disclosure is most clearly accomplished in Kant. Kant describes the aesthetic sentiment as a general structure capable of making a far-reaching discovery. The aesthetic sentiment reveals the attunement (*Einstimmung*) of the cognitive energies enabling all particular cognitions and "finds a reference in itself" to a "ground of unity."[12] Biemel has perceived the importance of this point. He writes:

> Kant allows to feeling, to mood, a revelatory function of judgment which was usually granted only to logical cognition. Kant has demonstrated in *The Critique of Judgment* how feeling is no "second-rate," incidental, merely emotional faculty, but on the contrary how it mediates for us an experience which has a claim on general validity. He implicitly lends to feeling a "veritative" significance which had not found its authentic justification until our time with Heidegger and Scheler.[13]

Biemel ought to stress the verbal form of Kant's discovery; Kant names aesthetic feeling in its formality and transparency with the decisive term *"Stimmung,"* mood.

The elaboration in Kant's third Critique of the dimension of mood in art is, I think, the single most important achievement of his aesthetics. Kant grasps the essential character of mood as non-purposive feeling, as the felt absence of a real-intentional character. Mood is self-reflexive.

Spitzer's monumental *Classical and Christian Ideas of World Harmony* is sub-titled *Prolegomena to an Interpretation of the Word "Stimmung"*. He breaks off just short of Kant. The history of mood in the modern period remains to be written. Rousseau would figure in it decisively, not least as the author of the *Confessions* who conceives his project as a "history of moods." "'J'écris moins l'histoire de ces éve[ne]mens en eux-mêmes que celle de l'état de mon âme, à mesure qu'ils sont arrivés."[14] Such a project requires the invention of "a new language," especially as the moods of his story are original.[15] Yet they are original not because they are particular but because they are general. Rousseau will need to capture this dimension of his moods; he will do so by including in his portrait the ideal dimension of the mood of writing: "I shall doubly portray my mood."[16] Rousseau's concern for moods having an ideal or general character is also the subject of the fifth *Revery*. The celebrated "sentiment de l'existence" may indeed have guided Kant's phenomenal description of the mood of aesthetic judgment.

The centrality of the term mood (*Stimmung*) (in its cognates *Gefühl, Gemütszustand, sentiment, état d'âme*) for the imaginative work of Rousseau and the systematic work of Kant exemplifies the importance of mood in the poetry and criticism of "Romantic" writers. The twenty-second letter of Schiller's *Aesthetic Education* correlates the "aesthetic mood" (*die ästhetische Stimmung des Gemüts*), "which contains the whole of humanity," with artistic form. For Hölderlin, for whom feeling constitutes "the best sobriety and reflection of the poet," "the inner ideal life can be grasped in various moods";[17] these moods may then function as the principles of poetic diction. Wordsworth's "mood of composition" transforms emotions recollected in tranquillity into the fictive emotions of his art. The theory of the last two writers helps to define the themes of their work as mood, temporality, and poetic language, and the form of their work (in Staiger's sense) as a certain form of temporality.[18] Their poetry exists as the movement through which lived moods are conducted into the moodful language of fiction.

The *history* of mood in the nineteenth century foreshadows the implicit inner connections in *Sein und Zeit* of the terms mood, historicity, and interpretation. A formulation from Lukács's *Theory of the Novel*, describing the alienated situation from which the novel-hero arises, suggests the necessity of these connections: "The nature of moods . . . presupposes the impossibility of an achieved and meaningful substance, the impossibility that the constitutive subject could find an appropriate constitutive object."[19] The impossibility of the coincidence of the subject with its world, evident in the fragility and strangeness of its moods, establishes the historicity of the subject. For, finally, it is this *"nécessité de parcourir le temps* [qu'] empêche l'esprit d'être maître de lui-même et de son contenu, de coincider avec soi dans la plénitude absolue d'une possession systématique et transparente du réel"* (italics mine).[20] The common property of post-Kantian philosophical anthropologies in Germany is the revelation through mood of human historicity and consequently of the necessarily interpretative relation of the self to its content, its "text". More particularly, when the source of literary language is grasped as mood, as the fundamental yet unstable reflex of the temporal self, the historical character of literary interpretation becomes explicit. "[Literary] understanding can be called complete only when it becomes aware of its own temporal predicament and realizes that the horizon within which the totalization can take place is time itself. The act of understanding is a temporal act that has its own history. . . . "[21] This situation helps originate the rich speculative tradition of nineteenth-century interpretation theory.

Kierkegaard, Dilthey, and Nietzsche are the chief figures of this tradition and Heidegger's immediate precursors. In each, a reflection on the category of mood profiles and organizes a poetics and hermeneutics. In Kierkegaard, moods are tones or voices comprising the "lyric dialectic" and exacting strenuous interpretations and choices. Dilthey's poetics, especially in *The Literary Imagination (Die Einbildungskraft des Dichters)* profiles mood as the entity enabling the passage of lived experience (*Erlebnis*) to its historical expression (*Ausdruck*) and its ultimate reconstitution in interpretation. This term heightens Dilthey's consciousness of the contingency of textual interpretation but also suggests to him the way in which meaning might be communicated across historical differences. Nietzsche meanwhile represents in the figure of moods that thinking which is not reflection but activity and play. The link between a mood-centered aesthetics and Nietzsche's panhermeneutical metaphysics is plain in Aphorism No. 119 from *The Dawn* (*Morgenröte*): "Can it be . . . that all our so-called consciousness is a more or less fantastic commentary on an unknown, perhaps unknowable, but felt text?"

Between the conceptions of mood in these writers there are vital differences. Yet the term persists tenaciously in modern European poetics in its crucial difference from that of sensation-bound feeling. Throughout the entire tradition, but at its clearest in Heidegger, mood stands for a disclosive power which cognitive understanding cannot sustain. The affirmation of the centrality of mood is at the same time inspired by a live reluctance to surrender truth to the "squint-eyed gaze" of irrationalism (see BT, 175). Perhaps something of the optimism engendered by the discovery attunes the mood which Kant makes exemplary for his demonstration. The aesthetic mood has the tonality of sociability, play, and delight, whereas for Heidegger the exemplary mood is anxiety.

What, then, is the force of Heidegger's connecting poetic discourse with mood in the system of *Sein und Zeit*? This demonstration is in principle as long as *Sein und Zeit* itself, for the scope of the terms "discourse," "communication," "existential," "possibility," "disclosure," and, finally, "state of mind" encompasses the entire existential analytic. Here I shall indicate only the features of Heidegger's description of these various terms which strike me as particularly interesting or as hitherto unnoted or unstressed.

1. *Discourse.* Discourse is first of all not to be equated with written or spoken language. Along with mood and understanding it constitutes a primordial disposition of being prior to language. Heidegger terms discourse "the articulation of intelligibility": it is how we "articulate 'significantly' the intelligibility of Being-in-the-world. . . . Vocal utterance, however, is not essential for discourse . . . " (BT, 204, 316). "At this stage of Heidegger's thought," writes Biemel,

> *logos* [i.e. discourse], in contra-distinction to the usual meaning of the word, is the constitutive moment, and language is merely the way in which *logos* gets expressed. Language is that through which the *logos* makes itself mundane; through language it becomes an element of the world and can be treated like other things found in the world.[22]

The force of this point is the depth at which Heidegger situates the poetic. It is first of all a fundamental orientation toward moods as toward intelligible existence as a whole. It is also the expression of meanings in words, but "in the factical linguistic form of any definite case of [such] discourse" not every constitutive element of the poetic may appear (BT, 206). To this extent literary language could not be grasped as an ensemble of word-things present-at-hand nor as a tool functional within a context of equipment. Literature is not an objective fact nor a social function. It would have to be understood principally in terms of an intention aiming at conformity with its source, a goal which it always falls short of. As Aler observes, "as soon as understanding manifests itself as a phonetic expression of significations — as an expression in words — one can observe that the project appears [in *Sein und Zeit*] in its being thrown."[23] In the way the poetic disclosure is expressed, there is already a certain opaque understanding deposited in it. "Dasein is constantly delivered over to this interpretedness, which controls and distributes the possibilities of average understanding and of the state-of-mind belonging to it" (BT, 211).

The original aspect of literary language, together with its ineluctable captivation by the "world," inspires the now well-known conception of literature in Paul de Man's *Blindness and Insight*:

> With respect to its own specificity (that is, as an existing entity susceptible to historical description), literature exists at the same time in modes of error and truth; it both betrays and obeys its own mode of being. . . . If literature rested at ease within its own self-definition, it could be studied according to methods that are scientific rather than historical. We are obliged to confine ourselves to history when this is no longer the case, when the entity steadily puts its own ontological status into question.[24]

An entity that aims to disclose being and yet exist as the "worldly expression" of significance courts "the desire to break out of literature toward the reality of the moment";[25] and whether as a movement of appropriation or of denial of the moment, it is prey, therefore, to the destiny of manipulation, of dissimulation, of idle talk.

Heidegger's poetics shares with Russian structuralism and certain types of French formalism the perception that the true subject of poetics is not poems but "poeticity." But with Heidegger the "poeticity" of literary language consists not in a calculable property but in an intention — one, moreover, which it is now possible to describe more richly than in the customary way as self-reflexive. The character of poetic language arises from its insistence on articulating states-of-mind, that is, moods, with a view toward their fullest possible disclosure; what they disclose are "existential possibilities," read, "existence."

The force of Heidegger's situating the poetic at the level of logos and not of language might be illustrated in another way. From a variety of critical standpoints, language is nowadays described as literary to the extent that it discloses its rhetoricity, its character as figurative speech. But following Heidegger the essence of figurative expression cannot be located in definite types of verbal entities having the character of objects present-at-hand — say, in metaphorical or metonymic figures. The depth of figurativeness arises from a primordial intention which language cannot realize but can only mediate. The source of poetic language is moods opened up to primary existential possibility, to authentically finite, temporal historical existence. But poetry, as language, is insistently problematic.

"Is [language] a kind of equipment ready-to-hand within-the-world, or has it Dasein's kind of Being, or is it neither of these?" (BT, 209). The possibility that language has *Dasein's* kind of being is by no means automatically auspicious. For this implies that language aiming to communicate the existential possibilities of moods will, like *Dasein*, find itself "equiprimordially in untruth," in error. Heidegger writes:

> It is not an accident that the earliest systematic Interpretation of affects that has come down to us is not treated in the framework of "psychology." Aristotle investigates the *pathe* (affects) in the second book of his *Rhetoric*. Contrary to the traditional orientation, according to which rhetoric is conceived as the kind of thing we "learn in school," this work of Aristotle must be taken as the first systematic hermeneutic of the everydayness of being with one another. Publicness, as the kind of Being which belongs to the "they," not only has in general its own way of having a mood, but needs moods and "makes" them for itself. It is into such a mood and out of such a mood that the orator speaks. He must understand the possibilities of moods in order to rouse them and guide them aright. (BT, 178)

Poetic discourse runs the peril of manipulating the inauthentic possibilities of moods and, as poetic *language*, has always already submitted to some extent to this peril. Poetic language is to the same extent rhetoric — but a rhetoric that functions as a *figure* for the original intention toward authenticity.

2. *Communication*. Heidegger's sentence speaks of poetic discourse as a type of *communication*. This point should not be passed over. It follows a full account of the meaning of communication apropos of assertion and interpretation, and the theme of communication is again

picked up in Heidegger's discussion of discourse and language. Here Heidegger writes:

> the phenomenon of *communication* must be understood in a sense which is ontologically broad. "Communication" in which one makes assertions — giving information, for instance — is a special case of that communication which is grasped in principle existentially. In this more general kind of communication, the Articulation of Being with one another understandingly is constituted. Through it a co-state-of-mind [*Mitbefindlichkeit*] gets "shared," and so does the understanding of Being-with. Communication is never anything like a conveying of experiences, such as opinions or wishes, from the interior of one subject into the interior of another. Dasein-with is already essentially manifest in a co-state of mind and a co-understanding. In discourse Being-with becomes "explicitly" *shared*; that is to say, it *is* already, but it is unshared as something that has not been taken hold of and appropriated." (BT, 205)

Poetic discourse is, for Heidegger, the privileged vehicle of a certain kind of communication. This kind of communication, which shares explicitly the existential possibilities of moods, looks to poetic discourse for its realization. Poetic discourse is informed by a communicative intent.

In this perspective it would be senseless to speak of an act of writing that had put aside the communicative function. As Fritz Kaufmann writes:

> Contact with the artist himself is not that of personal association, but that of super-personal participation in his work. For this participation is mediated of course by communication. But not so that the artist himself communicates his mood to us, manifests himself personally as the vehicle of the mood and the communication . . . ; the mood communicates itself to us from out of the work, in the manner in which it is precipitated in this work as an independent crystallization. Through being absorbed in a work — which in assuming the mood also frees itself from being a mere agency — artistic openness is protected from the danger of . . . personal exposure.[26]

The ineluctability of the communicative intent has been

(correctly) maintained even in the dominant schools of recent critical theory based on sociological and everyday linguistic analogues and, as such, most opposite to fundamental ontology. The insistence on the communicative character of literary discourse is therefore by no means the automatically polemical, anti-existentialist gesture which many suppose it to be. This point links Heidegger's program with Habermas's and Watzlawick's and can be paraphrased this way: "The one true *impossibility* of human communicative behavior [is] that *it is impossible not to communicate.*"[27]

Kept in mind, this point would discourage the tendency to describe modernism of the Flaubertian strain as "the attempt to escape from the circuit of communication, to make the text a written object and not the physical manifestation of a communicative act."[28] Such an approach — here it is Jonathan Culler's — flows from the persistent tendency in modern formalism to interpret the "logos in a way which is ontologically inadequate" wherein "the logos gets experienced as something present-at-hand and Interpreted as such, while at the same time the entities which it points out have the meaning of presence-at-hand" (BT, 203). Culler goes on to discredit the critic's supposition of the coherence of the literary work: "The notion that works of art must be unified and that the task of criticism is to demonstrate this unity derives, at least in part, from the communicative model and the metaphysics of presence on which it rests."[29] After *Sein und Zeit*, this makes strange reading indeed. The experience of thought to which "the metaphysics of presence" alludes — Heidegger's experience before Derrida's! — seems to have been occluded within the mere phrase. It is perfectly false that "the communicative model" need rest on a metaphysics of presence.

In *Sein und Zeit* the link is between a "communicative model" and a theory of historicity. As Aler observes:

> [In *Sein und Zeit*] in linguistic art the sensitive . . . explanation of our Being-in-the-world takes place in such a way that it also speaks to others. If this had not been touched on in principle, it would then have been impossible in *Sein und Zeit* to develop the phenomenon of being united by a common fate within the framework of man's historicity.[30]

3. *Mood*. The passage describing communication "in a sense which is ontologically broad" is vital to an understanding of Heidegger's characterization of poetic discourse. Poetic discourse turns on an act of communication; this act is essentially the sharing of a state-of-mind. To say of a certain kind of discourse that in it "the communication of the existential possibilities of one's state-of-mind can become an aim in itself" is not on the face of it to specify anything like "poetic discourse," since

110

such communication would apparently describe Section 40 of *Sein und Zeit*, in which Heidegger explains the existential possibilities of the basic state-of-mind of anxiety. This explanation occurs in the assertive mode, but it is the assertion which Heidegger, in the passage above, specifically designates "a special case" of communication and again as "not the primary 'locus' of truth" (BT, 269). "Indeed *from the ontological point of view* we must as a general principle leave the primary discovery of the world to 'bare mood' " (BT, 177). The distinctiveness and primordiality of poetic discourse are based on the fact that its truth is the truth of moods as it can be communicated *by a mood*.

To the extent that a poem is poetic it thus communicates a mood transparent to its own possibilities. These possibilities vary, of course, with the mood communicated. But at the basis of each such structure of possibilities is what Heidegger terms *"Geworfenheit"* (thrownness).

Literature reveals through moods the dimensions of thrownness. The French translations *"déjection"* (Wahl) and *"déréliction"* (de Waehlens) correctly convey something of its negative tonality. As "thrown," *Dasein* finds itself open to itself and its world but having to endure itself and its world as a burden. Both this openness and this oppression stem from the fact that *Dasein* does not know its origin or its goal: it is open only to the existence that it has to be in being already "there." When *Dasein* finds itself thrown, it finds itself moreover "in a way of finding which arises not so much from a direct seeking as rather from a fleeing" (BT, 174). In its states-of-mind *Dasein* turns uneasily away from the fact of its existence, its "that it is."

Poetic discourse thus brings *Dasein* face to face with the fact of its contingency, its "thralldom" in existence, brings it back from the "tranquillized supposition that it possesses everything, or that everything is within its reach" (BT, 223). It arrests the turbulence with which *Dasein* falls away from its own destination: its finitude, "the fact 'that it is, and that it has to be ... the entity which it is' " (BT, 321). As finite, *Dasein* is fundamentally thrown toward its death; it therefore knows the possibility of authentic existence. This possibility is the central disclosure of mood transparent to itself. Toward it is oriented the force of the poetic disclosure of the other "essential characteristics of states-of-mind": that *"mood has already disclosed, in every case, Being-in-the-world as a whole, and makes it possible first of all to direct oneself towards something. ... [Further it] implies a disclosive submission to the world, out of which we can encounter something that matters to us"* (BT, 176-77). Together, these revelations constitute a virtual origin for *Dasein*, from which it could redirect itself toward something or let something matter to it authentically.

The point is plausible, I think, if one grasps the literary work as a world. In an exemplary way the human beings "in" it are delivered over to that world and none other. The interpreter of literature who shares the existence of its "characters" has the exemplary experience of what it is to be enthralled by a world. At the same time he maintains an interpretative distance from his experience. This distance permits him to grasp the fact of his thralldom to his *own* world and at the same time to reorient himself toward it.

Literature thus becomes the vehicle of a possible authenticity. This point has often been asserted, especially by those readers of *Sein und Zeit* who from the very start were most interested in finding a connection between it and literature. As a rule, however, no attempt is made to find in *Sein und Zeit* the justification for the claim that literature profiles with any particular urgency or clarity the existential possibility of authenticity. But this argument is present in the work in various forms.

Poetic discourse seeks to share that articulation of moods which would amount to a disclosure of existence. It thus aims at *Dasein's* most *authentic* disclosedness, for "the most primordial, and indeed most authentic, disclosedness in which Dasein . . . can be, is the *truth of existence*" (BT, 264). This idea is confirmed by Heidegger's discussion of the discourse which takes a different aim — which issues into assertion and whose truth is *derivative* from existential-hermeneutical disclosure. One way of distinguishing between these two kinds of discourse is by distinguishing the moods that accompany them; linked to different modes of understanding, they are differently attuned. Poetic discourse elicits moods of various kinds, including the mood of anxiety. "Apophantical" discourse, issuing into the language of assertions, knows only the mood of theory — the tranquility of just tarrying alongside the world. But this mood is marked by its desire to be without moods. It would be proof against the disclosure which mood could accomplish, including the "quite distinctive" disclosure of anxiety: "that authenticity and inauthenticity are possibilities of [*Dasein's*] Being" (BT, 235).

In an important way, then, Heidegger's analysis of anxiety merely makes explicit the disclosure he first attributed to poetic discourse. Earlier, we noted the formal analogy: *Sein und Zeit* "listens in" to the possibilities of such distinctive entities as moods. This is the traditional project of poet and hearer. But the affinity is more revealing at the substantive level: Heidegger's analysis of the basic mood of anxiety provides him with "the phenomenal basis for explicitly grasping Dasein's primordial totality of Being" (BT, 227). This is exactly the basic function he earlier assigned to the phenomenon of poetic language: the poetic articulation of moods with communicative intent discloses existence. To prove this affinity, finally, it is not necessary to find that poetic understanding is anxiously attuned. For "along with the sober anxiety," writes Heidegger, "which brings us face to face with our individualized potentiality-for-Being, there goes an unshakable joy in this possibility" (BT, 358). This joy could be the essence of poetry.

Princeton University

NOTES

1 *Hölderlin und Heidegger*, 2nd ed. (Zurich: Atlantis, 1956), pp. 88-89. Additional references cited as: HH.

2 *Being and Time*, trans. J. Macquarrie and E. Robinson (New York and Evanston: Harper & Row, 1962), p. 243. Additional references cited as: BT.

3 See Jan Aler, "Heidegger's Conception of Language in *Being and Time*," in *On Heidegger and Language* (Evanston: Northwestern University Press, 1972), p. 44.

4 *Being and Time*, p. 205.

5 Hans Joachim Schrimpf, "Beitrag zu Forschungsproblemen: Hölderlin, Heidegger und die Literaturwissenschaft," *Euphorion*, 51 (1957), 313.

6 *The Critique of Judgement*, trans. James Creed Meredith (Oxford: Clarendon, 1952), p. 224.

7 "Beitrag," 313.

8 Guido Morpurgo-Tagliabue, *L'esthétique contemporaine* (Milan: Marzorati, 1960), p. 597.

9 *Poetics*, XIV, 5.

10 *Die Einbildungskraft des Dichters, Gesammelte Schriften*, 6 (Leipzig: Teubner, 1914), p. 138.

11 Cited in Pfeiffer, *Das Lyrische Gedicht als Ästhetisches Gebilde* (Halle: Niemeyer, 1931), p. 68.

12 *Critique*, pp. 224, 14.

13 Walter Biemel, *Die Bedeutung von Kants Begründung der Ästhetik für die Philosophie der Kunst, Kantstudien*, Ergänzungshefte, 77 (Köln: Kölner Universitäts-Verlag, 1959), p. 145.

14 *Oeuvres complètes*, Tome I, Bibliothèque de la Pléiade (Paris: Gallimard, 1959), p. 1150.

15 *Oeuvres*, p. 1153.

16 *Oeuvres*, p. 1154.

17 *Sämtliche Werke* (Frankfurt: Insel, 1961), pp. 960, 971.

18 *Die Zeit als Einbildungskraft des Dichters* (Zurich and Leipzig: Max Niehans, 1939), pp. 66-70 and "Schlusz."

19 *Die Theorie des Romans* (Neuwied: Luchterhand Verlag, 1965), p. 63.

20 Jacques Havet, *Kant et le problème du temps* (Paris: Gallimard, 1953), p. 10.

21   Paul de Man, *Blindness and Insight* (New York: Oxford University Press, 1971), p. 32.

22   Walter Biemel, "Poetry and Language in Heidegger," in *On Heidegger and Language*, pp. 70-71. See n. 3 above.

23   "Heidegger's Conception of Language," p. 50.

24   *Blindness and Insight*, pp. 163-64.

25   *Blindness and Insight*, p. 162.

26   "Die Bedeutung der künstlerischen Stimmung," *Jahrbuch für Philosophie und phänomenologische Forschung*, Ergänzungsband (1929), p. 214.

27   Dieter Krusche, *Kafka und Kafka-Deutung* (Munich: Fink, 1974), p. 156.

28   Jonathan Culler, *Flaubert: The Uses of Uncertainty* (Ithaca: Cornell University Press, 1974), p. 15.

29   *Flaubert*, p. 17.

30   "Heidegger's Conception of Language," p. 62.

Heidegger, Kierkegaard, and the Hermeneutic Circle:
Towards a Postmodern Theory of Interpretation as Dis-closure

William V. Spanos

I argue thus. If it be true that painting employs wholly different signs or means of imitation from poetry, — the one using forms and colors in space, the other articulate sounds in time, — and if signs must unquestionably stand in convenient relation with the thing signified, then signs arranged side by side can represent only objects existing side by side, or whose parts so exist, while consecutive signs can express only objects which succeed each other, or whose parts succeed each other, in time.

Objects which exist side by side, or whose parts so exist, are called bodies. Consequently bodies with their visible properties are the peculiar subjects of painting.

Objects which succeed each other, or whose parts succeed each other in time, are actions. Consequently actions are the peculiar subjects of poetry.

— Gotthold Lessing, *Laocoön*

The "Being-true" of the λόγος as ἀληθεύειν means that in λέγειν [to talk] as ἀποφαίνεσθαι [letting-something-be-seen] the entities *of which* one is talking must be taken out of their hiddenness; one must let them be seen as something unhidden (ἀληθές); that is, they must be *discovered*.

— Martin Heidegger, *Being and Time*

The following constitutes the second (and more or less autonomous) section of a long two-part essay attempting to articulate a post-Modern literary hermeneutics — a hermeneutics of discovery in the sense of dis-closure — grounded in Martin Heidegger's de-struction of the Western onto-theo-logical tradition and on the phenomenological/existential analytic of Being and Time. *In the first part, I attempt to show that "Modernism" in Western literature — and the New Critical and, more recently, Structuralist hermeneutics it has given rise to — is grounded in a strategy that spatializes the temporal process of existence. It is, in other words, a strategy that is subject to a vicious circularity that closes off the phenomenological/existential understanding of the temporal being of existence, and, analogously, of the temporal being — the sequence of words — of the literary text. It is no accident that the autotelic and in-clusive circle, that is,* the circle as image or icon, *is the essential symbol of high Modernism — for Proust (the recollection of things past); for Yeats (the unity of being in the cyclical theory of time); for Eliot (the mythical method) — and of the New Criticism and Structuralism. This attempt to "surpass" Modernism, then, is analogous to Heidegger's call for the surpassing of Western metaphysics — the traditional perception of Being* meta-ta-phusika *(beyond and thus from above the things themselves: all at once) which, Heidegger claims, in "achieving" its fulfillment in modern times, has forgotten the being of Being, i.e., has "come to its end": has become "the time of the world picture." The surpassing of criticism, like the surpassing of metaphysics, begins not in* presence *but in the temporality grounded in Nothing, the temporality of* Dasein. *This temporal, as opposed to spatial, orientation is the key not only to reading a literary text but to the discovery of a new literary history.*

Having re-established the ontological priority of temporality in human understanding by way of Heidegger's existential analytic of *Dasein*, we can now introduce explicitly into the hermeneutic process the concept of Being (or, to orient the discussion towards the literary argument, the concept of "the whole," of "form"), which, in fact, has always been present, but has been held in abeyance until now. Indeed, the reader has no doubt already remarked that an existential-ontological hermeneutics in the sense of its function as dis-covery or dis-closure implies that being is somehow already known in advance by the interpreter, just as the being

116

(or form) of a text that can be read again is known, and thus that the process is ultimately circular. Indeed, this is precisely and explicitly what Heidegger says about the hermeneutics of *Being and Time*: "Inquiry, as a kind of seeking, must be guided beforehand by what is sought. So the meaning of Being must already be available to us in some way."[1] And again: "Any interpretation which is to contribute understanding, must already have understood what is to be interpreted" (BT, 32, 194; SZ, 152). Hermeneutics, that is, does not discover anything radically new as such. It dis-covers what the interpreter (the inquirer) by his very nature as *Dasein* already has as a whole ("a totality of involvements") in advance, but is unaware of until the traditional interpretive instrument breaks down, i.e., until a rupture occurs in the referential surface, at which point the "as structure" (the something *as* something) that one has in advance but has "forgotten" *begins to achieve explicitness* (BT, 16, 104-107; SZ, 75-76).[2] "Whenever something is interpreted as something," Heidegger writes, "the interpretation will be founded essentially upon fore-having, fore-sight, and fore-conception. An interpretation is never [despite those committed to objectivity, including Husserl] a presuppositionless apprehending of something presented to us" (BT, 32, 191-92; SZ, 150).[3] Does this admission, indeed, this affirmation of circularity, therefore justify leaping to the conclusion that the hermeneutics of *Being and Time* is ultimately no different from that of metaphysics — and by extension, of the New Criticism and Structuralism? It should be clear from Heidegger's equation of circularity and the positional forestructure of *Dasein's* Being-in-the-world as well as from the previous argument as a whole (that the existential analysis of *Dasein* guides the ontological quest) that the answer is an emphatic no. For Heidegger's temporal hermeneutics in *Being and Time* does *not begin from the whole* in the same way — from the whole seen as *telos* or presence — that the spatial hermeneutics of the metaphysical and New Critical or Structuralist standpoint does.

In the last analysis, according to Heidegger, *all* human inquiry is circular. Indeed, as the passages quoted above suggest, the very notion of inquiry presupposes it. For the lack of a prior "awareness" of "what is sought" precludes the possibility of questioning. It is, in fact, precisely this argument that Heidegger presents at the outset of *Being and Time* (in the introductory section called "The Formal Structure of the Question of Being") as the ground for asking the question of what it means to be: "Thus to work out the question of Being adequately, we must make an entity — the inquirer — transparent in his own Being. The very asking of this question is an entity's mode of *Being*; and as such it gets its essential character from what is inquired about — namely Being" (BT, 2, 27; SZ, 7). The effort to avoid the hermeneutic circle, to achieve objectivity, a presuppositionless stance, therefore, is not only a futile gesture; it also does violence to the truth by way of concealing that which it is supposed to reveal. "What is decisive," Heidegger reiterates, "is not to get out of the circle but to come into it in the right way."[4] And the right way, as I have tried to suggest, is through the existential *Dasein*, the *Dasein* as being-in-the-world: "This circle of understanding is not an orbit in which any random kind of knowledge may move" — in other words, this is not the closed or spatial circle of the metaphysical standpoint, in which everything, including human beings, is simply an object present-at-hand. It is rather "the expression of the existential *fore-structure* of Dasein itself. It is not to be reduced to the level of a vicious circle, or even of a circle which is merely tolerated. In the circle is hidden a positive possibility of the most primordial kind of knowing" (BT, 32, 195; SZ, 153). Heidegger's culminating reaffirmation of the existential nature of the hermeneutic circle is presented not only as a refutation of the Husserlian charge that, because it is not "pre-suppositionless," the process is a vicious circle. In the process, he also implies a countercharge that, despite its claims to objectivity — its desire to protect the autonomy of the object of investigation — the metaphysical standpoint that makes the charge ("common sense," i.e. "public understanding," in the following quotation) becomes itself guilty of vicious circularity in being blind to its derivative status. Heidegger's interpretation of the hermeneutic circle is at the very heart of his version of the phenomenological return "to the things themselves," to origins as "groundless ground," and is crucial to a final understanding of the distinction I wish to draw between an existential/temporal literary hermeneutics and the metaphysical/spatial interpretive methodology of Modernist criticism. This culminating passage, therefore, deserves quotation at length. In answering the charge of circularity made from the standpoint of "common sense," Heidegger first differentiates between the "presuppositions" of his existential analytic and the "propositions" of logic:

> When it is objected that the existential Interpretation is "circular," it is said that we have "presupposed" the idea of existence and of Being in general, and that Dasein gets Interpreted "accordingly," so that the idea of Being may be obtained from it. But what does "presupposition" signify? In positing the idea of existence, do we also posit some proposition from which we deduce further propositions about the Being of Dasein, in accordance with formal rules of consistency? Or does this pre-supposing have the character of an understanding projection, in such a manner indeed that the Interpretation by which such an understanding gets developed, will let that which is to be interpreted [*Dasein*] *put itself into words for the first time, so that it may decide of its own accord whether, as the entity which it is, it has that state of Being for which it has*

been disclosed in the projection with regard to its formal aspects? Is there any other way at all by which an entity can put itself into words with regard to its Being? (BT, 63, 362-63; SZ, 314-15)

After thus implying that the hermeneutic circle, despite beginning with a presupposition, is not ontologically spatial, does not begin with derived propositions (public knowledge) but concretely and temporally (my-ownly, as it were), Heidegger then goes on to assert that "circularity" in research is unavoidable and that the effort on the part of "common sense" to avoid it, to be "objective," is an implicit strategy to negate Care, the existential intentionality which, as he makes emphatically clear, is the basic structure of the inquirer and has its source in his temporality:

> We cannot ever "avoid" a "circular" proof in the existential analytic, because such an analytic does not do *any* proving *at all* by the rules of the "logic of consistency." What common sense wishes to eliminate in avoiding the "circle," on the supposition that it is measuring up to the loftiest rigour of scientific investigation, is nothing less than the basic structure of care. Because it is primordially constituted by care, any Dasein is already ahead of itself. As being, it has in every case already projected itself upon definite possibilities of its existence; and in such existentiell projections [i.e., on the level of ontic (or ordinary) as opposed to ontological being] it has, in a pre-ontological manner, also projected something like existence and Being. *Like all research*, the research which wants to develop and conceptualize that kind of Being which belongs to existence, *is itself a kind of Being which disclosive Dasein possesses*; can such research be denied this projecting which is essential to Dasein? (BT, 63, 363; SZ, 315)

In fact, according to Heidegger, referring again to the strategy of "common sense" to annul Care and the understanding it discloses, the "disinterestedness" of common sense is itself an interested point of view:

> Yet the "charge of circularity" itself comes from a kind of Being which belongs to Dasein. . . . Common sense [which is grounded in "our concernful absorption" in the "they" (*das Man*), which interprets things as they are publically] concerns itself, whether "theoretically" or "practically," only with entities which can be surveyed at a glance circumspectively [i.e.

spatially]. *What is distinctive in common sense is that it has in view only the experiencing of "factual" entities, in order that it may be able to rid itself of an understanding of Being* [my emphasis]. It fails to recognize that entities can be experienced "factually" only when Being is already understood, even if it has not been conceptualized. [This is a reference to the derivative nature of propositional understanding as opposed to the originative nature of hermeneutic understanding.] Common sense misunderstands understanding. And *therefore* common sense must necessarily pass off as "violent" anything that lies beyond the reach of its understanding, or any attempt to go out so far. (BT, 63, 363; SZ, 315)

Thus, in his summation, Heidegger concludes:

When one talks of the "circle" in understanding, one expresses a failure to recognize two things: (1) that understanding as such makes up a basic kind of Dasein's Being, and (2) that this Being is constituted as care. To deny the circle, to make a secret of it [as "common sense" or, more philosophically, the metaphysical standpoint does], or even to want to overcome it, means finally to reinforce this failure. *We must rather endeavor to leap into the "circle," primordially and wholly, so that even at the start of the analysis of Dasein we make sure that we have a full view of Dasein's circular Being* [my emphasis].[5] (BT, 63, 363; SZ, 315-16)

What Heidegger implies throughout *Being and Time* is that, in beginning "omnisciently" from the end — disinterestedly or *care*-lessly, as it were — the radically logocentric metaphysical standpoint (whether in its naturalistic or its idealistic manifestation) "rids itself of" *Dasein's* authentic being by "closing off" his temporal existence. It thus generates the vicious circle. And in the process, the interpreter — like Kierkegaard's aesthetes, Dostoevsky's "straightforward" gentlemen in *Notes from Underground*, T.S. Eliot's Prufrock and Tiresias, Beckett's Vladimir and Estragon and Belacqua, Ionesco's Mr. and Mrs. Smith in *The Bald Soprano*, and the various aesthetes and "The Whole Sick Crew" (whose yo-yoing is a motion towards inanimateness) in Thomas Pynchon's *V.* — imprisons himself and eventually forgets his being inside its erosive bounding line. On the other hand, in "leaping into the 'circle,' primordially and wholly," in beginning consciously in the limited and contextual temporal standpoint

120

of being-in-the-world, the interpreter as ek-static and interested or *Care*ful *Dasein* "understands" being beforehand, not as a derived conceptual proposition, as finalized and spatial totality in which all "entities . . . can be surveyed at a glance," but only in a vague, a dim way, as that which has been "covered up" or "forgotten." The being "presupposed" in the forestructure of existential-ontological understanding is not a closed and static structure or form, a temporal existence *re-collected* in tranquillity, but, as we have seen, an open and freely expanding horizon. Thus, whereas the metaphysical perspective tends to understand or rather "misunderstand" being (and understanding) by interestedly negating the originary *interest* of the interpreter "on the supposition that it is measuring up to the loftiest rigour of scientific investigation," the existential/ontological standpoint of phenomenology is *"guided* and *regulated"* (BT, 63, 359; SZ, 312) by this vague primordial understanding of being, which, in belonging *"to the essential constitution of Dasein itself"* (BT, 2, 28; SZ, 8), makes "the idea of existence [temporal be-ing] . . . our clue [to] an ontologically clarified idea of Being" (BT, 63, 362; SZ, 314). In other words, phenomenological inquiry *moves* carefully and interestedly through time, "destroying" the metaphysical standpoint (disclosing its blindness, its impulse to spatialize time) and simultaneously thematizing — bringing out into the open — that which, to appropriate T.S. Eliot, "flickers in the corner of [our] eye"[6] — the vague and indefinite primordial understanding of being covered over and forgotten in *the tradition*. Ultimately, as I have suggested, it discovers that being resides in the temporal process itself, that what it means to be is be-ing. The hermeneutic circle is thus not a vicious circle, despite its presuppositions about being. For at the "end" of the temporal process of interpretive disclosure the "whole," the "form," it discovers, to put it mildly, is quite different from the whole, the form, as object of the beginning. It turns out, that is, to be "endless" — historical: not simply a fuller but a more problematic and dynamic experience: the concealing/unconcealing, truth/error process of being. What Heidegger says about the hermeneutic circle in the language of phenomenology, it is worth pointing out, is echoed in a remarkable way by A.R. Ammons in the language of postmodern poetry, a poetry that attempts to "surpass" the formalism, the closed or iconic form of Modernism in the seminal analogy of the Poundian *periplus*:

> the walk liberating, I was released from forms,
> from the perpendiculars,
>   straight lines, blocks, boxes, binds
> of thought
> into the hues, shadings, rises, flowing bends and blends
>   of sight:

I allow myself eddies of meaning:
yield to a direction of significance
running
like a stream through the geography of my work:
  you can find
in my sayings
                swerves of action
                like the inlet's cutting edge:
              there are dunes of motion
organizations of grass, white sandy paths of remembrance
in the overall wandering of mirroring mind:

but Overall is beyond me: is the sum of these events
I cannot draw, the ledger I cannot keep, the accounting
beyond the account. . . .[7]

As in Heidegger's *Being and Time*, time, in Ammon's circle of interpretation, is ontologically prior to being or form (the "Overall"), but not different from it.[8]

To put it positively, the hermeneutic circle is, paradoxically, *a liberating movement, an opening towards being*. It is finally, to use the important term that Heidegger borrows from Kierkegaard, a "repetition" or "retrieval" (*Wiederholen*),[9] a process of dis-covering and re-membering the primordial temporality of being and thus of the truth as *a-letheia* (un-hiddenness), which metaphysical understanding and interpretation (representation or, to anticipate, re-collection), in *closing time off* — in coercing temporality into spatial icon (the circle) — and hardening this closure into "tradition," covers over and forgets. The full significance for literary hermeneutics of the Kierkegaardian movement will be developed shortly. Here it will suffice merely to point, by way of orientation, to its ground in existential Care and to the paradoxical forwarding of remembrance. Retrieval or repetition, that is, is neither a process of re-cognizing a (historical) text in the tradition for its own sake; nor is it a process of re-collecting an absolute or privileged origin (logos as presence) as agency of judging a text in the tradition. It is rather a discovering of beginnings in the sense of rendering the present interpreter, as in the case of Ammons, a *homo viator,* of bringing him into an original, a careful explorative (open) relationship (a relationship of "anticipatory resoluteness") with the being of a text in the tradition. The hermeneutic circle as repetition, in short, involves the abandonment of a coercive methodology in favor of an unmethodical and generous dialogue: the my-ownly (*eigentliche*) "speech" act undertaken by the interpreter in Negative Capability or, in Heidegger's term, *Gelassenheit*, which *lets* the being of a text be, which lets it *say* how it stands with being. It is, in short, dialogic.

Heidegger does not explicitly apply the distinction between the hermeneutic circle of phenomenology and the vicious circle of metaphysics to literary creation or to literary exegesis as such in *Being and Time*. But that it is absolutely applicable is made clear by briefly recalling the fundamental, though too often overlooked, Kierkegaardian category I have just referred to: the existential concept of "Repetition," which he opposes to the Greek concept of "Recollection." This seminal distinction, which, along with Schleiermacher's and Dilthey's versions of the hermeneutic circle,[10] clearly influenced Heidegger's thinking about hermeneutics in a decisive way, sheds important light on the significance of the hermeneutics of *Being and Time* for aesthetics and, more specifically, for literature. Kierkegaard's distinction goes back as far as his important but neglected Master's dissertation, *The Concept of Irony*,[11] to which I will return. But it is given its fullest and, for my purposes, most accessible formulation in *Repetition*, his strange, "indecisive" novella about the violent — Jobian — dislodgement of a young man from the "aesthetic stage" into something like authentic existence (the "ethico-religious stage"). Thus the pseudonymous author Constantine Constantius, the "constant" and "steady" detached observer, who, therefore, despite his sympathy, cannot undergo repetition, writes near the beginning of his account of the young man's experience, perhaps better than he knows: "Repetition and recollection are the same movement, only in opposite directions; for what is recollection has been, is repeated backwards, whereas repetition properly so called is recollected forwards."[12] Somewhat later, in a remarkable prevision not only of Mircea Eliade's analysis of the myth and metaphysics of the eternal return[13] but also of the Postmodern critique of the doctrine of ironic inclusiveness, the fundamental structural principle of Modernist poetics, he "amplifies" this distinction, equating recollection with "the pagan life view" and ultimately with Greek — especially Platonic (and Hegelian) — metaphysics, and repetition with the "new," the existential, movement in philosophy:

> The dialectic of repetition is easy; for what is repeated has been, otherwise it could not be repeated, but precisely the fact that it has been *gives to repetition the character of novelty*. When the Greeks said that all *knowledge* is recollection [the reference is clearly to Plato's logocentric concept of the preexistent soul] they affirmed *that all that is has been*; when one says that *life* is a repetition one affirms *that existence which has been now becomes*. When one does not possess the categories of recollection or of repetition the whole of life is resolved into a void and empty noise. Recollection is the pagan life-view, repetition is the modern life-view;

repetition is the *interest* of metaphysics, and at the same
time the *interest* upon which metaphysics founders;
repetition is the solution contained in every ethical view,
repetition is a *conditio sine qua non* of every dogmatic
problem.[14]

The difficulty of these passages resides in the unfamiliarity to the Western
mind — tending as it does towards spatial form (or Being as substantive)
and thus towards the absolute epistemological value of *disinterestedness* —
of Kierkegaard's usage of the italicized word *"interest"* in the last
sentence. Kierkegaard understood this word — which he emphasizes to
distinguish it from metaphysical disinterestedness — in its etymological
sense. "Reflection ['knowledge' in the above quotation] is the possibility
of relationship," he says elsewhere. "This can also be stated thus:
Reflection is disinterested. Consciousness ['life' in the above quotation]
is relationship, and it brings with it interest or concern; a duality which is
perfectly expressed with pregnant double meaning by the word 'interest'
(Latin *interesse*, meaning (i) 'to be between,' (ii) 'to be a matter of
concern')."[15] Kierkegaard's "interest," in other words, in making a
difference is fundamentally similar to the existential/ontological "Care"
(*Sorge*) of Heidegger's *Dasein* as being-in-the-world. When the term is
understood in this way, the apparently difficult passage from *Repetition* —
indeed, the whole apparently unintelligible novel itself (which Constantius
writes "like Clemens Alexandrinus in such a way that the heretics cannot
understand what he writes"[16]) — becomes manifestly clear. The
distinction Kierkegaard is making between recollection and repetition is, if
we secularize his "eternity" as Heidegger's being (*Sein*), precisely the
distinction that Heidegger articulates between logos as Word or Presence
and logos as *legein* (*Rede*: speech); metaphysics and phenomeno-
logical/existential ontology; the hermeneutic circle of the temporal
or existential consciousness and the vicious circle of the spatial or
essentialist consciousness. There must be a prior "understanding" — a
presupposition — of being, since, if there were not, "the whole of life"
would resolve "into a void and empty noise," a sound and fury signifying
nothing. As in Heidegger, what is of primary importance, however, is how
one enters and remains in the circle. In fact, recollection and repetition are
both grounded in *interest*, i.e., the primordial need of the individual, the
existential man, for continuity and meaning. But in "recollecting
backward" — in recalling in the sense of re-collecting the unique temporal
experience from the point of view of an already fully established *concept*
of Being as realm of ideal Forms (as in Plato) or as ideal System (as in
Hegel) that is *prior* to the contingent experience, the recollection resolves
the contradictions and annuls the very interest that originally generates the
metaphysical question of what it means to be. In thus achieving
"dis-interestedness" ("objectivity" or in-difference), recollection finds

repose or, to use a favorite Modernist term, *stasis*, but it finally mistakes a distanced knowledge *about* (possibility) for authentic understanding. That is, it loses sight of, blinds itself to, the essential clue to the true meaning of being: the existence (ek-sistence) of the interpreter. It is in thus achieving the perspective *sub specie aeternitatis* or, as Kierkegaard puts it, *aeterno modo*, by "aesthetically" reconciling opposites in the inclusive whole of possibility and neutralizing the existential imperative to "choose" resolutely *in situation,* that metaphysics founders on interest. "Hang yourself, you will regret it; do not hang yourself, and you will also regret that; hang yourself or do not hang yourself, you will regret both; whether you hang yourself or do not hang yourself, you will regret both. This, gentlemen, is the sum and substance of all philosophy. It is not only at certain moments that I view everything *aeterno modo,* as Spinoza says, but I live constantly *aeterno modo"*: this is how the desperate metaphysical aesthete of *Diapsalmata* who will outdo Spinoza puts his "triumphant" transcendence of the ethical-existential either/or of temporal existence.[17] Aesthetic recollection, in other words, like the circularity of assertion in Heidegger's critique of metaphysics, is paradoxically a willful forgetting of being.

On the other hand, in "recollecting forward," repetition relies precisely on the *interest*, the intentionality of *inter esse*, of the unique, the existential individual as being-in-the-world, for its access into the meaning of being. It is not an objective mode, a contemplative act from without *aeterno modo*. It is, rather, a "subjective," a Care-ful, mode, in which the singular or, in Kierkegaard's preferred term, the *exceptional* interpreter (as opposed to a universal observer like Constantius himself) is guided beyond the present by the intimation of spirit (the primordial question of being) residing in his "memory." As such, repetition is *both* a mnemonic and an anticipatory — i.e. a de-structive and ek-static — movement. Though it presupposes being, it does so not tautologically but in such a way as to ground authentic understanding in "novelty," in "becoming," that is, in openness and anxious freedom, which is to say, in temporality. Thus, in a passage from the appended letter of explanation to "this book's real reader" that recalls Heidegger's hermeneutic quest for being in and through *Dasein*, Kierkegaard, speaking in his own voice (though retaining the pseudonym), writes:

> The exception thinks also the universal [read: the question of being] when it thinks itself, it labors also for the universal when it elaborates itself, it explains the universal when it explains itself. If one would study the universal thoroughly, one has only to look for the justified exception, which manifests everything more clearly than does the universal itself. . . . There are exceptions. If one cannot explain them, neither can one

explain the universal. Commonly one does not notice the difficulty because one does not think even the universal with passion but with an easygoing superficiality. On the other hand, the exception thinks the universal with serious passion.[18]

In thus entering the circle in the right way, leaping into it "primordially and wholly," Kierkegaard's repetition, like Heidegger's presuppositional hermeneutics, becomes, in the last analysis, *a remembering as dis-covering*. This, in fact, is precisely how Kierkegaard puts it in his unpublished polemic against the Hegelian J.L. Heiberg, who, in praise of *Repetition* in a review of the book, had utterly and, given his "metaphysical" perspective, his thinking about the universal with "an easygoing superficiality," inevitably misunderstood the italicized *"interest"*: "So step by step [the young man] discovers repetition, being educated by existence."[19]

My reason for invoking Kierkegaard's distinction between recollection and repetition is not, however, simply to draw attention to a supporting parallel with Heidegger's distinction between the hermeneutic and the vicious circle. In *Being and Time*, Heidegger restricts his overt discussion of the distinction to the level of philosophical discourse and the critique of the vicious circularity of traditional Western thought primarily, if not exclusively, to "common sense," i.e. the scientific tradition. As Vigilius Haufniensis's equation of the "disinterestedness" of metaphysics and Kantian aesthetics in the extended quotation from *Repetition* in *The Concept of Dread* suggests, Kierkegaard, on the other hand, explicitly subsumes the philosophical distinction under the broader and more radical category of the creative imagination. In so doing, he also subsumes the critique of the vicious circularity of "common sense" under the more radical category of metaphysics, which, in turn, is subsumed under the even more radical category of aestheticism. Thus in Kierkegaard the literary implications of the distinction between recollection and repetition, which in Heidegger would seem on the surface to point to a critique restricted to the well-made plot, the map structure of "positivistic" literature, include, indeed focus explicitly on, a critique of the iconic form of "Romantic" or Symbolist, i.e. Modernist, literature. It is this subsuming of metaphysics under aesthetics and the consequent recognition of the applicability of the de-struction to both phases of metaphysics, to idealism as well as to science, and analogously to Symbolist as well as to Realist literature, that, for purposes of literary hermeneutics, is important in the Kierkegaardian parallel with Heidegger. For it reminds us that despite its disarming critique of positivism and positivistic literary theory, the New Criticism — especially in its doctrine of ironic inclusiveness and its spatial exegetical methodology — is no less in the metaphysical tradition that it is the business of a Heideggerian phenomenological hermeneutics to "surpass."

Thus, as both volumes of *Either/Or* make especially clear, recollection, whether it takes the form of metaphysics or the literature of Romantic irony (i.e. Symbolism), is fundamentally the hermeneutic mode of the "aesthetic" stage. In contradistinction to the "ethical" and "religious" stages on life's way, the aesthetic, we recall, is the perspective *aeterno modo*, the perspective based, as Kierkegaard knew from his own experience as an artist, on the all too human impulse to neutralize the dread of existential time in the totalized present, the timeless moment, the epiphany, as it were:

> The life in recollection [the aesthete A observes in one of his *Diapsalmata* — the irony with which Kierkegaard infuses every word should not be overlooked] is the most complete life conceivable, recollection satisfies more richly than all reality, and has a security that no reality possesses. A recollected life-relation has already passed into eternity and has no more temporal interest.[20]

Or again, this time in the words of the aesthete William Afham of *Stages on Lifes Way*, who Louis Mackey calls "the most explicit champion . . . [of recollection] — its theorist, so to speak":[21] "Memory is immediacy . . . whereas recollection comes only by reflection. *Hence it is an art to recollect*." It "seeks to assert man's eternal continuity in life and to insure that his earthly existence shall be *uno tenore*, one breath, and capable of being expressed in one word" — which is, of course, the logos as the Word, the Omega — and thus, "consists in removing, putting at a distance" the immediate and contingent existence that is recalled. Thus "recollection is ideality."[22] Like Hegelian metaphysics, the *art* of recollection, in other words, is a logocentric art that purifies reflectively the existential reality, transforming the erratic and open-ended process of temporal events into a unified and inclusive spatial image. For, to bestow this "consecrating" ideality on existence and to achieve the distance it affords, the art of recollection must begin from the *end*. Beginning any other way, from the Alpha in the sense of *inter esse*, is the rock, so to speak, upon which ideality founders. "Properly speaking," Afham writes,

> only the essential is the object of recollection. . . . The essential is not simply essential in itself, but it is such by reason of the relation it has to the person concerned. He who has broken with the idea cannot act essentially, cannot undertake anything essential. . . . Outward

criteria notwithstanding, everything he does is unessential.[23]

These representative passages on the underlying aestheticism of recollection, freighted with echoes of the logocentric philosophies of presence extending from Plato through Spinoza to Kant and Hegel and pointing even to Nietzsche's Will to Power, recall the primary hermeneutic thrust of the entire history of metaphysics as Heidegger discloses it in his de-struction of the onto-theo-logical tradition. But they also allude to Sophocles' *Oedipus*, to Aristotle's *Poetics*,[24] to Friedrich Schlegel's *Lucinde*, and perhaps even to Wordsworth's "Preface to the Lyrical Ballads" — and point prophetically to the strategic spatial principle of recollection that "arrests," generates *"stasis"* or "repose" (circularity) in Worringer's *Abstraction and Empathy*, in T.E. Hulme's "Modern Art," in Proust's *A la recherche du temps perdu*, in Yeats' poetry of *A Vision*, in Joyce's *Ulysses*, in Eliot's "mythical method," indeed, in Symbolist Modernism at large. In so doing, they also lay bare the essential hermeneutic thrust of the whole history of Western literary criticism — especially of its highly self-conscious and "reflective" culmination in the ironic/inclusive mode of the "Neo-Kantian" modern critical tradition (and its extensions in the myth criticism of Northrop Frye and in the structuralist imperatives of Levi-Strauss: its defining impulse to objectify and thus annul the dread of being-in-the-world that has no-thing as its object or, to put it in another way, to spatialize time in order to gain aesthetic distance from it.[25] Commenting on Kierkegaard's analysis of recollection as the essential aesthetic category in a section entitled "Aesthetic Rest vs. Existential Movement" of a brilliant essay on Kierkegaard's pseudonymous writing, Stephen Crites observes in words that strike familiar Symbolist chords:

> The ideality bodied forth in a work of art is always an abstraction from experience. It arises out of the temporality of experience, but it achieves a purified form as a self-contained possibility, free of temporality. That is why both artist and his audience are able to come to rest in it. At least for this ideal moment of experience a man achieves integration, his consciousness drawn together by its concentration on a single purified possibility. Kierkegaard speaks of this moment of repose in ideal possibility as a recollection, in a sense of the term derived from Plato: here temporal reality is recollected, assimilated to atemporal forms that are logically prior to it. The recollected possibilities are logically prior in the sense that they give intelligible meaning to the reality of experience.

This important function of art is also performed by other operations of the mind and the imagination. Therefore Kierkegaard sometimes employs the term "aesthetic" in an extended sense that includes science and philosophy as well as art. For the cognitive grasp of an object, whether a purified object of experience or an ideal, logico-mathematical object, also enables consciousness to suspend its bewildering temporal peregrinations and to come to a satisfying moment of clarity: All knowledge is recollection.[26]

As the reference to Plato suggests, the "aesthete," or what for Kierkegaard is the same thing, the ironist who "lives poetically,"[27] achieves "rest" by irrealizing temporal existence, by transforming experiential time into cyclical space, that is, by entering into an inclusive and in-closed circle from the beginning. In this passage Crites is simply defining aesthetic recollection. What is left out of his account of Kierkegaard's analysis of the ironic transcendence of time or, as he usually puts it, of actuality is his insistence on the terrible consequences of this kind of circularity. As we see everywhere in the pseudonymous works, far from achieving an authentically liberating *stasis*, the aesthete, who by definition enters a *completed* circle from the beginning, enters an inexorable erosive process the deadliness of which not only estranges him from existence but eventually brings on despair and melancholy, that *accidia* or spiritual sloth in which rest is defined by an achieved timelessness that has atrophied the bodily and spiritual will to *move*, i.e. the existential self, or, rather, the memory of being. (This, of course, is a more radical version of Heidegger's *Seinsvergessenheit,* the oblivion of being.) Kierkegaard makes this point especially clear in his stunning portraits of the aesthetes in *Either/Or*: "How terrible tedium is — terribly tedious," A writes in *Diapsalmata,* "I know no stronger expression, none truer, for only the like is known by the like. If only there were some higher, stronger expression, then there would be at least a movement. I lie stretched out, inactive; the only thing I see is emptiness, the only thing I move about in is emptiness. I do not even suffer pain. The vulture constantly devoured Prometheus' liver; the poison constantly dripped down on Loki; that was at least an interruption, even though a monotonous one. Even pain has lost its refreshment for me."[28] But it receives its most significant expression, at least for our purposes, in his attack on Friedrich Schlegel's *Künstlerroman, Lucinde,* which, according to his description of its essential formal characteristics, makes it exactly a forerunner of the Modernist (poetic) novel of spatial form. "At the very outset," Kierkegaard observes,

Julian [the narrator] explains that along with the other conventions of reason and ethics he has also dispensed

129

with chronology. He then adds: "For me and for this book, for my love of it and for its internal formulation, there is no purpose more purposive than that right at the start I begin by abolishing what we call order, keep myself aloof from it, and appropriate to myself in word and deed the right to a charming confusion." With this he seeks to attain what is truly poetical. . . .[29]

After thus describing the novel in terms that might apply equally to any number of "de-temporalized" Modernist novels from Huysman's *A Rebours* to Virginia Woolf's *The Waves* — Kierkegaard is not unaware, of course, that what is "confusion" to the vulgar is the *aesthetic order* of the eternal imagination — he comments witheringly: "When the imagination is allowed to rule in this way it prostrates and anesthetizes the soul, robs it of all moral tension, and makes of life a dream. Yet this is exactly what *Lucinde* seeks to accomplish. . . ."[30] And again, after his brilliant analysis of the character of the "poetical" and melancholic Lisette, who (like young Stencil in Pynchon's *V* — the postmodern heir of Henry Adams) objectifies and distances her dread of life by referring to herself in the third person, Kierkegaard condemns the spatial mode of the aesthetic perspective: "Throughout the whole of *Lucinde*, however, it is this lapsing into an aesthetic stupor which appears as the designation for what it is to live poetically, and which, since it lulls the deeper ego into a somnambulant state, permits the arbitrary ego free latitude in ironic self-satisfaction."[31]

In thus tracing the "moral" history of circularity as recollection in the fate of the "ironic" — the inclusive — aesthete, Kierkegaard also prophecies the essential "moral" history of circularity as recollection not only in modern philosophy (from Nietzsche's annunciation of the saving eternal return to Heidegger's rejection of it), but also, and primarily, in modern literature, at least as this history is read by the main thrust of the contemporary avant-garde. (Though there has been a resurgence of cyclicalism in the structural anthropology of Levi-Strauss and in the poetry of a number of important contemporary American poets such as Jerome Rothenberg, Allen Ginsberg, Gary Snyder, and even Charles Olson, this new cyclicalism, with the exception of certain followers of Levi-Strauss, is at pains to acknowledge the priority of temporality by way of the priority of the body.) It is precisely this devastating "progression" we experience, for example, in the transition — generated by the foundering of metaphysics (and its aesthetic counterpart) on the rock of contemporary history — from W.B. Yeats's celebration of urobouric time to Samuel Beckett's grim recognition of its erosive horror. For the "Modern" Yeats, we recall, the epiphanic moment — when time has come around full circle (become space) — "integrates" or, to use his own vocabulary, *unifies being,* transforms the existential self into image and history, into Byzantium, the timeless Polis of Art:

> and after,
> Under the frenzy of the fourteenth moon,
> The soul begins to tremble into stillness,
> To die into the labyrinth of itself!
> . . . .
>
> All thought becomes an image and the soul
> Becomes a body: that body and that soul
> Too perfect at the full to lie in a cradle,
> Too lonely for the traffic of the world:
> Body and soul cast out and cast away
> Beyond the world.[32]

And again — the contrast with Kierkegaard, which is manifest even in the language, is startling in its absoluteness:

> The smithies break the flood,
> The golden smithies of the Emperor!
> Marbles of the dancing floor
> Break bitter furies of complexity,
> Those images that yet
> Fresh images beget,
> That dolphin-torn, that gong-tormented sea.[33]

For the postmodern Beckett, on the other hand, Yeats's aesthetic-metaphysical circle of perfection has become Clov's "zero zone," which, far from being a place of fulfillment, is where, as Gogo and Didi despairingly observe, there is "Nothing to be done."[34] Having "achieved" aesthetic *stasis*, the Belacqua figure of *More Pricks than Kicks*, of *Murphy*, of the *Molloy* novels — who is invariably a (Modern) artist and/or metaphysician — is thus doomed to wallow eternally, like "Sloth our own brother," in his willessness (his "freedom" from the desire and loathing, as it were, that Yeats and Joyce [in *Portrait*] want to transcend): "Being by nature sinfully indolent, bogged in indolence [Belacqua asked] nothing better than to stay put. . . ."[35] And despite their "art," the ground-down tramps of *Waiting for Godot* are doomed to "move" in endless circles until the entropic process, in running its course, utterly annuls their memory of being:

> Estragon: Well, shall we go?
> Vladimir: Yes, let's go.
> *They do not move*

> [Curtain, Act I]

131

. . . .

> Vladimir: Well, shall we go?
> Estragon: Yes, let's go.
> *They do not move*
>
> [Curtain, Act II] [36]

On the other hand, Kierkegaard does not, indeed, deliberately refuses to, define and systematically analyze the literary significance of the existential movement of repetition. And the reason for this is fundamental: whereas recollection is a mode of knowledge and thus accessible to the methodical language of analysis or "aesthetics," repetition is essentially a mode of existential "action," of uniquely human being. But, in fact, Kierkegaard does suggest, however indirectly, the implications of repetition for literary form and for literary hermeneutics in the very method of indirect communication of his pseudonymous works — and it turns out to be remarkably like Heidegger's in *Being and Time*. I mean his revolutionary transformation of a traditional literature of recollection, in which language as tautology stills temporal motion and thus neutralizes the selfhood of both author and reader, into a literature of "action," in which a language as dialectical movement (repetition) activates time, *moves* and thus generates the selfhood of, i.e. dialogue between, author and reader. In the pseudonymous works, in other words, Kierkegaard abandons the traditional sense of an ending, the *poetic* or *ironic* principle of closure. More specifically, the great ironist refuses to *resolve* the either/or of the existential situation into the neither/nor — what I.A. Richards would call the "inclusiveness" and Cleanth Brooks and W.K. Wimsatt the "ironic equilibrium" and Northrop Frye the "mythic total structure" — of the *aesthetic* perspective, the perspective *aeterno modo*.

As Stephen Crites observes, the creative process in Kierkegaard's pseudonymous works — it is, I take it, the process of an authentic, a "mastered irony" [37] — takes the form of a "dialectic of revocation," [38] a rupturing of the referential surface, as Heidegger would put it, or in terms of this essay, an icon-breaking act, in which an existential movement collides irreconcilably with the "aesthetic" frame of the book (the "spatial form" recollected from the "aesthetic" angle of vision) and disintegrates or, better, destroys its "objective" and conclusive authority. Thus, for example, in *Repetition*, where Kierkegaard's strategy is most representative,

> There are occasional hints about the meaning of repetition, but we are never permitted to see the movement itself [as it is "made" by the young man] except in the distorting mirror of the aesthetic. Constantine [the "objective" author, who recollects the

story *aeterno modo*] speaks of the affair as a "wrestling match" or a "breaking" (*brydning*): "the universal breaks with the exception, breaks with it in strife, and strengthens it [the exception] by this breaking." This break is what we are permitted to see in the book, but as it occurs the young man breaks out of the aesthetic frame of the book as well, and is lost from view. . . . The pseudonym and his book constitute a mirror reflecting from its angle and within its frame the existential movement as it breaks away. . . . The aesthetic medium is purely dialectic: it is simultaneously presented and obliterated.[39]

In thus destroying the aesthetic frame, the existential movement also breaks the reader's (interpreter's) privileged logocentric perspective. That is, it undermines his certain expectation of an aesthetic resolution — that "awaiting" (*Gewärtigens*) for an "end" which, according to Heidegger, unlike "anticipatory resoluteness," manifests itself psychologically as a calculative impulse to suspend the temporal process, to transform it into "a pure sequence of 'nows' " (BT, 65, 377; SZ, 329 and BT, 68, 389; SZ, 339), thus annulling the selfhood — and leaves him unaccomodated, "alone with the existential *movement* itself and whatever claim it may make on him."[40] The resolution, if there is to be one at all, must be achieved by the reader himself in an existential decision of his own. In "Guilty/Not Guilty?," the diary of a young man who has undergone something like an existential movement in the process of a love affair in which, like Kierkegaard, he abandons his beloved, the diarist expresses his utter uncertainty about the meaning of his act. He writes:

I have never been able to understand it in any other way than this, that every man is essentially assigned to himself, and that apart from this there is either an authority such as that of an apostle — the dialectical determination of which I cannot comprehend, and meanwhile out of respect for what has been handed down to me as holy I refrain from concluding anything from non-understanding — or there is chatter."[41]

Commenting on this crucial passage, Crites concludes about Kierkegaard's narrative method:

That, in the end, represents the standpoint of Kierkegaard's authorship as a whole . . . the pseudonymous writings are designed to throw every reader back on his own resources. There is not even an actual author to lay claim on him. They assign him to himself.

The pseudonymous works present their life-possibilities in this elusive form in order to evoke in the reader a movement that is entirely his own. They are not cookbooks that he could follow in concocting a novel but pretested pattern for life. . . . But each work is in its own way designed to create a quiet crisis in the life of a reader that can be resolved by his own decision.[42]

Precisely, though I would add to the "cookbook" the "icon" that annuls the imperative to engage oneself with the voice of the text and, by extension, with the world. Any effort, according to Kierkegaard, to explain the existential movement in discursive language or to "re-present" it in a literary art grounded in the traditional Western strategy of recollection is doomed to negate it. Given his commitment to the existential structures, it was inevitable that he should make the effort to assert the ontological priority of temporality in language. Thus for Kierkegaard literature, in the last analysis, becomes "anti-literature" in the same way that Heideggerian phenomenology is anti-metaphysical, an effort to surpass Western philosophy. To put it in terms of the hermeneutic argument of this essay, Kierkegaard withstands the enormous pressure of — and the security offered by — the Western metaphysical/aesthetic tradition to write author-ially (from a privileged origin) about existence, and chooses rather to write, with all the risks it entails, within the human — the temporal — situation of openness and uncertainty. Unlike his aesthetes (who, as we have seen, in their comportment towards the real world, bear a remarkable resemblance to the *fin de siècle* Symbolists in France and England) — and, in another way, with the aesthetic metaphysician *par excellence,* G.W.F. Hegel — Kierkegaard writes *in temporali modo*: exploratively or, what is the same thing, dialogically. He writes, that is, in such a way as to transform the reader's (interpreter's) impulse to objectivity into an *interest* (Care) that engages him dialogically with the text and with the ambiguous and anxiety provoking either/or of the temporal existence the text is exploring. Thus this "dialectic of revocation" or, as I prefer to call it, this iconoclastic strategy, in which the universal, far from "breaking" the "bitter furies of complexity . . . that gong-tormented sea," "breaks with the exception" in strife, becomes for aesthetics what, we recall, repetition, "the *interest* on which metaphysics founders," is for reflective thought.

In thus exploring the dialogic (and the "ethical") possibilities of an open, temporal, and existential form (as opposed to the distancing aestheticism of a closed, a spatial, form), Kierkegaard, of course, takes his place along with the Dostoevsky of *Notes from Underground*, the Pirandello of *Six Characters in Search of an Author*, and the Kafka of *The*

Trial as one of the most important immediate literary forebears of postmodern literature. For, as I have suggested, postmodern literature not only thematizes time in the breakdown of metaphysics following the "death of God" (or at any rate the death of God as Omega), but also makes the "medium" itself the "message" in the sense that its function is to perform a Heideggerian "de-struction" of the traditional metaphysical frame of reference, that is, to accomplish the phenomenological reduction of the spatial perspective by formal violence, thus, like Kierkegaard, leaving the reader *interesse* — a naked and unaccommodated being-in-the-world, a *Dasein* in the place of origins, where time is ontologically prior to being.[43] In other words, Kierkegaard's formal experiments, like Heidegger's experimental philosophy in *Being and Time*, is ultimately grounded in a profound intuition that, as Wallace Stevens puts it,

> we live in a place
> That is not our own and, much more, not ourselves[44]

and, therefore, that everything — the spiritual health of man — depends "not on [getting] out of the circle but [coming] into it in the right way," that is, hermeneutically.

It is true, of course — to return once more to Heidegger — that the Kierkegaardian repetition is a fictional strategy to engage the reader "ethically," not a theory of textual interpretation. But the difference is simply (if we bracket the religious dimension) that whereas Kierkegaard feels compelled to adopt a narrative strategy of hermeneutic violence against an age still "innocent" about metaphysics, a Heideggerian feels that "the rupture of the referential surface" of the metaphysical World Picture has taken or is taking place and thus that the modern reader has been prepared historically to accept this originative stance as a hermeneutic imperative (has "come of age," as it were). Seen in the light of the foregoing discussion, then, the relationship of Kierkegaard's repetition to a Heideggerian literary hermeneutics based on the phenomenological/existential analytic of *Being and Time* should now be obvious. What it suggests is that the Heideggerian hermeneutic circle as repetition or retrieval (*Wiederholen*) is finally a de-mystifying of the Modernist, especially the New Critical understanding of the hermeneutic situation. It is, in other words, an undermining of the privileged status of the interpreter, which, grounded as it is on the unexamined (derived) assumption that End is ontologically prior to process, justifies in the name of disinterestedness (and the autonomy of the text) the transformation of the be-ing of a text into a spatial form, a circle which, in the last analysis, becomes a *circulus vitiosus*, a circle that closes off temporality and thus "erodes" one's memory of the being of the text and, ultimately, in so far as language is the house of being, of being itself. Just as Kierkegaard's narrative strategy of repetition is a "dialectics of revocation," which in denying the reader an author-ial ground breaks the "metaphysical" circle of interpretation and "assigns him to himself," so a Heideggerian hermeneutic circle is a process of de-struction, of dis-closing, which dismantles the reader's metaphysical/spatial frame of reference and assigns the interpreter to himself, makes him a historical *Dasein*, a temporal being-in-the-world, in original and care-ful, i.e. in dialogic, relationship to the being of the text and ultimately to being itself. Just as the Kierkegaardian repetition is "the interest on which metaphysics founders," so the Heideggerian hermeneutic circle is the Care on which Spatial Form founders. Finally, as with Kierkegaard, for the Heideggerian interpreter repetition (unlike recollection [the vicious circle], which is "repeated backwards") is "recollected forwards." Although Heidegger, in the following passage, is referring to the history of the Western philosophical tradition, what he says about retrieval applies equally to the encounter with a particular literary text, since, as Lessing's distinction between the verbal and the plastic arts suggests, a literary text, by virtue of the temporality of words, is itself a "history" in little. Indeed, it is, I submit as a crucial point of contention against the Derridean deconstructors, this original temporal encounter with the literary text that generates the process of repetition on the larger level of the "text" of the tradition:

> To ask "How does it stand with being?" means nothing less than to recapture, to repeat (*wieder-holen*), the beginning of our historical-spiritual existence, in order to transform it into a new beginning. This is possible. It is indeed the crucial form of history, because it begins in the fundamental event. But we do not repeat a beginning by reducing it to something past and now known, which need merely be initiated; no, the beginning must be begun again, more radically, with all the strangeness, darkness, insecurity that attend a true beginning. Repetition as we understand it is anything but an improved continuation with the old method of what has been up to now.[45]

It is, finally, in the "Kierkegaardian" sense of the hermeneutic circle that we are to understand the phenomenological hermeneutics of Heidegger's existential analytic as lending itself to a literary hermeneutics of discovery or, what is the same thing though more explicit, of disclosure. I mean a literary hermeneutics which is simultaneously a dis-covering or dis-closing (present) of what has been covered over or closed-off and forgotten by the meta-physical imagination (past), and a Care-ful exploration of or opening oneself to *terra incognita* (future): or, more literally, a hermeneutics which makes the interpreter a being-in-the-world in dialogic relationship simultaneously with a particular literary text and, since the text enters history on being written, with the "text" of literary history, and, beyond that, with the "text" of the history of Western man. It is, further, in this sense of the hermeneutic circle that we are to understand the new literary hermeneutics of dis-closure to be post-Modern and thus postmodern.

In the epigraph of this essay, it will be recalled, I invoked Gotthold Lessing's famous distinction between poetry and painting in the *Laocoön* by way of orienting the reader towards the analogy I wish to develop between the literary text and the phenomenological/existential analytic of *Being and Time*. I also was implying that in defining the limits of poetry in terms of its temporal medium and the limits of painting in terms of its spatial medium, Lessing was sowing the seeds of an enormously important, if still to be fulfilled, development in literary criticism. Since the justification of this view depends on perceiving the transformation of meanings that it has undergone in the process of the ensuing discussion, the passage bears repeating:

> If it be true that painting employs wholly different signs
> or means of imitation from poetry, — the one using forms
> and colors in space, the other articulate sounds in time, —
> and if signs must unquestionably stand in convenient
> relation with the thing signified, then signs arranged side
> by side can represent only objects existing side by side,
> or whose parts so exist, while consecutive signs can
> express only objects which succeed each other, or whose
> parts succeed each other, in time.
>   Objects which exist side by side, or whose parts
> so exist, are called bodies. Consequently bodies with
> their visible properties are the peculiar subjects of
> painting.
>   Objects which succeed each other, or whose
> parts succeed each other in time, are actions.
> Consequently actions are the peculiar subjects of
> poetry.[46]

In the light of the foregoing interpretation of Heidegger's version of Husserl's phenomenological call to return *"Zu den Sachen selbst,"* it can now be seen, I think, why Lessing's distinction (which Joseph Frank in his influential essays on spatial form in modern literature dismisses as a critical judgment in favor of its importance "solely as instrument of analysis"[47]) is in fact a seminal insight. However at odds his existential intuition was with his conscious classical intentions, Lessing was engaged in an act of hermeneutic "de-struction" bent on recovering the ontological priority of temporality in the understanding of literature from the derivative — and spatial — metaphysical critical consciousness. To use the original and more precise terms of this discussion of hermeneutics, he was engaged in an act of iconoclasm intended to dis-cover the logos as *legein* (*Rede*) buried deeply and eventually forgotten by the Western spatial imagination when it interpreted man, the ζῶον λόγον ἔχον , as "rational animal." In insisting that words as temporal phenomena ("sounds in time") are the media of the expression of human actions ("objects which succeed each other, or whose parts succeed each other, in time"), Lessing was ultimately saying that the essential existential structure of human life is language as human speech — or, to recall Heidegger's terminology, that "Dasein, man's Being, is 'defined' as . . . that living thing whose Being is essentially determined by the potentiality for discourse" (BT, 6, 41; SZ, 20; see also BT, 7, 55; SZ, 32). And in so doing, he was reasserting against the grain of Western culture, and his own neoclassical inclinations, that, though literature is not life, it is, as radical medium, *equiprimordial* with the temporal existence of *Dasein* (*Befindlichkeit*) and the ek-static understanding of that existence (*Verstehen*).

In reading Lessing's aesthetic distinction in the light of Heidegger's phenomenological/existential hermeneutics, a postmodern generation awakens, with the shock of recognition (for it is, after all, a "commonplace"), to the fact that a literary work cannot, despite its repeatability, simply *be* in the sense that Archibald MacLeish speaks of it in "Ars Poetica" and the New Critics, and the Structuralists after them, deal with it in their brilliantly *superficial* (ontic as opposed to ontological) exegeses. Such a way of putting it, we can now see, betrays the fatal spatial prejudice that lies behind the crisis of Western man: that it reads logos not as *legein* — the "act of an instant," as the postmodern American poet Charles Olson puts it[48] — but as the Word and thus sees Form as Western metaphysics *sees* the Being of existence, i.e., as object, as image, *in-closing* time within the bounding line of space. To put it another way, what we discover is that modern literary criticism has concealed the primordial essence of literature: *that it uses words not pigments* to articulate experience and that words, "as consecutive signs," are radically temporal, at least in their authentic form, when they are "the act of an instant." In thus covering over the existential nature of language, it has also forgotten that, if a poem must "be," as the New Critics insist, it must "be" in the way that Heidegger's phenomenology dis-closes (opens up what has been in-closed) Being to be: as be-ing, as temporal process.[49]

If, therefore, the analogy that Lessing and Heidegger jointly suggest in giving parallel and equiprimordial status to Existence (*Befindlichkeit*), Understanding (*Verstehen*), and Speech (*Rede*) is allowed, the phenomenological stance demands a reorientation of perception in the reading process and thus a revision of the interpretive act similar to and as radical as that which Heidegger calls for in *Being and*

Time in the encounter with existence. For if a literary text is fundamentally a temporal phenomenon, if, that is, this temporality is ontologically prior to the Form of a text, then literary hermeneutics must abandon, or, more accurately, perhaps, must disengage, the prevailing and by now culturally ingrained habit of suspending the temporal dimension and its concurrent attitude of dis-interest in favor of the ontologically prior dynamic *process* conveyed by words in sequence. Literary interpretation, that is, must lay itself bare before the experience of language, the ongoing instants that, in following one another in rapid, if not always causal, succession, *engage* the reader's *interest* as Care — and in so doing constantly modify his temporal perception, his expectation of the future and understanding of the past, and, at the same time, always threaten his understanding of his own historical existence and being as he lives it in his mind and in his body or, as Merleau-Ponty would say, in his fingertips. To put it in another way, a postmodern interpreter must bracket the arrogant anthropomorphic frame of reference of the metaphysical imagination, the *Wille zum Willen*, and its synchronic perspective in favor of a "situated" or historical imagination and its diachronic standpoint, the standpoint of the ek-static *Dasein*. To return to the term that finally emerges as the inevitable definition of the hermeneutic act, the postmodern literary interpreter must become an explorer, a *Homo Viator*, in the place of origins. Here the author and the world of the literary text — whether it is Homer's *Odyssey* or Dante's *Divine Comedy* or Shakespeare's *King Lear* or Yeats's "Sailing to Byzantium" or Pound's *Cantos* or Beckett's *Malone* or Olson's *Maximus* — undergo a profound metamorphosis. The god indifferently "paring his fingernails" is transformed into a dialogic partner, a sharer. And what was conceived as an artifact to be read from a printed page, an image to be looked at from a distance, an It to be mastered, becomes "oral speech" to be heard immediately in time, a Thou. When we ask the question of its being in Care, the work of literature becomes in turn a voice that asks us the question of being. In the place of origins, as Hans-Georg Gadamer has persuasively reminded us, literature, ancient and modern, once more becomes fraught with risk — and possibility.[50]

SUNY-Binghamton

NOTES

1   Martin Heidegger, *Being and Time*, trans. John Macquarrie and Edward Robinson (New York: Harper & Row, 1962), Sect. 2, p. 25. Further references to *Being and Time* will be incorporated in the text in parentheses and will include the abbreviation BT, the section number, the page number. Since the translation is notoriously problematic, I will also include abbreviated references to the original German version, *Sein und Zeit*, 7th ed.(Tübingen: Neomarius Verlag, 1953), as, for example: BT, 2, 25; SZ, 5. While "Being" is consistently capitalized in the translation, and therefore in all quotations from

Being and Time, in my use I distinguish between being (or be-ing), when I mean to refer to its *verbal* (and new) sense, and Being when I refer to its *nominative* (traditional) sense.

2   See W.B. Macomber, *The Anatomy of Disillusion: Martin Heidegger's Notion of Truth* (Evanston, Ill.: Northwestern University Press, 1967), pp. 44 ff. The phrase is important for my purposes because its reference to inauthentic reality in spatial terms (map/icon) points to the causal relationship between the *spatialization of time* and the covering up and forgetting of being.

3   See also BT, 32, 188-92; SZ, 149-51. Specifically, the forestructure of the *Dasein* as interpreter consists of fore-having (*Vorhaben*); fore-sight or point of view (*Vorsicht*), which " 'takes the first cut' out of what has been taken into our fore-having, and . . . does so with a view to a definite way in which this can be interpreted"; and fore-conception (*Vorgriff*), the conceptualizability of that which "is held in our fore-having and toward which we set our sights 'foresightedly' " (BT, 32, 191; SZ, 150). The "fore-structure," that is, is another way of referring to the ek-static or temporal character of *Dasein*. The crucial point, as Michael Gelven points out, "is that the fore-structure comes from Dasein's involvement in the world as ready-to-hand; *not* as purely calculative function of the present-at-hand." *A Commentary on Heidegger's "Being and Time"* (New York: Harper Torchbooks, 1970), p. 95.

4   For another version of this crucial movement, see Heidegger's definition of the "leap" in *An Introduction to Metaphysics*, trans. Ralph Manheim (Garden City, N.Y.: Anchor Books, 1961), p. 5.

5   The great importance that Heidegger attributes to the hermeneutic circle is suggested by the fact that he invokes it as a governing concept of his theory of interpretation in an increasingly fuller way at least three times in *Being and Time*: BT, 5, 27-28; SZ, 7-8; BT, 32, 192-95; SZ, 151-53; and BT, 63, 362-63; SZ, 314-15.

6   T.S. Eliot, *The Family Reunion, The Complete Poems and Plays, 1909-1950,* (New York: Harcourt Brace, 1952), p. 250.

7   A.R. Ammons, "Corsons Inlet," *Collected Poems, 1951-1971,* (New York: Norton, 1972), p. 148.

8   As Paul de Man puts it in an important conversion of Heidegger's hermeneutics of understanding into literary interpretation:

> Literary "form" is the result of the dialectic interplay between the prefigurative structure of the foreknowledge and the intent at totality of the interpretative process. This dialectic is difficult to grasp. The idea of totality suggests closed forms that strive for ordered and consistent systems and have an almost irresistible tendency to transform themselves into objective structures. Yet, the temporal factor, so persistently forgotten, should remind us that the form is never anything but a process on the way to its completion. The completed form never exists as a concrete aspect of the work that could coincide with a sensorial or semantic dimension of the language. It is constituted in the mind of the interpreter as the work discloses itself in response to his questioning. But this dialogue between work and interpreter is

endless. The hermeneutic understanding is always, by its very nature, lagging behind: to understand something is to realize that one had always known it, but, at the same time, to face the mystery of this hidden knowledge. Understanding can be called complete only when it becomes aware of its own temporal predicament and realizes that the horizon within which the totalization can take place is time itself. The act of understanding is a temporal act that has its own history, but this history forever eludes totalization.

"Form and Intent in the American New Criticism," *Blindness and Insight: Essays in the Rhetoric of Contemporary Criticism* (New York: Oxford University Press, 1971), pp. 31-32. See also Stanley Romaine Hopper, "Introduction," *Interpretation: The Poetry of Meaning,* ed. Hopper and David L. Miller (New York: Harcourt, Brace & World, 1967), pp. xv-xvi. For another valuable account of Heidegger's version of the hermeneutic circle, see Gelven's *A Commentary on Heidegger's "Being and Time,"* pp. 176-81. In justifying the conclusion that the hermeneutic circle is not a vicious circle, however, Gelven invokes the analogy of the cumulative enrichment of meaning that comes with repeated listening to a Beethoven sonata. In so doing, he fails to point to the kind of temporality that is prior to the temporality of incremental repetition: the temporal process of listening to the sonata itself.

9   The translators of *Being and Time,* Macquarrie and Robinson, translate *"Wiederholen"* as "Repetition" (others, as "Retrieval") and add in a footnote:

this English word is hardly adequate to express Heidegger's meaning. Etymologically, "wiederholen" means "to fetch again;" in modern German usage, however, this is expressed by the cognate separable verb "wieder . . . holen," while "wieder-holen" means simply "to repeat" or "do over again." Heidegger departs from both these meanings, as he is careful to point out. For him, "wiederholen" does not mean either a mere mechanical repetition or an attempt to reconstitute the physical past; it means rather an attempt to go back to the past and retrieve former *possibilities,* which are thus "explicitly handed down" or "transmitted." (BT, 74, 437)

Neither they nor, as far as I know, his commentators refer to Heidegger's source as Kierkegaard. As a result a crucial dimension of the meaning of this important term is left out.

10   See Richard E. Palmer, *Hermeneutics: Interpretation Theory in Schleiermacher, Dilthey, Heidegger, and Gadamer* (Evanston, Ill.: Northwestern University Press, 1969), pp. 86-88, 118-21, 130-32. For the importance of Kierkegaard's critique of the aesthetic consciousness for Hans-Georg Gadamer's dialogic hermeneutics, see Gadamer's *Truth and Method* (New York: The Seabury Press, 1975), pp. 85 ff. and 112 ff.

11   Søren Kierkegaard, *The Concept of Irony, With Constant Reference to Socrates,* trans. with "Introduction" by Lee M. Capel (London: Collins, 1966), pp. 154-55.

12   Søren Kierkegaard, *Repetition: An Essay in Experimental Psychology,* trans. with "Introduction" and "Notes" by Walter Lowrie (New York: Harper Torchbooks, 1964), p. 33. See also Søren Kierkegaard, *Johannes Climacus or*

De Omnibus Dubitandum Est and A Sermon, trans. with an "Assessment" by T.H. Croxall (Stanford, Ca.: Stanford University Press, 1958). In distinguishing between the Cartesian/Hegelian methodology of systematic doubt and existential doubt (and extending this distinction to include that between disinterestedness and interest and between recollection and repetition), Kierkegaard in this seminal work (unpublished in his lifetime) remarkably prefigures Husserl's and especially Heidegger's interpretations of the phenomenological reduction, the principle of intentionality (Care), and the hermeneutic circle. See especially pp. 151-55.

13 See especially Eliade's account of the development of the primitive cyclical perspective, and its return to the timeless time (*in illo tempore*), into Plato's essentialist philosophy of Forms. *Cosmos and History: The Myth of the Eternal Return*, trans. Willard Trask (New York: Harper Torchbooks, 1959), pp. 34-35, 120-22.

14 *Repetition*, pp. 52-53. The emphasis is mine except for Kierkegaard's telling italicizing of both references to the word "interest."

15 *Johannes Climacus*, pp. 151-52. T. H. Croxall misses the connection with Heidegger's *Dasein* in his otherwise helpful introductory commentary on Kierkegaard's "interest":

> Philosophy "abstracts" life from factuality in order to think about it, and in doing so it pushes its way into the abstract sphere of "possibility" (the opposite of actuality). True philosophy uses both the term "possible" and "actual," but the actuality it deals with is really false because its content has been removed or "annulled." It is merely treated as something to be thought about idealistically and in the abstract. Such thinking is a dispassionate, disinterested process, involving no more than the Latin *interesse* in its root meaning of "being between," or being there. The "existing individual," on the other hand, is interested in the other sense of the Latin word, i.e. "being concerned." (p. 88)

16 *Repetition*, p. 131.

17 Søren Kierkegaard, *Either/Or: A Fragment of Life*, trans. David F. Swenson and Lillian Marvin Swenson (Princeton, N.J.: Princeton University Press, 1946), I, 31.

18 *Repetition*, pp. 133-34. The transitive use of the verb *to think* should not be overlooked.

19 "Editor's Introduction," *Repetition*, p. 4. The central importance that Kierkegaard attaches to the term "interest" (as opposed to "disinterest") and thus to the existential concept of repetition is made eminently clear not only in the polemic against Professor Heiberg's misunderstanding, which "occupies . . . 55 pages in Kierkegaard's Papers" (the crucial passage of which Walter Lowrie has translated and quoted at length in his introduction), but also in *The Concept of Dread* (Princeton, N.J.: Princeton University Press, 1957). In the latter Vigilius Haufniensis, the pseudonymous author, quotes the crucial passage from *Repetition* — and comments on the significance that Heiberg fails to understand — to lend authority to his thesis that "Sin [an

existential category] belongs to ethics [in this case a universal category] only in so far as upon this concept it [ethics] founders. . . .":

> "Repetition is the *interest* of metaphysics and at the same time the interest upon which metaphysics founders. Repetition is the solution in every ethical view [in this case an existential category]; repetition is a *conditio sine qua non* of every dogmatic problem." The first sentence [in *Repetition* all this is one sentence] contains an allusion to the thesis that metaphysics is disinterested, as Kant affirmed of aesthetics. As soon as the interest emerges, metaphysics steps to one side. For this reason the word interest is italicized. The whole interest of subjectivity [the existential self] emerges in real life, and then metaphysics founders. In case repetition is not posited, ethics [like metaphysics] remains a binding power [a principle that objectifies and determines existence]; presumably it is for this reason he [Constantius] says that "it is the solution in every ethical view. . . ." In the sphere of spirit . . . the problem is to transform repetition into something inward, into the proper task of freedom, into freedom's highest interest, as to whether, while everything changes, it can actually realize repetition. . . . All this Professor Heiberg has failed to observe. . . . (pp. 16-17)

20   Søren Kierkegaard, *Either/Or*, trans. David F. Swenson, Lilliam M. Swenson, and Walter Lowrie, with revisions by Howard A. Johnson (Garden City, N.Y.: Anchor Books, 1959), I, 31-32. The identity of metaphysics and aestheticism assumes even greater significance when one considers the relationship between A's definition of recollection and Hegel's term *aufgehoben*, which Kierkegaard interprets as one of the central concepts of the System. The word means "raised" or "taken up" but, as Robert Bretall points out in a note on its use by William Afham, the aesthete of Kierkegaard's *Stages on Life's Way*, "to render precisely its philosophical significance, we should have to say 'cancelled as a separate entity while preserved as part of a larger whole.' " *A Kierkegaard Anthology* (Princeton, N.J.: Princeton University Press, 1951), p. 189.

21   Louis Mackey, *Kierkegaard: A Kind of Poet* (Philadelphia: Pennsylvania University Press, 1971), p. 17.

22   Søren Kierkegaard, *Stages on Life's Way*, trans. Walter Lowrie (New York: Schocken Books, 1967). The quotations have been drawn from "The Prefatory Note" to "In Vino Veritas: A Recollection," pp. 27-36. My emphasis.

23   *Stages on Life's Way*, p. 29.

24   According to Kierkegaard, Greek (Aristotelian) tragedy is one of the purest forms of aesthetic recollection. This is why, in a number of places in his work, notably in *Fear and Trembling*, he conceives it as a literary form that, like metaphysics, must be surpassed. In this he is at one with the postmodern literary imagination, which rejects tragedy on the grounds that its evasive circularity (i.e. spatial form) is an especially virulent form of humanistic anthropomorphism that gains distance from death and finitude — the principle of Nothingness itself — by imposing a human order on and thus *justifying* in the teleology of form what is in fact meaningless. This is implicit in the drama of the absurd, but receives theoretical expression in Robbe-Grillet, "Nature,

Humanism, Tragedy," *For a New Novel: Essays on Fiction*, trans. Richard Howard (New York: Grove Press, 1963), pp. 49-75. This essay itself is an amplification of the following Brechtian epigraph from Roland Barthes: "Tragedy is merely a means of 'recovering' human misery, of subsuming and thereby justifying it in the form of necessity, a wisdom or a purification: to refuse this recuperation and to investigate the techniques of not treacherously succumbing to it (nothing is more insidious than tragedy) is today a necessary enterprise" (p. 49).

25   See my essays "Modern Literary Criticism and the Spatialization of Time: An Existential Critique," *Journal of Aesthetics and Art Criticism*, 29 (Fall 1970), 87-104; " 'Wanna Go Home, Baby?': *Sweeney Agonistes* as Drama of the Absurd," *PMLA* 85 (January 1970), 8-20; "Modern Drama and the Aristotelian Tradition: The Formal Imperatives of Absurd Time," *Contemporary Literature*, 12 (Summer 1971), 345-73; "The Detective and the Boundary: Some Notes on the Postmodern Literary Imagination," *boundary 2*, 1 (Fall 1972), 147-68.

26   Stephen Crites, "Pseudonymous Authorship as Art and as Act," in Josiah Thompson, ed., *Kierkegaard: A Collection of Critical Essays* (Garden City, N.Y.: Anchor Books, 1972), p. 210.

27   *The Concept of Irony*: "Irony is free . . . from all cares of actuality . . . when one is free in this way, only then does one live poetically, and it is well-known that irony's great demand was that one should *live poetically*" (pp. 296-97).

28   *Either/Or* (Princeton edition), I, 29. Note the similarity between the state of mind of Kierkegaard's aesthete (who spatializes according to an idealistic model) and that of Dostoevsky's "straightforward Gentlemen" in *Notes from Underground* (who spatialize according to a positivistic model).

29   *The Concept of Irony*, p. 308.

30   *The Concept of Irony*, p. 308.

31   *The Concept of Irony*, pp. 311-12.

32   W.B. Yeats, "The Phases of the Moon," *Collected Poems* (New York: Macmillan, 1956), p. 162.

33   "Byzantium," *Collected Poems*, p. 244. I read the last three lines of this stanza to be parallel with the preceding clause which has the expressive word "Break" as its predicate. The smithies and the marbles (the aesthetic recollection) thus "break" not only "bitter furies of complexity" (the imbalance of body and soul that is the source of "motion," i.e. the existential or ek-sistential self), but also "begotten" images and "that dolphin torn, that gong-tormented sea," i.e. generative life in time.

34   Samuel Beckett, *Waiting for Godot* (New York: Grove Press, 1954), p. 7. This phrase constitutes the first speech of the play and occurs repeatedly throughout at precisely and ironically the point where the circular process returns to its starting point, *in illo tempore*, as it were.

35   Samuel Beckett, "Ding-Dong," *More Pricks than Kicks* (New York: Grove Press, 1972), p. 31. The previous quotation is from *Purgatorio,* Canto IV, trans.

Dorothy Sayers (Baltimore: Penguin Books, 1955). Dante finds Belacqua on the second ledge of Anti-Purgatory sitting in a foetus position under the shade of a massive boulder:

> "Oh good my lord," said I, "pray look at this
> Bone-lazy lad, content to sit and settle
> Like sloth's own brother taking of his ease!"
>
> Then he gave heed, and turning just a little
> only his face upon his thigh, he grunted:
> "Go up then, thou, thou mighty man of mettle."

Dante recognizes him as Belacqua by "the grudging speech, and slow/ Gestures," and asks him "why dost thou resignedly/ Sit there?" Belacqua answers in words that betray his indolent nature:

> "Brother," said he, "what use to go up?
> He'd not admit me to the cleansing pain,
> That bird of God who perches at the gate.
>
> My lifetime long the heavens must wheel again
> Round me, that to my parting hour put off
> My healing sighs; and I meanwhile remain
>
> Outside, unless prayer hastens my remove —
> Prayer from a heart in grace; for who sets store
> By other kinds, which are not heard above?"

Though Belacqua is in Anti-Purgatory, the reference to Sloth suggests that Bekcett also has in mind Virgil's discourse on Love — the true agency of motion — in which Sloth is the fourth of the seven evil modes of love, exactly between the triad of hate (pride, envy, wrath) — the active absence of love — and the triad of excessive love of that which is good (avarice, gluttony, lust). Thus Sloth is definable as the neutralization of motion.

36   The "transitional" voice in this "moral" history of circularity in the modern period is the "existential" T.S. Eliot. See especially "The Love Song of J. Alfred Prufrock," *Sweeney Agonistes*, and above all the figure of Tiresias in *The Waste Land*.

37   See Josiah Thompson, "The Master of Irony," *Keirkegaard: A Collection of Critical Essays*:

> The task of the ironist, Kierkegaard suggests, is to master irony, indeed to overcome it [just as the task of the phenomenologist for Heidegger is to "overcome" metaphysics]. And this stage of mastered irony is described in the final section of the dissertation as a stage where actuality is again actualized. "Actuality will therefore not be rejected," Kierkegaard writes, "and longing shall be a healthy love, not a kittenish ruse for sneaking out of the world." (p. 120)

The quotation from *The Concept of Irony* occurs on p. 341.

38   "Pseudonymous Authorship as Art and as Act," p. 221. The phrase itself derives from the significantly titled *Concluding Unscientific Postscript*, trans. David F. Swenson and Walter Lowrie (Princeton: Princeton University Press, 1941), in which the pseudonymous Johannes Climacus, in an appendix ("For

an Understanding with the Reader"), writes that "everything [in the book] is so to be understood that it is understood to be revoked, and this book has not only a Conclusion but a Revocation" (p. 547). See also p. 548.

39   "Pseudonymous Authorship as Act and as Art," pp. 217-18. The quotation from Kierkegaard occurs in *Repetition*, p. 133. Like Pirandello's Manager in *Six Characters in Search of an Author* (another work that prefigures postmodernism), Constantine Constantius, the psychologist-observer, and other Kierkegaardian aesthetes, especially Johannes, the author of "Diary of the Seducer," take great pains to "arrange," to "plot," the unique and contingent lives of others into their recollections, their fictions orchestrated from the end. Kierkegaard also observes, in *The Concept of Irony*, the "poetic" Lisette's habit (in Schlegel's *Lucinde*) of referring to herself in the third person (which is equivalent to her furnishing her luxurious room with mirrors that reflect her image from every angle) to objectify her "unmanageable" life:

> When referring to her own person she usually called herself "Lisette," and often said that were she able to write she would then treat her story as though it were another's, although preferring to speak of herself in third person. This, evidently, was not because her earthly exploits were as world historical as a Caesar's. . . . It was simply because the weight of this *vita ante acta* was too heavy for her to bear. To come to herself concerning it, to allow its menacing shapes to pass judgment upon her, this would indeed be too serious to be poetical. (p. 311)

It is precisely this aesthetic impulse to objectify absurd existence that Beckett and Pynchon, for example, raise havoc with in their postmodern novels. This ob-jectivization is, of course, the aesthetic equivalent of Heidegger's analysis of the metaphysical *Vorstellung*. See "The Age of the World View," trans. Marjorie Greene, *Measure*, 2 (1951), 269-84; reprinted in this issue of *boundary 2*.

40   "Pseudonymous Authorship as Art and as Act," p. 218. My emphasis.

41   Søren Kierkegaard, *Stages on Life's Way*, trans. Walter Lowrie (Princeton: Princeton University Press, 1945), p. 314.

42   "Pseudonymous Authorship as Art and as Act," pp. 223-24.

43   This fundamental characteristic of Kierkegaard's "art" is virtually missed by Edith Kern in her study of his "existential fiction" in *Existential Thought and Fictional Techniques: Kierkegaard, Sartre, Beckett* (New Haven: Yale University Press, 1970). Despite her valuable discussion of Kierkegaard's elaborate use of personae to achieve distance from his characters, she fails to perceive the full implications of his disavowal of their views — especially of the views of his artists — which, as Josiah Thompson observes in "The Master of Irony," *Kierkegaard: A Collection of Critical Essays*, "if anything, . . . are the views he has outlived or outthought" (p. 112). She fails, in other words, to attend to Kierkegaard's avowal at the end of *The Concept of Dread* that irony must be mastered in behalf of the recovery of "actuality." Thus she sees his work as imperfect versions of the *Kunstlerroman* of the German Romantic tradition, in which the artist-hero transcends the messiness of temporal existence through the discovery of aesthetic form, i.e. an inclusive irony. In so

doing, she makes Kierkegaard, despite the imperfection of his form, a precursor of the "epiphanic" Modernist novel, of Proust's *A la recherche du temps perdu*, of Gide's *The Counterfeiters*, of James Joyce's *A Portrait of the Artist as a Young Man*, and even of Jean-Paul Sartre's *Nausea*, i.e., what I have called the novel of spatial form. One cannot help feeling that Ms. Kern has read Kierkegaard (and Sartre, for that matter) more from a Symbolist than from an existential point of view.

44   Wallace Stevens, "Notes toward a Supreme Fiction," *Collected Poems*, (New York: Alfred Knopf, 1961), p. 383.

45   *An Introduction to Metaphysics*, p. 32. For Heidegger's version of "repetition" as an aspect of the existential analytic (and for its dialogic implication for hermeneutics), see especially BT, 73, 432; SZ, 380-81.

46   Gotthold Lessing, *Laocoön: An Essay upon the Limits of Painting and Poetry*, trans. Ellen Frothingham (New York: Noonday Press, 1957), p. 91.

47   Joseph Frank, "Spatial Form in Modern Literature," *Sewanee Review*, 53 (Spring, Summer, Autumn 1945), 221-40, 433-45, 643-65; reprinted in *The Widening Gyre: Crisis and Mastery in Modern Literature* (New Brunswick, N.J.: Rutgers University Press, 1963), pp. 3-62. The quotation from Lessing occurs on page 7 of the latter.

48   Charles Olson, "The Human Universe," *Selected Writings*, ed. with introd. Robert Creeley (New York: New Directions, 1966), p. 54. The passage is worth quoting in full to suggest the remarkable parallel between the "postmodernism" of Heidegger and of the contemporary poet:

> We have lived long in a generalizing time, at least since 450 B.C. And it has had its effects on the best of men, on the best of things. Logos, or discourse [he means the derivative language of assertion], for example, has, in that time, so worked its abstractions into our concept and use of language that language's other function, speech, seems so in need of restoration that several of us go back to hieroglyphics or to ideograms to right the balance. (The distinction here is between language as the act of the instant and language as the act of thought about the instant.)

49   Here, of course, I am taking exception to Jacques Derrida's and Paul de Man's interpretation of the historical relationship between speech (*parole*) and writing (*écriture*). Where they find *presence* (a privileged origin) — and the model of Western literature — essentially in the speech act, I find presence (in the sense of spatializing time) — and the model of Western literary art — in writing, at least up until the present time. Thus whereas they call for the "free play" of *écriture* as the agency of surpassing metaphysics and metaphysical literature, I am suggesting with Heidegger in *Being and Time* and poets like Charles Olson that a postmodern literature and hermeneutics must ground itself in free speech, the speech which is the "act of an instant" of a being-in-the-world. Unlike the orality of, say, tribal ritual poetry, this kind of speech act, it must be emphasized, has its source not in presence (a substantial self), but, as Heidegger insists in *Being and Time,* in Nothingness, a groundless ground. I have, of course, vastly oversimplified a very complex issue — an issue that demands and hopefully will get fuller treatment soon. I refer to this issue here

147

simply to point out that Derrida's and de Man's Heidegger is not the Heidegger of *Being and Time* but a Heidegger interpreted (or deconstructed) through post-Structuralist eyes.

50   *Truth and Method*, see esp. pp. 330 ff., 344 ff., 487 ff. Indeed, this is the fundamental thesis of Gadamer's ironically entitled book. See also Richard Palmer, *Hermeneutics*, p. 168. It is especially the existential theologians — Barth, Bultmann, Fuchs, Ebeling, etc. — who have developed Heidegger's concept of Care into a dialogic hermeneutics. See, for example, James Robinson, "Hermeneutics since Barth," *The New Hermeneutic, New Frontiers in Theology*, II (New York: Harper and Row, 1964): With the development of hermeneutics from Karl Barth's *Romans* to Bultmann's "demythologizing,"

> the flow of the traditional relation between subject and object, in which the subject interrogates the object, and, if he masters it, obtains from it his answer, has been significantly reversed. For it is now the object — which should henceforth be called the subject matter — that puts the subject in question. This is true not simply at the formal level, in inquiring as to whether he understands himself aright, i.e., is serious, but also at the material level, in inquiring as to whether the text's answers illumine him. (pp. 23-24)

One of the most suggestive "theological" accounts of the "phenomenology of dialogue" is to be found in Heinrich Ott, "Hermeneutics and Personhood," in *Interpretation: The Poetry of Meaning*, pp. 14-33. Based on his "reading" of Dietrich Bonhoeffer, Ott's essay also presents the hermeneutic situation generated by the transformation of picture into voice as risk:

> It is not that I simply "consume" his thought. . . . In this case I simply would not yet have understood. Rather, my notions change and are forced open, my presuppositions are modified and my horizon widened; I gain new dimensions of understanding and expression. It is precisely by putting at stake what I bring with me into the encounter that I myself am changed and am lifted above what I bring as my own. (pp. 23-24)

Three Poems

by

Armand Schwerner

the point

don't be ambitious just do something you
are this calm person travelled you are this person
travelled by the grey rain cutting, you want
the blades of this rain cutting you, your left eye
pulses you are the servant of the pulse in your eye
you hold too tight to looking for what makes you move
when you walk when you eat your chicken-roll on rye
you are this person who walks and eats, flashing
from emptiness, no one
abandons you, there is no one
to abandon, you are simply this walker eating this eater
walking, one flash after another, the shoulders
shiver with awareness-pain, the hoarse throat
darkens, you forget your breathing which you had been,
every second you are at the point of death, can you imagine
stove or precipice or field of instantly killing mushrooms
but that's lust for a certification, where
is the ochre the brown world the comfort-giver, the securer
of breast and belly warmth? the beautiful lesson of Everything
Changes flashes in and out of nothingness
do you do your practice or do you find your practice
by discovering again every day how you walk, the
particular pressure on the right leg the rolling
of fear in the assertive swath you cannot
be abandoned there is no other life
to lust after can you imagine
the power of yourself center of the world, all
coming to you through your earned
emptiness? the blades of this rain
have nothing to pierce, you are this restfulness
of the constantly shifting water-body

blood

although this love appears as fresh water never there's
never been a drop of water never a drop
of water in it. but this blood, which transforms
the five poisons into the five knowledges, this blood
of great passion, passionless, free of passion,
this secret great blood, free of clinging. . . this blood
does not hanker after appearance. there's no giving, not any giving's
possible? the hungry ghost lusts for appearance. although
a hungry ghost appears as life-sap it wounds the space
as the secret great blood does not. is this true? this
I hate you draws a line. any authentic life
without a drawn line? no.
attack. fortification. self-gift. you/me, only this way, harshest giving
birth
not that there's no field for the giving, but the asking. . . the pus
tissues, neurone paths, body clamps, terror-heart heat firetongs,
sick old noble patience of understanding, compassion compassion
self-lies about ego-loss, noble noble noble
although the asking within the giving's infolded it is true
it must wound the space as it draws a line?
' if a man is not ready to face toil and risk
and in all gaiety of heart
his body will grow unshapely and his heart
lack the wild will that stirs desire.' or, 'we poets
begin in joy and gladness and descend therefrom
into despondency and madness.' or or or or or or.
or motto or proverb in the left rear pocket wallet or apothegm or or. dive
into your throat red thorough red be that red am I ready
to accept my throat as that throat
ready to accept me? all desire is shapely
when you see yourself as a god, when all your speech
is mantra, shapely viscous red lined cording throat.
to accept you as this person accepting herself, that's
the drawn line? red throat body chording. the secret
great blood turns the beautiful goddess body into
vibration. rainbow body. the school.

'a setting up in the unconcealed' (*Heidegger*)

'all works have this thingly character. what would they be without it?' care for
what you find, milk, wave, fluid air swim by Judith Weaver in Boulder doing Tai
Chi forms, blue streams of hunger and desperation from my body, sad wine of sadness
at giving up sadness, the peritonitis fear of giving up fear, my dog-whistle-pitch-
scream unassimilable by my body learning to be body. in the body the field of
desperation engenders the fruitful. so each day its own care? each day its own care.
sorge sorge sorge sorge. this poem-thing being poemed, can I 1975 be wisdom-poetry?
I can. 'to act compassionately is not to be overwhelmed by an emotion, but is always
to act feelingly and knowingly.' fill me I moan in the morning suck me cries the night
aloneness but the compassionate pirate stalks in his course which is his end.

by care,

the merit of the world, turn
the prose to singing, no holy whirlwind no
jubilee trumpet no blessed
gesture, but gesture shearing its own
possible names by the quick sword of its act
in the kitchen, let the holy blessed
whirlwind within the wind wither away and the ground
ground me, what I know I know in the vein
and the tendon, my other voices scare me I
let them my other voices
scare me I let them beautiful enemies my
lovers. high language again.
                a move-
ment dizzying motion nau-
sea seizure by verb radiant work
radiate act in the work act the work
see now seize the thing reveal in the
working in the working re-
turn within the work to heart and lymph *I was going to look for you
in the cafeteria* Margaret said, was going to look! o
language, darks of pastnesses in the tensions
of intentionality, was it hard? it pained? had it waited, this work,
on body decision, *sorge, sorge,* the unconcealment, to disclose? ask me I ask me me the endless stills
in the drunken mind ask
pardon. pardon me Margaret that I that is I say *now*
sudden heartfall knowledge you'd angered me it's me
could not tell *you.* bodhisattva bodhisattva I dream of you how
lock act and perception? me thingly or
me verbly bla bla, no, 'it,' the 'us' of the dark
sky of situation seizes in to-be-aware.

'had I left these images hidden
in the emotions, I might have been torn
to pieces by them.' dejection. sick of these
lessons will I never be quit
of these learnings not decent moral
gift sick charity but energy, 'to energy,' be the bad guy.
stomach pain of lies about letting my voices.
sick should should ought must sick ought should.
red heart *works* being poem white lymph
courses to *river* unconcealment.

Language and Silence:
Heidegger's Dialogue with Georg Trakl

Karsten Harries

I

Heidegger's interpretations of poetry have met with curiously mixed responses. This is particularly true of his Trakl essay, "Die Sprache im Gedicht" ("Language in the Poem").[1] Praised by some as offering profound insights into the work of the Austrian poet,[2] others have condemned it as a misinterpretation which presses fragments torn out of context into the service of Heidegger's own thought.[3] The task of deciding between such conflicting evaluations is made doubly difficult by the *hermetic* character of Trakl's poetry, which has invited and to some extent supported an extraordinary variety of often incompatible interpretations,[4] and by the circularity of Heidegger's *hermeneutic* approach, which may well lead one to wonder whether what is presented as a "thinking dialogue" between philosopher and poet is not rather a monologue in which Heidegger draws from Trakl's poetry only what he himself has placed there.

The mere fact that this poetry has invited so many different interpretations suggests at least that Trakl does not speak with just one voice. Even single poems are often too ambiguous to rule out different, even antithetical interpretations. Is such ambiguity only superficial, to be penetrated by more searching interpretation? Can we assume that a particular poem possesses one determinate meaning? Heidegger seems to deny this: to do justice to this poetry we have to do justice to its ambiguity (74). And yet, he himself tends to reduce the different voices of the poet to just one voice when he insists that the multiple meanings of what is said in different poems are gathered together by a deeper meaning which remains unspoken. Such single-mindedness, he asserts, provides a measure of the greatness of a poet: "Every great poet creates his poetry from one single poem" (37). It is this insight, or perhaps prejudice, which guides Heidegger's discussion and makes it an *Erörterung* in his sense, that is to say, an attempt "to consider (*erörtern*) the place (*Ort*) which gathers the poetic saying of Georg Trakl together into his poem, the place of his poem" (37).

If it is not to be arbitrary, such consideration must base itself on a careful listening to and interpreting of particular poems. But if Heidegger is right, such interpretation presupposes some consideration of the place of the poet's one poem. How is the interpreter to enter this circle? Must he not approach a particular poem with his own, perhaps inappropriate preconception, thus threatening to do violence to what the poem itself has to say? The question seems familiar. Is Heidegger's insistence on the "reciprocity between interpretation (*Erläuterung*) and consideration of the poem's place (*Erörterung*)" (38) more than a somewhat cryptically stated version of the by now familiar hermeneutic circle? Consider E. D. Hirsch's much clearer statement:

> The meaning of a text (or anything else) is a complex of submeanings or parts which hang together. . . . Thus the nature of a partial meaning is dependent on the nature of the whole meaning to which it belongs. From the standpoint of knowledge, therefore, we cannot perceive the meaning of a part until after we have grasped the meaning of the whole, since only then can we understand the function of the part within the whole. . . . Dilthey called this apparent paradox the hermeneutic circle and observed that it was not vicious because a genuine dialectic always occurs between our idea of the whole and our perception of the parts that constitute it. Once the dialectic has begun, neither side is totally determined by the other.[5]

The similarity between what Heidegger and Hirsch have to say is obvious enough: where Heidegger speaks of the reciprocity between the consideration of the place of the poet's one poem and the interpretation of particular poems, Hirsch speaks of the dialectic which "occurs between our idea of the whole and our perception of the parts that constitute it." There are, however, important differences. While Hirsch's statement of the hermeneutic circle is very general, Heidegger gives it a specific content and it is precisely this content which renders it questionable. By subordinating the unity of particular poems to the larger unity of the poet's one poem, Heidegger seems to challenge the traditional emphasis on the unity of the work of art. Should we approach the different poems of a poet as fragments demanding to be understood as parts of a larger whole? What lets us encounter a given manifold as a whole are expectations guided by established conventions. Thus a collection of sentences is read as a poem because of expectations guided by our idea of what a poem is. But what leads Heidegger to assume that to interpret a particular poem we must point beyond it to the place of the poet's one poem? Is this a hypothesis, to be verified by the poems themselves?

Any attempt at verification is discouraged by Heidegger's insistence that the poet's one poem remains unspoken. Heidegger's *Erörterung* claims to point towards what cannot finally be said and is yet the hidden meaning of the poet's work. There is nothing in Hirsch's formulation of the hermeneutic circle which suggests Heidegger's emphasis on the unspoken. Criticizing the "New Hermeneutic" of Heidegger and Gadamer, Hirsch insists that a literary text possesses a definite meaning which can be understood and expressed. Without this, interpretation could have no norms; criticism would turn itself into a kind of poetry. This is not to deny that our preliminary perception of what kind of a whole something is or what genre it belongs to will be vague and inarticulated.[6] But like a hypothesis in science, it can and should be made definite enough to be tested.

Heidegger would be the first not only to admit but to insist on the questionable character of his approach. His understanding of *Erörterung* is itself in need of interpretation and critical consideration. What justifies the assumption that a poem's true meaning remains unspoken? Must such an assumption not invite uncontrollable speculation and render interpretation without criteria and thus arbitrary? And what sense can we make of what Heidegger terms the place of the poet's one poem?

II

To answer the first question we have to consider, at least briefly, Heidegger's analysis of interpretation and language. In *Being and Time* Heidegger criticizes traditional ontology and its emphasis on the present, insisting instead on the importance of the future. Man, in his view, is essentially on the way, looking ahead and always engaged in some project or other. Similarly understanding is first of all not a detached noting of what is the case, but inseparably tied to what man is up to. Thus I understand the meaning of something when I know the different uses to which it can be put, when I can place it in the context of what Heidegger terms "the totality of such involvements." Every interpretation of what something is rests on an anticipation of such a context, where usually this context will be so intimately tied to our way of life that it is left unspoken and does not enter our explicit awareness. Unaware of the presuppositions guiding him, the interpreter may claim that he is simply exhibiting "what is there." But what is there "in the first instance is nothing other than the obvious undiscussed assumption of the person who does the interpreting."[7]

The circularity of interpretation cannot be avoided. It has its foundation in man's being, which is an anticipating being towards what he is to be. But even though we cannot step outside the hermeneutic circle, Heidegger denies that this circularity shuts us off from any real understanding of what is as it is.

> In the circle is hidden a positive possibility of the most primordial kind of knowing. To be sure, we genuinely take hold of this possibility only when, in our interpretation, we have understood that our first, last, and constant task is never to allow our fore-having, fore-sight, and fore-conception to be presented to us by fancies and popular conceptions, but rather to make the scientific theme secure by working out these fore-structures in terms of the things themselves.[8]

This last demand is difficult to meet, given the necessity of bringing to what is understood a preconception of the relevant context. There is a constant danger that our preconception will hide rather than reveal what is to be interpreted. Only as long as this preconception remains questionable and as such invites revision does the interpreter remain free to respond to what he is interpreting, does the interpretation remain a dialogue. Adequate interpretation must preserve the tension between what the interpreter brings to the interpretation and what is to be interpreted.

It is precisely in the preservation of this tension that authentic interpretation, indeed all authentic discourse, differs from our usual ways of interpreting. Usually language and being are so intimately tied together that the thought that language might be the prison rather than the house of being is not even entertained.

> In the language which is spoken when one expresses oneself, there lies an average intelligibility; and in accordance with this intelligibility the discourse which is communicated can be understood to a considerable

extent, even if the hearer does not bring himself into such a kind of Being towards what the discourse is about as to have a primordial understanding of it. We do not so much understand the entities which are talked about; we already are listening only to what is said-in-the-talk as such. What is said-in-the-talk gets understood; but what the talk is about is understood only approximately and superficially. We have *the same thing* in view, because it is in *the same* averageness that we have a common understanding of what is said.[9]

If Heidegger is right, language is first of all and most of the time *Gerede,* "idle talk." The term is somewhat unfortunate in that it suggests a particular misuse of language. Consider how often we speak, not because there is something to be said, but because we are expected to say something; so we speak of this and that, of the weather, of friends, of the marital problems of Mr. and Mrs. X — what we are talking about matters little. Thus when Wittgenstein likens the way philosophers use language to "an engine idling," he thinks of language which no longer functions as part of a language-game, where "language-game" is understood as "the whole, consisting of language and the actions into which it is woven."[10] Heidegger is thinking of a much more fundamental phenomenon. "Idle talk" refers to language which does function as part of a language-game which in its entirety is taken for granted. We do what one does, say what one says. The language of the everyday is "idle talk."

But what then is authentic discourse? Must we not speak as one speaks if we are to speak at all? It is difficult to find an answer in *Being and Time.* Heidegger does discuss the call of conscience as a mode of authentic discourse. Here the silent caller is the individual himself who calls himself back to his own essence. Should we say then that authentic discourse takes place in silence and is monological? Or can authentic discourse be understood in other ways? In *Being and Time* we find no more than a few hints which point towards the possibility of authentic dialogue.[11] What language would such dialogue use other than the inauthentic language of the everyday? Or does it use that language, placing it against the background of the unsaid so that language continuously suffers shipwreck? Think of the conversation of two people in love: it may seem difficult to imagine anything sillier and more superficial. Yet perhaps this is itself a superficial view which mistakes the verbal surface for the whole. The real meaning of such discourse remains unspoken.

Heidegger knows that man cannot rid himself of inauthenticity. Authenticity is only a way of taking up the inauthenticity which is constitutive of man as a being with others.[12] Similarly, authentic speech must base itself on established language, but in such a way that this establishment becomes questionable and its inadequacy is revealed.

Interpretation remains authentic only as long as it preserves the tension between an inevitably public language and what that language leaves unsaid. Such interpretation cannot pretend to adequacy, but must render itself questionable, and thus open itself to what the text to be interpreted has to say. Rendering itself questionable, interpretation becomes dialogue.[13] It is for this reason that Heidegger reminds his readers in the beginning of "Language in the Poem" that the most that his discussion of Trakl's poetry can accomplish is that it will make our listening to the poet "questionable," that is, open to the possibility that the preconceptions with which we approach this poetry may have to be abandoned. Thus our listening may become "more thoughtful" (39).

But if interpretation must preserve its own questionable character, it must also recognize that "because the understanding which develops in interpretation has the structure of a projection" it cannot but do violence to what is to be interpreted. But violence must also be turned against "the claims of everyday interpretation" and shake "its tranquillized obviousness."[14] Since the tendency to cover things up is inseparable from everyday understanding, an interpretation which seeks to penetrate the veil which such understanding casts over things must risk doing violence to what is usually taken for granted.

If the interpreter must preserve the tension between the spoken and the unspoken, this is even more true of the poet. Heidegger's insistence that to understand what is really said in the poem we have to listen beyond what our usual understanding would take to have been said and into the unspoken, follows from his view of poetry as authentic discourse. Caught up in idle talk, man is shut up in a prison which he himself has fashioned and from which there seems to be no exit. We can escape only if we open ourselves to the violence which language must do to what is, and thus pass beyond it. Heidegger understands poetry as discourse which, by preserving the silence in which the unspoken communicates itself, reveals the essential violence and thus the inadequacy of language.

III

All these considerations have done little to justify what is perhaps most questionable about Heidegger's Trakl interpretation: his presupposition that what remains unspoken in Trakl's different poems is the poet's one poem. Later I shall consider briefly the question whether this presupposition does indeed receive support from Trakl's poetry. But whether it does or not cannot finally establish or shake Heidegger's claim that the different poems of any great poet are gathered into one unspoken poem. What leads Heidegger to make this claim? In the present essay we are given neither justification nor explanation. Hints of an answer are, however, provided by the analysis of meaning offered in *Being and Time.*

As already pointed out, to understand the meaning of something I must be able to locate it in its proper context; I must know where it belongs, its place. E.g., to understand the point of a particular sequence of moves in a chess game I must not only know the rules of the game, but also anticipate what the players are up to. Only such anticipation allows me to gather what first presents itself as an opaque manifold into a meaningful whole. And yet, the meaning of this whole will itself remain obscure as long as I do not understand the point of playing chess. Such understanding demands that what is to be understood be placed in a wider context. I can push my search for meaning further and further until I arrive at a final context which cannot be surpassed: the way the individual exists in the world and pursues his own being. Man's being, pursued as a task, is the one unspoken meaning which gathers what would otherwise be a collection of fragments into one life. In Heidegger's view, man exists authentically when, in resolute anticipation of his death, he rescues himself from the tendency of the everyday to scatter him into different roles and activities, seizes himself in his entirety, and thus exists as a whole. There is thus a sense in which the different things the authentic person says and does have one meaning.

If poetry is a form of authentic discourse, the different poems of a poet are joined together by a common meaning. This is not to say that they should be considered parts of a whole in the sense in which sentences could be said to be parts of a poem. What Heidegger calls the poet's one poem is not a thing which could ever be. Yet if his interpretation of poetry as authentic discourse is right, the poet's different poems do belong together. Their interpretation must therefore base itself on a consideration of the place which is the hidden origin of this togetherness.

IV

Heidegger determines the place of Trakl's poetry as *die Abgeschiedenheit,* "apartness."

All saying of the poems of Georg Trakl remains oriented towards the wandering stranger. He is and is called "he who has parted" (*der Abgeschiedene*). Through and around him the poetic saying is tuned to a single song. Because the poems of this poet are gathered in the song of "him who has parted," we call the place of his poetry "apartness" (*die Abgeschiedenheit*). (52)

Who is *der Abgeschiedene*? What is this *Abgeschiedenheit* of which Trakl and Heidegger speak? A first answer to these questions is provided by fragments taken from Trakl's poetry. Interpreting them, Heidegger understands the *Abgeschiedene* as one who has taken leave from the community. He is no longer with us but stands alone and apart, a stranger. Interpreting Trakl, Heidegger calls what the *Abgeschiedene* has left behind *der bisherige Mensch,* "man as he has been up to now." "Man as he has been up to now falls apart (*verfällt*), in so far as he loses his essence (*Wesen*), i.e., decays (*verwest*)" (46). The term *verfällt* recalls Heidegger's thesis in *Being and Time* that, being with others, man is essentially falling (*verfallend*). The way we usually speak is witness to this fall. As pointed out above, to become the property of several, language "must make itself common," must become idle talk.[15] Losing himself to the common, man loses his essence, decays.

The *Abgeschiedene* listens to a silence which calls him from beyond the world of the everyday back to himself. Obedient to its call, he loses touch with the common sense of the established and accepted. Measured by this sense, what he thinks is nonsense. Thus he is called a madman.

> The madman thinks (*sinnt*), and he even thinks with an intensity shared by no one else. But he remains without the sense (*Sinn*) of the others. He is of another mind (*Sinn*). "*Sinnan*" means originally: to travel, to strive for . . . , to take a certain direction; the Indogermanic root *sent* and *set* means "way." "He who has parted" is also the madman, because he is on his way to quite another place. (53)

Where is the stranger going? His going is said to be a going under, a going unto death (46). Yet going under is not tied here to disintegration or destruction.

> Losing himself, he disappears *in* (*in der*), but in no way *into* (*in die*) the destruction wrought by November. He glides through it, away into the spiritual twilight of the blue, "to vesper," i.e., towards evening. (51)

Throughout this essay many of the words Heidegger uses are borrowed from Trakl while at the same time the way they are used and even the words themselves lead us back to Heidegger's own earlier works. This results in a certain ambiguity: who is speaking? The poet or the philosopher? There is no clear answer; the reader is left disoriented. As so often when reading the later Heidegger, we wish for a more precise statement or a translation. But although I will try to provide what may at times seem like such a translation, a warning is in order: what does it mean to offer a translation? To do so we have to use words which have their place in some familiar language, words whose meanings we already know. This poses the danger that the unspoken which is the soul of genuine dialogue and interpretation will be concealed by the familiarity of what has been said. The deliberate ambiguity of Heidegger's language helps to guard against this. While it appears to force the language of poetry and philosophy into an illegitimate fusion, it preserves their tension. This tension prevents the reader from resting content with what he is given. He is forced to struggle and only as long as this struggle is preserved is reading also genuine thinking. This discussion would serve Heidegger ill if it were to be read as an adequate translation of what has been said into a more readily understood idiom.

The wandering stranger is said to disappear *in*, but in no way *into* the destruction wrought by November. November is a time when what has been established by the preceding seasons is being torn away. It is the time of the year's approaching end. And yet, by his readiness to take leave from that world, the stranger appears to escape destruction. He moves through it, towards evening. "Evening" recalls November, but it suggests something more gentle; it also suggests more strongly the thought of repetition — an evening is one of many. Night, which follows evening, is not only the end of day, but also a period of rest which prepares for a new beginning.

Following Trakl, Heidegger speaks of *die geistliche Nacht*, "the spiritual night." Spiritual is related to spirit (*Geist*), spirit to flame. "The flaming is that which, being outside itself (*Ausser-sich*), opens and lights up the dark, but also can continue to attack and devour everything, leaving only the white of ashes" (60). Again the language suggests *Being and Time* as much as Trakl. In *Being and Time* temporality is called "the primodial 'outside-of-itself' in and for itself."[16] Ahead of himself anticipating the future, behind himself remembering the past, beyond himself putting himself in the place of others, man is essentially outside and at a distance from himself. Spirit is thus a name for the ecstatic essence of man. As ecstatic existence, man lights the world and lets it be seen. Thus he is the clearing of Being.

As Heidegger insists, this being open has to be understood not statically, as the metaphor of the clearing suggests,[17] but dynamically as care. Caring for himself and what he is to be, man is first of all ahead of himself. Ahead of himself he anticipates his own death. Spirit and death are thus linked: as spirit, man journeys unto death, even when in dread of this goal he hides the nature of this journey and thus his own essence from himself. And yet, the anticipation of death is not so much an anticipation of decay and destruction, as it is a leave-taking from the "decayed shape of man" (46). By revealing how inescapably man's life is his own, the anticipation of death prevents man from losing himself to the familiar world and to what one says and does. Man's dread of death creates a distance from things which lets him stand in their midst with more open eyes, while at the same time it recalls him to himself. Only by affirming himself in his being unto death can man exist as a whole.[18]

In the Trakl essay the blue night plays the part which in *Being and Time* is given to death: to heal man by calling him out of the world to which he has lost himself and back to his essence, i.e., spirit. In this sense night is called spiritual. But compared with death, night also has another and more positive meaning. Night not only means what puts an end to day; it means the limit of day which not only follows but precedes it. Thus it circumscribes day, making it visible in its entirety. Night is the origin and end of all establishment.[19]

Evening lets us anticipate the coming of night. Teaching us that things cannot go on as they have, it lets us see things differently. It creates a distance from established ways of life and speech and reveals them to have their ground in the night, although perhaps we should not speak here of "ground"; in that it withdraws whenever an attempt is made to grasp it, this ground is unlike what traditional philosophy sought when it asked for a ground, a firmly established foundation for further construction. If ground is understood in this way, the night is not *Grund,* but *Abgrund,* abyss.

The journey of the parted stranger has led him beyond the established and taken for granted towards what precedes and follows establishment. Since for man to be is to be with others, joined to them by a common established order, the wandering stranger cannot be. Thus he is called both, dead and unborn.

It should have become clear that when Heidegger, interpreting Trakl, is speaking of the *Abgeschiedene* or the wandering stranger he is not speaking of an individual who could ever exist. Perhaps we come closer to what he has in mind when we take the *Abgeschiedene* to express the ideal of an existence fully obedient to the call of the blue night. Certainly the *Abgeschiedene* is not the poet. The poet only follows his call.

> The poet becomes poet only in so far as he follows that "madman" who died away into the time of the beginning (*die Frühe*) and out of the apartness (*Abgeschiedenheit*) calls with melodious steps the brother following him. (73)

Poetry communicates the poet's journey away from the established community into the night. The language of poetry has its place in-between idle talk and silence.[20] It is a recovery of silence in the midst of idle talk. As this recovery, poetry presupposes more familiar language. Thus we may seem to know what the words of the poet mean, yet familiar words no longer function as they usually do; we know and don't know what is being said. In poetry, language reveals its essential ambiguity. The poem places what it names before a background of silence, yet not to hide that background, as would idle talk, but to return us to it. Thus its life resides in the tension between what has been said and what has remained unspoken.

The poem is like a vesper bell which breaks the silence of evening

164

and yet in breaking it lets it be heard; or like the steps of one disappearing into the night.

V

Again and again Heidegger speaks simply of "poetry" and "the poet." Is this to say that his determination of the place of Trakl's poetry is at the same time a determination of the place of poetry? This is at least suggested when Heidegger speaks in the plural of those who carry the silent music of the stranger into spoken language and thus become poets (70). But elsewhere Heidegger speaks of *Abgeschiedenheit* as the place of just one poem, of that poem which finds expression in Trakl's poetry. The reader is left with the ambiguity which announces itself already in the tension between the essay's title and subtitle: "Language in the Poem: A Discussion of Georg Trakl's Poem." Is Heidegger's determination of the essence of Trakl's poetry a determination of the essence of poetry?

Heidegger's own earlier attempts to exhibit the essence of poetry suggest a negative answer. In "Hölderlin and the Essence of Poetry," Heidegger defines poetry as "the inaugural naming of Being and of the essence of all things — not just any speech, but that particular kind which for the first time brings into the open all that which we then discuss and deal with in everyday language."[21] From this definition it follows that "poetry never takes language as a raw material ready to hand, rather it is poetry which first makes language possible."[22] Far from being a late luxury, parasitic on other language, our usual ways of speaking are said to have their foundation in poetry. And since man's dwelling in the world is also a dwelling in language, poetry can be said to reveal to man his world.

Heidegger has spelled out the revelatory power of poetry and art in a number of places, most completely perhaps in "The Origin of the Work of Art." In this essay Heidegger is speaking first of all of the visual arts, but all art is taken by him to be poetry in a wider sense, i.e., work revealing Being; furthermore all other work depends on poetry understood as the work of language. The latter follows if we agree with Heidegger that "language alone brings what is, as something that is, into the Open for the first time."[23]

Poetry in its wider sense is the establishment of Being in a work of art. Heidegger offers the example of a Greek temple. Establishing Being, such work establishes a world. "World" may not be understood here to mean the totality of facts. We come closer to what Heidegger has in mind if we think of a space of intelligibility: world is the context which assigns to man, to the gods, and to things their proper places. It is "the ever-nonobjective to which we are subject as long as the paths of birth and death, blessing and curse keep us transported into Being."[24]

As Heidegger emphasizes, only one side of the poetic establishment of Being is grasped when we understand it as an establishment of a world. Equally important is its other side: establishing a world, the work must also present the earth. What is meant here by earth? Perhaps more traditional formulations can help to point towards what Heidegger has in mind. To know what something is, is to know its place in some logical or linguistic space. This place is never so fully determined that it could not also be occupied by some other, very similar thing. The linguistic measures which we bring to reality, for instance when we call something a "tree," cannot capture what we see before us in its concrete individuality, but only in certain respects which make it comparable to other objects. This limitation is not a shortcoming of language, but its very point. In language, revelation and concealment must go together. Together they disclose the rift which separates language and reality. Just as the material presence of the object prevents language from fully penetrating and subjecting it so that some opacity will always remain, so by forcing what is to be known into our linguistic molds we prevent what is from showing itself to us as it is. Heidegger's term "earth" points towards the irreducible opacity which attends like a shadow all our knowledge of the real.

Poetry, according to Heidegger, is the instigation of a struggle between earth and world. He speaks of a struggle rather than of a resting together, because earth and world are unavoidably in tension. In so far as the establishment of a world is a making overt, it must also conceal the dimension of the hidden. Such concealment easily leads to a total forgetting of the earth, as it does, for instance, when science, misunderstanding its own essence, tries to grasp what is without loss.[25] Indeed all language poses a threat to the earth. Caught up in already established and taken for granted ways of speaking, we overhear the silent call of the other dimension. Having become a common and unquestioned possession, language tends to obscure the world's struggle with the earth. But this struggle must be preserved if man is to exist authentically, open to his own being and to the being of what is. Such preservation requires poetry.

How does Heidegger's determination of the place of Trakl's poetry agree with this twofold determination of the essence of poetry as establishment of a world and presentation of the earth? At least the latter is suggested by Heidegger's characterization of the poet as journeying towards the night. Night and earth point in the same direction. This relationship is made explicit by Heidegger's interpretation of Trakl's words: *Es ist die Seele ein Fremdes auf Erden.*

> The poet calls the soul "something strange on earth."
> The earth is precisely the place to which the soul in her wandering so far has not been able to get. The soul only *seeks* the earth, it does not flee from it. It wanders and thus seeks the earth so that it may build and dwell

poetically on the earth and only thus save the earth *as*
the earth: this fulfills the soul's essence. (41)

Since man has permitted himself to become absorbed in the established
and accepted, poetry, if it is to save the earth, has to bid us take leave
from our familiar ways of speaking. The poet must tear such language if he
is to let us hear the silence in which the earth communicates itself to us.

But can Trakl's poetry also be said to establish a world? The
answer would appear to be negative. "World" is used only once in the
essay to indicate the fallen world of modern man from which the poet bids
us to take leave (80). Take leave for what? Does Trakl offer us a new
world to take the place of that world which we are to leave behind?
Heidegger's characterization of Trakl as the poet of the still hidden
occident (*Abendland*) offers only an ambiguous answer.

VI

The going under of the stranger who has parted from the familiar
and accepted is a journeying towards the night. The land of his wandering
belongs thus to evening. "The location of the place which gathers Trakl's
poem into itself is the hidden essence of apartness and is called 'occident'
(*Abendland*)" (77). Once again Heidegger takes a critical term from Trakl,
who calls one of his poems "Abendland," a second "Abendländisches
Lied." Playing with the title of Oswald Spengler's *Der Untergang des
Abendlandes,* while opposing the pessimism expressed in that work,
Heidegger once more links the themes of ending and beginning, of going
under and crossing over.

The occident (*Abendland*) hidden in apartness
is not going under, but remains, waiting for its
inhabitants as the land of the going under into the
spiritual night. The land of the going under is the
crossing over into the beginning of the dawn which lies
hidden in it. (77)

Abendland no longer means here the Western world, but the land of
evening in Heidegger's sense. As such, it is the land of the transition from
day to night, where night has to be understood as end and as beginning.
Thus Heidegger calls apartness "the beginning of a rising world year, not
the abyss of decay" (77). This determines Trakl's place as a place
in-between: between the platonic Christian world and a world which
remains to be established and whose shape and essence are still hidden.
The poet lacks the strength to establish this world. He only prepares us for
such establishment by calling us out of our decayed world back to the
earth and to its silence. Measured by Heidegger's own determination of art

as the establishment of a world and the presentation of the earth, Trakl's work must be found lacking. But if Heidegger is right, this lack is not one the poet could have overcome. It has its foundation in his age, an age shaped by the triumph of metaphysics. What is metaphysics and what does it have to do with poetry? An adequate answer cannot be developed within the limits of this essay, but an answer must at least be sketched if we are to understand why Heidegger sees modern poetry and art tending towards silence.

Metaphysics is an attempt to grasp and to secure Being. The attack on the hidden, on what Heidegger terms the earth, is thus part of its essence. The metaphysical tendency reaches its final stage, decisive for the shape of our world, with Descartes. Man's reason is made the measure of reality: only what can be known clearly and distinctly can be said to be and what can be known in this manner can also be manipulated. Metaphysics triumphs over the earth, and thus over Being, in technology. Losing the earth, man loses his own essence to his domineering spirit and decays. "Today a man without uniform already makes the impression of the uncanny, which no longer belongs."[26]

If there is to be art in the full sense of the word, there must first be an openness to the earth. Having banished mystery and opacity from reality, we no longer live in a world which allows for such openness. Our world cannot offer a dimension which would allow the silent call of the earth to be heard. This makes the recovery of this other dimension a task which forces the artist to take leave from the world. Trakl's poetry communicates such a leave-taking.

If this analysis is accepted, it becomes difficult to consider the place which gathers Trakl's poems into one poem as the poet's own. It belongs as much to Heidegger's Hölderlin, and indeed to all who attempt to save the earth and man's essence in this age of need and thus form "*one* generation" (*E i n Geschlecht*) (78), joined by their willingness to follow the one who has parted and thus belonging to the land of evening.[27] Heidegger, too, belongs to this community. His own attempt to step beyond the history of metaphysics and to take leave from the "wasteland of the devastated earth"[28] makes him, too, a follower of the wandering stranger. The place of Trakl's poetry appears thus to be that of Heidegger's own thinking.

VII

By insisting on the violence of all interpretation, but also on the necessity of keeping ourselves open to "the things themselves," Heidegger invites us to question this conclusion. Are the place of poet and thinker really the same and is it this which makes their dialogue possible? Or has Heidegger done violence to Trakl's poetry? Is what is presented as a dialogue in fact a monologue?

168

Only a careful consideration of Trakl's work could do justice to these questions. But even a cursory look at particular poems suggests that Trakl is not of one mind and does not speak with one voice. Besides that in the end hopeful voice which Heidegger hears, there are others, often dark and despairing, linking decay to incest and a very personal guilt and suffering which no longer hopes for redemption. Heidegger does not hear this despair, perhaps because he is too ready to listen beyond the poet's words to his unspoken meaning. This leads us back to what is most questionable about Heidegger's interpretation. Not only in this essay do we meet with a tendency to sacrifice the multiplicity and tensions of what is to be interpreted to a higher unspoken unity which must remain abstract and empty.

Perhaps Heidegger's demand that the interpretation of particular poems be informed by a discussion of the place of the poet's one unspoken poem should be carried to this interpretation of Heidegger's essay. What is the place of Heidegger's own thought towards which all of his works point? I have suggested that the place which Heidegger assigns to Trakl is in fact his own. This is not to say that Heidegger is simply reading into Trakl's poetry his own subjective prejudice. The place of Heidegger's thinking can only be understood when it is linked to the place of his and Trakl's generation. As Karl Löwith points out, the power of Heidegger's analyses and interpretations is at least in part due to the fact that they always carry "the signature of our age."[29] The best interpretation of the place of Heidegger's thought is furnished by Heidegger himself. To the extent that our world is, as Heidegger describes it, a one-dimensional prison which shuts man off from the earth and thus from his own essence, man must take leave from that world if he is to save himself. And if this world is *the* world for us, this leave-taking must be a journey towards silence. The fascination with silence in modern music, art, and poetry suggests that this description of our world is not too far off the mark. Still, it is too one-sided to do justice to the different ways in which we are claimed and moved, often in incompatible directions. The metaphysical-technological world which Heidegger sketches is not the world in which we live, although it is perhaps the leading theme of our world and often the power of this theme is so great that it becomes difficult to hear other voices. Heidegger's dialogue with Georg Trakl is witness to this difficulty.

Yale University

NOTES

1   *Unterwegs zur Sprache* (Pfullingen: Günther Neske, 1959), pp. 37-82. Trans. Peter D. Hertz, "Language in the Poem. A Discussion on Georg Trakl's Poetic Work," *On the Way to Language* (New York: Harper & Row, 1971), pp.

159-198. Page references in the text are to the German edition. The translations are my own.

2   See Alfred Focke, *Georg Trakl. Liebe und Tod* (Wien und München: Herold, 1955), and Eduard Lachmann, *Kreuz und Abend. Eine Interpretation der Dichtungen Georg Trakls* (Salzburg: O. Müller, 1954).

3   See Walter Muschg, "Zerschwatzte Dichtung," *Die Zerstörung der deutschen Literatur* (München: List, n.d.), pp. 172-184, and W. H. Rey, "Heidegger — Trakl: Einstimmiges Zwiegespräch," *Deutsche Vierteljahrsschrift für Literaturwissenschaft und Geistesgeschichte,* 30 (1956), 89-136.

4   Helga Cierpka, "Interpretationstypen der Trakl-Literatur," Diss. Berlin, 1963.

5   E. D. Hirsch, Jr., *Validity in Interpretation* (New Haven and London: Yale University Press, 1967), p. 259.

6   *Validity in Interpretation*, p. 259.

7   *Sein und Zeit,* 7th ed. (Tübingen: M. Niemeyer Verlags 1953), p. 150. Trans. John Macquarrie and Edward Robinson (New York and Evanston: Harper & Row, 1962).

8   *Sein und Zeit,* p. 153.

9   *Sein und Zeit,* p. 168.

10   *Philosophical Investigations,* tr. G. E. M. Anscombe (New York: Macmillan, 1953), pars. 132 and 7.

11   See the suggestion that the resolute person can become the conscience of others (p. 298) and especially the claim that authentic existence requires communication and struggle to let the power of its destiny become free (pp. 384-5). Unfortunately, Heidegger has nothing to say about the nature of such communication.

12   *Sein und Zeit,* p. 179.

13   See *Was heisst Denken?* (Tübingen: M. Niemeyer, 1961), p. 110. "But authentic dialogue is never mere conversation. In mere conversation one glides along what has been said and does not get involved with the unspoken. Most interpretations of texts . . . remain in the realm of mere conversation, which is often many-sided and informative. In many cases this is sufficient."

14   *Sein und Zeit,* p. 311.

15   *Erläuterungen zu Hölderlins Dichtung,* 2nd ed. (Frankfurt: V. Klostermann, 1951), pp. 34-35.

16   *Sein und Zeit,* p. 329.

17   This metaphor shows particularly well the nature of Heidegger's own use of language. Traditionally, discussions of understanding and consciousness have always used a vocabulary of distance and of light, without making explicit its

170

metaphorical character. Heidegger joins these two themes in one metaphor and thereby forces us to consider what it is that they point to.

18   See *Sein und Zeit,* pp. 301-333.

19   See *Erläuterungen zu Hölderlins Dichtung,* p. 104.

20   Hugo Friedrich's analysis of the function of silence in modern poetry, especially in the poetry of Mallarmé, suggests that what Heidegger finds in Trakl's poetry is characteristic of much poetry in our time. See *Die Struktur der modernen Lyrik* (Hamburg: Rowohlt, 1956).

21   *Erläuterungen zu Hölderlins Dichtung,* p. 40. Trans. Douglas Scott, "Hölderlin and the Essence of Poetry," *Existence and Being* (Chicago: Henry Regnery, 1960), p. 283.

22   *Erläuterungen zu Hölderlins Dichtung,* p. 40, trans. p. 283.

23   *Holzwege* (Frankfurt: V. Klostermann, 1950), p. 60. Tr. Albert Hofstadter, *Poetry, Language, Thought* (New York: Harper & Row, 1971), p. 73.

24   *Holzwege,* p. 33, trans. p. 44.

25   See *Holzwege,* p. 36, tr. p. 47. "Earth thus shatters every attempt to penetrate into it. It causes every merely calculating importunity upon it to turn into a destruction. This destruction may herald itself under the appearance of mastery and of progress in the form of the technical-scientific objectivation of nature, but this mastery nevertheless remains an impotence of will. The earth appears openly cleared as itself only when it is perceived and preserved as that which is by nature undisclosable, that which shrinks from every disclosure and constantly keeps itself closed up."

26   *Vorträge und Aufsätze* (Pfullingen: Günther Neske, 1954), p. 26

27   See W. H. Rey's very critical discussion of Heidegger's interpretation of Trakl's *Abendländisches Lied,* an interpretation which places all the emphasis on just two words: *Ein Geschlecht.* "Heidegger — Trakl: Einstimmiges Zwiegespräch," p. 131.

28   *Vorträge und Aufsätze,* p. 97.

29   Heidegger, *Denker in dürftiger Zeit,* 2nd ed. (Göttingen: Vandenhoeck & Ruprecht, 1960), p. 110.

Situating René Char:
Hölderlin, Heidegger, Char and the "There Is"

Reiner Schürmann

> To *situate* means here first of all to point out the
> proper place or site of something. Secondly it means,
> to heed that place or site. These two methods, placing
> and heeding, are both preliminaries to a topology.
> And yet it will require all our daring to take no more
> than these preliminary steps in what follows. The
> topology, as befits a path of thought, ends in a
> question. That question asks for the location of the
> site.
>
> — Martin Heidegger

We want to situate Char's poetry. Neither the poet himself nor
the literary critic raises the question of the site. To situate a script, that is,
a way of writing determined by an understanding of being, one has to give
some thought to the locus out of which the poet speaks and writes. Where
do poets like René Char and Saint John Perse or, also, novelists like Peter
Handke stand if their script and speech hint at an experience with language
that seems already somehow familiar to us and yet still foreign, strange,
too "avant-garde"? To situate a work of prose or poetry is to raise the
question of its beginning: where is the place from which the script
originates? Although such an elucidation cannot be the explicit
preoccupation of the poet himself, this does not deny him any reflective
knowledge of his own undertakings; he is not the dumb mouth of destiny.
Rather his experience with language is probably more immediate than the
philosopher's — so immediate that the question of the origin of the poetic
script will finally throw us back upon the humble, historically
conditioned, always over-determined experience with our mother-tongue.

To situate René Char's poetry, to question the place or site from
which it arises, requires a historical framework. Even within contemporary
literature, a post-war poet cannot write any longer as did Rimbaud, or a
post-war novelist as did Musil: in half a century our experience with
language has mutated. In poetry René Char is among those today whose
script manifests the threshold between a former ("modern" and therefore
still metaphysical or representational) experience of language and a
present or perhaps imminent ("postmodern," beyond metaphysical,
non-representational) experience of language and being. The historical
framework of this topology of René Char's poetry will remain somehow
implicit; it is that of the history of metaphysics. Char's script is localized
in relation to this history and to its end.

Henri Matisse, "The Shark and the Gull"

"In May 1946 I sent the manuscript of the poem 'The Shark and the Gull' to Henri Matisse at Vence. During the visit that I had paid to the great painter we had not spoken of any poem in particular. I had convinced myself that Matisse was well and that his treasures continued being executed with the same sumptuous regularity as usual. Back at l'Isle-sur-Sorgue I sent him the manuscript of my poem (I love Matisse and his discrete goodness: this poem to thank him for a precise act). He answered me that in a recent series of drawings he had *discovered* the same theme. Here is one of these drawings."

René Char*

Here is one of Char's best known poems, "Le requin et la mouette" ("The Shark and the Gull"), not previously translated into English:[1]

Je vois enfin la mer dans sa triple harmonie, la mer qui tranche de son croissant la dynastie des douleurs absurdes, la grande voilère sauvage, la mer crédule comme un liseron.

Quand je dis: *j'ai levé la loi, j'ai franchi la morale, j'ai maillé le coeur*, ce n'est pas pour me donner raison devant ce pèse-néant dont la rumeur étend sa palme au delà de ma persuasion. Mais rien de ce qui m'a vu vivre et agir jusqu'ici n'est témoin alentour. Mon épaule peut bien sommeiller, ma jeunesse accourir. C'est de cela seul qu'il faut tirer richesse immédiate et opérante. Ainsi, il y a un jour de pur dans l'année, un jour qui creuse sa galerie merveilleuse dans l'écume de la mer, un jour qui monte aux yeux pour couronner midi. Hier la noblesse était déserte, le rameau était distant de ses bourgeons. Le requin et la mouette ne communiquaient pas.

O Vous, arc-en-ciel de ce rivage polisseur, approchez le navire de son espérance. Faites que toute fin supposée soit une neuve innocence, un fiévreux en avant pour ceux qui trébuchent dans la matinale lourdeur. (FM, 197)[2]

(At last I see the triple harmony of the sea, whose crescent cuts the dynasty of absurd sufferings, the great wild aviary, the sea, credulous as a bindweed.

When I say: *I overcame the law, I transgressed morality, I unfurled the heart*, it is not to justify myself before this weigher of nothingness whose murmur extends its victory palm beyond my persuasion. But nothing that has seen me live and act hitherto is witness here. My shoulder may well sleep, my youth come running. From these alone immediate and operative riches must be drawn. Thus there is one day of purity in the year, a day that hollows its marvelous gallery into the sea-foam, a day that mounts into the eyes to crown the noon. Yesterday nobility was desert, the branch was distant from its swelling buds. The shark and the gull did not communicate.

Oh You, rainbow of this polishing shore, bring the ship closer to its hope. Make every supposed end be a new innocence, a feverish advance for those who stumble in the morning heaviness.)

A first group of images speaks of the sea which appears triply immense: by the thickness of its water, the width of its front, and the depth of the horizon. The "crescent" of the sea cuts suffering: it traces a bulging line like a woman before childbirth. The sea is the "great wild aviary," it encloses life. Here everything is heavy. The water attracts the stroller and invites him to plunge. Gravitation makes his sufferings fall. At the same time the water is soft. It offers no resistance. It is "credulous as a bindweed." These little winding lilies with slender, twining stems bend and yield to the wind, and when the breeze is strong they even roll themselves up. Thus the sea. Its waves follow the impulses of the atmosphere. The sea is straight horizontality, the continuous shelter, the volume of one piece whose docility welcomes living beings as a refuge. This insistence on the weightiness in which life originates and is regenerated does not go beyond traditional figures of aquatic symbolism. In Char it is inspired by the sight of the Mediterranean.[3] We shall see that the entire oceanic symbolism is here a pre-text before the real text.

This first type of imagery is opposed by another. *"I overcame the law. . . ."* This sentence is printed in italics. To overcome, to transgress, to unfurl: these verbs break the oceanic horizontality. They indicate a rebellion. The law overcome, morality transgressed: thus the maternal order represented by the sea is broken. Aquatic symbols are ambiguous, since the water gives life and purifies but also drowns and kills. Char calls the sea the "weigher of nothingness." No shelter resembles the matrix more than the tomb. "I unfurled the heart": against the seductive rumor the "I" stands up as if about to leap. In René Char the "heart" represents precisely this sudden rise and affirmation. Another poem, "The Swift," begins thus: "Martinet aux ailes trop larges, qui vire et crie sa joie autour de la maison. Tel est le coeur" (FM, 223). (Swift with wings too wide, who turns and cries his joy around the house. Such is the heart.) The bird that turns and cries is opposed to stability, to the established order of the house. The heart bears the impulse to destroy all cycles. Impromptu, it becomes infatuated. As such, Char praises a woman: "Seins pourris par ton coeur" (NP, 40) (breasts rotten by your heart). Any repose, anything that rests and stays put, every familiarity, threatens the heart. "Qui a creusé le puits et hisse l'eau gisante/ Risque son coeur dans l'écart de ses mains" (NP, 30). (Whoever has dug a well and raises the resting waters/ Risks his heart in the spread of his hands.) When fingers spread and imitate the formless waters, the danger of drowsiness becomes most alarming. The timeless protection that the water recalls and offers must be broken by a mutinous heart. Into all systems of security, the poem seems to say, man introduces discontinuity.

These are the two dimensions within which Char's poetry speaks: gravity and transgression. The arrival at the seashore is one of those moments in which they may unite. "Nothing that has seen me live and act hitherto is witness here." Yesterday's dullness is forgotten. No one is there to recall torpidities. The past is no longer. The extended time, the time that lingers, is the last fabric to be torn. Duration is the most captivating of all dwellings, the narrowest of all prisons. Its dismissal is forcefully urged. Char cherishes the dawns. The early morning, the moment without precedent, makes the world rise anew, immaculate. The moment of waking is much more than the rediscovery of things familiar. It makes the world begin, absolutely. "Nous sommes une fois encore sans expérience antérieure, nouveaux venus, épris" (PA, 48). (We are once again without previous experience, newcomers, infatuated.) The arrival upon the seashore has something of the morning insurrection: once again we begin. It is fatal to settle down, any establishment sacrifices the instant to duration. "La sagesse est de ne pas s'agglomérer" (PP, 237). (Wisdom is not to agglomerate.) Erosion and degradation threaten the freshness of the heart. Even the reverie on the waterfront is perilous if it lasts. In "The Word in Archipelago," Char says, "Ne regardez qu'une fois la vague jeter l'ancre dans la mer" (PA, 152). (Give but a quick look on the wave casting its anchor in the sea.) Everything that stablizes itself diminishes.

The symbols of the shoulder and of youth, curiously associated in the poem, signify the same departure. "My shoulder may well sleep, my youth come running." They belong together. The shoulder, the angle of the torso, points upwards as a volcano does, says the "Pulverized Poem": "Violente l'épaule s'entr'ouvre;/ Muet apparaît le volcan" (FM, 178). (With violence the shoulder opens partway;/ the volcano appears, mute.) To be a child, to be constantly on the edge of a departure, is Char's "privilege." In a commentary on the "Pulverized Poem" he writes: "Moi qui jouis du privilège de sentir tout ensemble accablement et confiance, défection et courage, je n'ai retenu personne sinon l'angle fusant d'une Recontre" (A-H, 20). (I enjoy the privilege of feeling all together dejection and confidence, defection and courage; still I have never retained anyone except *the spurting angle of an Encounter* [italics added].) Rare are the lives that resemble an eruption, new at each moment; rare is the resolution of duration into the instant. "There is one day of purity in the year."

The key to this poem is the opposition between duration and instant, massive horizontality and vertical takeoff. Actually it is a poem about poetry. The one pure day "hollows its marvelous gallery into the sea-foam, a day that mounts into the eyes to crown the noon." This rare day, this instant, *reconciles* weight and lightness, submission and transgression, the dive and the flight, or again the oceanic spread and man's freedom. The docile sea and man in revolt belong to each other in the poem. The entire poem hastens the union of the two dimensions. It is a call to fuse sedentary life and departure, to establish oneself on the road. "Epouse et n'épouse pas ta maison" (FM, 99). (Espouse and do not espouse your home.)

The Now of the poem abolishes yesterday's dispersions and separations. "Yesterday . . . the shark and the gull did not communicate."

In the now of the poem the shark and the gull do communicate at last. The gull is constant leaving, vertical flight, whereas the shark settles in the depth, gravity is its shelter. The gull has no refuge. When both communicate, the rainbow appears, offspring of the light and water drops. The sky and the ocean mingle. The poem aspires to the union of the two opposite dimensions down to the prayer that concludes it: "Make every supposed end be a new innocence, a feverish advance for those who stumble in the morning heaviness." The morning heaviness — this is the supreme paradox which translates Char's dream of unity. The morning is the hour of rising, of innocent beginning, of the gull. Heaviness is of the impenetrable sea, of the house, of the shark. As if a lightning flash, the poem makes me a unifier. Reality is antinomic, but the heart, man, or the poet unites. The language of the poem is the multiple matter in which things diverse and opposite enter into relation.

Not One Origin, Two

We now possess a first element for a topology of Char's poetry. We asked: where is the place from which it speaks? Where is its origin? The answer is clearer now: the origin lies somehow within the poem itself. Only when and insofar as the poem is spoken or understood do the dimensions of the shark and the gull communicate. The realm of the poem begins with its utterance. For a brief moment a world is opened in which the opposite is one — even more: in which the world is "world," that is, *there* for man. In Char's poetry an experience comes to language which is properly an experience of the origin. However, this origin is not distinct from the script of the poem itself. In or with the poem the world begins. Char's language is originary in the sense that it is itself the origin of what the poem achieves. We take the word "origin" literally: *oriri*, to rise, to appear, to come forth. Thus we say that language here gives rise to poetry which in turn gives rise to a world unified. Yet to claim that Char's script is originary implies no reference to anything mythical; the origin is not the inception of some process or history. Rather, when the poem is said and understood, the world just begins. But its world lasts as briefly as the poem itself. "La vitalité du poète n'est pas une vitalité de l'au-delà mais un point diamenté *actuel* de présences transcendantes et d'orages pèlerins" (FM, 78). (The vitality of the poet is not a vitality of the beyond, but an actual diamond point of transcending presences and migrating storms.) Thus this poetry is entirely of the earth; it has no other ground, no mythical foundation: it refers to language alone as its provenance; it founds a world which is inseparable from its speech. To understand Char is to see that this passionate celebration of the pure "there is" and this violent exclusion of any "it was" constitute the very structure of his script. If poetry still remains mysterious, if the presence is still called "transcending," this points solely towards the unspeakable subject-matter of poems such as "The Shark and the Gull," namely the mere presence of what is present. The subject-matter here is the visibility of the visible. "Quoique affaire terrestre, comme la vie dont elle est l'endroit victorieux du temps, claire ou opaque, la poésie reste un mystère en acte" (A-H, 11). (Although it is a matter of the earth, just as life whose right side, victorious over time, it is, poetry, whether clear or opaque, remains a mystery in act.)

Two notions of the origin appear to be phenomenologically defensible: the origin as the presence of what is present, and the origin as cause. The first may be described as nuptial: Char's poem announces the nuptials of the shark and the gull. The second may be called natal: cosmogonies speak of the cause or nascency of the world. Both notions imply an event, but nuptials occur in the present whereas nascency is a happening of the past, of the beginning of an era. It should be understood that Char's situation — the origin is not remote but is the presence of the present — disrupts the epistemological continuity that, in the eyes of theoreticians of symbolic forms, links poetic to mythological language. This kind of epistemological continuity may still characterize modern poetry, but it becomes undone already with Rimbaud. A myth relates events that occurred *in illo tempore*. The ritual by which the myth is celebrated revives these events for today so that history begins again: *incipit vita nova*. The important point is that in the innumerable manifestations of the sacred, the origin addresses man according to either temporal mode: the myth recalls and thus calls upon its believer. This double temporality belongs to the essence of any myth, at least to its basic forms, which are cosmogonic and soteriological. On the one hand such a myth remembers: "In the beginning there was . . ."; on the other hand it exhorts: "This is the day. . . ." The myth's double temporality, recalling and calling, is due to its essentially etiological intent. Recollection instates a duration, namely the time since those early days when the gods made or visited or saved the earth. Exhortation yields a presence, a renewed existence. Birth and rebirth, the origin as nascency and as nuptials, constitute properly the mythological time-structure. The word "religion," whether understood as *re-legere* or as *re-ligare*, suggests this link between present and past. All forms of the sacred draw their energy from the conjunction of these two modes in which the origin shows itself: the preservation of a message from the past and the exigency of a new hearing and a new existence in the present.

Thus, phenomenologically, "origin" designates two events. Char is so important to us because his poetry excludes violently any such amphibology. He rejects mythical or religious etiologies and turns deliberately to the actual happening in language of the presence of things present. His script reflects a particular understanding of time. The divine is no more; duration, which tied man back to his beginnings, is expunged from time. "Quand s'ébranla le barrage de l'homme, aspiré par la faille géante de l'abandon du divin, des mots dans le lointain, des mots qui ne voulaient pas se perdre, tentèrent de résister à l'exorbitante poussée" (A-H, 29). (When man's dam was shaken, sucked in by the giant rift of the desertion of the divine, words afar, words that did not want to get lost, tried to resist the exorbitant thrust.) The words of poetry have thus come to be simple words of the earth, words of today. Cut off from their numinous roots they have no glorious history to extol but only that glory which human eyes can see. The poet fulfills his task of manifesting the visible with "l'effort, le courage et l'amour" (A-H, 29) (with effort, courage and love). However, he is not the only one to bring the visible to speech. The fullness of language is not entrusted to him alone. He is only one of "les rescapés en si petit nombre" (A-H, 29) (the rescued in so small a number). Who are the others, his companions? Those who know how to converse. Language is primarily dialogue. In an era deprived of the divine, language manifests its essence in the discourse between humans. The rescued ones (from the collapse of religious creed into technological dogma) experience the unique sense of "mystery" or "transcendence" that remains in Char's poetry: the simple presence of one dialogue partner to the other. This presence, as that of the shark to the gull, although it occurs in language, is irreducible to the words exchanged in dialogue.

The difference between the presence and what is present does not construct a new afterworld, a new beyond; and yet, the unity that language establishes between the shark and the gull or between two speakers is not simply the sum of the beings that it brings together. Char's language is mundane, it is deprived of otherworldly roots, but it is not one-dimensional. It operates a communication that is not limited to man. A poem is a "mystère qui intronise" (FM, 83) (a mystery that enthrones). Perhaps we are to understand poetry in a very large sense here: "Tu es dans ton essence constamment poète" (A-H, 47). (You are in your essence constantly a poet.) In the collection *Formal Divide*, many sentences begin with "In poetry . . . ," as if poetry were some separate domain of language. But elsewhere Char simply says, "Man. . . ." "Il y a un homme à présent debout, un homme dans un champ de seigle, un champ pareil à un choeur mitraillé, un champs sauvé" (FM, 40). (There is man now, standing, a man in a field of rye, a field similar to a choir peppered with gunfire, a field that is saved.) The man who saves the field here is evidently the poet. But not necessarily the professional versemaker: any word that gathers together (in German *dichten*, to poetize, suggests *dicht*, intense, together, concentrated) is poetic. Language is at home in the now that gathers together. In "The Shark and the Gull," this gathering is symbolized by the "marvelous gallery" hollowed in sea-foam. Other texts suggest that here again the symbol is meant to evoke the poem itself: Char calls the poem "le tunnel dérobé," "la chambre d'harmonie," "la piste captieuse" (the hidden tunnel, the chamber of harmony, the captious track) and the poet "dans la chambre devenue légère, le donneur de liberté" (FM, 37) (the giver of freedom in the chamber now turned light). In that sense any human whose speech is responsible deserves the epitaph written for a poet: "Enlevé par l'oiseu à l'éparse douleur,/ Et laissé aux forêts pour un travail d'amour" (PA, 92). (Taken away by the bird from the scattered suffering/ And left to the forests for a work of love.)

The poem thus realizes the unity of the world that it signifies. It does not only press for a new existence. If man constantly poetizes, his speech brings together the dimensions of the world, the lightness of the bird and the gravity of the forest. But the poem realizes the unity that it signifies only for the moment of its articulation. Its world springs up and founders immediately. Success here does not abolish desire: "le poème est l'amour réalisé du désir demeuré désir" (FM, 76). (The poem is the realized love of desire remaining desire.) By its nature the poem is an ephemeral victory over dispersion and dislocation.

In the poem all things just begin. "Le poète, grand Commenceur" (FM, 83) (the poet, great Beginner), says Char. Again, this beginning is neither mythical nor religious. The presence that it inaugurates neither founds anything nor even lasts. The poem only lends a voice to the presence of things, it *is* the elocution of their pure presence. It opens for them a space where they belong to each other. The poem lets them be. It lets be whatever is. Thus it operates the identity of the non-identical. "Le poète peut alors voir les contraires . . . aboutir, poésie et vérité, comme nous savons, étant synonymes" (FM, 72). (The poet can then see things contrary come to their end . . . poetry and truth, as we know, being synonymous.)

The truth of things, their instantaneous blooming, does not last in a poetry whose origin is nothing divine but only language itself. Truth realizes itself "sometimes": "L'homme n'est qu'une fleur de l'air tenue par la terre . . . ; le souffle et l'ombre de cette coalition, certaines fois, le surélèvent" (PA, 81). (Man is only a flower of the air held by the earth . . . ; the breath and the shadow of this coalition sometimes elevate him.) Hardly achieved, this presence is already regretted: "Oiseaux qui confiez votre gracilité, votre sommeil périlleux à un ramas de roseaux, le froid venu, comme nous nous ressemblons!" (NT, 43). (You, bird, who entrust your frailty, your perilous sleep to a heep of reeds, when the cold has come how we resemble one another!)

The Hymn to the Rhine

With René Char the origin of poetic script lies in the mere present: the poet, "great Beginner," discloses a meaning which is always new. The origin appears as nuptials. Char spells "Beginner" with a capital letter: the poet's ministry is to establish an order. In the poem, the shark and the gull are present, belong at last to each other. When silence cornes back, chaos rules again: "Le poète ne retient pas ce qu'il découvre; l'ayant transcrit, il le perd aussitôt. En cela réside sa nouveauté" (PA, 73). (The poet does not retain what he discloses; as soon as he has transcribed it he loses it. In that lies his novelty.) The Beginning is to be understood as instantaneous novelty. It is to this sudden nakedness of the world that Char dedicates his effort. "Great Beginner" is a polemic title: Char's battle is delivered against mythological origins, against any reference to ancestral incipiencies. It is on this decisive understanding of the origin that Char differs radically from another poet, Hölderlin, whom he otherwise resembles in many respects. Char and Hölderlin know of only one subject-matter of poetry, poetry itself. They share the same predilection for rivers. But running waters as a symbol of the poem do not mean the same thing in one and the other. The situation of Hölderlin is not the same as Char's.

"Quand on a mission d'éveiller, on commence par faire sa toilette dans la rivière" (PP, 237). (When one has the mission to rouse, one begins with washing in the river.) The rouser begins, and so does the river. No one enters twice the same river, Heraclitus is reported to have said. The running water is at every moment young. Each dive is like a dive into a fountain of youth: the coolness *begins*, as violent as a child. The same is true for the poet. The communion that he institutes appears suddenly and immediately dissolves. "La poésie est de toutes les eaux claires celle qui s'attarde le moins aux reflets de ses ponts" (PP, 94). (Poetry is of all clear waters the one that lingers the least with the reflections of its bridges.) The poet dwells in white waters, as the trout. He settles in unhabitable elements. "L'éclair me dure" (PA, 72). (Lightning makes me last.) Char calls the Sorgue River of his native Vaucluse "rivière où l'éclair finit et où commence ma maison" (FM, 218) (the river where lightning ends and where my house begins). He wants all humans to dare to choose the unstable. "Donne aux enfants de mon pays le visage de ta passion" (FM, 218). (Give the children of my country the face of your passion.) The Sorgue River operates a departure, everything it touches becomes effulgence. Even the earth splinters into thousands of particles and movements: "Rivière, en toi terre est frisson" (FM, 218). (River, in you the earth is shiver.) The praise of the Sorgue ends with this request: "Rivière au coeur jamais détruit dans ce monde fou de prisons,/ Garde-nous violent et ami des abeilles de l'horizon" (FM, 219). (You, river, whose heart is never destroyed in this world mad with prisons, keep us violent and friends of the bees on the horizon.) Only an indestructible heart can will the anti-compact, the explosive fever of a swarm of bees. And such a heart alone can ally a pulverized systole with a sedentary, earthy diastole. Such a heart is made to the image of the river: violent in the fragmentations that it operates and nevertheless constant in its run. Such is also the paradox of poetic language: "obscurité prénatale et lumière" (PA, 73) (prenatal obscurity as well as light).

Let us now listen to Hölderlin. In 1801 he finished the hymn entitled "The Rhine." Here are its first lines:

Im dunkeln Efeu sass ich, an der Pforte
Des Waldes, eben, da der goldene Mittag,
Den Quell besuchend, herunterkam
Von Treppen des Alpengebirges,
Das mir die göttlichgebaute,
Die Burg der Himmlischen heisst
Nach alter Meinung, wo aber
Geheim noch manches entschieden
Zu Menschen gelanget; von da
Vernahm ich ohne Vermuten
Ein Schicksal. . . .
Jetzt aber, drin im Gebirg,
Tief unter den silbernen Gipfeln
Und unter fröhlichem Grün,
Wo die Wälder schauernd zu ihm
Und der Felsen Häupter übereinander
Hinabschaun, taglang, dort
Im kältesten Abgrund hört'
Ich um Erlösung jammern
Den Jüngling, es hörten ihn, wie er tobt',
Und die Mutter Erd 'anklagt'
Und den Donnerer, der ihn gezeuget,
Erbarmend die Eltern, doch
Die Sterblichen flohn von dem Ort,
Denn furchtbar war, da lichtlos er
In den Fesseln sich wälzte,
Das Rasen des Halbgotts.
Die Stimme wars des edelsten der Ströme,
Des freigeborenen Rheins. . . .[4]

(I sat among dark ivy at the forest's gate just as golden noon, to visit the source, descended from the steps of the Alpine ranges, for me the divinely-built, the castle of the Heavenly, following old opinion, whence even yet many a secred decree reaches men; and thus I unsuspectingly received a destiny. . . . Amidst the mountains, deep down below the snowy summits and under the jubilant green, where the shuddering forests and, craning over each other, the crags look down upon him all day long, I now heard in the coldest abyss the youth wail for release; there, as he raged, accusing Mother Earth and the Thunderer who begot him, his pitying parents heard him, too; but the mortals fled from the place, for as he writhed without light in his fetters, terrible was the demi-god's raving. It was the voice of the noblest of rivers, the free-born Rhine.)

The hymn begins with a description of the Alps. According to the myth, they are the fortress of the gods, of heavenly architecture. From these heights the gods still send decrees whose destiny or "mittance" (*Schicksal*, from *schicken*, to send) the poet, "I," receives and grasps (*So vernahm ich ohne Vermuthen ein Schicksal*). These decrees are rough; within the desolate scenery of rocks a youth, son of the Earth and the Thunderer, writhes in his chains. It is the Rhine who fights furiously his way through the rocky masses. Hölderlin calls him the "noblest of rivers," a demi-god. In Hölderlin as in Char, the river symbolizes the poem; in both cases also it unites duration and instant, the solid and the light or the lightning. The son of the gods is "saxifragous," the rock breaker. Char dedicated a poem to Hölderlin entitled "Pour un Prométhée saxifrage. En touchant la main éolienne de Hölderlin" (PA, 125) ("For a Saxifragous Prometheus. Touching the Eolian Hand of Hölderlin"). It begins thus: "La réalité sans l'énergie disloquante de la poésie, qu'est-ce?" (Reality without the dislocating energy of poetry, what would that be?) The violence of the young and raving Rhine symbolizes the violent rise of the poetic word. Char probably also has Hölderlin in mind when he writes in *Formal Divide*: "Fureur et mystère tour à le séduisirent et le consumèrent. Puis vint l'année qui acheva son agonie de saxifrage" (FM, 70). (Furor and mystery seduced and consumed him by turns. Then came the year that concluded his saxifragous agony.) It was fatal for Hölderlin to unite lightning and the earth, furor and mystery. Five years after he had finished "The Rhine" he fell into madness. One has even the impression that Char paraphrases the first lines of the hymn: "Nous regardions couler devant nous l'eau grandissante. Elle effaçait d'un coup la montagne, se chassant de ses flancs maternels. Ce n'était pas un torrent qui s'offrait à son destin mais une bête ineffable dont nous devenions la parole et la substance" (FM, 222). (We watched the growing water flow before us. It wiped out the mountain in a single blow, breaking forth from its motherly womb. It was not a torrent that offered itself to its destiny, but an ineffable beast whose word and substance we became.)

If examined more closely, however, the difference between Char's and Hölderlin's use of the river symbol, and therefore the difference between their ways to understand the poem, is radical. All along its current the Rhine is seen by Hölderlin *close to its source*. The poet's mediation remains near the origin of the divine decrees: "Ein Rätsel ist Reinentsprungenes. Auch/ Der Gesang kaum darf es enthüllen" (*Werke*, 315). (A riddle is what is of pure origin, song itself may hardly disclose it.)

Wherever the Rhine passes, it is "pure origin." The poet's utterances remain thoroughly faithful to the "heavenly" messages which, "beyond question," reach mankind by his mediation. "Ein Rätsel ist Reinentsprungenes" — this means something different now from "poète, grand Commenceur," the poet, great Beginner. If Char's ministry consists merely in lending a voice to what is present in as much as present, Hölderlin's hermeneutic function is one of translating and transmitting. The origin that addresses man in Hölderlin's poetry is sacred, arises from elsewhere. Whereas Char announces the nuptials of what is visible, Hölderlin turns back towards the invisible nascency of which he is the servant and the herald. The entire hymn exalts this presence of the natal, not yet nuptial origin; it is a hymn to man's wandering identity with his birth.

> Und schön ists, wie er drauf,
> Nachdem er die Berge verlassen,
> Stillwandelnd sich im deutschen Lande
> Begnügt. . . .
> Doch nimmer, nimmer vergisst ers.
> Denn eher muss die Wohnung vergehn,
> Und die Satzung und zum Unbild werden
> Der Tag der Menschen, ehe vergessen
> Ein solcher dürfte den Ursprung
> Und die reine Stimme der Jugend. (*Werke*, 316-7)

(How fair is the way he now, after leaving the mountains, glides onward in calm content. . . . But he never, never forgets. For sooner the dwelling shall perish, and the laws, and the day of men become a calamity, than such as he forget the origin and the pure voice of youth.)

These lines express Hölderlin's human ideal: the nearness of the past inception and the memory of the pure voice of our early years. The poem speaks of the ideal itself as much as of its loss. Hölderlin's time, our time, is the one where the gods seem to be no more. Rivers have become factors of calculus in the navigation business and cheap means of industrial evacuation and refrigeration. This is the age of the night to which Hölderlin opposes the age of the day, that is, early Greece.

> Aber weh! es wandelt in Nacht, es wohnt, wie im Orkus,
> Ohne Göttliches unser Geschlecht. Ans eigene Treiben
> Sind sie geschmiedet allein, und sich in der tosenden Werkstatt
> Höret jeglicher nur. . . . (*Werke*, 290)

(But alas! today's mankind errs through the night, it dwells as though in hades, deprived of the divine. They all are solely enchained to their own agitation, and in the middle of the boisterous workshop everyone hears only himself.)

An age such as ours must again learn how to listen. Hence the sanctity of Hölderlin's mediations. A human being close to the source, the poet, does what the river does. He transmits the life-giving decrees of the gods to the mortal inhabitants of the valleys. At each step he remembers his early beginnings. He remains impetuous. He is the mediator who consumes himself in his task. When Hölderlin feels madness imminent, he compares himself to the demi-god Tantalus "who received from the gods more than he could digest." To be a poet is not a matter of talent. The poem succeeds when the natal origin, the mystery of birth, becomes language. The saying of the poem *is* the arrival of the gods. As a demi-god, the poet experiences the lasting nearness of the *arché*. Only when the gods grant their presence do his stammerings become a poem. The hymn "Patmos" says: "Nah ist/ Und schwer zu fassen der Gott" (*Werke*, 328). (Near, and yet hard to grasp, is the god.) In fact, the poet does not seize. Rather he is seized, "struck by Apollo."

Hölderlin's poems thus preserve a certain past; they enunciate both the ancientness and the nearness of our provenance: the ancient glory of language as incantation is the terrible privilege of those who dare remember. The origin is here understood as proximity of the divine, forgotten though it is in needy times. The man of this proximity is necessarily a stranger. Only in that condition can he, "like the god of wine, render intelligible to the heart the language of the purest ones," that is, of the gods (*Werke*, 318). The poem is divine speech, the only one that we still possess. By such an elevation of everyday words into hymnic song, language comes into its own.

Hölderlin's situation is that of the end of metaphysics: the divine ground holds no more, the foundations appear shaken. What used to be the most powerful presence, the divine, has fallen into oblivion. Only the poet remembers. What, then, is Char's situation? In his poetry there is no regretfulness of sacred decrees, no recollection. The site from which he speaks is nothing mythical, not "a stronghold of the Heavenly," no "sacred Alps," but man's own language in its humble event. Char's situation is properly postmodern, perhaps beyond metaphysics altogether. It may be that Char says less than Hölderlin: no holy injunctions are transmitted. It may be that he says also less than Nietzsche: no madman cries after God. But in saying apparently less, does he not speak from another locus, still too novel to think of, a place beyond representations and beyond that threshold where the overcoming of metaphysics is still the dominant problem? In that case Hölderlin would have experienced the decline of the truth of being, and particularly the decline of the truth of the supreme being. Since the very quest for certainty, security, and salvation has become meaningless in his situation, Char points more decidedly towards a new beginning. Yet Char's project has nothing to do with the simplifying label "atheism," but very much with a new thought of being. The truth of being lies no more in the principle of reason and in logic, but in the *princeps*, the beginning, which the logos as poetic speech is itself.

Both Hölderlin and Char poetize the origin. But in Char the dimensions of the visible communicate due to his script; his poem exists when the visibility of the visible alone becomes language. In Hölderlin a restoration occurs; the natal origin — in the mythical sense, as he states explicitly — addresses a mortal race that has forgotten its own essence. The task of Hölderlin's hymn is to recall the divine as one calls back a fugitive. "The Rhine" ends precisely with the wedding between the mortals and the immortals:

> Dann feiern das Brautfest Menschen und Götter,
> Es feiern die Lebenden all,
> Und ausgeglichen ist eine Weile das Schicksal.   (*Werke*, 319)

> (Then gods and men celebrate their nuptials, all the
> living celebrate, and Destiny becomes equal for a while.)

For the time of the poem the difference between mortal and immortal is abolished. It is not by chance that Hölderlin composes "hymns," whereas Char renounces any kind of praise or acclamation. *Hymnos*, in Greek, designates primitively the "hymen" songs that were accompanied by flutes and lyres. The songs are started off by the friends that guide the young couple to the bridegroom's house. Hölderlin's hymns are hymeneals of the mortal and the immortal. In contrast, the only wedding Char admits of is that of the dimensions of the earth, of the shark and the gull, but never of heaven and earth. Char's ontological situation lies above — or underneath — whatever might resemble "une vitalité de l'au-delà" (FM, 78) (a vitality of the beyond).

In Hölderlin's view a double giving takes place in poetry. On the one hand the poet assists the mortals, to whom he points out the originary road to follow:

> Nachdem er lächelnd auch
> Der Menschen geschäftiges Leben
> Das odemarme, wie Segel
> Mit seinen Lüften gelenkt hat. . . . (*Werke*, 319)

> (He steers the busy life of men, short-breathed as it is,
> like sails, with his own inexhaustible breezes.)

But on the other hand, as a mediator, the poet also gives to the gods. The wedding that he calls for also profits the immortals: to the "most-blessed" he offers his fragility. This fulfills their only need:

> Bedürfen die Himmlischen eines Dings,
> So sind's . . . Sterbliche. Dann
> Muss wohl, wenn solches zu sagen
> Erlaubt ist, in der Götter Namen
> Teilnehmend fühlen ein andrer,
> Den brauchen sie. . . . (*Werke*, 317)

"If one need remains to the Celestials, that need is for mortals." Gods are impassible, suffering is unknown to them. Therefore, "if to say such a thing is permitted, another must be compassionate and feel on their behalf." In need of mortals, the gods use, *brauchen*, the poet. To bear such usage and such usury he has only his endurance to count upon. His happiness is of the weightiest kind.

> Nur hat ein jeder sein Mass.
> Denn schwer ist zu tragen
> Das Unglück, aber schwerer das Glück. (*Werke,* 319)

> (Each has his measure. For hard though to bear is
> unhappiness, still harder is happiness.)

Around him men breathlessly render the night more comfortable. But the poet "knows God." He has been measured with the double gauge of divine and human needs. He remains the wailing youth, guardian of the source and guarded by it. As the hermeneuts, the priests at Delphi, he goes back and forth between the oracle and the people's square. His sayings are essentially interpretative.

> Denn schonend rührt des Masses allzeit kundig
> Nur einen Augenblick die Wohnungen der Menschen
> Ein Gott an. . . . (*Werke*, 308)

> (A god, always heedful of measure, touches as a guard in
> a single moment upon the dwellings of man.)

Man's dwelling, language, which is thus "touched" by the divine, is the poem.

Hölderlin's concept of origin is both mythical (mainly in the hymns) and historical (in his translations and aesthetic writings). In either case, though, what he recalls is early Greece. The contrast with Char is evident. There is no sacred dimension of existence or of history that speaks through Char's poems and whose recollection would be entrusted to the poet. What does speak in Char's verse is the ephemeral harmony of mortal speech which for an unsettled existence builds and unbuilds instantaneous dwellings.

"There Is" in the Poem

It is not enough to say that in Hölderlin's poetry the origin appears as mythical and remote, and in Char's as actual and present. Nor have we understood the situation of Char once his script has been labeled post-metaphysical. The event of language by which the origin manifests itself in his poetry needs to be questioned for its own sake. Hölderlin thinks the era of Western history and tries to renew its early vitality, its divine infancy. In this sense his poetry is a memorial. As a recollection and as a revival it opens the space of a second beginning. Char seems to retain only the contemporaneous part of the essentially ambivalent language of the origin, smothering its romantic overtones. Only the present instant remains: "La lumière a un âge. La nuit n'en a pas. Mais quel fut l'instant de cette source entière?" (NT, 34). (Light has an age. The night has none. But which was the instant of that integral source?)

In the poem there is the sea; there are the Sorgue River and the Rhine; there is the shark communicating with the gull. But prior to all this there is in the poem the "there is" itself. Since Rimbaud, the poem has said: whatever is, is. Sometimes it takes a more pressing tone, when it says: whatever is, may that be. But this wish that it formulates is fulfilled right away. What is at stake in the poem is the presence of everything to everything. Only the presence. Not an intention, but the intonation alone. Rimbaud is the poet of poetry when he writes in his *Illuminations*:

> There is a clock that does not ring.
> There is a quagmire with a nest of white birds.
> There is a cathedral. . . .
> There is a small car. . . . [5]

The same celebration of what is purely present is found in Apollinaire's *Calligraphies*:

> There is a vessel that has taken away my beloved.
> There are six sausages in the sky. . . .
> There is an enemy submarine. . . .

and so on, for twenty-four "there is's."[6]

Is all this to say that poems such as these and Char's eliminate any *difference* from language? Is their verse content with the beautiful sequences of auditory and visual elements? Against theories of structural

189

linguists, it is clear that the "there is" introduces by itself a difference, a mystery, if that is the word, which neither turns our eyes away (as it does in Hölderlin) from the purely visible and audible nor keeps them riveted to the order of words and things that make up the poem (as, for instance, in Roman Jakobson's theory). Thus the question of the situation of René Char's poetry, the question of how the origin has to be understood in his script, becomes the question of identity and difference in the "there is." We may even be entitled to go a step beyond Char, to risk the defoliation of our anthologies, and to concentrate our attention not upon the things shown, but upon the showing itself. When the poem is said, things are present, reconciled, called together by its speech. This recognition of their being-there is probably common to all poetry we know of. But being-there *is not* the being that is there. The present is different from the thing present, as the visibility of the thing shown is different from the shark and the gull that the poem makes visible.

The poem is the burning articulation of a desire: may all things be there. May pure presence be. Even more, it announces and already realizes what it desires. The dimensions of the earth communicate, but this communication *is not* the water and the sky, or gravity and transgression. The poem is the tangible sign, offered to our eyes, our ears, our lips, that all is one, that mere presence *is*. The poem is the color of hereness, its fulgor and its splendor. The difference that the "there is" introduces into the poem is the difference between the presence and the things present or the visibility and what is rendered visible.

The German idiomatic expression *es gibt*, "there is," means literally "it gives." "Among dark ivy at the forest's gate" there is the river. Hölderlin thinks the *es gibt* literally when he continues: "A riddle is what is of pure origin." One may ask: what is it that gives? The Alps give the Rhine. The gods give destiny. However, that which gives cannot be properly named. But out of that region, we are told, "secretly much, beyond question, still reaches man." That which gives is the origin of presence. It gives presence. When the poem calls all things together, they are mysteriously granted to us, bestowed by That which gives. In order to understand the essence of poetry, solely the provenance of this giving deserves to be questioned. Heidegger sees in this idiomatic turn *es gibt* the possibility of a new examination of ontology: "the memorable is what gives food for thought. . . . The memorable grants."[7] The source of a river is memorable, it remains so down to the estuary. "As you began you remain" ("The Rhine"). Heidegger comments: "We try to carry our sight towards that which gives and towards its giving, and we spell the 'It' with a capital letter."[8] That which gives is different from what it gives.

There are thus three semantic layers that we have to distinguish carefully: the things present (the shark and the gull), their presence (the poetic speech or script), and the event of the presencing (the essence of poetic language). In the vocabulary of Heidegger's writings of the 1930's:

beings, beingness, and Being. Or in the vocabulary of *On Time and Being: das Anwesende, das* Anwesen*lassen, das Anwesen*lassen. Based upon the difference that the German expression "there is" suggests, this threefold layer gives an answer to any inquiry into the way things and words are present in a poem. Both Hölderlin and Heidegger give witness to this Germanic way of speaking and therefore of thinking.

Superficially the *"es gibt"* of Heidegger (commenting on Hölderlin) resembles Rimbaud's *"il y a"* and the English "there is." But the similarity is deceptive, as the kinship between Hölderlin and Char is deceptive. *"Es gibt"* and "there is" belong to two different worlds. Both the English "there is" and the French *"il y a"* eliminate any mythical reminiscence from the poem. This is not so with *"es gibt,"* particularly when spelled with a capital letter. Hence the danger of misunderstanding some of Heidegger's latest writings. The invitation to silence before the mystery of That which gives, as well as Heidegger's reference to Hölderlin, may easily mislead the reader. Even in his texts about the event of presencing, it is still the visibility of the visible that is thought of. Thus he is closer to the way of thinking that says "there is" or *"il y a"* than to Hölderlin's hymn "The Rhine" and the recollection into divine mittances as implied by *"es gibt."* If Heidegger still speaks of the sacred and of the mystery, this must be understood in Char's way: the communication of the dimensions of the earth is sacred; the presencing of the essence of language that renders things present is mysterious. "There is" and *"il y a"* tell more humbly the proximity of being than Heidegger's own mother-language.

Char's poetry is far from any celebration of non-human grantings, from any grace or giving. It expresses nothing more than the spectacle of what is. Hölderlin's poetry, or the *"Es gibt,"* implies a stretched-out temporality, a return to the beginnings. Char's poetry, or the *"il y a"* and the "there is," in the purely vertical temporality of the instant, consumes horizontal history as the lightning consumes the day. On this point some of Char's titles may lead to confusion: "Retour amont," or "Le nu perdu" ("Return Upstream," "Nudity Lost"). But in no way does Char display the nostalgia for a lost paradisaic nudity, and the return upstream is not an ascent to the causes. Rather, "amont éclate" (NP, 48) (upstream bursts). The only path that Char traces for us leads to the being-there of what is there.

Char's situation is beyond metaphysics insofar as the pure "there is" to which he gives voice destroys causal scaffoldings. Thus the armistices concluded both by Hölderlin and by Char are of opposite terms. Hölderlin's hymns are the script of an Absent. They are the presence of this Absent qua absent. That which grants Hölderlin's poems to be the locus of reconciliation between man and his origin arises from elsewhere. Hölderlin's poetry settles a momentary armistice between man and the sacred. In Char the armistice is between a carnivorous beast, the shark, and the light-feathered gull, both of which *are there* in his poetry, belonging to each other and appropriating each other. In Hölderlin the cities founded by the legislating stream are *from elsewhere*, from the gods. "Then man and gods celebrate their nuptials." Heidegger's interpretation of this line refers again to the Absent which, through the text, becomes present. These weddings, he writes, celebrate "the encounter of those among men and gods who give birth to the mediators between men and gods and who endure this intermediacy."[9] In other words, out of this wedlock the poet is born. The offspring carries the mark of what is absent into the present.

Poetry is that section of language in which being lets itself be explicitly experienced as event and as appropriation. But each native tongue prepares for this event and this appropriation a dwelling which is particular to it. The German *"es gibt"* comprises a difference between what is shown and its origin; this language lives from such a reference to what is absent, or from the manifestation of the non-manifest. It is a metaphysical language. The German language experiences the appropriating event as the intrusion of a distinct and forgotten origin into the customary proximity. The poet's saying is here understood as a translation: he translates to our ears the anonymous gift by which the poem lets whatever is be present. The poet is the guard of this gift, and inversely this gift guards (*schont, hütet*) him.

The French and English languages stay among what they show — but radically. *"Il y a"* and "there is" open a difference between what is and its presence. The poem makes the purity of the *there* be seen. It is as mysterious as the sun at noon, which is the sun "and" which is there. Without involving any double, any invisible afterworld, Char's poetry and the tongue in which it is written live within this difference, between things of the earth and their being-there. Char is the poet of the visible mystery for whom and by whom presence is different from things present but not other than they, hence also identical with them.

As for the English language, one nuance is striking in this context: "there is" applies in English both to human existence (*Dasein, être-là*) and to the more general presence of beings (*Es gibt, il y a*). The lack of this distinction in English reveals perhaps another kind of ontology which would have to be worked out from contemporary poetry in that language.

New School for Social Research

NOTES

1   All translations which follow the original texts in parentheses are mine.

2   In the references to René Char's works, the following abbreviations are used:
PP *Poèmes et Prose choisis*. Paris: Gallimard, NRF, 1957.
FM *Fureur et Mystère*. Paris: Gallimard, NRF, 1962.

PA *La Parole en archipel.* Paris: Gallimard, NRF, 1962.
NP *Le nu perdu.* Paris: Gallimard, NRF, 1971.
A-H *Arrière-Histoire du Poème pulvérisé.* Paris: Jean Hugues, 1972.
NT *La Nuit talismanique.* Genève: A. Skira, 1972.

3   Char writes about this poem: "It was at Trayas on the border of the Mediterranean in the winter of 1946 that the theme of "The Shark and the Gull" imposed itself on me. I went to see Henri Matisse at Vence, and we spoke of it. That perfect wedding haunted him. — This poem has fulfilled itself by the foaming charm that it has procured me long after its flight, like a cock's crowing: brutal to the soul, and master of the silence that follows" (A-H, 40).

4   Friedrich Hölderlin, *Sämtliche Werke*, ed. Paul Stapf (Berlin und Darmstadt: Tempel, 1958), p. 314 f., hereafter referred to as *Werke*. Franz Mayer, 'René Char et Hölderlin," *Cahiers de l'Herne* 15 (1971), 81-88, has attempted a comparison between the two poets. He sees the function of modern and postmodern poetry in the anticipation of a historical reality to come: "L'avenir est ainsi, pour Char comme pour Hölderlin . . . une réalité historique" (p. 88). It seems to me that the kinship between the two poets lies, on the contrary, in the attention that both give to an origin that arises within the poem, neither before nor after. For both Hölderlin and Char the future is *advenir*, a present event, rather than *à venir*, to come. Virginia La Charite, *The Poetics and the Poetry of René Char*, (Chapel Hill: University of North Carolina Press, 1968), sees the time-structure of Char's poetry also as derived from an attitude of hope, turned towards the future; according to her interpretation "the great Beginner" would mean hope "for a better future" (p. 93). This line of interpretation was first that of Maurice Blanchot, "René Char," *La part du feu* (Paris: Gallimard, 1949), p. 17. Read in such a way, poetry would again found some kind of duration, a new era, whereas for Char and Hölderlin no inception occurs in the poem, but only its own rise and death in the present now.

5   Arthur Rimbaud, *Oeuvres* (Paris: Garnier, 1960), pp. 256-7:

Au bois il y a un oiseau, son chant vous arrête et vous fait rougir.
Il y a une horloge qui ne sonne pas.
Il y a une fondrière avec un nid de bêtes blanches.
Il y a une cathédrale qui descent et un lac qui monte.
Il y a une petite voiture abandonnée dans le taillis,
ou qui descend le sentier en courant, enrubannée.
Il y a une troupe de petits comédiens en costumes,
aperçus sur la route à travers la lisière du bois.
Il y a enfin, quand l'on a faim et soif, quelqu'un qui vous chasse.

6   Guillaume Apollinaire, *Oeuvres poétiques complètes* (Paris: Pléiade, 1969), p. 817:

Il y a un vaisseau qui a emporté ma bien-aimée.
Il y a dans le ciel six saucisses. . . .
Il y a un sous-marin ennemi. . . .

7   "Das Bedenkliche ist das, was zu denken gibt. . . . Das Bedenkliche gibt." Martin Heidegger, *Vorträge und Aufsätze* (Pfullingen: Neske, 1954), p. 132.

8   "Wir versuchen, das Es und sein Geben in die Sicht zu bringen und schreiben das 'Es' gross." Martin Heidegger, *Zur Sache des Denkens* (Tübingen: M. Niemeyer, 1969), p. 5.

9   *"Das Brautfest* ist das Begegnen jener Menschen und Götter, dem die Geburt derjenigen entstammt, die zwischen den Menschen und den Göttern stehen und dieses 'Zwischen' ausstehen." Martin Heidegger, *Erläuterungen zu Hölderlins Dichtung* (Frankfurt: V. Klostermann, 1963), p. 98.

*"J'adressais, au mois de mai 1946, à Henri Matisse, à Vence, le manuscrit du poème 'Le requin et la mouette' composé quelques semaines auparavant au Trayas. Au cours de la visite que j'avais faite au grand peintre il n'avait pas été question d'un poème plutôt que d'un autre. Je m'étais persuadé que Matisse allait bien, que ses trésors continuaient à s'élaborer avec la même somptueuse régularité qu'à l'ordinaire. De retour à l'Isle-sur-Sorgue je lui adressais donc le manuscrit de mon poème (J'aime Matisse et sa bonté discrète: ce poème pour le remercier d'un acte précis). Il me répondit qu'il avait dans une série de dessins récents *découvert* le même thème. Voici l'un de ces dessins." The drawing and the accompanying lines are reproduced from: *Cahiers d'Art*, Paris 1945/46, p. 77. By permission of the editors of the *Cahiers d'Art*.

"The Being of Language and the Language of Being": Heidegger and Modern Poetics

Alvin H. Rosenfeld

J: How would you present the hermeneutic circle today?

I: I would avoid a presentation as resolutely as I would avoid speaking *about* language.

J: Then everything would hinge on reaching a corresponding saying of language.

I: Only a dialogue could be such a saying correspondence.

. . . .

J: The course of such a dialogue would have to have a character all its own, with more silence than talk.

I: Above all silence about silence. . . .

J: Because to talk and write about silence is what produces the most obnoxious chatter.

I: Who could simply be silent of silence?

J: That would be authentic saying . . .

I: . . . and would remain the constant prologue to the authentic dialogue *of* language.

J: Are we not attempting the impossible?

The conversation cited above, which is excerpted from "A Dialogue on Language," the opening selection of Martin Heidegger's *On the Way to Language*,[1] provides a hint of the subject that I wish to take up in the pages that follow. More than likely, it is "attempting the impossible," as Heidegger's interlocutor cautioned in their conversation. Nevertheless, in the belief that the impossible is an attractive and even necessary part of any meaningful discussion about modern poetry, I propose to venture into an area of poetics that Heidegger himself has done much to open up, namely, that area in which we approach the abiding but still largely undetermined relationship that seems to exist between poetry and ontology, or, in Heidegger's more imaginative formulation, between "the being of language and the language of being," (p. 76). Admittedly, this is a danger zone for critical thinking, and the characteristic excesses and frequent failures of Heidegger's own thought should serve to warn us away from it. Nonetheless, it seems worthwhile to try to make a beginning, taking Heidegger as guide, and for three reasons: one, I am convinced that much of the most interesting poetry written by twentieth century poets locates itself within a sphere of concern that touches at many points, and thus helps to define, "the being of language and the language of being"; two, because I want to draw attention, if only in a preliminary way, to the fairly recent introduction of hermeneutical thinking into literary criticism and to test, through practice, some of its advantages and disadvantages to the working critic; and three, because I think this is a good time to re-examine the ancient enmity between philosophy and poetry, an enmity that may find some relief, if not yet reconciliation, in the kinds of attention presently being focused on language.

The earliest use of the term "hermeneutics" in Heidegger appears in *Being and Time* (1927), but in order to grasp the full import of the term, it is necessary to go to such later works as "A Dialogue on Language" (1953/54) and "Words" (undated). In the first of these, Heidegger quotes Schleiermacher to the effect that hermeneutics is "the art of understanding rightly another man's language" (p. 11), but it is clear that he himself intends something of far greater scope and will not settle for a definition that limits hermeneutics to "a science that deals with the goals, ways, and rules of the interpretation of literary works" (p. 10). Rather, he speaks in terms of a "vastness that springs from originary being" (p. 11), a vastness which he claims language alone can lead us to and reveal. "The matter is enigmatic," he confesses, and perhaps not "a matter at all" (p. 11), but for this very reason it demands thought and interpretation. Yet far from being an "art" or a "science" of

196

interpretation, hermeneutics appears within Heidegger's writing as a process of searching, and, as he remarks, "how is one to give a name to what he is still searching for?" (p. 20). Nevertheless, names are not altogether lacking, and in a typical turn of thought, Heidegger looks to classical etymology for clarification. This is what he discovers:

> The expression "hermeneutic" derives from the Greek verb *hermeneuein*. That verb is related to the noun of *hermeneus*, which is referable to the name of the god Hermes by a playful thinking that is more compelling than the rigor of science. Hermes is the divine messenger. He brings the message of destiny; *hermeneuein* is that exposition which brings tidings because it can listen to a message. Such exposition becomes an interpretation of what has been said earlier by the poets who, according to Socrates in Plato's *Ion* (534e), *hermenes eisin ton theon* — "are interpreters of the gods." (p. 29)

Heidegger stresses this original sense of hermeneutics because it "brings out the Being of beings" and not "in the manner of metaphysics, but such that Being itself will shine out" (p. 30). He goes on to affirm that it is "language [that] defines the hermeneutic relation," calling man himself to essential being.

Most of the characteristics and concerns of Heidegger's thought are recognizable in these passages: a return to philosophy's origins in early Greek thought; a fondness for etymological definition; the strain of anti-scientism and an expressed lack of sympathy for Western metaphysics on the one hand and, on the other, an invocation of the gods and the poets as more reliable arbiters and interpreters of human knowledge and fate; a central stress on the ontological properties of language; and the touchstones of radiance and luminosity as confirmation of powerful and authentic presence. Taken together, these elements of style and stress reveal Heidegger's well-known biases against the traditional methods of ratiocination, and for what one can only call poetic thinking. Poetic thinking, at least when it is strong, always has only a single object in mind, as Heidegger himself confirms when he writes, in an essay on Trakl ("Language in the Poem"), that "every great poet creates his poetry out of one single poetic statement only" (p. 160). In an attempt to locate this central poem in Heidegger, it will be useful to turn to "Words," one of Heidegger's more successful meditations on "the being of language and the language of being."

The occasion for this essay — its major provocation to thought — is "Worte," a brief lyric poem by Stefan George about the power of language to enact discoveries that prove to be as frail and evanescent as words themselves. Heidegger fastens onto the poem's concluding line —

"Where word breaks off no thing may be" — and, in contemplating it, comes to formulate the kinds of questions that characterize his thought at its most rewarding:

"What are words, that they have the power to endow things with Being?"

"What are things, that they need words in order to be?"

"What does Being mean here, that it appears like an endowment which is dedicated to the thing from the word?" (p. 141)

The questions are not original with Heidegger, of course, but as old as philosophy itself. Nevertheless, they are invoked anew and with a special urgency in Heidegger's thought and, what is most important, placed within the context of a phenomenological hermeneutics. By that I mean a kind of interpretive thinking that is less immediately concerned with texts than with the ground out of which texts arise, with, in other words, "originary being" as it finds its way to us through language. Here, from "Words," is Heidegger's own formulation of this idea:

The word's rule springs to light as that which makes the thing be a thing. . . .

The oldest word for the rule of the word thus thought, for Saying, is *logos*: Saying which, in showing, lets beings appear in their "it is."

The same word, however, the word for Saying, is also the word for *Being*, that is, for the presencing of beings. Saying and Being, word and thing, belong to each other in a veiled way which has hardly been thought and is not to be thought out to the end. (p. 155)

This passage is notable both for the precision of its formulations and, at the very same time, for the thinker's confessed awareness that his thought will not penetrate far enough to allow him precise answers. It is as if the veil that enwraps Saying and Being, the word and the thing, in unity and concealment can be illuminated but finally not pierced by thought. Yet what we have here is less a matter of ultimate frustration and failure as it is an acknowledgement of awe before a presence too vast to be contained within conceptual categories. Heidegger's expressed sense of the vastness and immediacy of being, of the palpable presentness of presence, far from acting as a discouragement to his thinking, has been its major spur, and ever since *Being and Time* has provided its unity as well. The search all along has been for a "hermeneutic of *Dasein*," by which things will disclose themselves to us in their being in such a way as to reveal Being itself. What makes this kind of inquiry attractive, and also a rich base for a new poetics, is the conviction on Heidegger's part that being is intimately and necessarily bound up with saying, that "it is in language that things first come into being and are." The statement, which is analogous to every poet's credo, whether expressly stated or not, recalls Wallace Stevens's proposition that "a poet's words are of things that do not exist without the words." One thinks as well of Heidegger's own elaboration of this idea in one of his Hölderlin essays:

> The poet . . . names all things in that which they are. This naming does not consist merely in something already known being supplied with a name; it is rather that when he speaks the essential word, the existent is by this naming nominated as what it is. So it becomes known *as* existent. Poetry is the establishing of being by means of the word.[2]

Hermeneutics, then, in this sense of it, is, in Richard E. Palmer's definition, "really a theory of ontological disclosure,"[3] and as a result language, which Heidegger majestically defines as "the house of Being" (p. 63), comes to receive a paramount and compelling attention. Since in Heidegger's view the poets are "the shepherds of Being," it is to poetic language in particular that Heidegger has been drawn, and in his powerful reflections on Hölderlin, Rilke, George, and Trakl, he has extended thinking well beyond its familiar limits in most schools of literary criticism and established a model for the ways in which poetics, existential ontology, and phenomenology might join in a new and more inclusive hermeneutics.

What would characterize such a poetics and which poets in particular might be newly and profitably understood by following Heidegger's lead? The emphasis, first of all, would remain, as it must, on text interpretation, but in such a way as to treat language as revelatory *less* of the nature and workings of consciousness than as the unfolding and disclosure of being which *precedes* consciousness. If saying is to be understood as *showing*, the discovery of a world made possible through words, then attention must shift away from the solitary and autonomous power of poetic consciousness to what brings it first to birth and comes to shine through it. The ground of a new critical hermeneutics, therefore, lies "not in subjectivity but in the facticity of world and the historicality of understanding."[4] The interpretive quest, following Heidegger's own quest, is for nothing less than an articulated access to being, and since it is through language, and most especially through the language of poetry, that being comes to light, the hermeneutical process must focus on what emerges from the darkness that precedes words and plunges back into concealment. Revealment and concealment, the two poles of

199

phenomenological disclosure, thus become a central focus of the critical act, which, like the poetic act itself, searches for meaning in the repetition and retrieval of originary being. Just as, in Heidegger's view, thinking is *listening* (p. 123), so proper reading, interpreting, and understanding are parallel ways of being creatively open to what manifests itself in the poem, to both the said and the unsaid of the world as it enters and departs from language. If, as Heidegger says, "the whole sphere of presence is present in saying" and "only where there is language is there world,"[5] then it is not a tautology to maintain the obvious, namely, that what manifests itself in the poem is first and foremost *language*. And what manifests itself in and through language? For answers I turn to the poets, to Bialik, for instance, who tells us that "language contains no word so slight that the hour of its birth was not one of powerful and awesome self-revealment. . . . How much of profound philosophy, of divine revealment was there in that small word 'I' that the first man uttered!"[6] Any contemporary poem that could recapture that primary moment of discovery would be eligible for greatness, just as would be any interpretive poetics that could present it coherently. Octavio Paz advances our thinking a bit further in his essay on "The Poetic Revelation":

> By a path that, in its own way, is also negative, the poet comes to the brink of language. And that brink is called silence, blank page. A silence that is like a lake, a smooth and compact surface. Down below, submerged, the words are waiting. And one must descend, go to the bottom, be silent, wait. Sterility precedes inspiration, as emptiness precedes plenitude. The poetic word crops out after periods of drought. But whatever its express content may be, whatever its concrete meaning, the poetic word affirms the life of this life. I mean: the poetic act, poetizing, the poet's utterance — independently of the particular content of that utterance — is an act that, originally at least, does not constitute an interpretation, but rather a revelation of our condition.[7]

In the same way, any criticism that, by rightly interpreting language, could bring us to approach "the life of this life" would obviously, and meaningfully, be in the service of more than rhetoric. Just what it is we *are* in the service of as critics, incidentally, is a nice question, and a seldom asked one. A possible reply is provided us once more by Octavio Paz, when he asks a similar question about the work of poets. This is his answer:

> The poet is not served by words. He is their servant. In serving them, he returns them to the plenitude of their

nature, makes them recover their being. Thanks to poetry, language reconquers its original state. (p. 37)

To return us there, so that we might know the place and be in it as if for the first time, would put us in the employ of the gods and, like Hermes, we too would be the bearers of the message of destiny. Can we, as critics, also be its interpreters? We can be if we rightly heed the message of our vocation, which affirms the simultaneity of word and world. In pointing to this simultaneity, and, furthermore, in insisting upon it, Heidegger has wrought a considerable change in the concept and scope of hermeneutics, which prior to him had been understood chiefly in the narrower terms of a philological discipline strictly limited to text interpretation. As Richard Palmer has argued, "the subject-object schema, objectivity, norms of validation, the text as an expression of life — all are foreign to Heidegger's approach, [which is dedicated instead to clarifying] the moment that meaning comes to light."[8]

To a poet *as* poet, this moment comes as an experience with and through language. What does it mean "to undergo an experience with language"? The question is implicit in much of Heidegger's late writings but is raised explicitly in "The Nature of Language." It will be useful to look briefly at what he says in this important but exceptionally difficult essay and then go on to examine some poems that attempt to express, as a major part of their progress into poetry, what it means to undergo an experience with language.

"To undergo an experience," writes Heidegger,

means that something befalls us, strikes us, comes over us, overwhelms and transforms us. . . . The experience is not of our own making; to undergo here means that we endure it, suffer it, receive it as it strikes us and submit to it. . . .

To undergo an experience with language, then, means to let ourselves be properly concerned by the claim of language by entering into and submitting to it. If it is true that man finds the proper abode of his existence in language — whether he is aware of it or not — then an experience we undergo with language will touch the innermost nexus of our existence. (p. 57)

By the forcefulness of this description, it is clear that Heidegger has in mind a more than ordinary relation to language. "It could be," he conjectures, "that an experience we undergo with language is too much for us moderns" (p. 58), that we prefer instead a more distant or more strictly utilitarian relationship to language, one in which *we* use it rather than have *it* possess us. But such an attitude reduces language to something less than itself — Heidegger calls it "metalanguage," the information gathering and distributing medium of a technologized civilization — and consequently reduces us to something less than ourselves. For if language cannot be brought to voice more purely and authentically, then something in us goes mute as well.

Yet Heidegger maintains that from time to time, and especially "when the issue is to put into language something which never yet has been spoken," words may come to life in unexpected and particularly striking ways. At such times poetry is born, and "a poet might even come to the point where he is compelled — in his own way, that is, poetically — to put into language the experience he undergoes with language" (p. 59).

It is precisely this experience that I am interested in searching out in poetry, a poetry full enough and close enough to "touch the innermost nexus of our existence." Where does one find such poetry?

Within modern poetry one finds it, surprisingly enough, in abundance, so much so that one can select from a large body of literature written in several languages. In French poetry, one would look to Mallarmé and Valéry, in German poetry to Hölderlin, Rilke, Hofmannsthal, and Celan, in American poetry to that central tradition that begins with Emerson and Whitman and comes into the twentieth century to include such figures as Stevens, Eliot, Crane, and Williams. In all cases, one would look for, and find amply exhibited, poetic reflections on the nature of poetry, which especially in our time would of necessity have to include reflections on silence as well as on language, on the distances between words and things as well as on their proximity, on the void as well as on plenitude. In carrying out such a study, one would begin to take cognizance of two movements in particular that have tended to dominate modern poetry and shape its prevailing ideas of language. Following Gerald L. Bruns, who has recently and usefully given us just such a study in his *Modern Poetry and the Idea of Language*, we can define these two "extremes of speech" as "hermetic" and "Orphic" movements, keeping in mind that they do not ever perform entirely exclusive roles but rather alter dialectically within the play of language that is poetry. It will be convenient to adopt Bruns's definitions:

> We can call the first idea 'hermetic' because the direction of the poet's activity is toward the literary work as such, that is, the work as a self-contained linguistic structure. . . . We can call the second idea 'Orphic,' after Orpheus, the primordial singer whose sphere of activity is governed by a mythical or ideal unity of word and being, and whose power extends therefore beyond the formation of a work toward the creation of the world.[9]

Following Heidegger, it is necessarily to the second of these two movements that we must direct our discussion. For Heidegger's central poet, like Orpheus, is a poet of the earth, in whose song being comes to blossom. The finest Orphic poetry of the century is Rilke's, but for present purposes I want to look to the work of a more recent poet, to Denise Levertov. Let me admit from the outset that I do not regard her as a figure anywhere comparable in achievement or stature to Rilke and do not come to her for the reasons that Heidegger gave for his choice of Hölderlin, namely, that he "is in a preeminent sense *the poet of the poet*. That is why he compels a decision." Denise Levertov has written some admirable poems and one that is possibly great, but in no way is she a poet of the front rank who "compels a decision." Rather, I come to her partly because today we *have* no poets of the front rank — and I am interested in exploring the ground of that notable lack — poets who, like Hölderlin, write because they feel "borne on by the poetic vocation to write expressly of the essence of poetry."[10] Poetry in our time may on occasion pretend to such a station but nowhere has it attained it, at least in part because it has been compromised by the "metalanguage" of the age. Octavio Paz, one of the more strenuous interrogators of the condition of poetry today, is once more acute in his observations:

> Many contemporary poets, wishing to cross the barrier of emptiness that the modern world puts before them, have tried to seek out the lost audience: to go to the people. But now there are no people: there are organized masses. And so, "to go to the people" means to occupy a place among the "organizers" of the masses. The poet becomes a functionary. This change is quite astonishing. . . . The poet has a "place" in society today. But does poetry? (p. 30)

Denise Levertov is notable as a poet who has won a prominent place for herself, a prominence gained through the publication of a dozen books and numerous public readings of her poetry. Given the pressures that accompany success in American life, it would be unusual for a poet not to have been hurt some by the kinds of activity that one has to engage in to establish prominence, and Denise Levertov is merely one of many who show in their work the compromises and erosions of language exacted by success. We shall examine the nature and possibly also the origins of these failings shortly, but first I want to briefly sketch some of the brighter moments of the poetry, moments in which language comes to light more clearly in its own terms. A useful way to do that is to look at a few of the many versions of her still developing *ars poetica*, to those poems in which the poet takes cognizance of her relation to language, poems in which poetry voices its own deepest hopes for a native and authentic speech. In *Overland to the Islands* (1958), her third collection, for instance, one finds this happy account of "Illustrious Ancestors":

> The Rav
> of Northern White Russia declined,
> in his youth, to learn the
> language of birds, because
> the extraneous did not interest him; nevertheless
> when he grew old it was found
> he understood them anyway, having
> listened well, and as it is said, 'prayed
>   with the bench and the floor.' He used
> what was at hand — as did
> Angel Jones of Mold, whose meditations
> were sewn into coats and britches.
>   Well, I would like to make,
> thinking some line still taut between me and them,
> poems direct as what the birds said,
> hard as a floor, sound as a bench,
> mysterious as the silence when the tailor
> would pause with his needle in the air.

In an interesting autobiographical note on this poem, Miss Levertov identified "the Rav of Northern White Russia" as Schneour Zalman, the founder of Chabad Chassidism, from whom her father claimed descent, and Angel Jones of Mold as a "Welsh tailor and mystic," from whom her mother descended. It is keeping with this very special genealogy, therefore, that the idea of language expressed in the poem is likewise special, invested as it is with the properties of silent communication and magical transmission. One need not look to the esoteric traditions to understand the poet's hope for a vital and informed speech, however, but rather just to another poem — to this one, "A Common Ground," for instance, from *The Jacob's Ladder* (1961):

> Not 'common speech'
> a dead level
> but the uncommon speech of paradise,
> tongue in which oracles
> speak to beggars and pilgrims:
>
> not illusion but what Whitman called
> 'the path
> between reality and the soul,'
> a language
> excelling itself to be itself,

speech akin to the light
with which at day's end and day's
renewal, mountains
sing to each other across the cold valleys.

The two poems both end on a common note of mystery, a mystery wedded to language, which is coterminous in the first poem with silence and in the second with light. What arrests the imagination in both cases, therefore, and brings it to song is, quite astonishingly, the speechless — that momentary pause before and after words *in which* words have their birth. Like the song of the mountains, which issues only at the twilight moments of transition ("at day's end and day's/ renewal"), poetry exists at its purest in those intervals of change and transference, momentary openings that it looks to penetrate and fill with song. Bialik considered such openings danger zones, and declared, in fact, that "the most dangerous moment — both in speech and in life — is that between concealments, when the void looms." Yet such moments, he continued reassuringly, "are very rare both in speech and in life, and for the most part men skip over them unawares."[11] Men might but poets cannot, for it is precisely out of this void, out of the wordless, that words come. Like the rare but everyday disclosure of the mountain peaks in the fading and renewal of light, language continually re-enters and emerges from silence, thus becoming itself by excelling itself. It is this manifestation of language "between concealments" that I take to be the principle interest of these two poems.

For Denise Levertov's fullest elaboration of this idea we must look to a later and longer poem, one in which the classical agent of transmutation and disclosure is himself directly invoked by name. I refer, of course, to Orpheus and to an extraordinary poem in Miss Levertov's eighth book of poems, *Relearning the Alphabet* (1970), a poem in which we confront, in Heidegger's words, "a poet [who has] come to the point where he is compelled to put into language the experience he undergoes with language." "A Tree Telling of Orpheus" is Denise Levertov's most forceful and direct presentation of this experience, so forceful and so direct, in fact, that in reading it one comes to know exactly what Heidegger meant when he defined experience as something that "befalls us, strikes us, comes over us, overwhelms and transforms us." The poem is too long to be quoted in full and too much of a piece to be easily cited in selection, but here nevertheless is a sample of it:

Then as he sang
it was no longer sounds only that made the music:
he spoke, and as no tree listens I listened, and language
        came into my roots
                out of the earth,

```
              into my bark
                            out of the air,
              into the pores of my greenest shoots
                            gently as dew
     and there was no word he sang but I knew its meaning.
     He told of journeys,
                of where sun and moon go while we stand in the dark,
           of an earth-journey he dreamed he would take some day
     deeper than roots. . . .
     He told of the dreams of man, wars, passions, griefs,
                and I, a tree, understood words — ah, it seemed
     my thick bark would split like a sapling's that
                                   grew too fast in the spring
     when a late frost wounds it.
```

Song, when it is this intense, "bowls us over . . . transmutes our relation to language" (p. 107), as Heidegger knowingly says. In the Rilkean formulation, *Gesang ist Dasein*: poetry is existence. Language aroused rouses us, conjures up a world in which we dance in the fullness and joy of being alive. Denise Levertov's poem succeeds more so than any other contemporary American poem I know in bodying forth this dynamic of disclosure. It records and *is* a coming-into-being of heightened and primary experience; it records and *is* the lyrical unfolding and possession of a world. In an earlier poem, "The Unknown," we find this poetic credo: "The awakening is/ to transformation,/ word after word." In "A Tree Telling of Orpheus," the awakening is no abstraction but part of a familiar and powerful moment, the moment of creative inspiration, which, to a poet, is identical with the breath of life itself. As word after word ripples into full-throated song, then lapses back once more into feintness and finally and inevitably into silence, we come to see that the emotional arc of this poem is one and the same with its meaning. Both may be described in terms of that central Heideggerian insight with which we began: at their fullest and most expressive, language and being are coterminous: "the being of language" and "the language of being" coalesce. It is poetry that unites them, hallows and celebrates the union, then retreats back into the wordless, where it resides until summoned again by a new Orpheus. The moment of inspiration and insight runs its course, and both speech and the world return to their more common levels.

"But what we have lived/ comes back to us," as Miss Levertov's poem persuades us so movingly, so that "we see more" and "feel" more, and hence *are* more, precisely in the sense of being able *to be* at all. Language is the house of Being, and we owe a large debt to such a poem as this one for permitting us the privilege of inhabiting it so fully.

Relearning the Alphabet is notable for containing not only "A Tree Telling of Orpheus," Denise Levertov's largest achievement to date as a poet, but also some of her weakest poems. The phenomenon of excellent and poor poetry mingling in the same collection is not rare, to be sure, but in *Relearning the Alphabet* the best is so good and the poorest so bad as to provoke us to thought. The situation calls to mind one of the most challenging questions raised by Heidegger in *Being and Time*: "What kind of Being does language have, if there can be such a thing as a 'dead' language? What do the 'rise' and 'decline' of a language mean ontologically?"[12] Set within the context of historical languages, these questions might evince some far-reaching conclusions about the respective strengths of national cultures and their abilities to posit a future tense for themselves. If "language is the house of Being," where is the present domicile of, say, Gaelic? Or, more tragically, of Yiddish? On the other hand, there is the singular example of Hebrew reborn and the concurrent return of the Jews to their homeland. The intertwinings of linguistic and national revival in this instance are too striking to be ignored, and one would want to know more than we perhaps do know about the ontological relationship between Hebrew resurrected and Jerusalem restored.

Yet despite the presence of "the Rav of Northern White Russia" among her esteemed and "Illustrious Ancestors," it would appear that Denise Levertov has not been much moved as a poet by the richness of the revival just alluded to, for, as she writes in one of her later poems, "Without a terrain in which, to which, I belong,/ language itself is my one home, my Jerusalem." Language being the medium of poetry, the statement is in one sense true, of course, for all poets, yet precisely because Jerusalem is no longer a mere metaphor — precisely, that is to say, because it has taken on new ontological status — the level of abstraction in this poetic credo is disturbingly weak, as is the notable flatness of speech in which the credo itself is formulated. One is moved, then, to try to transfer Heidegger's questions out of their historical context and into the sphere of poetry. More specifically, if our interest remains that of exploring the relationship between "the being of language" and "the language of being," how do we account for the simultaneous presence of "live" and "dead" language in a single collection of poems? Put another way, if language is always revelatory, and we know that it is, what is revealed in insincere or uninspired or merely imitative speech? What is the precise nature of that ontological unease that exists, for instance, between "A Tree Telling of Orpheus" and "From a Notebook," the poem from which the Jerusalem line has been taken?

"From a Notebook: October '68-May '69" is too long and too uninteresting a poem to quote at any length, but here, from Part I, is a small sample of what it is like:

> Revolution or death. Revolution or death.
> Wheels would sing it
>   but railroads are obsolete,

we are among the clouds, gliding, the roar
a toneless constant.
                    Which side are you on?
Revolution, of course. Death is Mayor Daley.
This revolution has no blueprints, and
                    ('What makes this night different
                    from all other nights?')
is the first that laughter and pleasure aren't shot down in.

Life that
          wants to live.
                              (Unlived life
                    of which one can die.)
          I want the world to go on
          unfolding. The brain
not gray except in death, the photo I saw
of prismatic radiance pulsing from live tissue.
          I see Dennis Riordan and de Courcy Squire,
          gentle David Worstell, instransigent Chuck Matthei
          blowing angel horns at the imagined corners.
          Jennie Orvino singing
          beatitudes in the cold wind

                    outside a Milwaukee courthouse.
I want their world — in which they already live,
they're not waiting for demolition and reconstruction.
                              'Begin here.'
Of course I choose
revolution.

This kind of doggerel, a weak imitation of Berkeley Bravura, winds on for
some twenty pages, during which time the poem courses raggedly through
the rhetorical wrecks of American campus life of the late 1960's. One feels
embarrassed for a poet who strains so hard to enlist her language for the
revolutionary "cause," a cause that enters her poetry like some tired
locomotive, puffing and chugging its way along until it comes to an
exhausted halt:

                    I choose
                              revolution but my words
          often already don't reach forward
                    into it —
                              (perhaps)

Poetry collapses limpidly onto such terrain, which is familiar enough to

208

the poet, no doubt, but does not belong to her, and least of all to her *as* poet. The poem acknowledges as much:

> Whom I would touch
> I may not,
> whom I may
> I would
> but often do not.
>
> My diction marks me
> untrue to my time;
> change it, I'd be
> untrue to myself.

Yet change it she did — "The words came through, transistor/turned up loud" — and in the change we witness the abandonment of poetry to politics, an abandonment made almost inevitable, at least within the context of present-day American culture, when a poet seeks so ardently and willfully "to go to the people." The result for the poet is that he risks becoming a "functionary . . . a high-ranking employee of the 'cultural front,' " as Octavio Paz explains it. For "poetry lives on the deepest levels of being, while ideologies and everything that we call ideas and opinions constitute the most superficial layers of consciousness. . . . Modern political [movements] turn the poet into a propagandist and thus degrade him" (pp. 30-31). No wonder that, after the batterings of ideology, Denise Levertov felt impelled as a poet to start all over again, to "relearn the alphabet,/ relearn the world," to "go stumbling back/ to [her] origins," which are as distant from the meta-language of her "Notebook" poem as "the uncommon speech of paradise" is from the rhetoric of revolution. To such a poet as this one, the only authentic revolution is Orphic, a transmutation that "is not under the will's rule." Poetry learns its lessons from the depths of language, or not at all.[13]

The issue involved here is not one of any inevitable confrontation between poetry and politics per se — in the case of a Brecht, for example, there was no conflict between the two — but rather that of recognizing and living out of one's most authentic creative sources. In Denise Levertov's case, such sources are not naturally located in or even near the external pressures of political activity; no matter how pressing political demands may seem, they will yield little "poetry" to an imagination shaped, as this poet's has been, by the traditions of Romantic aestheticism and Modernist sensibility. The *person* one is may respond to the slogans of the campus and street; the *poet* one is will not, at least not in any way that will be beneficial for poetry. This split between "poet" and "person" is not one that is readily or easily acknowledged, but the refusal to acknowledge it will only insure a continuation of damaging results for both poet *and*

209

person. All poets strive mightily against such bifurcation, but only the great among them — a Milton, a Goethe, a Rilke — seem to be able to raise the quarrel of divided allegiances into true poetic argument. For the rest, the imagination either succumbs or is condemned to hobble along on crippled feet.

There is a philosophic side to these concerns, which may be illuminated by reference to the struggles of an earlier poet.

In a letter that he wrote to his friend Neuffer (November 12, 1798), Hölderlin described a different kind of disorientation that he was suffering through as a poet, and it is one that we would do well to remember today:

> From my early youth onwards the world drove my spirit back into itself, and I am still suffering from this. There is, of course, a hospital where wrecked poets of my kind can take refuge honorably, that is philosophy. But I cannot leave my first love, the hopes of my youth, and I should rather perish without any claim to distinction than part from the sweet home of the Muses, from which only chance has banned me. If you know some good advice for me, which will, as soon as possible, lead me to the true way, give it to me. I lack facility more than strength, *nuances* more than ideas, manifoldly ordered sounds more than a keynote, shadows more than light, and all this for one reason: I avoid the commonplace and the vulgar too much in real life. I am truly a pedant, if you like.[14]

The crisis that Hölderlin describes here could only have been written by a poet of the Enlightenment, or by a Romantic poet still laboring under the burden of Enlightenment thought. If poetry is in a condition of crisis today, it is for altogether different reasons, reasons not attributable to an excess of thought but rather to its deficiency. Heidegger has made the charge that "man today is in flight from thinking,"[15] and, with but few exceptions, the work of most of our poets would tend to bear him out. Within American poetry of the twentieth century, the most notable exception has been Wallace Stevens, who confessed to having "the most intense interest in defining . . . the place of poetry in thought and . . . the special thinking of poetry."[16] On occasion, Eliot shared a somewhat similar interest but confined it strictly to his writings as an essayist. Pound, Williams, and Cummings seem not to have shared it at all and more often than not were openly antipathetic to ideas in poetry. Hart Crane, perhaps the saddest case of all, partially wrecked himself, in good Romantic fashion, against the shores of a thinking that receded from his grasp the more eagerly he strained to reach them. There are others that one could cite as well, but it suffices to stop with these and remark what is by now a truism, namely, that poetry in our day, at least within its American context, has not been very much bothered by the kinds of problems that weighed so heavily on a Hölderlin. The hospitals to which wrecked poets of recent years have carted themselves have been much flimsier structures than philosophy. Far from avoiding "the commonplace and the vulgar," they have sought refuge in these places, as they have in popular psychology, evangelical politics, and the various forms of self-indulgence that go to make up much of cultural life today. In almost exactly inverse proportion to Hölderlin's complaints, ours has been a poetry conspicuously *lacking* in strength more than facility, a keynote more than manifoldly ordered sounds, light more than shadows, and, most seriously of all, lacking ideas more than nuances. What other period could bring a poet of maturity to utter such lines as these: "Revolution or death. Revolution or death.... Of course I choose/ revolution." Yet this same poet, reduced here to the level of silliness, has also given us some of the most subtly nuanced poems we have, poems of a finely attuned sensibility and an inherently elegant grace.

With respect to sensibility, in fact, ours has been a rich and even daring poetry, marked by a gift for the most detailed and exploratory kinds of perception. Yet ever since the Romantic period, poets of sensibility have come up against the limits of private perception, and when these are reached and exhausted, there is nowhere to go but down, which has meant, quite literally, into a silence so absolute as to have suicide as its neighboring and welcoming end. Self-destruction, the refuge to which more and more of our ailing poets have taken themselves, becomes a final option only when poetry has closed itself off from thought, or at least from the kind of thought that has Being as its end.

If it is true, as Leigh Hunt observed, that "thought by itself makes no poet at all," it is also true that, lacking thought, poetry in our day will not be able to advance much further at all. It has gone about as far as it can meaningfully go in exploring the range of private sensibility, to the point where what it now needs is not a further push along this same path but re-direction, and in this effort thinking has a role to play. I look to Heidegger to define it:

> There is the danger that we will overstrain a poem . . . by thinking too much into it, and thereby debar ourselves from being moved by its poetry. Much greater of course — but who today would admit it? — is the danger that we will think too little. . . . The lofty poetry of all great poetic work always vibrates within a realm of thinking. . . . Thinking in turn goes its way in the neighborhood of poetry. It is well, therefore, to give thought to the neighbor. . . . Poetry and thought, each

needs the other in its neighborhood, each in its fashion, when it comes to ultimates. In what region the neighborhood itself has its domain, each of them, thought and poetry, will define differently, but always so that they will find themselves within the same domain. But because we are caught in the prejudice nurtured through centuries that thinking is a matter of ratiocination, that is, of calculation in the widest sense, the mere talk of a neighborhood of thinking to poetry is suspect. (pp. 69-70)

This is not the place to rehearse at any length that ancient quarrel between philosophy and poetry to which Heidegger alludes, but it is in keeping with our subject to remark that criticism can have a role today in helping to ease that quarrel by making poetry and thinking more compatible with one another. By defining their common domain as within the sphere of language — language understood in the Heideggerian terms of opening up an access to being — criticism can render discussion of the relationship between poetry and philosophy less suspect. Both would profit from a rapprochement, for just as poetry stands in need of more thoughtful perceptions, so does thinking need to come to grips with the more pleasurable perceptions. As it is, each now presently resists the other, but between poetry and philosophy "there exists a secret kinship because in the service of language both [can] intercede and give lavishly of themselves."[17] Criticism, positioned as it is between the two, is by nature in the service of both, and if by performing its work well it "makes a good poet's work even more difficult for him to perform," that is only in keeping with its vocation, "since only the overcoming of genuine difficulties can result in poems wholly adequate to the age."[18]

Indiana University

NOTES

1 Martin Heidegger, *On the Way to Language* (New York: Harper & Row, 1971), pp. 51-52. Henceforth all citations from this book will be given in the body of the text itself immediately following the quotation.

2 Martin Heidegger, *Existence and Being* (Chicago: Henry Regnery Company, 1949), p. 281.

3 Richard E. Palmer, *Hermeneutics: Interpretation Theory in Schleiermacher, Dilthey, Heidegger, and Gadamer* (Evanston: Northwestern University Press, 1969), p. 137.

4 *Hermeneutics*, p. 137.

5 *Existence and Being*, p. 276.

212

6 Chaim Nachman Bialik, "Revealment and Concealment in Language," in *An Anthology of Hebrew Essays* (Tel Aviv: Institute for the Translation of Hebrew Literature, 1966), I, 128-129.

7 Octavio Paz, *The Bow and the Lyre* (Austin: University of Texas Press, 1973), p. 13. Henceforth all citations from this book will be given in the body of the text itself immediately following the quotation.

8 *Hermeneutics*, p. 156.

9 Gerald L. Bruns, *Modern Poetry and the Idea of Language* (New Haven: Yale University Press, 1974), p. 1.

10 *Existence and Being*, p. 271.

11 *An Anthology of Hebrew Essays*, I, 134.

12 Martin Heidegger, *Being and Time* (New York: Harper & Row, 1962), p. 209.

13 Denise Levertov has addressed herself to the tensions that exist between the private vision of a poet and his public commitments in her collection of essays, *The Poet in the World* (New York: New Directions, 1973), where she writes, "I believe in the essential interrelatedness and mutual reinforcement of the meditative and the active.... I hope to show the reader something of that relation I feel exists, and must exist, for the poet, between the inner and outer life, and which may not be denied without imperiling both." Whatever one thinks of her striving for such a connection, the poetry itself nowhere shows her success in achieving it.

14 Quoted in Michael Hamburger, *Hölderlin* (New York: Pantheon, 1952), p. 34.

15 Martin Heidegger, *Discourse on Thinking* (New York: Harper & Row, 1966), p. 45.

16 Wallace Stevens, *Letters of Wallace Stevens* (New York: Alfred A. Knopf, 1966), pp. 500-501.

17 Martin Heidegger, *What Is Philosophy?* (New Haven: College and University Press, 1956), p. 95.

18 Harold Bloom, *A Map of Misreading* (New Haven: Yale University Press, 1975), p. 10.

Heidegger and Tragedy

Michael Gelven

Neither in his specific analyses of the particular arts nor in his ontological inquiries into human existence does Martin Heidegger anywhere develop what might be called a "theory" of tragedy. To be sure, he quotes from tragedy, and in the case of his interpretation of the Chorus in *Antigone*, which we find in his *Introduction to Metaphysics*, he goes far to show us how to read the tragic passage. Yet on the meaning of tragedy as such, Heidegger is strangely silent. His thinking, however, both in terms of his existential ontology and of his works on the nature of the arts, is peculiarly well suited for examining tragedy as an art form, and even more, of throwing light on that mysterious paradox of tragedy — why we thrill to the grim failures of great men.

But it is not only that Heidegger can throw light on tragedy, but tragedy can throw light on our understanding of Heidegger's philosophy. For it is the peculiar characteristic of tragic genius to teach us how to see worth — and hence *meaning* — in noble *existence* without relying upon fortuitous circumstances or even moral excellence to prompt our approval. Just as Heidegger struggles to show us how to *think* about what it means *to be*[1] without reference to substances or even moral judgments, so do the

215

great tragedians teach us to respect the *being* of the hero even as he suffers and brings about misfortune through his actions.

Both Heidegger and the tragedians struggle with a similar problem: how to focus our attention on *being* rather than things; how to understand the meaning of existence and not merely our actions and their consequences. What is not so obvious, however, is that the philosophical inquiry which Heidegger carries out on the problems of existence constitutes a rich response to the paradox of tragedy; and the insights into the nature of the tragic art in turn provides us with a profound understanding of the chief tenets of Heidegger's philosophy. In this article I intend to think through the paradox and the nature of tragedy under the influence and inspiration of Heidegger's teachings — but in addition I intend to show how our native grasp of the meaning of tragedy reveals *in concreto* some of the more spectacular elements of Heidegger's thought. Furthermore, I shall show how this analysis of tragedy provides the best example possible of how one can understand that remarkable doctrine of Heidegger aesthetics: that art, particularly poetic art, *speaks the truth.*[2] For tragedy is not just another instance of an "art form"; its emphasis upon the *ritual of being* characterizes it as an elemental way of *thinking*. It is not by accident that tragedy, above all other arts, has fascinated the great philosophers.

The interrogation of tragedy must always proceed from a profound realization of the paradox inherent in our obvious appreciation of what should seemingly be censured and rejected: the suffering of a noble person. How is it possible to be so uplifted and so inspired to greatness at our witnessing the madness of Lear, the death of Hamlet, the damnation of Faustus, the desperate dilemma of Antigone? In order to show what this paradox means, we must avoid every attempt to *dissolve* the paradox by treating the suffering as morally deserved (Antigone ought not to have irritated Creon; Hamlet was too weak to avenge his father, hence he should have been killed; Desdemona was just too stupid, hence she deserved to be killed; etc.). For our experience of tragedy is not that of moral satisfaction — but on the contrary, there is a sense of greatness and boldness, if you will, purchased at the price of moral dissatisfaction. It is precisely because Desdemona does *not* deserve to die that we are deeply disturbed and enthralled at our *acceptance* of her murder as a part of that experience which satisfies on a different and indeed transmoral level.

In order to show how carefully the great tragedians *remove* from us our moral sentiments in interpreting the play, a close look at a particular tragedy may help to show the true nature of that strange "affirmation" which is the result of all truly great tragedy. Only in the actual working-out of a concrete instance of the tragedian's art can their emphasis upon the meaning of being (*Sinn von Sein*) be fully realized.

Few scenes in the repertoire of tragedy have greater dramatic force or power to provoke a truly tragic response than the three scenes in

Othello which show the painful development of the Moor's accusation against his innocent wife. A consideration of these three scenes (III, 4; IV, 1; IV, 2) in light of their emphasis upon the question of being will show the point better than any purely abstract arguments. The three scenes reveal the rapidly intensifying passion with which Othello confronts Desdemona with her "guilt." The first of these scenes describes his famous request for the handkerchief; the second provides the indecent sight of Othello striking his wife in public; the third shows us, almost with relief, Othello finally accusing her of infidelity, thus changing her terrible confusion to an even more terrible injury. Our perception of these events is almost unbearable, and we are usually grateful that most actors botch them rather badly with over-frenzied theatricality, for their effect done well might be beyond our capacity. There are several reasons why these scenes are so compelling. In the first place, Shakespeare has made us rather fond of both lovers, and this fondness is due in part to their respective weaknesses. We love Desdemona for her innocence and feminine sweetness, even though this is precisely what we curse in her, since these attributes become rather foolish and inadequate in terms of the enormity of her danger. A little *less* trusting, a little *less* innocent in the ways of the world, and Desdemona could easily have avoided her fate. Her innocence is at times almost startling, for she is quite serious when she asks:

> Dost thou in conscience, think, tell me, Emilia,
> That there be women do abuse their husbands
> In such gross kind?

and we are most relieved by Emilia's earthy response. The same can be said for Othello's noble but irritating sense of honor. We understand it quite well. It is that about him which attracts us to him even as it is that which brings him to disaster. For he is not boasting when he says:

> My parts, my title, and my perfect soul
> Shall manifest me rightly.

And it is Othello himself who recognizes that this characteristic is the cause of his downfall. His famous line,

> then must you speak
> Of one that loved not wisely but too well,

does not tell us that his love was too passionate, but too honorable. For Othello, to love well just *means* to love with honor, and his virtue in so doing has become his vice. In addition to these vicious virtues or virtuous vices which constitute the lovers' characters, there is the problem of justice. We know Desdemona is innocent, we also know that Othello firmly believes *he* is just in thinking her guilty, and we have a natural concern for justice. We do not want to see injustice triumph, and so the approach of such injustice grips us as we desperately hope that the wrongdoing can be avoided. If there can be such a thing as a hopeless hope, it is ours as we find ourselves caring so intensely for justice to occur when we *know* that it will not. We find ourselves, too, confused as to who suffers more, who deserves our greater sympathy; and in spite of the fact that it is Desdemona who suffers unjustly, it is Othello's agonies which, I think, touch us the more deeply.

Shakespeare's skill in developing the three-stage intensity of these gruesome confrontations between suspicious husband and injured wife is simply magnificent. In the first of these scenes, the absence of the handkerchief is unsettling; we see it as part of Iago's planning, an incident which could easily be rectified by disclosure of certain facts. Thus, although it makes us anxious, its alleviation is so palpable that our response is chiefly one of frustration. Our sentiments are, at this early stage, with Desdemona's simple and uncomplicated worry:

> Sure, there's some wonder in this handkerchief;
> I am most unhappy at the loss of it.

Unhappy, indeed! But in the second of these three scenes, Othello's physical savagery is unforgiveable. We are no longer dealing with a situation which can be rectified by proper information. His fury and anger are blinding him and hurting both himself and his wife. Our reaction to his actions, unlike the mere frustration in the previous scene, is now one of moral censure. We are led to wonder with Lodovico:

> Is this the noble Moor, whom our full senate
> Call all-in-all sufficient? Is this the nature
> Whom passion could not shake? Whose solid virtue
> The shot of accident nor dart of chance
> Could neither graze nor pierce?

In short, we are overwhelmed with outrage. But Shakespeare has not yet reached the zenith of his development of this confrontation. In the third of these dreadful encounters, we find her protestations of innocence totally inadequate. His sense of outraged honor and her sense of outraged innocence can compel no longer our sympathy but our *shock*. We are no longer compassionate or even outraged, but aghast. We tremble as he says:

> But there, where I have garnered up my heart,
> Where either I must live or bear no life,
> The fountain from the which my current runs

218

Or else dries up; to be discarded thence!
Or keep it as a cistern for foul toads
To knot and gender in!

As we hear this, we know it is too late. We are now prepared to watch in stunned horror at the inevitable destruction of these two whom we have learned to love far too dearly. When he kills her, he protests that her word "murder" is inaccurate: he calls it "sacrifice"!

Now what is the nature of this series of responses on the part of the audience? Our sense of concern for those we admire, our sense of justice, our sympathy with suffering, our outrage, even our own vicarious suffering — what is the nature of these responses? And what does it mean to *go beyond* them? We can identify these feelings loosely as *moral,* for they all belong to our sensitivity to human need. These responses constitute our moral level, and on these responses alone the play *Othello* warrants our appreciation. For if we find ourselves experiencing such emotions they may well increase our moral sensitivity, and as such be beneficial. The character of these responses can be called moral because they consist of our spiritual identification with the hero. We see his character in its flawed state, but we realize how genuinely he suffers, and we share with him his agonies. This attests to the worth of such suffering and to our natural hatred of misery. Because we feel with the hero we know how much he is hurt, and so our protest of his situation ennobles our sensitivity. These feelings identify us with the human condition, and as such they are moral.

But if we were to interrupt our participation in any of these scenes with a request for our true response, would it indeed be one of sympathy for the suffering we are witnessing? If that were so, our basic impulse would be to stop what is going on. Moral responses necessitate action. If we could, we would shout to Othello that it was Iago who stole the handkerchief; we would rush to tell Desdemona not to press her suit on Cassio's behalf; we would urge Emilia not to leave her mistress on that fateful night. Now to be sure, these instincts are present when we watch the play. But if our watching were interrupted, would our first response be to lament, How sad? How unfortunate? Is not rather our primary response to such scenes the revealing utterance, How beautiful! And with this utterance, is not the whole complexion of our experience radically altered?

"How beautiful!" we say, as we watch Othello's noble character unravel into violent jealousy; "How beautiful!" we say, as their mutual loves lead husband and wife to their fateful undoing; "How beautiful!" we say, as we watch Shakespeare so develop the scenes that our *moral* responses are totally exhausted, and we are purged of any and all moral censure or sentiment. And what does this utterance signify? It does not signify our willingness to act, as does the moral instinct, *but to let the thing go on*, to thrill to its unfolding. The moral impulse would put us on

219

the stage to keep injustice from conquering, it binds us to the sharing of those all-too-human griefs; but our exclamation, "How beautiful!" keeps us in our seats, absolves us from lamentation, and emphasizes not our humanity but that thin and insecure participation in a kind of Dionysian divinity. For in a perspective which is almost wicked from the human point of view, we find ourselves *affirming* the steady march toward doom which our beloved heroes on the stage must inevitably take. This perspective cannot be justified by the moral order, for it violates that order; but it *is* justified by the single word: beauty.

Thus, in tragedy, it is the triumph of our love of beauty over our concern for the good that thrills us. The essence of tragedy might therefore be identified as the triumph of eros over ethos: our appreciation of beauty is actually enhanced when all other forms of support and affirmation are removed. By the careful work of the tragedian we are led to abandon our purely moral perspective of what is going on, so that our appreciation of its beauty will stand alone. We *need* to have our moral sense offended lest we make the otherwise inevitable error of justifying beauty on moral grounds. But many great philosophers have assured us that beauty is precisely that form of affirmation which is autonomous — that, as Kant says: the beautiful is that which we appreciate *without interest.*[3]

But if our love is of the beautiful, and if beauty is without interest or benefit or even moral approval, what is beauty *about*? What is it that I *affirm* in the love of the beautiful even when all other forms of support are removed? The answer is: *existence.* A beautiful woman is she who is appreciated not for what she does but simply for what she is. Reverence for beauty therefore is the ancient and classical way of getting at the *meaning of being.*

When an architect makes beautiful a house, what he has done through his art is to show us *what it means to dwell* — and he has done so by showing that "dwelling" is precisely that dimension to our going and staying in buildings which is *not necessary.* A warm and dry hovel which protects us from the elements provides us with the basic necessities — it is why we build the house in the first place. But once this basic aspect is provided for, whatever *else* we do, whether it is to taper the supporting posts and thus make them pillars, or arch a doorway so that what is a mere aperture in a wall becomes an entranceway; whatever is in addition to the needs is of the order of beauty, i.e., that from which we learn *meaning.* The architect teaches us, through his art, *what it means to dwell.* Thus we see how beauty reveals meaning.[4]

Now, in tragedy, the artist's skill, by doing violence to the basic needs and instincts (comfort and morals) forces our attention solely to the realization of the worth of our *existence.* The nobility of the hero (which is an aesthetic, and not a moral virtue) becomes emphasized when I cannot find any other source to affirm what I see.

Tragedy began as a part of the Dionysian festival. Its etymology (literally: the song of the goat) suggests the close connection between the plays and the celebration of beauty *for its own sake* — for Dionysius is that god whose riggish indifference to moral restraint deifies our love (eros) for things beautiful. Upon analysis we see that beauty teaches us the *meaning* (rather than the use or the cause) of a thing. What a dwelling *means* is accomplished by the architect making the building beautiful. Hence, even as early as the ancients, beauty was seen as that by which the mere existence of a thing is appreciated on its own. This is precisely what Heidegger teaches in his existential ontology.

What Heidegger argues is that our existence *as such* is open to rational inquiry, and is hence meaningful in and of itself. But furthermore, Heidegger's analyses show us that what makes our existence meaningful is: *first*, that the modes or ways in which we exist are either authentic or inauthentic; and *second*, that the basis for authenticity and inauthenticity is our capacity to *fail* at being, or *to be* as the basis of nullity in guilt. This means that one's being guilty is the basis by which one's existence can be *thought about*. (Since whatever is *thought about* is thereby meaningful, to be able to be guilty is the basis of our existence being meaningful.) Being guilty — and the reticent projection of this guilt toward our own possibilities, which is the meaning of authenticity — is not a moral predicate which reveals the worth of action, but is an ontological term which reveals the meaning of being as such. Thus without this profound sense of being the basis of my own failure (and the resolute acceptance of this being guilty in authenticity), my existence could not be thought about, and as such, could not be meaningful. But the question is, How can I think about my being? Must not I first determine the question of substance (by asking, What *kind* of thing am I?) or at least must I not first determine the principles by which I can make *moral judgments*? Heidegger has shown, however, that I *can* think about being, prior to and independently of these questions, and indeed, by realizing the fundamental and irreducible capacity to fail at existing. But since this very capacity to *be* negatively is the principle by which meaning is possible, I learn to affirm, to accept, indeed, to *celebrate* my being precisely in the light of this capacity to fail. However, this is surely the same thing which *King Lear* provides for the sensitive audience.

By carefully expurgating any possibility of moral satisfaction or approval, the only thing left we have to approve is the worth of Lear's *being*. (And in so doing, we approve too of our own being.) His suffering, madness, and even his death repudiate *meaninglessness* because we see these things which are done beautifully, as dimensions which matter. Lear, though he falls, does so in such splendid terms that we realize there is meaning to his very existence which all his agony and misery can never erase.

Both Heidegger's thinking and the tragedian's art are intensely affirmative in this singular sense — they both refute nihilism. In spite of Stanley Rosen's miserable and petty misinterpretation,[5] Heidegger's works teach us how to confront the nihilist — by showing that the meaning of existence can indeed be thought about. For the nihilist need not join with either the sceptic or the relativist: he could accept the claims of certain knowledge, and even admit there are certain duties which one should do; but the nihilist simply adds that the validity of such reasoning *does not matter*. He says this for a simple reason: there is no way, he claims, in which my existence can be rationally thought about. Both Heidegger and the tragedian show the nihilist's position to be untenable. Heidegger does so by actually developing successfully a thematic analysis of the ways in which we exist and grounding them in the reality of our being. The tragedian counfounds the nihilist by showing our affirmation of the nobility of being, even when all *other* sources of affirmation, such as pleasure, well-being, utility, and even moral approval, are violated.

The mutual confrontation with nihilism by Heidegger and the tragedian manifests a similarity in their ultimate attitudes toward the reality of being. The ability to-be-guilty, our ultimate and non-transferable power to be the basis of our own success and failure, is celebrated by both philosopher and artist. Whether the burden of being guilty is due to our own moral weakness (Macbeth) or to the circumstances of our fate (Antigone), what is affirmed is the meaning of existence as such. Although Antigone may not be as directly responsible for her misery as Macbeth, it is still her own existence which is made meaningful by her dilemma, a dilemma which is due to *who* she is.

A slightly different nomenclature from more classical times evokes a similar response. Of the great trinity of being — the true, the good, and the beautiful — it could be said that *truth* is that through which we can think and ground *facts* and *actuality*: i.e., truth tells us about the world. *Goodness* is that through which we think and ground our *acts* and our *duties*: i.e., goodness tells us what we ought to do. But *beauty* is that through which we think and ground *meaning*: i.e., to see a thing as beautiful is to see what it means, or to see it in the light of its meaning. The classical emphasis upon the beautiful as that which reveals meaning accounts for Heidegger's "shift" from doing existential analyses to his "later" concern for the arts. For one who truly understands Heidegger and classical views toward beauty, however, this "shift" is as natural, indeed as inevitable as thought itself. For beauty speaks of the meaning of being — which is precisely the concern of Heidegger's early *Being and Time*. Perhaps the "turning" from ontology to poetry is simply the result of the courageous recognition of the importance of beauty in revealing philosophical meaning.

In the above analysis of the three scenes from *Othello*, we see how our responses are very carefully manipulated so that we go through various stages: first our sense of frustration, then moral outrage, and

222

finally shock. Our interests, then, shift from a concern for mere physical conditions (the location of the handkerchief) to moral judgments (the censure of Othello's anger) to the aesthetic response of numbed but deeply thrilling acceptability of the inevitable. By forcing us through these stages, Shakespeare succeeds as a tragedian, and leaves us with a profound sense of reverence for our *being*. Heidegger, on the other hand, in articulating in his existential analysis how true being is grasped in authenticity, carefully leads us through a similar journey. We are first led through the rejection of the Cartesian world and subject — i.e., rejection of substance as the basis of being. Then, by showing that moral actions *presuppose* the existential situation — i.e., that one must first *be able to be guilty* before one can be held responsible for an action — he removes us from establishing moral judgments as the basis of meaning. Both Shakespeare's development of Othello's grand but guilty existence and Heidegger's insistence upon the fundamental priority of guilt as the basis for reasoning about human meaning succeed in showing us how we stand in thrall of our own being. Unless such an awareness of being *were* possible, as seen either through the tragedian's art or through Heidegger's philosophy, the *nihilist*, in his denying the thinkability of existence, would ultimately be right.

Heidegger's analysis of guilt is especially helpful in seeing this point. For his analysis shows that guilt is not something we can understand as a mere feeling or as a response to action, but is rather that essential mode of being which makes us the basis of that nullity which is necessary for a rational understanding of being. He writes:

> When human existence understandingly lets itself be called forth to the possibility of guilt, this includes its becoming free for the call. In understanding the call, human existence is in thrall to its ownmost possibility of existence.[6]

Thus, only by being fundamentally guilty is the human person capable of being aware of the meaning of existence, for only then does this existence matter.

Tragedy makes the same point. Why are we so thrilled and uplifted (or, Why are we put "in thrall to our ownmost possibility of existence") by the grim suffering and abject failure of King Lear? Because the tragedy shows us that such ultimate guilt is the basis of our meaning — that Lear's greatness and nobility, in spite of his other losses, saves him (and hence, us) from *meaninglessness*. Such salvation can only be the source of the deepest kind of joy, the profoundest kind of affirmation. For all the pleasantness, justice, and well-being in the world can turn sour for us if we sense the basis of our meaning slip away — just as there is no suffering too great, not even death itself, that can ultimately conquer the tragic triumph of beauty over mere fortuity and happiness. It is not by accident that tragedy flourishes in eras and epochs charged with great fervor and enormity of the affirmative spirit: Periclean Athens, Elizabethean England, and nineteenth century Germany. Far from being morbid times, they are periods of affirmation, for tragedy shows us that even if all else is lost, the dignity and grandeur of our existence as such can be loved as beautiful.

If Heidegger does nothing else but show (1) that it is possible to inquire into the meaning of existence as such and (2) that death and guilt provide the basis for an understanding of such meaning, his thought would greatly illuminate the paradox of tragedy. But Heidegger's careful and profound analysis of the nature of art as truth does even more in throwing light upon the meaning of tragedy. For Heidegger, truth is not a matter of propositions, but rather should be seen as that by which the meaning of being is manifest. (And surely, such a definition of truth does represent what we normally mean when we use the word.) Now art, particularly the poet's art, makes us aware of what it means to be (through language) and hence, the poet literally *speaks the truth*. This is a truly amazing thing to say; indeed, as a principle of aesthetics it can almost be called spectacular. Rather than seeing art as that which makes something pleasant to look at or to otherwise sense, art is seen as concerned with truth itself. According to this remarkable theory, poets can be said to speak the truth, not because their attractively designed propositions refer to facts which happen to be the case, but because their language reveals what it means to be.

The impressive if somewhat startling advantage of this theory of aesthetics is that it breaks through the time-stiffened distinction between *what* is said and *how* it is said. This dubious distinction has often led one to believe that the inelegant vernacular could speak the same truth as brilliant poetry but without the fancy "externals." This has led many English teachers to urge their students to disregard the *meaning* of a poem and note rather the mere felicity of how nicely something, no matter what, is said. According to Heidegger, however, beautifully spoken language reveals more meaning than nonpoetic speech, and hence, *is more true*. In fact, what makes the speech of the poet beautiful is that it reveals greater truth. *How* I say something, therefore, becomes a part of *what* I say. The great poet can thus reveal certain truths which cannot be revealed outside his art. If such a point can be made, then the nature of language is not essentially that of *reference*: language does not refer to facts; rather, *language articulates meaning*. Referring to facts is only one (and indeed a derived) way of articulating meaning.

But can we believe such a theory? As much as we might like to accept Heidegger's development of language, in which poetry speaks a truth unattainable through prose, how are we to *understand* such a claim? What is it about poetry (and the arts in general) that provides it with the special qualities for uncovering the meaning of being? It is only when we realize that tragedy is a ritual, and that tragic language or poetry *performs a rite*, that the full significance of this theory for our understanding of tragedy can be seen.

The purpose of tragic poetry is not to reveal the facts, but to establish respect for the meaning of human existence. It takes just three words to inform someone that Romeo loves Juliet, but the knowledge of such a fact is not the purpose of Shakespeare's art. Through his art he *establishes* the meaning of such a love. His language is true, not because it is accurate, but because it is *performative*. That is to say, we attend the theatre, not to find out what is going to happen, but to celebrate its meaning. The very formality and structure of metered lines, for example, gives a stately atmosphere of pomp and ritual. Through such solemnity of language our attention is drawn by the power of language to *establish* meaning. In tragedy, language does not reveal what is the case, it establishes an order of meaning, for its nature is performative. This needs further comment.

Let us take an example of a non-dramatic instance of performative language. The philosophers tell us that uses of language such as the making of promises, the taking of oaths, or the utterance of marriage vows are special kinds of language which are not *about* the world but become an important *part* of the world. Thus when I utter sayings such as "I hereby take thee as wife," or "I hereby promise that . . . ," one understands that a certain order or structure of meaning is established by the language. In the same way, religious ceremonies are performative; they do not merely remind us of certain beliefs, they establish such beliefs by official ceremony. The breaking of bread, the baptizing of an infant, the incantations at burial, exorcisms, all establish a reality by means of performative language. Reality itself is altered by the utterance. Performative language makes real certain objects of meaning. For language to be able to do this, it must have certain characteristics: it must, for example, be extraordinary; it must inspire our respect; it must be stately and formal since it itself establishes a form and a state; it must present itself with the authority necessary to establish binding influence on the mind. In tragedy, such performative language establishes the triumph of "eros over ethos"[7]; i.e., it celebrates our understanding of *what it means to be* over our mere knowledge of facts: it establishes meaning to existence.

A rite is the symbolic but concrete performance of an action which gives meaning and evokes the sentiments of reverence, awe, and fear. Because a rite is performative and not descriptive, it establishes meaning rather than merely refers to it. Often rites have legal significance, as in the case of oaths and the rites of marriage; but even when they do not, they possess a kind of authority which cannot be found in purely symbolic acts or in sentiments of nostalgia. It is sometimes said that a certain act is a "mere ritual"; i.e., that someone has done something merely out of concern for etiquette or habit. The phrase sometimes even means that someone has done something without thinking. Such uses of the term are inaccurate and manifest a profound misunderstanding of the etymology and tradition behind rites. A rite, rather than being something less than real, is actually that which determines reality. Its etymology (Latin *ritus*) shows the close connection between a rite and a religious ceremony. In fact, even in modern usage there is often the suggestion of religiosity about a rite.

Ritual provokes the sentiments of reverence, awe, and fear. Fear, because the power of that which validates the rite — i.e., the godhead, the state, or an institution — with authority, is greater than those who perform the rite. Rites put us in the presence of forces greater than ourselves, or at least provoke dimensions in ourselves (such as the moral law) which outrank our individual desires. To have ritualistically promised something is to put one's commitment beyond the influence of mere desire and the concern for pleasure. Hence, the rite produces fear, for the forces unleashed by the rite can destroy our tranquility or even our lives. It produces reverence for the same reason: we are in the presence of a reality which demands our respect and prompts our humility. And it evokes awe because a rite orients our consciousness towards dimensions of greatness. A rite prompts a kind of thinking which reveals the enormity of our being in the world. The sentiments of reverence, awe, and fear are proper responses to rites, for the performative language of a rite establishes an order to reality which binds us to the *meaning* of our existence *as* whatever it is the rite suggests.

To what extent, then, can we understand tragedy as the performance of a rite? As we have seen, tragedy is the triumph of eros over ethos; but this triumph is accomplished as a ritual. The plays of Sophocles and Shakespeare are rites performed in the temple of Dionysius — the theatre — where we *participate* in the affirmation of the autonomous worth of the beautiful, of the meaning of being as such. Such an affirmation must be established by the performative power of a rite, since no basis for affirmation can be found in a mere description or experience of the world. When we leave the performance of a successful tragedy, we sense that our own reality has been formally sanctioned by the persuasive power of greatness.

This is because the audience in a tragedy is not a group of mere observers looking on, but *participants* in the ritual. It is *we* the audience, and not the *dramatis personae*, who thrill to the grim violation of our moral instincts for the sake of participating in the worship of the autonomous worth of beauty. When Romeo first sees Juliet, the beauty of his language evokes in us an affirmation: we do not merely *hear* Romeo and thus become *informed* of his love, rather the poetry provokes in us our performance of the *rite* by which we *sanction* Romeo's commitment to Juliet:

If I profane with my unworthiest hand
This holy shrine, the gentle sin is this;
My lips, two blushing pilgrims ready stand
To smooth that rough touch with a gentle kiss.

But within just a few lines of this, our ritualistic approval of their young love is checked by our discovery (through Juliet's lines) that their love — and hence our sanction — is cursed:

My only love sprung from my only hate!
Too early seen unknown and known too late!
Prodigious birth of love it is to me,
That I must love a loathed enemy.

But, rather than merely *lamenting* the situation, *we thrill to it*, we affirm it, indeed, we participate in this frustration of happiness and thus celebrate the triumph of eros over ethos — we perform the rite by which we establish our meaning as higher than our happiness. Thus tragic poetry shows us how the poet can *speak the truth*. Heidegger's seemingly outrageous claim is here seen to be valid.

A final word should be said about the roots of tragedy in the Dionysian festival and the significance this has for Heidegger's philosophy. In celebrating eros over ethos, or the meaning of existence over a concern for the world, the Dionysians praise three things which simply confound most other thinkers. In tragedy we have seen how the Dionysians teach us to understand human suffering and even death. But suffering is not the only enigma: there is also foolishness. This they celebrate in Comedy (the song of the Fool). Comedy teaches us how to affirm our own foolishness. But the third enigma which the Dionysian teaches us to accept is perhaps the greatest of all: ignorance. Philosophy teaches us to celebrate our own ignorance. For the true philosopher, like Socrates, is he who realizes that his wisdom lies in the recognition of ignorance. Ignorance for a philosopher is that from which one can *inquire* (for knowledge *ends* inquiry: if I know, I have no need to inquire further). Thus the Dionysian celebration of ignorance is the philosophical realization of finitude. Socrates learns that he does not *possess* wisdom but that he loves it, and it is thus his self-realized ignorance that leads him to inquire and which validates the oracle's claim that he is the "wisest" of men.

These three enigmas — suffering, foolishness, and ignorance — are celebrated by the three worshippers of Dionysius: the tragedian, the comedian, and the philosopher. Martin Heidegger is a true philosopher in this special and exalted sense.

Northern Illinois University

227

NOTES

1   I translate Heidegger's phrase "Die Frage nach dem Sinn vom Sein" by "The question of what it means to be." For a defense and discussion of this translation, see my *A Commentary on Heidegger's "Being and Time"* (New York: Harper & Row, 1970), p. 18.

2   See "The Origin of the Art-work" by Heidegger, finely translated by Prof. Albert Hofstadter in *Poetry, Language and Thought* (New York: Harper & Row, 1971).

3   See Kant, I, *Critique of Judgment.*

4   For a further discussion of how beauty is the rational basis for thinking about meaning, see my *Winter, Friendship and Guilt* (New York: Harper & Row, 1973).

5   S. Rosen, *Nihilism, a Philosophical Essay* (New Haven: Yale University Press, 1970).

6   Heidegger, *Being and Time,* trans. Macquarrie and Robinson (New York: Harper & Row, 1962), p. 334.

7   For a further discussion of the definition of tragedy as "eros over ethos" see my forthcoming book, *Eros and Tragedy.*

From Heidegger to Derrida to Chance:
Doubling and (Poetic) Language

Joseph N. Riddel

> "You have a quarrel on hand, I see," said I, "with some
> of the algebraists of Paris; but proceed."
>
> — Poe, "The Purloined Letter"

I

American criticism has come to Heidegger, or he to it, very late, and for the most part by indirection. The detour produces a certain, inevitable distortion, like the itinerary of a translation, though it may be no more than the inevitable misinterpretation already posited in the Heideggerean hermeneutic. On the other hand, this lateness circumvents not a few historical distractions. While our philosophers have had to confront the politics as well as the "language" of Heidegger, literary criticism has been able to ignore the kind of resistances which, according to Jacques Derrida, mark in one way or another almost every "reading" of Heidegger in Europe — the political resistances which conceal deeper resistances, and reciprocally. Derrida remarks in various places upon the apparent obligation to begin a consideration of Heidegger with a kind of apologetics for the political and/or ideological contaminations that threaten his readers. We have been spared this for the most part, only perhaps because we have been spared a direct Heideggereanism.

But we have not been spared the problems of a certain historical seam-liness. What historians of modern thought have come to distinguish as two Heideggers (the existentialist-phenomenologist destroyer of metaphysics; and the celebrant of poetic "dwelling"), we have received in a more or less single package of transcriptions which tend to suppress the difference, or at least to remove it as a primary concern for literary criticism. Beyond that question, however, another one arises. Presuming two Heideggers, even if one is continuous with the other, do the two lend themselves to a unified hermeneutical method? It is not my concern here to take up the question of this historical placing of an early and late Heidegger, and certainly not to consider the sameness and difference in any "evolution" of his thought.

The task here is much more modest — to remark the "place" of Heidegger in certain "projects" of literary criticism. But for this purpose, one cannot ignore that the commercial (Heidegger might say, technological) chance of his translation into English texts has provided his thought with a kind of interpretive framing — the appearance in the early fifties of parts of the Hölderlin book, combined with the more recent translations of Heidegger on language and poesis, bookending the earliest and basic text, *Being and Time*. Setting this historical dislocation aside, there is the other fact that whatever impact Heidegger has had on literary criticism comes not so much directly from his own critical writings, via comparatist critics alert to the intellectual dialogue in Europe, as by another indirection: the absorption of the Heideggerean hermeneutic into various European criticisms, from existentialism to the "criticism of consciousness" to structuralism. In particular, one would have to say that the so-called Geneva School, which has had an indelible impact on American criticism, again by a certain indirection, is situated in a critique of "consciousness" and "place" which is at the same time undergirded and undermined by Heidegger's early writing. But at the very moment that a "criticism of consciousness," with its phenomenological orientation, had begun to offer a fruitful alternative to American formalist and thematic criticism, another kind of formalism known as structuralism and directed explicitly at the "ground" of phenomenology, the priority of consciousness, had begun to be translated into a variety of American methodologies.

What has been missing from the American debate, however, except in the work of a few critics with deep continental roots, is the considerable history of hermeneutical thinking which has crisscrossed Europe in the last hundred years. At the center of that thinking has been the Heideggerean destruction of metaphysics, but no less the retrieval and reinterpretation of Hegelian and Nietzschean thought, the appropriation of psychoanalysis by philosophy, and the centering of criticism on the problematics of language opened up by the new linguistics. The history is familiar enough in its broader outlines, though for the most part the American critic's awareness of the dialogue between phenomenology and structuralism has been so foreshortened (condensed largely within the past decade) that the intellectual consequences of the confrontation have been repressed. The dialogue has come so late to the American academy that, with certain powerful exceptions, we find ourselves in a "post-structuralist" period without having suffered the rites of initiation into that which it has displaced. This can lead to superficial jokes about the abbreviated half-life of the Parisian element of ideas. It is disconcerting, after all, to be reminded that within a singular deployment of a hermeneutical method derived in part from Heidegger (and from Nietzsche and Freud), translated as a "destruction," or more precisely, "deconstruction" of metaphysics, we may find lumped into one grand "metaphysical" heap: not only Platonic idealism and Aristotelian formalism but all of the varieties of subjectivism from Descartes through Hegel and Nietzsche as well, which we recognize in one form or other of romanticism or dialectical thought; not to say phenomenology (which thought to escape the subject-object problem), existentialism, and even structuralism itself; and finally, even the deconstructors themselves (especially Heidegger). In short, all of Western (Heidegger called it onto-theological) thought, including even the thinking of the thinkers who have tried to "overthrow" metaphysics, are combined into a "deconstruction," as in the Derridean analysis, that only reveals the historical "net" of "white mythology."

Every "move" of this (non-)history of ideas surpasses and displaces a previous move which it appropriates, surpasses and displaces that which has no history itself, since it is coexistent not only with the history of the West but with the history of history (that is, the history of meaning) itself. In a succession of "moves" that now reveal something more like a game of chess (Derrida says, somewhere, played upon a multi-leveled board without bottom) than an advance, we experience the foreshortened history of ideas which culminate in a variety of attempts to "close" metaphysics and "overthrow" it, appropriate it, or, more radically, step outside it: Nietzsche's naming of Hegel as the end of metaphysics; Husserl's dream to write its closure; Heidegger's reading of Nietzsche's will to power as the ultimate subjectivism; and the revival of the Nietzschean question of interpretation in the recent work of Michel Foucault, Gilles Deleuze, and, in a certain "advanced" sense, Jacques Derrida. Derrida, in fact, in an essay entitled "Les Fins de l'homme," calls this latest overthrow by the name of "France" or "French thought" (in contrast, obviously, to the closures of German thought, particularly Heidegger's).[1] Have we, in and through these names, arrived at the "end of philosophy" which Heidegger long since announced as Nietzsche's *capital* achievement?

233

arrived there by the disruption achieved in the Derridean deconstruction of Heidegger's destruction? The question, which could be made portentous, is obviously beyond our asking here. But a more modest question can be posed. Translated over into a more limited field, what does this "deconstruction of metaphysics," or what does deconstruction as a method, portend for literary criticism which in one way or another has to embrace all the assumptions of an "aesthetic" that is part and parcel metaphysical, an aesthetic which assumes the indissoluble relation between poetry and truth, and thus privileges form, consciousness, and even "poetic language" itself? In one way or another, as Derrida has indicated in a series of essays,[2] literature is considered a metaphor (for) (of) truth, of meaning or sense, or is inflated into the kerygmatic utterance of the single "word" which all metaphysical thinking in one way or the other pursues as its lost origin.

Geoffrey Hartman has recently posed the desperate question (or is it a plea?) for the humanist "crisis" of our time: "Is it too late, or can our age, like every previous one, protect the concept of art?"[3] (One deploys "crisis" in quotation marks, mindful of Paul de Man's alignment of the terms "crisis" and "criticism" as nearly interchangeable.[4]) Art, of course, is a "concept" and *as such* takes its meaning within the horizon of the very metaphysics which is under attack by those who would save art from metaphysics. The fact that Hartman's question (rhetorical) is posed most desperately in the face of the "baroquely elaborated asceticism of the School of Derrida" is revealing, for it is a plea (almost certain to have a rippling or doubling effect) to maintain the fiction of "self-presencing" even in the face of a questioning which forces his recognition that the fiction is only itself a simulacrum. Hartman's plea may sound Heideggerean in urging a return to "wonder" and therefore to an "authentic" art which will preserve us against an inauthentic (ascetic) (deconstructive) thought. And it may well share something with the early Heidegger, though with a difference which is of no point here. Heidegger surely does make a last, late defense of the "concept" of art, displacing as it were the classical conception of representation (which Hartman, following his master Auerbach, has reappropriated) with another (presencing), but in no way moving beyond the implication of art in the concept presence, as Derrida has repeatedly shown. Is Derrida, then, the great disenchanter, who in making a game of the concept has placed the concept *hors jeu*? that is, declared it offside? Has Derrida's disruption of the "play of language," which Heidegger so eloquently proclaims as "bound to the hidden rule"[5] that commands the reciprocal difference of poetry and thinking and thus governs *aletheia* — has Derrida's "play," by revealing the "hidden rule" as the law of all metaphoricity, destroyed the concept of art and perhaps given us back "literature" (again, in quotation marks)? In a way (not Heideggerean) this essay will concern itself with the different paths broken by this figure of language's "play" in Heidegger and

Derrida, since it is within the parentheses of these names that the future of the metaphor "(poetic) language" (as an illusion?) turns (tropes).

II

Even for the literary critic, the basic Heidegger text remains *Being and Time*,[6] appropriately incomplete, almost a pre-text to a writing that would appear in another, fragmentary form, primarily as "lectures" or "essays." *Being and Time* is, in a sense, a clearing of obstacles (classical ontology) in a path that will lead "to" language — a methodology which destroys by overcoming, that is, reappropriating. But it has turned up in literary criticism in a number of ways in-different to its methodology: as an existential analytic, as a text of modern "thematics," with its identification of care, anxiety, fallenness, being-toward-death, being-in-the-world, and so on, the themes, in short, of a phenomenology. Its method, however, has tended to undermine "thematics," which is always tied to the ontology against which the book was directed. Thus Heidegger begins with a hermeneutic already situated within a "tradition" of conceptualization, and proposes to clear that "history" as a way of gaining "access" to the "primordial 'sources' from which the categories and concepts handed down to us have been in part genuinely drawn" (BT, 43). His delineation of a method which will "destroy the traditional content of ancient ontology" (BT, 44) proceeds through the matrix of a philosophical metaphoricity which presents itself as a "content." It is an exercise in language, in "translation," an etymological un-weaving which finally comes to the point of declaring its own theme as the problematics of "language." (The English version of the text thus might appear as the translation of a text on translation, a text composed originally in the "possibilities for thought" Heidegger finds inherent in the German language. Heidegger thus employs this "power" to unveil the same originating "spirit" and "power" of the Greek language, long obscured and dulled in the metaphysical translation of pre-Socratic concepts.[7])

As he protested in later texts, the "destructive" hermeneutic was easily misinterpreted, as a kind of etymological retreat in search of the archaic origin of conceptuality and even for the origin of language (see QB, 93 — where he says that, despite hostile misinterpretations, the "destruction" did not "desire to win back the original experiences of metaphysics . . ."). The clearing projected a reappropriation, not a philological archaism. The development of what would later become the poetics of Being, of the metaphysical forgetting of Being as the unconcealed, of *logos* as the reciprocal difference of *physis*, of the Same that marks the difference between thinking and saying, does seem implicit in the "destruction." Certainly the figure of "breaking" a "path," of opening the "way" to language, and therefore of achieving an "authentic" language or "articulating" the "proximity" of Being and being, is anticipated by a destruction which no more advocates a return to some ideal or primordial philosophisizing than it suggests a full recuperation of some lost essence or truth. Heidegger's early discourse on his method locates his search clearly within the temporal horizon of *Dasein*, and thus within the "limits" of interpretation.

The "theme" of language emerges rather late in the first section of *Being and Time*, and then as language in general, or more accurately, as the speech or discourse of "interpretation" through which *Dasein* discloses itself. The interpretation of Greek ontology uncovers the "definition" of *Dasein* as that "living thing whose Being is essentially determined by the potentiality for discourse" (BT, 47). Language as such becomes the relation of the temporal unfolding of the Being of *Dasein*. Thus when Heidegger finally arrives at language as "theme" (BT, 203), he must preoccupy himself largely with a "destruction" of the concept language as the "deposited" understanding of historical knowledge (*Gerede* or "idle talk"), but reserves the privileged concept of speech or discourse as the "structure" of *Dasein*. As Derrida reveals in a "reading" of Heidegger's famous footnote on time (see BT, 500), this early Heideggerean separation of the authentic and inauthentic, of the primordial and the derivative, of discourse as the structure of the Being of *Dasein* and "idle talk," of *Verfallen* as the passage from one temporality to the other, constitutes a reappropriation of metaphysics: "Is there not at least some Platonism in the notion of *Verfallen*. . .?"[8] If the "destruction" suspends nostalgia, as Derrida indicates elsewhere, and repudiates the dream of some recovery of archaic concepts, it produces on the other side of nostalgia the figure of the potential return of presence, a figure that always effaces itself, producing in Heidegger a kind of metaphysical "hope," the "quest for the proper word and the unique name."[9]

The "destructive" method of *Being and Time* employs a hermeneutical violence or a systematic interrogation of the onto-theological concepts which reside within and govern the structure of Western thought: particularly the concepts that define the relation between Being and beings. Thus the crucial concept of "time." This interrogation differs from "understanding," as Heidegger presents it in Section 32 of *Being and Time* (pp. 188 ff.), in the sense of a "development" that overthrows the concept understanding. The development is disruptive — a disruption of any significance that may be presumed to inhere in the already interpreted (the present-at-hand), and thus disruptive of the habit of imposing significance upon the present as if that significance were immanent in the thing. Interpretation as reappropriation is grounded in understanding, but always goes beyond it, breaking the interpreted free from its circumspect context of involvements. Interpretation always involves a putting in question, the assumption of a point of view (not in this case subjective); the displacement effected in interpretation is a kind of "articulation," an

236

assertion that communicates, and thus a "retelling" that is shared with Others (sometimes viewed as a theory of intersubjectivity). Interpretation is therefore grounded in what Heidegger calls "fore-having" (*Vorhabe*, or "what is before us" or "what we have in advance"), "fore-sight" (*Vorsicht*, or "what we see in advance"), and "fore-conception" (*Vorgriff*, or anticipation, "what we grasp in advance"). This Heideggerean foreplay as anticipation disrupts the concept of the a priori. It presents the present-at-hand to be interpreted as the already interpreted, as already appropriated in the structure of discourse that is at the same time originary and fore-structured. Language is always involved in interpretation, in an always incomplete disclosure.

For literary criticism this projection of the "fore-knowledge" may be the literary text itself, as Paul de Man has argued — and thus what de Man interprets as authentic or literary language is that language which has already achieved the highest form of "self-understanding" or the fullest possible interpretation (a kind of totalized understanding).[10] This "text" is situated in a "context," a language within language, a text which is at the same time concealed and unconcealed, an interpretation demanding interpretation. Every interpretation already presumes a meaning (or "operates in the forestructure," as Heidegger writes), but more significantly, it presumes a point (a proximity) between the concealed knowledge of the text and that knowledge which interpretation can disclose: "Any interpretation which is to contribute understanding, must already have understood what is to be interpreted" (BT, 194).

Heidegger's hermeneutic circle, however, is not a vicious circle, not closed. It is a circle which in its approximation of closure allows the text to become fully disclosed, though such an ideal disclosure would also lead to a disappearance or effacement of the text as a fore-structure.[11] Thus the hermeneutic circle, though inescapable, is liberating. It embraces the limitations of the "existential constitution of Dasein" (BT, 195). "What is decisive," Heidegger writes, "is not to get out of the circle but to come into it the right way," by a deliberate process of determining the fore-structure; for once the circle is defined as the potential for interpretation, we discover that it hides within itself a "positive possibility of the most primordial kind of knowing" (BT, 195). But as de Man further indicates, the possibility of a full disclosure, or an ideal commentary, is already denied. Interpretation bears within its structure an always deferred end.

At the point in *Being and Time* where assertion as predication and communication become the way of "methodological foresight," Heidegger introduces language as his "theme *for the first time*" (BT, 203), language "which already hides in itself a developed way of conceiving" (BT, 199). Language here is the structure of *Dasein*, and not yet, as it will become, the "house of Being," poetic language. But even here, language as discourse is identified with the presencing of speech and not the secondariness of writing: *"The existential-ontological foundation of language is discourse or talk"* (BT, 203). Talk as communication is always about something, but this something is not simply a thing explained or defined: "What the discourse is about is a structural item that it necessarily possesses, and its own structure is modelled upon this basic state of Dasein" (BT, 205). Language is the structure of Man.[12] (At this point in the text, page 202, Heidegger projects the full development of the question of Being in a later section, which he did not write, except in the sense of the later fragments, essays, lectures on language as the "house of Being.") But language is not the ontological structure of man as subject. As Heidegger indicates in the "Letter on Humanism," the "proximity" of man and language confirms the proximity (nearness) of man and Being, not in the sense of two existences but in the sense of their sharing the same structure of presencing. In *Being and Time*, however, the particular nature of poetic language is defined as a very special form of communication: "In 'poetical' discourse, the communication of the existential possibilities of one's state-of-mind can become an aim in itself, and this amounts to a disclosing of existence" (BT, 205).

The seeds of a phenomenological poetics lies within this kind of "possibility," though "state-of-mind" here is not pure consciousness or cogito, but a consciousness of consciousness, an interpretation of consciousness as projected in the structure of language. In the later Heidegger, poetry will become the purest mode of interpretation of poetry because as the primal form of discourse or talk it is a disclosure of the "structural item that it necessarily possesses." The destruction of metaphysics, then, clears the way for the later meditations on the "way to language," by a discourse that reveals the structure hidden within "idle talk" or received historical understanding. As a method, the "destruction" can only be the reverse form of the later interpretation of poetry or "authentic" language, since as an interpretation of the "inauthentic" it is an interpretation of the world as "text," as fallenness, the "world" as already interpreted. The destruction makes way for "thinking," and for a kind of interpretative commentary which is reciprocal with the "saying" of poetry, with poetry as originary naming.

It is the status of the "language of Being," or language which situates the "nearness" of man and Being, that has been the object of Derrida's most severe questioning. (As he puts it in "Les Fins de l'homme," this "proximity" does not mark the relation between two ontological beings but between the "sense" of being and the "sense" of man — a kind of security that today is being displaced by a thinking that announces the "end of man" to be implicit in the language of Being.[13]) And ironically, as Heidegger has moved more and more toward the prophetic and oracular celebration of a "poetic" language as the "house of Being," and man as the "shepherd of Being," *Dasein* has tended to be displaced, and with "him" the structural model of discourse as "communication." Heidegger's later method, fully embracing poetic language as originary speech, has become increasingly less useful for literary criticism. Paul de Man, for example, has been one of the subtlest interpreters of Heideggerean hermeneutics for American criticism, arguing for the privilege, the "authenticity," of "poetic language."[14] But he stops short of embracing the "prophetic poeticism" of the later Heidegger.[15] Instead, he begins with Heidegger's interpretation of the "positive possibility for the most primordial kind of knowledge," which is hidden within language, and derives from it a view of the irreducible doubleness of "literary language" which he can accommodate to even the most severe post-structuralist critiques of Heidegger.

De Man's interpretation of "literary language" as that which forever names the void lying between sign and meaning derives from Heidegger's non-expressive view of a discourse that names the "existential possibilities of one's state of mind," in the sense that it always names the difference of understanding, of mediation. Thus literature, for de Man, always names itself as "fiction." It is the fore-knowledge of our understanding of the special nature of language. For de Man as for Heidegger, literary language is never self-deceived about the problematic that opens between the word and the thing; though unlike Heidegger, de Man will not pre-figure what literary language does name, the void, as the site of an emerging "truth." De Man is a negative Heideggerean, like Maurice Blanchot. The privileging of literary language for de Man is not derived from its power of unconcealing but lies in its resistance to self-mystification, its refusal to name presence and its repeated naming of distance that is "nothing." (Perhaps de Man's use of "literary" language rather than "poetic" language is one evidence of this difference; he comes close to identifying literature with Derrida's rhetoric or grammatology rather than with Heidegger's presencing speech.[16]) For de Man there is the "void" rather than "proximity" or the "site." The "authenticity" of literary language lies in its persistent naming of itself as "fiction," and thus of its unique double function as the origin of the "self" and the naming of the self's nothingness, the naming of the "subject" as a necessary function.

III

De Man, then, begins as a "critic of consciousness" intent on putting that criticism within definite parentheses, marking the limits which govern the strengths (the blindness and insight) of the phenomenological critique. For de Man there can be an authentic criticism as well as an authentic literature, so long as that criticism is oriented toward the literary text as a kind of foreknowledge, as a totalized understanding of the absolute fissure between language and what it is presumed to name or to disclose. Inauthentic criticism, on the other hand, idealizes or mystifies poetry. And Heidegger's late "prophetic poeticism" is for him a form of this self-mystification.

De Man's reappropriation of Heidegger is not offered here simply as one form of American mistranslation, but because it points up some of the possible directions criticism takes from Heidegger's overthrowing of metaphysics. But de Man's interpretation of "literary" language as authentic does not derive solely from *Being and Time*; it comes as much by way of some intermediary texts. Both Blanchot's hermeneutics and de Man's move by way of the insertion of the "nothing" into the Heideggerean critique, the "nothing" of "What Is Metaphysics?" which is conceived as the "pure 'Other'" and as the "veil of Being." Heidegger's own philosophical "turn" (*Kehre*) from language as the structure of *Dasein* to language as the "house of Being" depends on his thinking of the abyss and thus on the thinking of "nothing" as a productive principle.

The consequences of this for his thinking of the nature of language is revealed in another early lecture, "The Origin of the Work of Art" (first read in 1935),[17] a deconstruction of the concept aesthetics as it is implicated in classical ontology. Though a bridge to the later thinking of poetry as the presencing of presence, the essay has not yet adopted the full-throated kerygmatic tones of the later meditations, perhaps because the essay's concern is as much with the "work" as "thing" as with the problem of origins. Still, Heidegger's ultimate concern is with art as truth (*aletheia*). Therefore, the opening of Being through language, while set against the metaphysical concept of the "subject" as origin and so against all theories of art as expression or representation, is presented as a metaphorical "rift." This is not the basic dualism of a subject become exterior, or an idea fallen into form, but the double nature of unconcealedness. Metaphorically, Heidegger presents this rift as between "earth" and "world," between the closed and the open, opposites always in conflict, reciprocal differences: "Truth is un-truth, insofar as there belongs to it the reservoir of the not-yet-uncovered, the un-covered, in the sense of concealment. In unconcealedness, as truth, there occurs also the other 'un-' of a double restraint or refusal. Truth occurs as such in the opposition of clearing and double concealing" (PLT, 60). One recalls the figural "place" of the poet in the Hölderlin essays, situated in the "time" of the "double-Not" (need) of the old gods who have disappeared and the new ones who have "not yet" come.

The "rift" is a "between" that is a "measure." The conflictual situation of "earth" and "world," which seems to anticipate the later redefinitions of *physis* and *logos* in *An Introduction to Metaphysics* and elsewhere, is a "figural" place — the place as figure, the figure as place. "Createdness of the work means: truth's being fixed in place of the figure. Figure is the structure in whose shape the rift composes and submits itself" (PLT, 64). In the later essays, this place of poetry's opening will be presented figurally (as the "house of Being" or "bourne of Being," etc.),

240

but a figure that is already doubly effaced and rendered as the Being of language (beyond metaphor). In this essay, the figure is double-faced, a Gestalt, a form of writing. Thus Heidegger opens up the possibility of a "figural" analysis of the kind proposed by de Man, in which the "rift" of the figure is the nothing it names, the distance between sign and meaning. But in Heidegger the figure is the "appearance," as opposed to the "expression," of truth. Language now appears as something other than the vehicle of communication: "language is not only and not primarily an audible and written expression of what is to be communicated. It not only puts forth in words and statements what is overtly or covertly intended to be communicated; language alone brings what is, as something that is, into the Open for the first time" (PLT, 73). Thus the reification of poetry as "inaugural naming."

In the same gesture, language for Heidegger is turned into a figure for some primal signification: "Language is not poetry because it is primal poesy" (PLT, 74); that is, poetry is the secondary sign, words, in which a primary language, poesy, takes its place. The primal is not the primitive but the originating. Art is historical for Heidegger in the sense that it reinvents the beginning of history as an opening. It is an appropriation and an overthrowing of the historical, and thus an original beginning (origin as *Ursprung* or "primal leap"). Poetic language overthrows "actual language," of which it is the origin; yet in its appearance it doubly effaces itself. Poetic language cannot be analyzed and criticized as a system of signs, but only prompted to bespeak itself. Veiled in a figural shape that has already disrupted the metaphoricity of actual language, it speaks of Being as at once inside and outside of metaphor. It introduces us to a "history" that holds out the hope for some full recovery of presence, as Derrida indicates in "La Différance," pointing to the evocation of "the first word of Being" in "Der Spruch des Anaximander." To "find a single word, the unique word," is the possibility harbored in "every language."[18]

Poetic language, then, portends a text that overthrows its own temporality. (Poetic) language is a metaphor of that which is the "author" of all metaphor, the non-metaphoric Being. It is the "first word" without which the origin of language, Being, could not have its Being. Thus Being must also be metaphoric, already inscribed in the system as the name of the origin of the system — a system in Heidegger's case which fully declares itself as "language." (See Derrida's discussion of philosophical metaphorics in "La Mythologie blanche."[19]) Heidegger admits to the "mystery of language" which "admits to two things": "One, that it be reduced to a mere system of signs, uniformly available to everybody . . .; and two, that language at one great moment says one unique thing, for one time only, which remains inexhaustible because it is ordinary . . ." (WICT, 191-92).[20] The first recalls the "idle talk" of *Being and Time*, or "actual language," but even these "signs" do not submit to the materiality of linguistic description. Both written language and acoustical sounds are

241

for him "abstractions." "Words" are "well-springs" (WICT, 130), and they can be named only metaphorically. They must be repeatedly "dug up." Thus poetic language is the excavation of language by language.

This operation, the gift of Being, can only be accomplished metaphorically: one can only dig in a "place." Things only bloom in a "field": "the saying [of poetic utterance or authentic thinking] *speaks* where there are no words, in the field between words . . ." (WICT, 186). The remark comes in regard to a commentary on a text of Parmenides, and emphasizes the "paratactic" grammar of this pre-Socratic style of thinking, including the significance of the graphic sign of punctuation, the colon. But contrary to the reading of such signs in modern linguistics or grammatology, Heidegger reads them as figural measures of a saying which speaks in silence. Thinking and saying *speak* in a "place" marked figuratively by the sign, but they speak a "proper word" to which "words" are related as Being is related (or articulated) to beings. Writing, or "script," on the other hand, is for Heidegger a near total repression of the "saying" of speech. Writing of Nietzsche, and of the sometime need to resort to writing, Heidegger remarks on the Nietzschean style as a generative violence directed against philosophical writing. If originary saying is related to speech, a response to some "call" or "appeal," there are occasions, says Heidegger, when only a "scream" will answer the "call." But the "scream" is difficult to achieve in writing:

> Script easily smothers the scream, especially if the script exhausts itself in description, and aims to keep men's imaginations busy by supplying it constantly with new matter. The burden of thought is swallowed up in the written script, unless the writing is capable of remaining, even in the script itself, a progress of thinking, a way. (WICT, 49)

The privileging of speech over writing (speech as presenting-saying and not speech as acoustic sign, another form of writing) is, as Derrida points out, persistent and massive in Heidegger, and is consistent with the valorization of presence which entangles him in the very metaphysical network he has so methodically overthrown and announced as ended. (Derrida thus marks the difference between the "closure" of metaphysics and the "end" of philosophy, as Heidegger announces it in his book on Nietzsche.) More of this later. But at this point it is necessary to consider the consequences for literary criticism of the suppression of the "text" explicit in Heidegger's view of (poetic) language. Quite obviously the idea of a "text" has always included not only the idea of totalization but also the economy of the signifier — the "text" not only as scripted writing, as Derrida says, but as a "re-mark," a re-inscription of a previous discourse and its conceptualization. "Text" is therefore itself a metaphor for a totalization of elements which reveals itself as a metaphor of this totality.[21] For Heidegger, poetry or even "literature" cannot be this kind of re-marking, since it is original, the original speech of the (not-yet-disclosed) "proper word."

"Script," which smothers the "scream," is for Heidegger a kind of second-order language, representational, unless the style can overcome itself. Heidegger's example of Nietzschean writing which overcomes the "script" is an "aphorism," the writing of a poetic utterance which overthrows sense or ordinary understanding. The writing-speech of aphorism is therefore the utterance of the "one thought" that every true thinker repeatedly thinks, or the "one unique thing" that authentic language says "at one great moment" (WICT, 191). It is not rhetoric. Like the "single poetic statement" which at once rises from and remains concealed in the "site" (as "source") of every poet's saying, and "always remains in the realm of the unspoken" (OWTL, 160),[22] (poetic) language is a silence which speaks Being but has no being. The "source" of metaphor, the "site" of figure, it is non-figural. And its origin is "natural," in the sense of *physis*. The poetic text, then, is only a kind of veil, or the rhythm of a passage, a trace of Being, a metaphoric detour which at the same time turns the "thinker" of the text toward the "site" and prevents his looking directly into its full light. (Poetic) language cannot be destroyed, or appropriated, in the sense of overthrowing the metaphysical concept; any interrogation of it must take the form of a "dialogue," a "poetic dialogue," that emerges in the "reciprocity between discussion and clarification" (OWTL, 160).

There is an "authentic" criticism, then, or an ideal commentary as de Man says, already posited in Heidegger's early writing, that emerges as a proximal possibility in his later work. If poets think the "holy," the true dialogue would be like a "conversation" between poets. On the other hand, there is the "dialogue" between "thinking" and poetry (as "saying"), or between two different kinds of discourse which share a "proper" "relation to language." But even in the conflictual reciprocity of this dialogue, Heidegger returns to the caution of the Hölderlin essays, that the critical statement must open a way to the pure utterance of the poem and in that act annihilate itself, or become the silence of the "unique word": "in order that what has been purely written of in the poem may stand forth a little clearer, the explanatory speech must break up each time both itself and what it has attempted. The final, but at the same time the most difficult, step of every exposition consists in vanishing away together with its explanation in the face of the pure existence of the poem," allowing the poem to "throw light directly on the other poems" (EB, 234-35).[23]

Taken as a description of the critical discourse, this kind of statement might point toward a criticism which begins with individual poems but evolves into a study of the unitary metaphorics of the poetic canon, a criticism of consciousness as the exploration of the one poet's site. But this figural site is the site of all authentic poets, the site of "poetry" itself. Commentary, Heidegger writes, should ultimately sound like the "fall of snow on the bell" (EB, 234), the figure itself derived from Hölderlin, from authentic language. In the poetic fragment from which it is drawn, the metaphor of snow falling on bell is a figure of dissonance, of that which smothers the "tune" of the bell which calls one to meals, to sustenance. (We might as well vulgarize Heidegger here, and say that he considers most explanation a snow-job.) Heidegger's deployment of this figure appears in a "Prefatory Remark to a Repetition of the Address," itself an explanation of his own repeated "smothering" of the pure self-interpretation of poetic language, and is thus a fore-structuring of his own "lecture" as that which will vanish in his utterance, re-membering the "poet" in the silence of its own end. Heidegger's essays on poets and poetry regularly "end" in the poet's words, with the poem which is the first and last word. Heidegger's dialogue with Hölderlin turns out to be an effort in self-annihilating "thinking," an apology for the reappropriation of pure "saying" in the explanation which transcribes, translates, and transgresses poetic language, turning it into its other. Thus Heidegger's "Preface" turns his after-word into a fore-word that fore-warns of its own dulling of the pure tones of the "holy." It marks off the critical text as a by-path to the poetry which has already explored the by-path of poetic homecoming.

The "Preface," then, repeats the essay's own theme of incompleteness, of the poetic deferral of the naming of the "holy." It repeats for us the poet's theme of poetic foreknowledge: "his knowledge of the mystery of the reserving proximity" (EB, 269). This site of "proximity" or place of mystery is the place of the "double-Not" (EB, 289). The "mystery" is not revealed by the poet, but is only protected. This "mystery" as "reserving proximity" is the mystery of language, its generative power or Being, that must be protected from writing. The poet, whose "singing" still lacks the proper word or "naming word," offers a "song without words," a song which holds open, by deferring, the "end" in which the "others" (the non-poets) may also have their "homecoming," the ultimate "understanding" of the proper word. As Heidegger interprets Hölderlin, the poet protects the "reserving proximity" so that the "others," those "of writing *and* of thinking," may always be directed towards the true source of language and not be side-tracked by its historical mis-adventures. The poet protects the "mystery" by calling to the others, by calling their thinking to his saying, thus re-membering the "community" of man.

IV

Derrida's critique of Heidegger's "metaphorics" takes not only the form of systematic questioning, but consists in itself of a methodological doubling of the "destruction," a strategy, as he warns, which must go beyond the fundamental "inversion" of basic concepts and mark a "divergence" which will prevent the conceptual reappropriation of those same concepts. Derrida finds the Heideggerean error to lie in this "destruction" which inverts and reappropriates, thus overthrowing metaphysics and reinscribing it fully within the thinking of presence. The question of the "resemblance" between their two methods — the "destruction" and the "deconstruction" — has compelled Derrida toward a statement on the nature of "écart" and "renversement."[24] Heidegger presents a problem for Derrida at every turn. He has been the subject of two essays in particular, but the "name" reverberates everywhere in the Derridean canon, as an example of the problematics involved in any metaphysical reappropriation or in any overthrow of metaphysics, not the least being the "inflation" of language and the relating of "literature" and truth in Heideggerean thinking.[25]

Derrida never underplays the difficulty of reading Heidegger, nor ignores the implications of turning a methodology against itself, of deconstructing the deconstructor. One might say, then, that Derrida *underwrites* Heidegger, in the various and contradictory senses of that word: to place the thinking of presence in italics, to become a signatory to the difference, to re-mark the metaphysical implications of writing an "end" to metaphysics, to submit Heidegger's valorization of speech to the mark of a *proto-écriture* which it tries to conceal, etc. Derrida's relentless questioning of the metaphysical hierarchy which places speech in a privileged relation to presence, and reduces writing to a secondary function, is literally an *underwriting* of the idea of a "poetic language," of language that claims to escape the double sense of the metaphoric.

In "La Différance," Derrida submits the Heideggerean text, "Der Spruch des Anaximander," to an extensive deconstruction, concentrating on the Heideggerean language of presence and the difference "between pre*sence* and pre*sent*" (SP, 155-60).[26] The thrust of the Derridean critique inserts a double mark into Heidegger's attack on metaphysics which has, as Heidegger notes, "forgotten" the difference between Being and beings. Derrida submits the Heideggerean figure of the "trace" of the difference, which must be effaced in the appearance of being-present, to an irruptive discourse. What Heidegger calls the "matinal trace" (*Spur*) of the difference which effaces itself in the moment of Being's appearance, in order that Being might maintain its essence or its difference from beings, is also a figure analogous to what he calls the "mystery" of poetic language: the "difference between Being and beings" can be forgotten only if it is already "sealed in a trace that remains preserved in the language which Being appropriates" (quoted in SP, 156-57). Derrida's questioning of this "trace" traces it to its source in another language. In repeating the Heideggerean step, he disrupts the Heideggerean "way." The "trace" as "sustaining use" is a simulacrum of the name of Being, and not the appearance of the difference itself.

In this classic of deconstruction, Derrida interrupts the Heideggerean text in order to reveal that Heidegger's deployment of the concept "difference" reappropriates the metaphysical text it seems to disrupt; and in the same gesture, Derrida disrupts the thinking of hierarchical difference. "There is no essence of difference," he writes, and thus no "trace" or name for it that is not already a metaphysical inscription or another trace, the trace of a trace. Thus Derrida, who has already coined the name of "différance" as a trace of the concept difference which turns out to be a trace, a trace which has already effaced itself, provides a model of a critique which resists the reappropriation of the concept through inversion; he re-marks the divergence of a name that is not a word, not a concept, though it may simulate the concept (which is already a trace). (Derrida's neologism is *coined* in a manner to reveal the hidden functioning of priority in ontological concepts, wherein the phonetism of the letter "e" marks no "différence" from the letter "a," a *différance* marked only in writing.) Rather than examining a "text" for its concealed sense, or for its thematic differences which trace a hidden unity or promise a recovered word, Derrida inserts another language into the text, in order to reveal that the "text" is composed of different orders of signs and not signs which trace a single sense. The language of *différance* under*writes* the concept difference and renders it a "simulacrum" or "undecidable." It names the *name* of the difference, the word which is the name for all the possible substitutions for any of the commanding or privileged concepts which might govern the differences of the text — whereas Heidegger sees the metaphysical "forgetting" of the difference to be the determining movement of Being, and can thus promise in his own text what is always deferred in his interrogations of language, the ultimate overcoming of the difference of Being and being in the "proper name." But as Derrida concludes, the writing of *différance* reveals that there never was a "proper name" but only the "unnamable" play that produces "nominal effects," just as "the false beginning or end of a game is still part of the game" (SP, 159).

Now, it is not so much this interrogation of Heidegger which should instruct us here, as it is the Derridean thinking of textuality itself — though in this particular case, Derrida's critique of the Heideggerean "language of Being" is also a critique of the authenticity of poetic "speech." If poets are, as Heidegger wrote in "The Origin of the Work of Art," those who "sense the trace of the fugitive gods" and thus trace the realm of the "holy," they provide only traces of traces, and thus protect the "mystery" of the source (PLT, 94). "Language," which is "not poetry because it is primal poesy," is itself only a trace, a figural play of irreducible differences. Thus the expanding network of Heideggerean figures for present and presencing — site, house, bridge, etc. — might be analyzed as metaphorical traces of a word that is always already metaphorical, the name of the origin, the name that is already inscribed in every system as the "center." Language, for Heidegger, is the "name" of Being as presence, the name of naming. "Language" not only "gathers" the two-fold, it is an already doubled metaphor. Heidegger features the double function of the *present* participial, at once noun and verb, as the temporal naming of Being — gathering, thinging, thinking, saying, bridging, dwelling, building, showing, relating, blooming, etc.

In *The Question of Being*, Heidegger speaks of authentic language as a "meaning-fullness." Its plenitude of sense is not an historical accumulation, but a "play" of unfolding, a "play which, the more richly it unfolds, the more strictly it is bound by the hidden rules" (QB, 105). The "play" of meaning is always commanded by an origin it can never fully name; the "meaning-fullness" of the word is determined by a rule that is fuller than meaning, by Being which appropriates that which in every appearance leaves it behind in bringing it to light. This is a "play" easily comprehended within the "tradition" in which we measure the depth of the work of art, a fathomless, resource-ful text which interpretation can never exhaust. Derrida, on the other hand, inserts into the thinking of the "text" and interpretation a more playful figure of "play," in which the production of meanings turns upon a meaning-lessness, an absence of the commanding, originating word, and the play of the *supplément* which stands for that word (that center) in the text. In doing so, Derrida deprives us of literature in its relation to truth, only to give us back "literature" already in quotation marks, a text whose meaningfullness resides in its play of differences, including the insertion within it always of disruptive re-marks, other texts, signs that are not filled with meaning but are always already doubled and mark the double play of the text. Criticism begins with an insertion of a question into the opening provided by the text, into the double sense of the operative signifier; an operation which often consists of raising the illusory governing concept or "proper word" from the text in order to re-mark it, to mark its double sense and doubling function, and to trace its itinerary as a simulacrum. Thus Derrida's own (non-) concepts: *trace, différance, supplément, pharmakon, dissémination, écart, hymen, gramme*, etc., which he calls "undecidables" or "simulacra," words and concepts that are only the semantic mirage of real words and concepts, as if there were "real" words and concepts.

As example, we might point to the two complementary essays, "La Mythologie blanche"[27] and "La Double séance,"[28] which are both implicitly and explicitly deconstructions of the Heideggerean principle of "thinking" and "saying." "La Mythologie blanche" is a rigorous interrogation of metaphor in philosophy; "La Double séance" is a systematic disruption of the "idea" of literature as truth, either as representation or as *aletheia*, at once a disruptive reading of an imaginative text (Mallarmé's *Mimique*) and of idealized or totalized readings of that text. Characteristically, Derrida's strategy is to approach one text through another, whether the second text is a reading of the first or not. The indirection or detour is consistent within the "nature" of all textuality — that is, a text is never self-sufficient or self-present, never in itself a totalization of meaning or a concealment/unconcealment of a unitary sense. "La Mythologie blanche" introduces the problematics of philosophical language through the imaginary dialogue of a "literary" or fictional text (by Anatole France), itself already a kind of parody of the philosophical dialogue. "La Double séance" opens in the "field" between a philosophical (Platonic) and an imaginative (Mallarmean) text, texts which in their way mark the opening and closing of metaphysics and in which is posed the question of the absolute reciprocal "difference" between two modes of "truth." This involves Derrida in an examination of various rhetorical strategies — including the placement and function of operational elements, both verbal and non-verbal, in the text, the deployment of the title, the use of epigraph, the function of grammatological marks. (The essay is the middle one in a "book," *La Dissémination*, which is introduced by a "Preface" about the function of prefaces, a preface with its own doubled title, "Hors Livre.")

The "central" text of "La Double séance" is Mallarmé's, the title of which already provides a *capital* instance of the question of representation and "what is represented?" But Derrida does not submit the work of "literature" to criticism. His "reading" is a re-marking of the text within other "readings" of it, in particular the impressive book of J.-P. Richard which incorporates the coherent thematic play of this one Mallarmé work into a totalized reading of the Mallarmé canon as an imaginary "world": a "world" or unity evident in the intricate play of thematic differences which dialectically unfold and enfold the unity of "consciousness" or "imagination." For Derrida, such readings of the thematic or semantic richness of work only reveal that the depth of the text is a semantic mirage generated by the play of heterogeneous signifiers which refuse to be commanded by any single element within (meaning) or without (author) the text. Thus Derrida deconstructs Richard's and other critical readings of Mallarmé by raising the textual undecidable, the "hymen," from its thematic role in order to show how it works as a grammatological function to disrupt the concept of mimesis named in the title and already displaced as an initiatory key to the text. It functions as a mark, a slash (/), and as a title with two faces; it functions always to disrupt the positioning of any representation that is not itself a representation of a representation. Thus it functions to upset the illusion that in literature there can be truth, or the "appearance" of an unrepresented in the represented, the concealed which is unconcealed yet hidden, a unity of consciousness or the "reality" of an imaginary "world."

There is nothing represented that is not already a representation, just as in "La Mythologie blanche" there is no pure or natural origin of metaphor which stands behind or beneath the play of traces, but only metaphorical play itself. Derrida's strategic re-marking of concepts, by a forceful inversion followed, as he says, by a divergence, is necessary to keep his own undecidables in play, and to resist the overpowering tendency of the "names" to be reconceptualized. Thus Derrida's artful footwork of renaming his "positions" so as to avoid any one of his "names" falling into a position of initiatory concept: most obviously, the undecidable *écriture* which many critics of Derrida have tried to locate as his privileged position. (He has even been called a nominalist, even though nominalism is a classical form of representation, the privileging of the word-concept.) All of his undecidables recall, like a distant echo or a veiled shape, some etymological legacy which they at the same time *underwrite*, trace, and efface. Thus, the conflictual nature of the Derridean text inverts the Heideggerean conflict, and diverges from it; Derrida's gap or break or hymen redoubles Heidegger's rift; his dissemination disrupts Heideggerean flowering.

Écriture is not the name for the physical mark of writing, but the doubleness of which the physical mark is always a sign — a sign that has no signified except another sign. Thus the productive function of *écriture* which, like *différance*, initiates by an instant re-play. The limitlessness of "literature" is not the concealed fullness of language, but its disruptive and temporalizing function. "Literature" is neither a full text nor an empty text, neither a presence nor an absence. There is no "literary language," not even in de Man's sense, for there can be no privileged language. Derrida's critique disrupts the classical play of difference which always begins or ends with one of the two terms in a "position" of "authority." "Literature" can be privileged, then, only because it is the purest function of the self-dissimulating movement of writing. "Literature" is writing — the "figure" of a productive function for which the produced text is only a simulacrum, a facsimile, a fac-simile, a "factor." The literary text is a play of textuality, not simply in the obvious sense that a "work" of art always originates in the historical field of predecessors. Its own play of differences mirrors its displacement and reappropriation of other texts, and anticipates the necessary critical text which must "supplement" it, insert into it the undecidable or raise the undecidable which is dissimulated in it as a unique word. The Derridean rhetoric names the double-play of chance as the (non-) law of "literature." Thus Derrida threatens to disrupt the whole cultural order which has given literature a "place" at the center because it could assume that literature was the *arche* and *eidos* of order. But then, he gives us back "literature" as the double-name of man, who makes metaphor, who interprets.

Derrida is a kind of Dupin, whose literary function he explores in a recently published essay, "Le Facteur de la vérité"[29] — a de-cipherer in pursuit of a letter which is always moving, always displaced, always doubled, always at hand and underhanded, an "author" who is already only the sign of another (pre-) text.

Dupin who:

> observed them [the edges of the exterior of the letter] to be more *chafed* than seemed necessary. They presented the *broken* appearance which is manifested when a stiff paper, having once been folded and pressed with a folder, is refolded in a reversed direction, in the same creases or edges which had formed the original fold. This discovery was sufficient. It was clear to me that the letter had been turned, as a glove, inside out, re-directed, and re-sealed.

Dupin who: through the distracting ruse of some "pretended lunatic" reappropriates the letter and replaces it with a *"fac-simile* (so far as regards externals)," but with an inside which is a sign reappropriated from literature and marking its transgressions.

Dupin who: is the double of the narrator, shares the sign ("D——") of the thief, and is the double-name of author-interpreter-seducer, who cannot *write* either a beginning or end to literature, who cannot escape the circuit of the sign as the "factoring" (bearing, like a mailman) of a "truth" that never gets outside "literature," and is never fully delivered.

University of California, Los Angeles

NOTES

1   "Les Fins de l'homme," *Marges, de la philosophie* (Paris: Editions de Minuit, 1972), pp. 135-36, 161. Translated as "The Ends of Man," *Philosophy and Phenomenological Research*, 30 (Sept. 1969), 31-57.

2   See, for example, "La Parole soufflée," *L'Écriture et la différence* (Paris: Éditions du Seuil, 1967), pp. 253-92; and "La Double séance," *La Dissémination* (Paris: Éditions du Seuil, 1972), pp. 199-317.

3   *The Fate of Reading, and Other Essays* (Chicago: Univ. of Chicago Press, 1975), p. 107.

4   See "Criticism and Crisis," *Blindness and Insight, Essays in the Rhetoric of Contemporary Criticism* (New York: Oxford Univ. Press, 1971), pp. 3-19. First published in 1967, this essay situates the present "crisis" in criticism, the challenge of structuralism to a criticism of consciousness or to a criticism which privileges the subject, within Mallarmé's pronouncement almost a century earlier of a "crisis" in poetry, and concludes that creative periods are always critical, marked by pronouncements of rupture, displacements, violent

changes, discontinuities, etc., enacted upon and within received conventions. So, in any such pronouncement, the crisis lies in the criticism.

5   *The Question of Being*, trans. and introd. William Kluback and Jean T. Wilde (New Haven, Conn.: College and University Press, 1958), p. 105. Hereafter noted in text as: QB.

6   *Being and Time (Sein und Zeit)*, trans. John Macquarrie and Edward Robinson (New York: Harper & Row, 1962). Hereafter noted in text as: BT.

7   See *An Introduction to Metaphysics*, trans. Ralph Mannheim (New York: Anchor Books, 1961), p. 47.

8   "Ousia et Grammé," *Marges*, pp. 73-74. Translated by Edward S. Casey, in *Phenomenology in Perspective*, ed. F. J. Smith (The Hague: Martinus Nijhoff, 1970), pp. 54-93; see esp. p. 89.

9   "La Différance," *Marges*, p. 29. Translated as "Differance" in *Speech and Phenomena, and Other Essays on Husserl's Theory of Signs*, trans. and introd. David B. Allison (Evanston, Ill.: Northwestern Univ. Press, 1973), pp. 129-60; see esp. pp. 159-60.

10   *Blindness and Insight*, pp. 30-31.

11   *Blindness and Insight*, pp. 30-31.

12   See Derrida, "Les Fins de l'homme," *Marges*, pp. 160-61 ("The Ends of Man," pp. 54-55), on this restoration of "humanism" as the determination of the "end" of man in the thinking of Being. The major thrust of the essay is a deconstruction of Heidegger's thinking of proximity. In his conclusion, Derrida offers a project of two kinds of deconstructive thinking, and thus marks the difference between Heidegger's and his own. I will discuss this in the last section of the essay.

13   *Marges*, pp. 160-61 ("The Ends of Man," pp. 54-55).

14   *Blindness and Insight*, pp. 29-32, 76, and *passim*.

15   *Blindness and Insight*, p. 100.

16   See also Paul de Man, "The Rhetoric of Temporality," *Interpretation: Theory and Practice*, ed. Charles Singleton (Baltimore: Johns Hopkins Univ. Press, 1969), pp. 173-209; and "Semiology and Rhetoric," *Diacritics*, 3 (Fall 1973), 27-33.

17   In *Poetry, Language, Thought*, trans. and introd. Albert Hofstadter (New York: Harper & Row, 1971), pp. 17-87. Hereafter noted in text as: PLT.

18   *Marges*, p. 29; *Speech*, p. 160.

19   *Marges*, pp. 247-324. Translated as "White Mythology," in *New Literary History*, 6 (Autumn 1974), 5-74.

20   *What Is Called Thinking*, trans. Fred D. Wieck and J. Glenn Gray (New York: Harper Torchbooks, 1968). Cited in text as: WICT.

21   See Jacques Derrida, *Positions* (Paris: Éditions de Minuit, 1972), pp. 81-82, and *passim*. Parts of this text are translated in *Diacritics*, 2 (Winter 1972), 35-43; and *Diacritics*, 3 (Spring 1973), 33-46.

22   *On the Way to Language*, trans. Peter D. Hertz (New York: Harper & Row, 1971). Cited in text as OWTL.

23   *Existence and Being*, trans., introd., and analysis by Werner Brock (Chicago: Gateway ed., 1949). Cited in text as: EB.

24   *Positions*, pp. 73, 81; see *Diacritics*, 2 (Winter 1972), 40-43. See also *Marges*, pp. 162-64 ("The Ends of Man," pp. 56-57).

25   See *De la grammatologie* (Paris: Éditions de Minuit, 1967), pp. 33 ff.; and references in footnote 2.

26   *Marges*, pp. 24-29.

27   *Marges*, pp. 247-324. (See footnote 19.)

28   *La Dissémination*, pp. 199-317.

29   "Le Facteur de la vérité," *Poetique*, 21 (1975), 96-147. This essay, which is soon to be translated in *Yale French Studies*, is a "reading" of the Lacanian "Seminar" on "The Purloined Letter," and thus a reading of the psycho-analytic appropriation of literature as truth. Derrida reads "The Purloined Letter" in and through the interpretations of Marie Bonapart and Jacques Lacan, and in the context of Freud's reading of a "literary" text.

Reading Heidegger:
Paul De Man and Jacques Derrida

Frances C. Ferguson

Still, to talk about language is presumably even worse
than to write about silence.

— Martin Heidegger

Imagine two men. Each reads the work of a major philosopher of
their time, and, suddenly, philosophical literary criticism — in the
philosopher's image — is born in each of them. Such an account as this
predominates in the traditional schemes of the "history of ideas," which
inform us that Burke formed the consciousnesses behind the literature of
the English Romantic sublime and that Godwin and Hartley spawned the
young Wordsworth, who somehow recapitulated the course of English
philosophy by poetically overthrowing them. Philosophy and
philosophers, in this kind of account, are themselves a priori; they always
seem to have gotten to the "big ideas" first. And all of the deceptions
which literary language would foist upon us are curiously redeemed
because they are buttressed simply by intersecting with the philosophers'
avowed aim to speak the truth. We mark — and justify — literary and

intellectual time by our philosophers, so that Locke becomes the rationale for the existence of the eighteenth century in England, so that it seems inevitable for scholars to search for the philosophers whom Shakespeare read. Milton's description of Shakespeare as "Fancy's child," warbling "his native wood-notes wild," becomes simply one poet "covering" for another, feigning ignorance of those true sources in philosophy which gave him a purchase on the language.

Neither Paul de Man nor Jacques Derrida is a poet — except in a rather loose sense of the word — but I have drawn this (admittedly simplified) sketch of one conception of the relationship between philosophy and literature to insist upon my distance from it. Philosophy is not — any more than literature — transmitted whole, with some kind of magical power to influence and create the character of all other varieties of language of its time. So I cannot speak of the influence of Heidegger upon de Man and Derrida, as if they somehow imitated him or borrowed from him. Instead, it seems appropriate to speak of their readings of Heidegger — in order to get at the notion of the mutual availability of language which constitutes the process of any text being read. In fact, I shall only touch peripherally upon Derrida's direct analysis of Heidegger (in "Ousia et Grammé," for example), because I am far less interested in expounding his position or de Man's position towards Heidegger than in exploring the ways in which Heidegger's texts are subsumed in a constellation of texts and concerns for both de Man and Derrida.

But the fact of the matter — or of my matter, at any rate — is that Heidegger, Derrida, and de Man are writers who involve us less in what can be said than in a consciousness of what cannot — or ought not to — be said. When Heidegger and Derrida formulate their critiques of the history of philosophy, when de Man and Derrida present their critiques of literary history, the project is one of subtraction, of clearing away the weight of false problems, false presuppositions, false answers which encumber the possibility of inquiry. "Our provisional aim is the Interpretation of *time* as the possible horizon for any understanding whatsoever of Being," Heidegger announces in his introduction to the "Introduction" of *Being and Time*.[1] And it is in the starkness of that Heideggerian project that we can locate the work of both de Man and Derrida: what does it mean to think the time of language and of the literary text?

With de Man figurative language and something called "literary language" provide access to time in literary terms. In the opening sentences of "The Rhetoric of Temporality," one of his most important essays, de Man in fact immediately pits rhetorical language against a naively subjectivist account of literature in the following terms:

> Since the advent, in the course of the
> nineteenth century, of a subjectivistic critical
> vocabulary, the traditional forms of rhetoric have fallen

into disrepute. It is becoming increasingly clear, however, that this was only a temporary eclipse: recent developments in criticism reveal the possibility of a rhetoric that would no longer be normative or descriptive but that would more or less openly raise the question of the intentionality of rhetorical figures.[2]

With the use of "intentionality," as opposed to "intention," de Man moves his discourse outside of a literary tradition that imagines the subject to be the arbiter of truth — the presumably solipsistic tradition of the Romantics who resolved their supposed difficulties with a subject-object dialectic by asserting the subject as a last resort, or, at least, a final word. And de Man's division of the essay into discussions of "Symbol and Allegory," on the one hand, and "Irony," on the other, involves a choice of rhetorical figures which have traditionally been discussed in terms of temporal movement. But the most interesting complication in de Man's discussion of symbol and allegory occurs when he argues that not even the discussions of rhetorical figures — those constructs which mean what they say *differently* — can say what they mean.

"We find in Coleridge what appears to be, at first sight, an unqualified assertion of the superiority of the symbol over allegory." And for de Man the superiority — and even the distinction — which separates symbol from allegory begins to vanish as soon as one examines the terms of Coleridge's description:

> In truth, the spiritualization of the symbol has been carried so far that the moment of material existence by which it was originally defined has now become altogether unimportant: symbol and allegory alike now have a common origin beyond the world of matter. The reference, in both cases, to a transcendental source, is now more important than the kind of relationship that exists between the reflection and its source. It becomes of secondary importance whether this relationship is based, as in the case of the symbol, on the organic coherence of the synecdoche, or whether, as in the case of allegory, it is a pure decision of the mind. (p. 177)

Even by this rather early point in the argument, de Man's implication is that Coleridge cannot mean what generations of commentators have understood him to say; the dream of totalization — even in the guise of synecdoche which is associated with the symbol — plays havoc with the alleged value of the symbol. And de Man might perhaps say that the symbol cannot maintain any privilege or priority over allegory precisely because the synecdochal relationship of part to whole also implies a negative, that remainder which is always by definition left out in the synecdoche. Yet there is more. For de Man proceeds to speak of the primary repository of Romantic imagery, Nature, and that very movement into apparent concreteness becomes the means through which the dissolution of even a unified subject for "Romantic" subjectivism occurs. Romantic nature imagery continually generates "ambivalences derived from an illusionary priority of a subject that had, in fact, to borrow from the outside world a temporal stability which it lacked within itself" (p. 184). Coleridge's gestures towards unification, towards merging subject and object, become a misguided reduction of the object to another self, so that nature appears available to the accommodation of a "purely intersubjective pattern."

Allegory finally emerges as the victor in its dialogue with the symbol, after several examples designed by de Man to demonstrate the allegorical nature of Rousseau's *La Nouvelle Héloise* and of Wordsworth's poetry.

> Whether it occurs in the form of an ethical conflict, as in *La Nouvelle Héloise*, or as an allegorization of the geographical site, as in Wordsworth, the prevalence of allegory always corresponds to the unveiling of an authentically temporal destiny. This unveiling takes place in a subject that has sought refuge against the impact of time in a natural world to which, in truth, it bears no resemblance. (p. 190)

And whereas allegory has been seen as a system of connections which derived their force from the edicts of dogma, it becomes for de Man (with the aid of the early Romantics) precisely the obverse of dogma. Rather, allegory hovers as an abyss which would register the virtual impossibility of all and any belief.

> Whereas the symbol postulates the possibility of an identity or identification, allegory designates primarily a distance in relation to its own origin, and, renouncing the nostalgia and the desire to coincide, it establishes its language in the void of this temporal difference. In so doing, it prevents the self from an illusory identification with the non-self, which is now fully, though painfully, recognized as a non-self. (p. 191)

As de Man concludes the "Symbol and Allegory" section, he offers "an historical scheme that differs entirely from the customary picture."

> The dialectical relationship between subject and object is

> no longer the central statement of romantic thought, but
> this dialectic is now located entirely in the temporal
> relationships that exist within a system of allegorical
> signs. It becomes a conflict between a conception of the
> self seen in its authentically temporal predicament and a
> defensive strategy that tries to hide from this negative
> self-knowledge. (p. 191)

Rousseau and Wordsworth (among others) participate in a recovery of allegory which involves a recognition of the temporal dismantling of the self. Yet the "lucidity" of these early Romantics becomes obscured, lost in the self-mystifications of an aesthetic rhetoric which keeps symbolizing itself to death — or into an avoidance of death and the multiple deaths which time obtrudes upon the subject that keeps willing itself whole. But how did the critical obfuscation take place? And what difference does it make that critical *idées réçues* repeatedly attempted to restrict allegorical writers like Wordsworth and Rousseau to a symbolic scheme which substitutes a vocabulary of simultaneity and spatiality for "an authentically temporal destiny"? The critical obfuscation derives, perhaps, from a desire to see aesthetic pronouncements purely as statements of position — statements which are direct and non-literary enough to be taken quite literally as the theory from which literary practice stems. But while de Man is quite persuasive on this point, the impact of "distorted readings" must ultimately be beside the point. And the division between writers like Coleridge and the critics who have valorized the symbol, on the one hand, and allegorical writers like Wordsworth and Rousseau, on the other, provides a clarity to de Man's argument by establishing in its turn the illusion of a choice between rhetorical and non-rhetorical texts. Rhetoric, saying better and meaning differently, has become allegory in the process of de Man's argument. But both rhetoric and allegory are credited with being such fundamental insights and operations that no writer can really avoid them (whether by choice or unconsciousness). In that sense, not even Coleridge, the English founder of the "Romantic" comparison between symbol and allegory, can really maintain the priority of the symbol. And the only possibility of distinguishing between Coleridge and the allegorical Romantics involves denying Coleridge the possibility of rhetoric (or, perhaps, of any consciousness of his own rhetoric) — a tack which the opening gesture towards an analysis of the intentional structures of rhetorical figures would seem to disqualify.

An examination of Coleridge is probably useful at this point — not as an exercise in apologetics, but rather as an attempt to describe the difficulties in submitting Coleridge's text to a static position even for polemical purposes. The distinction which Coleridge makes between symbol and allegory occurs in the context of a discussion of reading under the aspect of religious belief, but we must suspend the temptation to condemn it as onto-theological (for that would be to lend too much authority to the theological by our attack). In fact, this distinction in the *Statesman's Manual* is perhaps more accessible in connection with an even more famous passage from the *Biographia Literaria* — the discussion of imagination and fancy.

> The IMAGINATION, then, I consider either as primary, or secondary. The primary IMAGINATION I hold to be the living Power and prime Agent of all human Perception, and as a repetition in the finite mind of the eternal act of creation in the infinite I AM. The secondary Imagination I consider as an echo of the former, co-existing with the conscious will, yet still as identical with the primary in the *kind* of its agency, and differing only in *degree*, and in the *mode* of its operation. It dissolves, diffuses, dissipates, in order to re-create; or where this process is rendered impossible, yet still at all events it struggles to idealize and to unify. It is essentially *vital*, even as all objects (*as* objects) are essentially fixed and dead.
>
> FANCY, on the contrary, has no other counters to play with, but fixities and definites. The Fancy is indeed no other than a mode of Memory emancipated from the order of time and space; while it is blended with, and modified by that empirical phenomenon of the will, which we express by the word CHOICE. But equally with the ordinary memory the Fancy must receive all its material ready made from the law of association. . . .

Like most passages in Coleridge, this presents a basic problem of reading — as if an imagined web of misreadings had already made it impossible for the discussion even to appear to say what it means. But we may hazard a few observations. The primary imagination, as the "agent of all human perception" seems intelligible enough in its comprehensiveness. As a recapitulation of the infinite "I AM," the specific perceptions which are the finite repetition of that "I AM" are symptoms of the infinite creative word rather than independently meaningful creations. But although imagination in this sense — as perception — is inevitable, it does, however, lack specific form. A pure language of the primary imagination would be a language composed entirely of "I AM."

Perhaps the most striking feature of Coleridge's discussion of the primary imagination, however, is that temporal terms define the human word. Human perception exists in a synecdochal relationship to the divine creative word, and the link between finite and infinite occurs explicitly in the temporal terms of "repetition." But whereas Coleridge does not stress the temporal disparity between the finite word of human perception and the infinite word of divine creation, an exaggerated version of that disparity becomes the specific feature of the secondary imagination. If the primary imagination seems, in Coleridge's account, to represent an hypostatized unity between the infinite "I AM" and its finite repetition, the secondary imagination would seem to have crossed over some imaginary temporal boundary beyond which division is inevitable.

It is at the point at which Coleridge proceeds to a discussion of the fancy that his polemical prescriptivism becomes troublesome. Although Coleridge identifies numerous instances of the fancy throughout his prose writings, his exposition here, in the thirteenth chapter of the *Biographia*, renders fancy more chimerical than real. He has granted so much to the primary and secondary imaginations that it is difficult to see how the fancy can exist at all, except as a debased or parodic form of the secondary imagination. If the creative perception of the primary imagination is as inevitable as it earlier seemed to be, the fancy can only have received its materials — those "counters" of "fixities and definites" to play with — originally from perception. On the other hand, fancy seems to involve only a slavish adherence to the denominative aspect of the secondary imagination without the redeeming balance of conceptualization. As such, it seems to be as much beyond the realm of human language as the primary imagination itself; although the primary imagination appears as pre-linguistic because of its total integration into the conceptualizing-idealizing aspect of language, the fancy appears as curiously alinguistic because of its total dependence upon the exclusively denominative aspect of language. The fancy is, as Coleridge presents it, post-linguistic. Both disjunct and disjunctive, the fancy would seem to consist in infinite relationships based on pure contiguity; it is, as Coleridge says, associationism.

Thus far our account presents very few obstacles to a critique of Coleridge's definition of imagination and fancy which might parallel de Man's critique of the discussion of symbol and allegory. Fancy, in fact, represents a metonymic process which is curiously aligned with allegory, for the fancy is precisely a recognition of the impossibility of coincidence with a transcendental source which allegory repeatedly asserts. Yet, even while Coleridge apparently condemns the fancy as a degraded and empty form of thought, he also provides the means for an ironic reversal of the entire schema. As is well known, the discussion of imagination and fancy occurs after a lengthy buildup which is interrupted by a letter which Coleridge received from a friend "whose practical judgement [he had] had ample reason to estimate and revere." Just as in the case of "Kubla Khan," that poem which might have been completed had Coleridge not been interrupted by a person from Porlock, the letter serves as an emblem of the fancy itself — a Shandean spoof of the mind "getting off the track" through an associationism which invades it. Thus, for Coleridge's distinction between imagination and fancy, the inevitability of a detour into fancy is established before the distinction is even underway, and Coleridge's disparagement of the fancy occurs merely as a self-ironizing gesture which casts suspicion upon the insistence on the connectedness of the imagination.

In this light, Coleridge's argument shifts from its role of willful self-blindedness to an approximation of what de Man describes as "irony." Using Baudelaire's *De l'essence du rire*, de Man suggests that "the notion of self-duplication or self-multiplication" emerges as "the key concept" of Baudelaire's article, and the nature of the ironic duplication involves "a relationship, within consciousness, between two selves, yet it is not an intersubjective relationship" (p. 195). If we view Coleridge's esteemed friend in the *Biographia* and the person from Porlock in "Kubla Khan" not as persons but as flimsy personifications of Coleridge's own fancy, that ironic self-multiplication which can only register "the distance in reflection" becomes a central feature of the text. But now it appears that we are suggesting that Coleridge is redeemed by fitting into de Man's conception of irony — even if he may not be conspicuously allegorical. And that brings us to another problem: can allegory and irony really be distinguished in de Man's treatment of them? Irony "relates to its source only in terms of distance and difference and allows for no end, for no totality"; allegory and irony are linked "in their common discovery of a truly temporal predicament"; and "the temporal void that [irony] reveals is the same void we encountered when we found allegory always implying an unreachable anteriority" (p. 203). Despite the resemblances between the two, however, de Man maintains a distinction between them and proceeds to search for "meta-ironical texts" which have "transcended irony without falling into the myth of an organic totality or bypassing the temporality of all language" (p. 204). But the very text on which de Man anchors his discussion of irony, Baudelaire's *De l'essence du rire*, complicates de Man's separation between the narrative expansiveness of allegory and the "unsettling speed" of irony. De Man focusses on the fall as instrumental in creating the possibility of the division of the subject into a multiple consciousness — the man who falls, who is an object, and the man who laughs in recognition of his previous self-mystification in seeing himself as superior to nature. "Nature can at all times treat him as if he were a thing and remind him of his factitiousness, whereas he is quite powerless to convert even the smallest particle of nature into something human" (p. 196). But although de Man embarks upon his own narrative account of Baudelaire's fall on the sidewalk, and even though he introduces the notion of the Fall of Man as an incipiently allegorical connection with the ironist's fall, he still maintains that irony is distinct from allegory in occurring within an instant, like a conversion to negativity. Yet Baudelaire's "little" fall contains within it the seeds of its own extension, for the fall occurs specifically through the power of gravity. And the ironist cannot confine himself merely to the recognition that his being objectified into a falling object once implies the possibility of his falling in the future, because such a view would restrict the character of the threat from nature in the form of gravity, would reinstate the self-delusion of a superiority to nature by implying that a fall would teach you all you needed to know and fear about nature. Rather, the force of the ironist's fall proceeds from the allegorical and unacknowledged aspect of the situation — that this fall, and any others which occur in an instant, are merely blatant illustrations of a temporal process: gravity is not just continually but continuously pulling one down. One can warn himself or someone else against falling, but who would warn anyone against aging? Thus, when de Man describes irony as "essentially the mode of the present, knowing neither memory nor prefigurative duration," whereas allegory "appears as a successive mode capable of engendering duration as the illusion of a continuity that it knows to be illusionary" (p. 207), the examples of Coleridge and Baudelaire argue that irony and allegory are not exactly mirror images of the same process but rather operations which inevitably involve one another.

Toward the end of the article, de Man suggests that "the dialectical play between the two modes [allegory and irony], as well as their common interplay with mystified forms of language (such as symbolic or mimetic representation), which it is not in their power to eradicate, make up what is called literary history" (p. 207). Chronological literary history, like symbolic or mimetic representation, is a delusion, an attempt to objectify a literary language which is so thoroughly rhetorical that it can only ironize its objectifiers. Literary language for de Man becomes language which in

> accounting for the "rhetoricity" of its own mode . . . also postulates the necessity of its own misreading. . . . In accordance with its own language, [the text] can only tell its story as a fiction, knowing full well that the fiction will be taken for fact and the fact for fiction; such is the necessarily ambivalent nature of literary language.[3]

Now, several things are at stake here: a version of Heideggerian temporality, in which incompleteness empties time of specific content, banishes literary history as a falsely chronological, objective version of an underlying myth of progress; the possibility of a unified authorial self is undermined by the discontinuity of literary, or rhetorical, language; and the notion of mimesis as a recapturing of an essential unity vanishes as the subject to be imitated loses all semblance of presence and as language is revealed to be so devious in its windings that it could not recapture any presence if it did exist. In such a context, however, the role of the literary critic becomes suspect. For the infinite extension of the literary, in theory, collides with the exclusions of certain texts in practice. De Man calls " 'literary,' in the full sense of the term, any text that implicitly or explicitly signifies its own rhetorical mode and prefigures its own misunderstanding as the correlative of its rhetorical nature. . . . It can do so by declarative statement or by poetic inference."[4] A discursive, critical, or philosophical text which operates by means of statements is just as "literary" as any poetic text. But if all language is rhetorical in nature, how is it that any and all rhetoric, all language, is not the "intentional structure" of "rhetoricity"? Once one has subverted the possibility that an extended "literary language" could make a mistake which would count as a mistake, how is it any longer possible to suggest that any text could *really* be self-blinded or mystified, as symbolic or mimetic representation is said to be? The choice *between* keeps vitiating the choice *of*. As de Man says, "The rhetorical character of literary language opens up the possibility of archetypal error: the recurrent confusion of sign and substance."[5] But the avoidance of that confusion, the eschewing of literalism, in practice involves attributing that literalism to another. The process of opposition thus covertly reinstates an objectivity to error which the appeal to literary language attempted to avoid.

In a recent essay, Joseph Riddel replies to Hillis Miller's review of his latest book by seeing Miller as an emanation of de Man. And Riddel views de Man as engaged in an "effort to contain the Derridean question, to restore the 'subject' (if only as a function) and with it the privilege of 'literature' and 'literary language,' and thus to save, just at the moment it seemed most heinously vented, the valorized 'text.' "

> De Man's is a heroic task, and nearly irresistible for those of us concerned with "literature" as (the ground of) an institution. Miller's adoption of it, however, presumes that the deed has already been done — that Derrida's deconstructions have already redefined the nature of the "text" which can never be present to itself, and that de Man has already contained the problem by demonstrating that "literary language" was ever thus, and was never self-deceived in claiming for itself a unitary, idealistic, referential truth-value. For de Man, then, as for Miller, that literature which but a short time ago could be thought of as the phenomenological "sign" of a unified origin, the constitutive and constituted *cogito*, becomes the already doubled Word, never self-deceived, prior to all other forms of discourse.[6]

Riddel's account is forceful and cogent, and yet it raises anew the question of how to deal with de Man. For de Man's notion of "literary language" seems (to me at least) less an assertion of the value of the literary text and the "subject (if only as a function)" than a demolition of those concepts. "Literary language" appears as an extension and an undelineated consolidation of those figures of allegory and irony which he discussed in "The Rhetoric of Temporality." For the ironic use to which de Man puts literary history — the history of reading — implies that not even de Man's uncovering of previous misreadings can be a final stance. The text of any sign which can be read or assimilated in more than one way (i.e., most things with the possible exception of things like a stop sign by the side of the road, which bears a certain relation to the force of gravity) must be literary, since only misreadings or contradictory readings are potential indices to the very rhetoricity or literariness of which de Man speaks. But to speak of misreadings as testimony to literariness is not to valorize the literary text, but rather to insist that the bottom drop out of it. The apparent hypostatization of the text is itself rhetorical; it serves a polemical purpose by countering both the notion of the author as a unified subject who says what he thinks and the notion of an historical development or progression in which ideas become clearer (or conversely, a decline, in which they are less clear). But further, this apparent elevation of the literary text casts an ironic light upon a recurrent delusion which readers pass upon themselves. The problems of reading any literary text are not to be resolved easily, or else the anecdote about the white Southerner leaping to the stage to defend Desdemona against Othello would not be so clearly a joke. Reading becomes a complicated process as soon as one recognizes that distinguishing between truth and fiction, or presence and absence, (ad infinitum) is never enough. For the difficulty is always in trying to imagine that the text means something different from what I think it means. And whereas de Man continually submits himself to the delusion which we all open ourselves to in reading and writing about reading as if we had, finally, "got it right," his version of the text — as an empty meaning which lends itself to a variety of "full meanings" — exercises an ironic function. Like gravity in Baudelaire's *De l'essence du rire*, the language of a text continually and continuously exerts a force that leads to a fall; precisely at the moment at which any reader or any critic imagines that he has distinguished the figurative from the literal, the "real" meaning of the text, he asserts its presence as his subjectivity. And precisely at that moment, he is mocked by the text, which does not, and cannot, yield up any immutable classification of its figurativeness or its literalness.

De Man's essay "The Rhetoric of Blindness," on Derrida's *De la grammatologie*, signals several differences between these two writers — whether through de Man's containment of the Derridean question, as Riddel suggests, or whether through a different way of framing the questions of language and literary language. Whereas de Man asserts that "it is a historical fact that irony becomes increasingly conscious of itself in the course of demonstrating the impossibility of our being historical" (p. 194), Derrida opens *De la grammatologie* with a deconstruction of the history of the Word in the Western tradition. Thus, while de Man sees history as an ironic text, so that history is already emptied of content, Derrida feels the gravity (the weight and the pull) of history enough to imagine both that a deconstruction (like Heidegger's) of the metaphysical tradition and a utilization of the "errors" of that tradition are possible and necessary. Derrida's project involves, then, an attempt both to examine language as a kind of supplemental consciousness and to question the ways in which *this* language seems to have been ever thus to those who live in its domain.

If ethnocentrism plays an inevitable part in Derrida's account of the history of the logos and *écriture*, he never allows the ethnocentrism of language to be merely a puzzle, an arbitrary end to questioning, or merely an anecdote, like Jakobson's story of the German woman who, on learning of the French word *fromage*, replied (*auf Deutsch*) that "*cheese* is more natural."[7] Nor does he suggest that "logocentrism" (the metaphysic of phonetic writing) is a mere accident which can be reversed by a simple decision to banish it. These elementary points demand some rehearsal largely because they are continually being minimized. Jonathan Culler, in his provocative book *Structuralist Poetics*, asserts that Derrida,

> having maintained that writing cannot be treated on the model of speech, [wants to] show that the features which he has first isolated in writing are already present in speech, which must, therefore, be conceived according to the new model of writing. But this further move is a purely logical point, which someone concerned with the social facts can afford to neglect: even if Derrida shows that we ought to think of speech as a kind of writing, we may arrest the play of his concepts by saying, simply, that within Western culture there are crucial differences between the conventions of oral communication and those of literature which deserve study whatever their ideological basis. To replace a metaphysic of presence by a metaphysic of absence, to invert the relation between speech and writing so that writing engulfs speech, is to lose the distinction which translates a fact of our culture. Communication does take place. Many instances of language are firmly situated in the circuit of communication.[8]

Culler is, of course, making a shrewd appeal to all of those who responded to Fredric Jameson's complaint that Derrida would involve us in a process

264

of infinite regress; and he raises a viable suspicion toward the Derridean project: how is it possible to be sure that the "free-play" which Derrida counsels is any less a blind alley than the metaphysics of presence which it was designed to counter? Derrida would reply that the "facts of our culture" constitute a less solid ground than Culler suggests they do. But this quite obvious disparity between the two writers raises a question of belief which may account for some of the melodrama which surrounds the opening sections of *De la grammatologie*, in which Derrida beckons his readers toward the "future" by describing its possible horrors in the form of a challenge.

> L'avenir ne peut s'anticiper que dans la forme du danger absolu. Il est ce qui rompt absolument avec la normalité constituée et ne peut donc s'announcer, se *présenter*, que sous l'espèce de la monstruosité. Pour ce monde à venir et pour ce qui en lui aura fait trembler les valeurs de signe, de parole et d'écriture, pour ce qui conduit ici notre futur antérieur, il n'est pas encore d'exergue.[9]

> (The future cannot anticipate itself except in the form of absolute danger. It is that which breaks absolutely with what is constituted as normality and it thus cannot announce itself, present itself, except under the aspect of monstrosity. For the world to come and for that in it which will have made the values of the sign, the word, and writing tremble, for that which draws here our anterior future, there is no more evidence.)

Thought, or the attempt to write about language, becomes science fiction which provides a *frisson* of horrified delight that is reminiscent of *Frankenstein*, in which knowledge seems to become wholly other as it shifts from the figure of Victor Frankenstein to the figure of his monster (the future?).

This conflation of science (knowledge) and science fiction determines the mutually contradictory elements of *De la grammatologie*, in which Derrida is continually announcing an apocalyptic shift in Western thought which can occasionally seem to be merely a substitution of old myths for new. For the idea of a new age remains contaminated by carrying with it the implicit promise of presence which all of those old "new ages" once proffered — "Bliss will it be in that dawn to be alive." But what does the old age of Western civilization look like? The concept of writing has been governed by a phonetic derivation for it which obscures writing's history of its own production. The history of metaphysics has always suggested that the word (logos) is the origin of truth, and has disparaged writing in the search for a "full" speech. And the

265

concept of science (or of the "scientificity" of science) has been determined as logic, in all of its obvious derivation from logos. But the historico-metaphysical epoch of these notions is drawing to a close. A Word which imagined itself to be creative is about to self-destruct, out of sheer exhaustion at having to maintain a tremendous web of fictions as truth.

For some of the writers around *Tel Quel*, Derrida's postulation of the closure of metaphysics has become a scheme which appears to have empirical validity. And with a strikingly uncomplicated comprehension of Derrida's "toujours déjà" ("always already"), they see that closure as having occurred with Mallarmé, which, of course, leaves them with a body of literature upon which to work the millenarian program of affirming absence. For Derrida, however, the historical schema in which "presence" is continually being ferreted out tells a rather different story. For although the notion of "presence" occasionally seems to function as a kind of villain, a newly discovered version of a Cartesian evil genius, Derrida carves the territory of his account from the recognition of a confrontation between the words for presence and the seeming presence of words. The very act of describing Heidegger's deconstruction of metaphysics enmeshes him in a welter of words which cannot be confined to a simple disclosing of a history of easily expunged bad faith. On the one hand "c'est la *question* de l'être que Heidegger pose à la métaphysique. Et avec elle la question de la vérité, du sens, du logos. La méditation incessante de cette question ne restaure pas des assurances."[10] (. . . it is the *question* of being which Heidegger poses to metaphysics. And with it the question of truth, of meaning, of the word. The incessant meditation upon that question does not restore the assurances.) But on the other hand, Heidegger wants to exempt "being" from the movement of the sign. Instead he evokes the "voice of being":

> La voix des sources se n'entend pas. Rupture entre le sens originaire de l'être et le mot, entre le sens et la voix, entre la "voix de l'être" et la *"phonè,"* entre "l'appel de l'être" et le son articulé; une telle rupture, qui confirm à la fois une métaphore fondamentale et la suspecte en accusant le décalage métaphorique, traduit bien l'ambiguité de la situation heideggerienne au regard de la métaphysique de la présence et du logocentrisme.[11]

> (The voice of sources does not hear [or, comprehend] itself. A break between the originary sense of being and the word, between meaning and voice, between the "voice of being" and the "spoken," between the "call of being" and the articulated sound; such a rupture, which

at the same time confirms a fundamental metaphor and suspects it in attacking the metaphorical displacement, translates well the ambiguity of the Heideggerian situation with regard to the metaphysics of presence and of logocentrism.)

Yet if the tradition of thinking about writing generally involves a repression or a refusal to face the full consequences of the differences within self-divided selves and self-divided words, it is also impossible to imagine a progress or a decline within the tradition. For the passion upon which Rousseau bases his claim that the first language was figurative (as Derrida underscores) cannot be evaded: it is both the non-coincidence of the subject with itself and the non-coincidence of *signifiant* and *signifié*. Derrida's merger of "science" (thought) and science fiction attempts to imply the inevitability of passion within the most apparently dispassionate thought. For the extension of a narrative or grammatical string of words must necessarily disclose its own internal disjunctions through that very extension in time, so that the repression of the word into a false consistency or a false insistence upon presence is self-defeating (which is perhaps the reason why de Man utilizes Jakobson's categories of metaphor and metonymy, to dissolve metaphor into metonymy, as a linguistic version of empty allegory).[12] Neither ordinary language nor literary language can, then, become in itself the statement of repression, because both are continually implicated in a temporal predicament of being caught in the very passion which they would contain. And being implicated, they imply that passion. In that sense, no text can affirm presence or deny it; the question becomes one not of position but of implicitness or explicitness, as those categories (like the ones of "literality" and "figurality") constantly shift in their relationships. *"Différance"* cannot divide time into historical periods or epochs; rather, it suspends and thus transforms the notion of history.

Derrida repeatedly speaks of "force" and "energy," and his attempt to see language in terms of "free play" involves an effort to disclose and liberate the passion within writing. But the project is illimitable, as illimitable as Derrida would wish. For the passion which is non-coincidence keeps constituting difference in terms of objects; Rousseau's savage who calls a man a "giant" reveals a disjunction within himself in that moment of passion, but the passion not only constitutes the other man as an object but *overconstitutes* him as an object. He may learn "in time," as Rousseau says, that the "giant" is a "man," but that does not exempt him from an infinitude of analogous errors.[13] The passion which repeatedly institutes difference also acts to reify difference, so that the problem of trying to face the emptiness of thought continually reasserts itself as a problem. A few years ago *Time Magazine* circulated a series of witticisms printed on little cardboard plaques, one of which said, "If you haven't got anything to say, why don't you just shut up?" The dilemma which Derrida presents us with is that he urges us to think of the emptying of thought — not having any*thing* to say — while also reminding us of the passion which keeps leading to an unending constitution of *things*.

Puttenham, in *The Arte of English Poesie*, speaks of rhetoric as ornament which can be lent — through *enargia* (from "*argos*, because it geveth a glorious lustre and light") and through *energia* (from "*ergon*," because it works "with a strong and vertuous operation").[14] But if he talks as though rhetoric is an *addition* to language, he also performs the curious gesture of naming his tropes so that they become personifications — like "Micterismus, or the Fleering Frumpe," "Hiperbaton, or the Trespasser," "Prozeugma, or the Ringleader," and "Hiperbole, or the Over reacher, otherwise called the loud lyer." And through that personification, rhetoric comes to seem like passion within the subject — a division into a proliferation of characters with doubled names. The deconstruction of specific forms of passion always remains a necessary exercise, but a major question about literary language is why any reader ever commits himself to the delusion which he or the text will separatedly, or together, deconstruct. In Shelley's brief essay "On Love," he simulates a demand from the reader: "Thou demandest what is love?" And he responds to this imaginary, objectified, and idealized reader:

> It is that powerful attraction towards all that we conceive, or fear, or hope beyond ourselves, when we find within our own thoughts the chasm of an insufficient void, and seek to awaken in all things that are, a community with what we experience within ourselves. If we reason, we would be understood; if we imagine, we would that the airy children of our brain were born anew within another's; if we feel, we would that another's nerves should vibrate to our own, that the beams of their eyes should kindle at once and mix and melt into our own, that lips of motionless ice should not reply to lips quivering and burning with the heart's best blood.[15]

It would take a lengthy analysis of the text of the essay and of various poems to demonstrate that Shelley — or his texts — does not merely fall into willful blindness about the possibility of the correspondences of which he speaks. But let us take it, temporarily, on faith that love (like any variety of passion) is seen as a conspicuous delusion, the self's attempt not just to mirror itself but to magnify itself. The lover is to be the reader who supplements the writing. Yet that delusion is continually readmitted in an imaginary constellation in which the language of the text, the reader, and the writer do not create an intersubjective relationship but an objectification in which the objectified other is supplementary and greater (like Rousseau's "giant"). To speak of the subjectivity of the author, to valorize the text, to read with temporary unconcern for the false presence of the text — these are the submissions to the delusion of any passion which recur so often that they become, in conjunction with their deconstruction, another version of the fall of the ironist. Language cannot extend itself in time without offering the pretext for deconstruction, and writing is never read without the delusion which creates the imagination of mistakenly enlarged objects. It is, perhaps, in this sense that Wordsworth speaks of poetry as the "history or science of feelings" and of tautology or repetition in poetic language in terms of "our passion for words as *things*, active and efficient."[16]

Wordsworth, in his "Poems Founded on the Affections" and most clearly in the "Blest Babe" passage of *The Prelude*, creates a mythic progress for perception and language in which the infant, in his passionate attachment to the mother, sees the world and himself as *inside* her eyes. He is her best pupil as he sees his own reflection in the pupil of her eye. And that passionate delusion leads to an unwitting education to perception and language — an acceptance of the importance of the forms because they *are* the mother. When the mother dies (whether literally or through a recognition of the child's separateness from her), the child is

> left alone
> Seeking the visible world, nor knowing why.
> The props of my affections were removed,
> And yet the building stood. . . . (*Prelude*, II, II. 277-80)

The world of perception and of language has lost its motivating principle, that one central love object, and Nature becomes a substitute mother both as an inadequate and empty substitute and as a desperately embraced surrogate. For the delusion of passion keeps generating an unwilled belief — that the world of visible form may be an implicit legacy, a text through which to reimagine that fall which seemed to be a paradise. Only for the purest (i.e. inhuman) thought can an intersubjective relationship be imaginable, because the passion within divided language and the divided self recapitulates precisely the kind of unwieldy movement into passion's constitution of objects which de Man describes as Coleridge's reduction of a theocentric to an interpersonal relationship: "To make the object one with us, we must become one with the object — ergo, an object. Ergo, the object must be itself a subject — partially a favorite dog, principally a friend, wholly God, *the* Friend." The subject here is not a subject — not even subjects — but rather a proliferation of objects.

The Johns Hopkins University

NOTES

1   Martin Heidegger, *Being and Time*, trans. John Macquarrie and Edward Robinson (Oxford: Basil Blackwell, 1967), p. 19.

2   Paul de Man, "The Rhetoric of Temporality," in *Interpretation: Theory and Practice*, ed. Charles Singleton (Baltimore: The Johns Hopkins University Press, 1969), p. 173. Additional references cited in text.

3   Paul de Man, "The Rhetoric of Blindness," in *Blindness and Insight: Essays in the Rhetoric of Contemporary Criticism* (New York: Oxford University Press, 1971), p. 136.

4   *Blindness and Insight*, p. 136.

5   *Blindness and Insight*, p. 136.

6   Joseph N. Riddel, "A Miller's Tale," *Diacritics*, 5 (Fall 1975), 56-65, esp. 56.

7   Roman Jakobson, "Quest for the Essence of Language," *Diogenes*, 51 (1965), 24.

8   Jonathan Culler, *Structuralist Poetics: Structuralism, Linguistics, and the Study of Literature* (Ithaca: Cornell University Press, 1975), p. 133.

9   Jacques Derrida, *De la Grammatologie* (Paris: Les Editions de Minuit, 1967), p. 14. Translations are my own.

10   *Grammatologie*, p. 35.

11   *Grammatologie*, p. 36.

12   Paul de Man, "Semiology and Rhetoric," *Diacritics*, 3 (Fall 1973), 27-33.

13   Jean-Jacques Rousseau, *Sur l'origine des langues*, (1817; rpt. Paris: Bibliotheque du graphe, 1970), p. 506.

14   George Puttenham, *The Arte of English Poesie*, (rpt. 1906; rpt. Kent: The Kent State University Press, 1970), p. 155.

15   Percy Bysshe Shelley, "On Love," in *Shelley's Prose, or The Trumpet of a Prophecy*, ed. David Lee Clark (Albuquerque: The University of New Mexico Press, 1954), p. 170.

16   William Wordsworth, "Note to 'The Thorn,'" in *Lyrical Ballads*, ed. R. L. Brett and A. R. Jones (London: Methuen and Co., 1963), p. 283.

The Ontology of the Literary Sign:
Notes toward a Heideggerian Revision of Semiology

Donald G. Marshall

Renaissance linguistics is "etymological" in a strong sense. Each thing rests on God's creating *logos*: "Adamic" naming grasps this creating *logos* as a proper essence. The humanist slogan *"ad fontes"* yielded a preference for ancient "pure latinity" over modern barbarism; and (in theory, but rarely in practice) a preference for even more ancient Greek over Latin. Pagan languages could contain wisdom, for they were closer to God's original institution of meaning in the Book of Nature. The practical aim of linguistic research was constantly to recover original meaning by purifying a text of accumulated corruptions. Such restoration cancels history, which is conceived as error or fall.

Vico's *New Science*[1] inaugurates "philological" linguistics. Rejecting Renaissance attributions of wisdom to the ancients, Vico contends that primitive men were brute giants, all robust sense and imagination. Their language conceals no wisdom; rather these men use real objects and mute gestures to express the unmediated certainty of their sensations and feelings. Only slowly do men develop the capacity to form "imaginative universals," pictorial hieroglyphs where a particular is made

271

to stand for a class of similar particulars. Finally, men form "intelligible universals," class concepts with abstract names, expressed in vocal sounds and "vulgar letters" (that is, alphabetic script). This development, repeated in each individual, is the only way Divine Providence could have brought mere sensual brutes to that pre-eminence of reflective mind which can accept a Christian revelation, transcending and controlling sense. As a methodological principle, linguistics aims not at the recovery of an original essence in the word, but at tracing a providentially guided "progress" of language in its double relation to changing institutions and to a mankind which itself changes. For Vico's philology, language becomes the scene on which is played out "Ideal History," the providential progress of mankind.

With various qualifications and transformations, this program dominates 19th-century philology. Against it, Ferdinand de Saussure's *Course in General Linguistics*[2] asserts, "Everything in language is basically psychological" (GL, 6). Saussure does not mean to oppose to history the psychology of the empirical individual, which is the domain of what he calls *parole*, "speech." In *langue*, "language" as system, the sign "in some way . . . always eludes the individual or social will" (GL, 17). Actually, Saussure wants a phenomenology of the sign, a structural and transcendental descriptive psychology of signification. He recognizes seventeenth- and eighteenth-century rational grammar as a forerunner of this approach (GL, 82). Replacing the certitude of faith with the certitude of conscious reflection, Cartesian rationalism left consciousness as the origin of signification.[3] Rationalism repeats the structure of etymological linguistics, but shifts the locus of authority. The project of a "real character," a graphic representation of the object's essence, already shows the dominance of rationalized technology over the linguistic sign. Saussure's linguistics completes this process by taking the word not as the transcription of a thing, but as itself a thing. Having established its object, linguistics becomes the scientific analysis of that object's necessary constituent structure.

The general "science that studies the life of signs within society" is semiology (GL, 16). Semiology is the transcendental psychology of signification which underlies *langue*, just as *langue* is the system which grounds the empirical psychology of the speaking individual (*parole*). Semiology founds the objectivity of linguistics by establishing both its object and its structure; and hence it supplies the criterion of descriptive adequacy, which, by grounding the mutual relation of object and structure, transforms taxonomy into explanation. Speaking of the role of abstract entities in grammar, Saussure says that "the sum of the conscious and methodical classifications made by the grammarian who studies a language-state without bringing in history must coincide with the associations, conscious or not, that are set up in speaking" (GL, 137-38). The end of the section makes explicit what the phrase "conscious or not" implies, that the "associations" are a transcendental rather than empirical ground for classification: "A material unit exists only through its meaning and function" ("meaning" and "function" stand wholly within structure) (GL, 139). Hence, a technical term like "motivation" looks like empirical psychology. In fact, it means "structural reduplication," either within a single level or between levels of analysis: English numbers like seven-teen, eigh-teen, nine-teen follow a basic pattern. "Motivation" is not "intention" or "volition" in an empirical sense, but rather a feature of structure (GL, 132-34).

This brief sketch has been largely guided by Heidegger's analysis of the history of metaphysics. In what follows, I will concentrate on three approaches to the literary sign in the theories of Roman Jakobson, W. K. Wimsatt, and Heidegger. I would wish to suggest a certain contrast between Heidegger and any "structuralism" deriving from Saussure (and from the rationalism culminating in Kant which lies behind him). At the same time, I hope to persuade the reader of a possibly fruitful contact. In "Logic as Semiotic,"[4] C. S. Peirce distinguishes three sorts of signs: the "symbol," an arbitrary rule for consciousness which connects the sign with what it stands for; the "icon," in which the sign stands for something in virtue of a property the sign actually possesses; and the "index," in which an existential relation connects sign to signified. Heidegger's conception of the literary sign profoundly radicalizes the historical thinking of philological linguistics. By doing so, his conception can help us understand the importance of the "indexical" in language. Heidegger helps us grasp the existential (and therefore historical) relation of sign to signified. Language becomes the place where there endures the call of Being as an appropriation and man's response to that call as expropriation.

I

For Saussure, the linguistic "sign" is a value (GL, 79-81, 111-22) established by its use in the "speech-circuit" (GL, 11-12). Two speakers exchange signs either for other signs or for the "things" or "concepts" they represent. The nature of the sign is determined by the practical economics of communication. Roman Jakobson diagrams this "communication situation" into a structure of constituents in the exchange of signs:[5]

CONTEXT

ADDRESSER————————MESSAGE————————ADDRESSEE
CONTACT

CODE

273

This apparently obvious description of ordinary communication is in fact already dominated by the technological conceptions of semiology. The "addresser" and "addressee" are not empirical subjectivities, but rather the pronouns "I" and "you," conceived as indexes, the existential "subject" of the utterance and the existential "non-subject" of the utterance ("existential" here means "determined by the utterance itself as utterance").[6] "Context" is not a world of things (*Bedeutungen*, objects of intention), but only of "signifieds" (*Sinne*, intentional objects). These "signifieds" are determined by their arbitrary association with the "signifiers" which make up the "message." Arbitrariness is the first principle of the sign, according to Saussure (GL, 67-70), and in Jakobson's "contact," we see the second principle, linearity (temporal in the case of the spoken, phonetic representation of the signifier; spatial in the case of its graphic, written representation). "Code" is the system of a language, the *langue* internalized by the two speakers. To bring out the semiological conception which determines how language can come to appearance within structural linguistics, we can now relabel Jakobson's diagram:

SIGNIFIED

EXISTENTIAL		EXISTENTIAL
SUBJECT OF	SIGNIFIER (arbitrary)	NON-SUBJECT OF
ENUNCIATION ("I")	SIGNIFIER (linear)	ENUNCIATION ("you")

LANGUE

In semiology, the linguistic sign is brought to stand as an object. It is a "means of communication," where communication is thought technologically as a distributional economics of exchange within the place of exchange ("marketplace").

Jakobson retranscribes the positions in his diagram to yield a linguistics of "functions of language":

REFERENTIAL

EMOTIVE ——————— POETIC ——————— CONATIVE
PHATIC

METALINGUAL

Again, ordinary-language terms somewhat mask the essential technological conception indicated by the notion of "functions." Jakobson makes clear that a particular utterance is not to be assigned wholly to one or another category in the diagrammatic map. "Functions" are internal constituents of any utterance. Nevertheless, one function "dominates": that is, the functions are present in some determinate, hierarchical order. "Function" is not conceived empirically as "use," but mathematically as the weight, relative to each other, of constituent factors ($f(x,y, \ldots)$). Within the terms of the diagram, Jakobson then answers the main question of the essay in which he introduces them: what is the *differentia specifica* of verbal art? The structural principle of the "poetic function" is the dominance of or "set" toward the message itself for its own sake.

Jakobson's theory here follows the earliest thinking of Russian formalism. Victor Shklovsky conceived art as a way of breaking up automatized perception and thinking (I. A. Richards' "stock responses").[7] The poem used a linguistic sign as a "device," making its perceptual qualities prominent instead of effacing the sign in the service of ordinary communication. In such a use, both the sign and the thing it stands for become "strange," so that we "recover the sensation of life." Art makes "the stone *stony*" (AT, 12). The poem is a technique for transforming a sign from an instrument of knowing and communicating to an object of perception: "Gore in art is not necessarily gory; it rhymes with *amor* — it is either the substance of the tonal structure or material for the construction of figures of speech" (AT, 44, see 18). In Jakobson's words, the poetic function "by promoting the palpability of signs, deepens the fundamental dichotomy of signs and objects" (CS, 356). By drawing on language's self-referential capacity, poetic function makes the linguistic sign into a reflexively self-constituting object. Thus purged of "extralinguistic" entities like reference, such a sign occupies a privileged status in Jakobson's linguistics: the poetic sign is the pure sign; poetry is discourse generated out of pure signs.

Poetic function constitutes a discourse by projecting "the principle of equivalence from the axis of selection into the axis of combination" (CS, 358). (This is, in Jakobson, an empirical criterion for recognizing poetic function, and not a generative principle.) This formula is best understood through Saussure's distinction between the paradigmatic and the syntagmatic.[8] A sign occurring at a given point in a speech chain is simultaneously the member of various classes: *enseignement* is part of the series "nouns ending in -ment," of the series "nouns having to do with education," of the series "words formed from the root theme *enseign-*," and others. These series or classes of equivalent items are "paradigms." A sign is also linked in the speech chain to the signs preceding and succeeding it, which, in their sequentiality, constitute the "syntagm." In poetic function, paradigm dominates over syntagm, so that equivalence becomes the constitutive device of the sequence. In simpler terms, some perceptible unit recurs in the sequence of speech. That unit may be a certain clause-structure (the parallelism of Hebrew psalms), a certain number of syllables (French verse), a certain sound repeated in roughly equal-time intervals (Old English verse), and so forth. Some perceptible rhythm is the fundamental fact of poetic speech, and the rhythmic units become "equivalent."

In this conception, the poetic function of language mirrors linguistic analysis. The metalingual function is used to establish a code, that is, to find equivalences in the sequence of speech, to determine exchange values. Poetic function reverses the process, making sequences out of equivalences of all kinds. Through reflexivity, the poetic sign makes the signifier its own signified, so that an arbitrary association of different entities (an ontologically heterogeneous sign) becomes a pure autonomous object, self-establishing as a self-same substance. At the same time, the distinction between significant and non-significant features in the sign's structure disappears.[9] In utterances, poetic function maximizes "motivation," the internal reduplication of structure. Both the signified (the relation of arbitrariness) and the sequence (the relation of linearity) here derive directly from the autonomous sign. Like the aesthetic object for Kant, the poetic sign dissolves the fundamental antinomies of structuralist thought.[10] When language is thought wholly within the pragmatics of communication, the poetic sign is not so much a deviation from the model of communication as it is a revelation of the most fundamental and constitutive truth of signs. In poetic function, the sign re-presents itself purely as technique. The poetic sign is an autotelic, bare perceptual particular. Standing forth in its essential purity, the poetic sign validates structural linguistics by its own internal consistency: poetry is pure, autonomous grammar.

Since the poetic sign is autonomous from all "extralinguistic" entities, a structuralist criticism essentially reduces articulation to taxonomy. There cannot even be a qualitative difference among signs: the fundamental principle is equivalence. Within poetry, signs must be related symmetrically, and symmetries must be parallel.[11] Criticism is the taxonomic analysis of verbal structure, designed to exhibit the maximum of perceptible technique. "Perceptible" has no meaning from empirical psychology (just as the phrase "how X is made" in Russian formalism is not a matter of empirical generation): it means simply the pure possibility of representing a symmetry.

II

Against Jakobson's theory may be set a later stage in Russian formalism itself. With Tomashevsky, the art-work began to be conceived as a sub-system analogous to language.[12] A concern for relation of part to whole replaces a definition of the art-work in terms of the immanent structure of the pure sign. The key notion is "motivation." Again, as in Saussure, the term seems to cover loosely any conceivable or formulable reason for the appearance of anything in a work. But its more strictly technical sense is "structural reduplication." Tomashevsky tried to analyze the whole work into various levels or strata, infra-structures within the work conceived as a whole. "Motivation" mainly registers the various relations between elements in different infrastructures. The work becomes a totality constituted by complex interactions between autonomous infrastructures (sound, diction, syntax, rhetoric, image pattern, theme, character, plot, and the like). "Autonomy" has meaning only in the relation of one infrastructure to another. Mediated by the whole, one stratum can "dominate." The combination of "dominance" with the mediated autonomy of strata permits relations of asymmetry within the textual totality. Roman Ingarden's *The Literary Work of Art*[13] develops a similar conception from a purely phenomenological standpoint. He describes rigorously four strata, whose "polyphonic" interrelations are integrated within the whole work.

The fullest development of this conception occurs in American formalist criticism. Like Jakobson, Cleanth Brooks assumes that communication in propositional statements is the basic form of language.[14] Poetry deviates from this form toward "dramatic" structure, where the individual sign is not constituted by its relation to an external reality, but to the whole structure of the poem. This relation Brooks calls "propriety," contrasting it with scientific "truth" (HP, 205). "Irony" is Brooks's broadest term for poetic structure; he defines it as the qualification any element receives from its context (HP, 209). The poetic sign, for Brooks, retains a constitutive heterogeneity, but he substitutes the heterogeneity of part and whole for the heterogeneity of word and thing (or concept) characteristic of ordinary communication.

In the essays in *The Verbal Icon*,[15] W. K. Wimsatt overcomes even this dichotomy of heterogeneities and thus achieves the most comprehensive (I believe, the most comprehensive possible) structural conception of poetry. The book's title, as Wimsatt explains in a note, preserves the conception of the poem as a total structure, but only as related to the structure of a denoted object. The poem as verbal icon is "a bright picture" or "image," but also "an interpretation of reality in its [presumably the poem's] metaphoric and symbolic dimensions" (VI, x). The poem's internal structure is "coherence"; its relation to external structure or structures is "correspondence." Combining both sorts of structure, Wimsatt's definition of poetry differs sharply from Jacobson's:

> Poetry is a complex kind of verbal construction in which
> the dimension of coherence is by various techniques of
> implication greatly enhanced and thus generates an extra
> dimension of correspondence to reality, the symbolic or
> analogical. (VI, 241)

The poem does not diverge from reference, but enhances reference into interpretation. The "total structure of verbal meaning" ranges from a basic stratum of substantive "stated meaning" (roughly, "denotation," itself complex and stratified), shading toward varieties of "intimated meaning," and finally thinning into "purely verbal style" (VI, 202-03). Though relatively rare and limited, directly iconic words illustrate purely verbal style: onomatopoeia or autologism ("polysyllable," "word"), that is, words which exhibit the sound or property they name. More usually in poems, verbal patterns function "counterlogically": they cannot generate a substantive meaning nor make a false one true, but they help concentrate on substantive meaning "whatever propriety there may be" in it (VI, 208). The referential force of words remains fundamental and irreducible. "Counterlogical" verbal patterns do not present substantive meaning by direct iconic echo, but rather by diagrammatic representation of substantive meaning's own relational properties. Such diagrammatic iconicity is made possible by the systemic nature of language. Because language tends to distinguish different meanings by different sounds, the repetition of sounds invites an attention to possible similarities of meaning, as in the pun or various other "lurking and oblique elements of homophonic harmony" (VI, 216). If "language is a system of conventional norms" (VI, 215), it may nonetheless follow "certain laws of analogy and propriety in the relation of sound to meaning." The arbitrary relation of signifier to signified is constrained by an analogical determination of the signifier mediated by the totality of the linguistic system.[16]

In a "poetic situation" (VI, 215), the systemic properties of a linguistic sign correspond to properties — real or plausibly supposable — in objects ("there has to be some fact behind a pun" [VI, 214]). In the open totality of language, the propriety of verbal pattern to substantive meaning is logical iconicity. Attention is concentrated onto substantive meaning. But since the poem is a conventionally closed totality, it can concentrate and multiply systemic relations between words, as in such devices as meter. The poem's system must not violate the prior language system — a poet cannot shift a word's accent for his own metric convenience. Rather, precisely because it concentrates in a finite compass the "poetic situations" or systemic properties of a language, a poem augments our double awareness of language's native systematicity and of its potential for analogical relation to substantive meaning. Hence, poetic symbols "invite evaluation" (VI, 217) precisely of this analogical, iconic presentation of meaning. And at the same time, they encourage our awareness of verbal structure as *verbal* and therefore autonomous:

> Poetry by thickening the medium increases the disparity
> between itself and its referents. . . . The symbol has
> more substance than a noniconic symbol and hence is
> more clearly realized as a thing separate from its

> referents and as one of the productions of our own
> spirit.[17]   (VI, 217)

In its structural autonomy, the poem is different from its referents; in its iconicity, it is like them. By mediating this simultaneous difference and likeness, the poetic symbol achieves "the total metaphoric relation between a good poem and the reality or the many circles of reality to which it refers" (VI, 217). As an iconic *sign*, the poetic symbol refers to something else; as an *iconic* sign, it must actually possess in its own right the property in virtue of which it refers; and these properties in the case of the poetic sign are mainly relational within the poem.

In ordinary language, the relation of word to referent is mediated by a concept. Poetic structure presents this concept indirectly in virtue of its own structural properties. Metaphor is a concrete abstraction which discloses a more general third class by asserting a relation of resemblance between members of two other classes. "This (third) class," Wimsatt says, "is unnamed and most likely remains unnamed and is apprehended only through the metaphor. It is a new conception for which there is no other expression" (VI, 79). By approximate descriptions of the poem's internal structure or "coherence," the critic helps the reader approach that "something (an individual intuition — or a concept) which can never be expressed in other terms" (VI, 83). This internal structure is an interrelation of likeness and difference between two terms. Wimsatt departs from classical rhetoric, insofar as the latter takes metaphor to be a trope on a single word, the substitution of a less frequent for a more familiar name. Quoting Coleridge, Wimsatt asserts that metaphor is "the mesothesis of identity and difference."[18] The word in a poem retains its "proper" meanings, precisely so that in confrontation with other words it can release "indefinite radiations of meaning" (VI, 127). The multiplicity of a poem's particulars does not collapse into sameness or equivalence, as in Jakobson. Poetic structure holds particulars distinct, but only so that by their interrelations within the poem those particulars can present indirectly a quasi-concept released by the intimation of likeness (this intimation is meter's main role). In return, the quasi-concept mediates the coalescence of particulars into a unified whole. This identifying unity must therefore be based on two kinds of difference: the distinctness of particulars and the distinct autonomy of the poetic structure in relation to meaning.

In Jakobson, the self-reflexivity of language is reduced to equivalence, an absolute self-sameness which eliminates the difference necessary for meaning and models the sign on a pure perceptual object in itself. This is the final outcome of the technologization of the linguistic sign. Wimsatt founds poetic structure on a different model, which becomes explicit in the essay "The Concrete Universal." Speaking of the "rounded" and substantially existing character Falstaff, Wimsatt suggests that his attributes make a circuit and connection. A kind of awareness of self (a high and human characteristic), with a pleasure in the fact, is perhaps the central principle which instead of simplifying the attributes gives each one a special function in the whole, a double or reflex value. (VI, 79)

Wimsatt here recovers the rational tradition which begins with Descartes and which in Kant reaches a formulation that founds technological thinking and is then largely forgotten (or is reduced to pure method instead of a metaphysics of the object based on an analysis of the constitutive structure of experience). Probably most pertinent to Wimsatt is the formulation of this tradition in the ten theses from Chapter XII of Coleridge's *Biographia Literaria.*[19]

Coleridge seeks some principle in which "object and subject, being and knowing" are identical. He finds it in self-consciousness: "Only in the self-consciousness of a spirit is there the required identity of object and of representation; for herein consists the essence of spirit, that it is self-representative" (BL, 153). This is not a passive registration of sameness, for the spirit must dissolve its self-sameness in order to become conscious of itself as object. This it does by an "act": "it follows therefore that intelligence or self-consciousness is impossible, except by and in a will" (BL, 153). Striving toward self-representation, spirit generates the subject-object contradiction: "In the existence, in the reconciling and the recurrence of this contradiction consists the process and mystery of production and life" (BL, 153). The generation and reconciliation of the subject-object contradiction rests on "will or primary act of self-duplication." Intelligence is therefore engaged in "a process of self-construction," tending "to objectize itself" and then "to know itself in the object" (BL, 156).

The will to self-representation founds knowledge in the reconciliation of opposites. In the poem, imagination is first put in action by will and understanding and "reveals itself in the balance or reconciliation of opposite or discordant qualities" (BL, 174). The synthesizing power of imagination binds part to whole in the poem. The holistic integrity of the poem is modeled on the holistic integrity of self-consciousness in perception. For perception is not the passive registration of sense impressions, as, Coleridge says, it is for the empirical tradition. Rather, "sensation itself is but vision nascent, not the cause of intelligence but intelligence itself revealed as an earlier power in the process of self-construction" (BL, 155). Perception effects its object by force of representation within the transitional or progressively unfolding subject, unified by the self-attribution of its own experience.[20]

In Wimsatt, the poetic sign is an act of consciousness. The poem as a whole is the symbolic intuition of a concept that does not permit schematic intuition. In the *Critique of Judgement*, Kant gives the example of a monarchical state, which is incapable of direct sensible intuition, but may be represented as a living body when governed by a constitution or as a mere machine if ruled tyranically. The agreement thus instituted between a concept and an intuition, Kant says, is merely the rule of the procedure which supplies the symbol, and hence lies solely in the form of reflection upon both the concept and the symbol.[21] As with Falstaff, the poetic sign in metaphoric structure achieves a "double or reflex value": the internal coherence of self-consciousness and a grasp through symbolic intuition of poetry's "subject matter," "the moral realm," in a broad sense (VI, 82). "Complexity of form is sophistication of content," Wimsatt argues, returning us to Kant's assertion that "the beautiful is the symbol of the morally good." It is through complex form that the moral realm, transcending sense, is represented as harmonious with the understanding, which is not free. "Imagination, even in its freedom," Kant says, is represented "as amenable to a final determination for understanding." By returning to this Kantian model, Wimsatt surpasses Jakobson; for he grasps (even better than Ingarden) the structural integrity and yet ontological heterogeneity of the poetic sign, a double value modeled on and effected in self-consciousness.

III

To expound Heidegger on signs is complicated by the fact that his thinking passes through several stages, which are, I judge, consistent but distinct. I will begin with Articles 17 and 18 from *Being and Time*.[22] Heidegger rejects any formalized classification of signs or of kinds or species of referring. He tries instead to interpret the sign ontologically, in order to approach an analysis of "reference" or "assignment." Signs are a special kind of equipment for showing or indicating. They are "ready-to-hand within-the-world in [a] whole equipment-context" (BT, 109). An automobile's turn-signal, for instance, acquires its significance within the whole context of automobile, driving, traffic regulations, and the like; and that significance is manifested not as an abstract formal relationship between thing (turn-signal) and some other thing (direction of movement), but rather by the on-going activity in which the driver of an automobile and drivers of other automobiles make use of the sign. Heidegger thereby connects the sign with two key constituent elements: a totality within which the sign acquires its significance; and an ongoing activity within which the sign is established and used. The sign achieves "an orientation within our environment" (BT, 110). Hence, "A sign is not a Thing which stands to another Thing in the relationship of indicating" (BT, 110). Rather, it is an item of equipment through which we can perceive that any item ready-to-hand, any item we use in our ordinary activities, is involved in a totality or ordered world.

In the process of "establishing a sign" we can see a little more clearly the nature of the relationship between sign and what it signifies. A sign is some ready-to-hand equipment which "takes over the 'work' of *letting* something ready-to-hand *become conspicuous*" (BT, 111). Heidegger had previously mentioned some ways in which a piece of equipment becomes conspicuous: when we cannot find the equipment we need, for instance, or when a piece of equipment is broken. A sign is a piece of equipment which in its own conspicuousness makes available by revealing it another piece of equipment or even the environment in general. "Revealing" is here an active process, making the signified available to us in our ongoing (and ultimately directed, including goal-oriented) involvement with an environing world. Hence, the totality within which the sign signifies is not just a heap: the indicating the sign does has a particular orientation founded on an "in-order-to." The sign is especially helpful for Heidegger as a piece of equipment whose very being allows us to see that "reference or assignment" is constitutive for anything ready-to-hand. The power of the sign to indicate is not something added to its "mere" existence, but is rather its ontological foundation as what it is.

Reference essentially involves a "with . . . in" structure. Any entity has "with" it an involvement, namely, a "towards-which" of serviceability and a "for-which" of usability. Such ontologically constitutive purposiveness is framed by a totality of involvements. This totality rests ultimately on something different from a particular entity or thing and from a totality of involvements. This further foundation is a "for-the-sake-of," a determinate "potentiality-for-Being" through which human existence (*Dasein*) establishes a world as an orientation of itself toward its own Being. The ordered totality of these relations — beginning with human existence's establishment of a world and proceeding to the freeing of particular entities encountered within the world — is "signifying," and this in turn makes up the structure of the world (BT, 120). Human existence grasps this structure in an act of understanding. "The Being of words and of language" rests upon the disclosure of "significations" in acts of understanding and interpreting (BT, 121). "The significance thus disclosed is an existential state of Dasein," Heidegger adds (BT, 121). "Signifying" is therefore not just a formal relation of sign to signified nor does it exist simply as "something thought." It is the ontological foundation for the existence of every actual entity. Heidegger thus argues that signification involves the totality of world; that such totality rests ultimately on human existence and the comportment it takes up toward its own Being; and that — by implication — words and language do not transcribe arbitrarily posited relations nor even pure "concepts" of thought,[23] but rather serve to disclose signification as ontologically fundamental for every entity.

Heidegger's analysis in these early sections of *Being and Time* may seem oriented chiefly toward "significations" which are practical in nature or at most limited to purposes of understanding. A more complete exegesis would need to pursue the fuller characterization of "discourse" as that which articulates (segments, structures, and makes manifest) the "disclosedness" of human existence's essential "Being-there," which is constituted by the unity of understanding, mood, and falling, these three moments exhibiting respectively the temporal characteristics of futurality, the "having been," and the present. Such an exegesis would acquit Heidegger of any charge that his view is narrowly practical or intellectualist.[24] For our purposes here, I think it will be more helpful to turn to a somewhat later stage in Heidegger's thought and to the specifically aesthetic concerns of "The Origin of the Work of Art" (published 1950; based on lectures given in 1936-37).[25]

Heidegger begins with the two-sided character of the art-work: in it, "something other is brought together with the thing that is made" (OW, 652). This bringing together is, in Greek, $\sigma \upsilon \mu \beta\,'\alpha\lambda\lambda\epsilon\iota\nu$: "The work is a symbol." The art-work has a thingly character of its own, but this character is not a substructure to which some "higher" element is added. The nature of the art-work as a thing lies in its character as work: "the path toward the determination of the thingly reality of the work does not lead from thing to work but from work to thing" (OW, 667). Heidegger then explores the nature of "work." Through work, a world is set up. This "world" is the open but ordered whole within which human beings live: "Wherever the essential decisions of our history are made, are taken up and abandoned by us, mistaken and re-examined, there the world worlds" (OW, 671). "World" is then essentially a verb, an active process of human existence and comportment, founded on human comportment toward the fundamental matter of its own existence. "Work" establishes the "place" of worlding: it liberates and establishes world. At the same time that work sets up world, it "sets forth" world. In ordinary equipment, its material is used up in serviceability: the equipment "wears out." In the art-work, "world" is set back into a material medium which is persistingly manifested in its own nature and persistingly manifests world. This material medium is "earth." The "work" is then a setting up (of world) and a setting forth (of earth). The relation between world and earth is a "struggle" (OW, 675); that is, the "art-work" never devolves into an inert thing, but maintains "the continually self-overreaching composing of the movement of the work," what Heidegger calls "the intimacy of strife" (OW, 675).

In this striving intimacy, Heidegger finds, "the truth is set into work" (OW, 675). The art-work as truth discloses what *is*, and "what *is* is never, as may all too easily appear, our handiwork or even merely our representation" (OW, 678). Truth can be set into work in the art-work only because the unified strife of world with earth establishes a symbol.

Any entity we encounter seems "familiar, reliable, ordinary" (OW, 679). But the entity is disclosed only through a twofold concealment: the entity refuses itself and dissembles or hides something else. Heidegger does not offer a detailed example. I take him as meaning something like this: normally, a word is "used up" in the process of naming. We pay no attention to it. In a poem — in a metaphor, for instance — the word "refuses itself" in its normal function. In that refusal, what it *is* stands forth. At the same time, the metaphoric word dissembles, standing in front of something else which it manifests. For instance, Heidegger frequently remarks that language is "the house of Being." Is "house" a metaphor? Not in the classical sense of "metaphor": "To talk of the house of Being is not to transfer the image of 'house' to Being, but from the materially understood essence of Being we shall some day be more easily able to think what 'house' and 'dwelling' are."[26] The word "house" here refuses itself in its "ordinary" sense; at the same time, it dissembles or stands in front of the sense it manifests in this phrase. Its showing forth of a signification is ineluctably tied up with this double concealment. But we are not to think that "house" has a "proper" meaning which the phrase deviates from. The "proper" or "ordinary" meaning is itself taken within a world, and only once we begin to grasp "the materially understood essence of Being" will we be able to think "house" as a word used with the utmost exactness and precision in this phrase, and not as a rhetorically motivated deviation from conceptual meaning nor as the symbolic intuition of a thing not capable of schematic intuition — that is, neither as a way of supplying a gap in the set of names nor as a way of supplying a gap in sensory presentations. Rather, "Language is the clearing-and-concealing advent of Being itself" (LH, 279). The metaphoric literary sign records "a mode of thinking more rigorous than the conceptual" (LH, 297), because it always shows forth its revealing within the existential frame of human existence and its Being-in-the-world.

The active advent of Being in the art-work Heidegger sees as the "happening of truth," where "truth" is understood as disclosing or un-concealing. The "happening of truth" comprises both "creating" and "preserving." Heidegger understands creating as the establishing of conflict (between disclosure and double concealment) in the figure (the Gestalt, the structure or placing as framing and ordering) by means of the "rift" (*Riss*). "Rift" is that "intimacy of strife" which "draws the opponents (here, world and earth) together into the source of their unity" (OW, 686). Truth as conflict brings into itself an entity constituted by the setting forth of the conflict and the setting of the conflict back into earth. Thus, "Truth is present (in the work) only as the conflict between lighting and concealing in the opposition of world and earth" (OW, 685). Artistic creation is "an employment of the earth in the establishment of truth in the figure" (OW, 687). The other side of the "Happening of truth" in the art-work is "preserving." Like creating, it is a knowing, again not as representation (either by copy or by concept). It is rather a maintaining of the conflict between unconcealment and double concealment which is already established by creation in the work's earth. Just as the answer to a question "remains in effect as answer only as long as it is rooted in questioning" (OW, 692), so the art-work retains its character as art-work only so long as the establishing effected in creation is preserved in its essence as the working of truth. The art-work as doubly creation and preservation "is then the becoming and happening of truth" (OW, 693).

Such an art, Heidegger says, is "essentially poetry" (OW, 693). Not that the other arts are to be reduced to "poesy" (German *Poesie*, opposed to *Dichtung*). Rather, "poesy makes its advent in language because language preserves the original essence of poetry" (OW, 695). That original essence is to bring "what *is* as something that *is* into the Open for the first time" (OW, 694). "This naming," Heidegger adds, "nominates what *is, to* its being *from out of* its being" (OW, 694). (That is, it should not be mistaken as a merely subjective process on the part of the naming human.) Naming here becomes "saying," which is not just the speaking of words, but a "projecting" which transforms the ordinary by first disclosing what *is* and by serving as the occasion for us to "enter into what is disclosed by the work," into its "world," and thus to "bring our essence itself to a stand in the truth of what *is*" (OW, 695). The stand we achieve by preservingly entering the work's world has the force of disclosing or unconcealing truth (about what *is* and about our own existence), and is not any merely self-amused toying with a "different way of looking at things." As "projective speech," "poetry is the saga of the unconcealment of what *is*" (OW, 695).

In the essay "The Way to Language,"[27] Heidegger applies the same terms to language, in particular connecting "sign" to *Riss* ("rift" or "rift-design"). The "unity of the being of language," Heidegger says, is "design" (*Aufriss*). "The 'sign' [*Riss*] in design (Latin *signum*) is related to *secare*, to cut — as in saw, sector, segment. To design is to cut a trace" (WL, 121). The sign articulates within the wholeness of world. Heidegger continues,

> The design is the whole of the traits of that drawing
> [*Zeichnung*] which structures and prevails throughout the
> open, unlocked freedom of language, the structure of a
> show [*Zeigen*] in which are joined the speakers and their
> speaking: what is spoken and what of it is unspoken in
> all that is given in the speaking. (WL, 121)

The sign as a showing is not here seen as an instrument in a "communication situation" between causally prior speakers. Signs "arise from a showing," for "the essential being of language is Saying as Showing" (WL, 123). Showing saying is not a "linguistic expression added to the phenomena after they have appeared" (WL, 126). Only insofar as he himself abides in saying can the human speaker show forth through signs what *is*. The "moving force" which brings forward what is and grants the showing power of saying is "Appropriation" (WL, 127): "Appropriation is the way-making for Saying to come into language" (WL, 130). In modern technology, Appropriation shows itself in the mode of "Framing," which provokes man "to order and set up all that is present being [sic] as technical inventory" (WL, 131). "Within Framing," Heidegger continues, "speaking turns into information" (WL, 132). But the "most proper mode of Appropriating" is saying as showing (WL, 131). Since the way-making of appropriating is temporal even more than spatial, "All language is historical" (WL, 133). In the remainder of this essay, I will follow a somewhat indirect but, I think, necessary path toward a fuller characterization of the absolutely fundamental event of Appropriation and the consequent historicity of language.

Despite important shifts in emphasis and vocabulary, Heidegger's assertions here are consistent with *Being and Time*. He always insisted that entities were never simply inertly "there," but were primordially encountered as distinct and synthesized, that is, articulated in a structured world or whole, a "reference totality." The articulation of totality by discourse is more fundamental or prior to any "putting into words," even though it becomes most acutely visible in this further process. Ultimately, such totalities must be referred back to human existence. *"Hence,"* Heidegger insists, *"only Dasein can be meaningful or meaningless"* (BT, 193). Linguistic communication "speaks forth" an entity; what it shares with an other is not just the entity, but "our *Being towards* what has been pointed out" (BT, 197). This sharing may widen the availability of the entity pointed out or may tend to veil it, as in hearsay or rumor. Language "has its roots in the existential constitution of Dasein's disclosedness. *The existential-ontological foundation of language is discourse or talk"* (BT, 203). "Discourse" is here just as fundamental as ''state-of-mind'' or ''understanding.'' It is, Heidegger says, the "Articulation of intelligibility" (BT, 203). The ontological foundation of language denies that mere entities exist and that mere words exist and that the two get somehow "related" arbitrarily (or even mediated by some purely mental "concept"). The power of the word to disclose a thing rests on the articulation of human existence's Being-in-the-world. "In 'poetical' discourse," Heidegger adds, "the communication of the existential possibilities of one's state-of-mind can become an aim in itself, and this amounts to a disclosing of existence" (BT, 205). "The Origin of the Work of Art," insofar as it focuses on poetry in the narrower sense, essentially works out these ideas.

"Poetic language" cannot be described merely as some linguistic deviation from ordinary language — that is, it cannot be described adequately in Jakobson's purely technological terms. Nor can it be described adequately in the more comprehensive terms of Wimsatt, though the conception of verbal art as presenting analogically certain truths or realities of the human, moral world — truths either too complicated or too experiential to be grasped conceptually — comes much closer. Poetic language can be adequately characterized only on the basis of a fully worked-out analysis of human existence and "the ontologico-existential whole" of the structure of its discourse. In Peirce's terms, poetic language is not to be conceived on the model of the symbol, as an arbitrary rule for the understanding associating the sign with what it signifies; nor is it to be conceived as icon, where the sign in virtue of properties it possesses in itself or by its organization into an autonomous system presents (by analogy) experiential realities of what it signifies. If we adopt the remaining alternative, that poetic language reveals more clearly than any other the existential foundation of any "putting into words" of articulated discourse, we must understand the "existential" connection of sign to signified in other than simply causal terms. Peirce says that a "rhematic indexical legisign" (for instance, a demonstrative pronoun), "is any general type or law, however established, which requires each instance of it to be really affected by its Object in such a manner as merely to draw attention to that Object" (LS, 116). The phrase "really affected by its Object" may have a narrowly causal interpretation. But if we take the "existentiality" of relations between sign and signified in the index to cover a broader conception, then we approach Heidegger's argument that the power of a sign to disclose an object ("draw attention" to it, but in a much stronger sense) rests on the articulation of human existence's understanding of its world. In "The Origin of the Work of Art," Heidegger helps us see poetic language as the place where "the happening of truth," that is, the disclosure of what *is* within the establishment and preservation of human being's world, can be most clearly grasped.

Heidegger's notion of a "discourse" which, in its intimate connection with human existence, lies beneath ordinary language, finds a striking anticipation in Vico's philology. Vico rejects the rationalist characterization of the word as an arbitrary concrete mark calling to mind by association an intelligible universal which can then be used to grasp a perceptual particular conceptually. Such propositional thinking, Vico asserts, is a late achievement of the philosophers. Instead, language historically went through three stages: first, a mute language of ritual gestures, including signification through real, existing objects; second, visual hieroglyphics, the heroic blazoning of signification in *imprese* or coats of arms; and finally, vocal language recorded in vulgar letters. The operative principle in the first stage is that in ignorance men attribute to things the feelings of their own minds (NS, pars. 120-23). Vico certainly does not intend any deliberate "animism": the primitive does not first clearly grasp his internal feeling and then predicate it externally. Rather, he first grasps his own feeling in an alienated form which returns to him within ritual gesture. Hence, ritual gesture allows external reality to appear in a relation to human being. The primitive auspices constitute this gestural language which brings the hidden to appearance. The real is disclosed in its relatedness to man, but not as subjective. Gesture allows a god to signify to man by bringing the object indicated in the gesture to stand as a disclosure (rather than as the "objective" object of rationalism).

In "A Dialogue on Language," Heidegger's thought is remarkably similar to Vico's.[28] Heidegger says that "gesture is the gathering of a bearing." Heidegger notices explicitly that the bearing, which includes an idea of orientation within a structured whole, is both toward us and borne by us toward an encounter with what bears toward us. What is fundamental is not one or the other "side" of such an encounter, but the gathering disclosed in gesture. This gathering gesture opens the clearing within which each thing comes to appearance, and gesture becomes thereby the foundation of language. It is a primordial articulation by discourse, and to the opening or clearing it establishes, an actual name gets attached.

Heidegger develops this line of thought in his later writings, using a vocabulary that is difficult because it avoids most of the terms which have emerged in the historical tradition of philosophy. I will concentrate on the "Conversation on a Country Path about Thinking," which seems to me to present in a concentrated way many of the later Heidegger's central positions.[29] From the point of view of language, Heidegger distinguishes between "designation" and a different sort of naming, one "in which the nameable, the name and the named occur altogether" (CC, 71). Designation belongs essentially to representational thinking, which takes as assumed a framework or "transcendental horizon" within which emerge "objects" possessing an essence or "typical appearance" in relation to subjectivity (as in the traditional philosophical description of perception). Both Jakobson and Wimsatt stand within this kind of thinking, Jakobson one-sidedly emphasizing the object, Wimsatt grasping more fully the emergence of the object within experience, making self-consciousness the basic model of knowing.

Instead, Heidegger proposes a "recollective thinking" characterized by a "releasement toward things." The terms and moves of Heidegger's argument are not easy to follow here. But I take it the line of thought is to understand "releasement" as something precise and directed toward "things," not just as a loose passivity or will-less indifference, and then to ask what makes such a releasement possible. The answer is "regioning." It is important to notice that the word is a verb, containing a temporal component, though this verbal base tends to get lost in translation. A region, Heidegger says, "holds what comes forward to meet us." But we should avoid characterizing the region "through its relation to us" (CC, 65). By exploring the root meanings of the word "region," Heidegger comes to a sort of definition: "That-which-regions is an abiding expanse which, gathering all, opens itself, so that in it openness is halted and held, letting everything merge in its own resting" (CC, 66). Many of these terms we have already encountered. In one sense, Heidegger is here trying to characterize more cautiously and yet more rigorously the notion of "world" in *Being and Time* and the further notion of "clearing" or "open" we saw in "The Origin of the Work of Art." "Regioning" now becomes the key term, for "Releasement comes out of that-which-regions" (CC, 73). Releasement occurs insofar as man "originally belongs" to that-which-regions, that is, "insofar as he is *appropriated* initially to that-which-regions and, indeed, through this itself." The relation between regioning and releasement is "neither . . . ontic nor . . . ontological" (CC, 76). And the same is true of the relation of regioning to the thing.

In a short exploration, Heidegger also asks about the relation of man to thing. The goal of this question is evidently to conceive "knowledge" within the kind of thinking whose nature is emerging slowly out of this discussion of releasement and regioning. The relation of man to thing, Heidegger asserts, is historical. It "belongs to the history of man's nature" (CC, 78). This assertion is immediately qualified: "Only so far as man's *nature* does *not* receive its stamp from man, but from what we call that-which-regions and its regioning, does the history you presage become the history of that-which-regions" (CC, 78). Again, despite the change of terms, this remark bears a clear relation to Heidegger's program in the 1930's for exploring the "history of Being." History emerges from the temporal nature of regioning, and hence, the more limited linguistic theory which takes names as designations (that is, takes them solely within the relation of ego to object), is inevitably founded on and traversed by history. Historical change as well as the temporal "stamp" of language is not an accident that occurs to a system, even when the system is conceived as generative rather than "synchronic." On the contrary, the historicity of existence is fundamental to language, is, in fact, precisely what makes language possible.

Heidegger does not elaborate this discussion, but continues toward the topic of knowledge: "Here the concept of the historical signifies a mode of knowing and is understood broadly" (CC, 79). He returns to a further discussion of releasement, first bringing forward a revised version of the notion "resolve" from *Being and Time*. There is "a steadfastness hidden in releasement," which shows itself in the "composure of releasement." Heidegger proposes the word "in-dwelling" for this composed steadfastness. Secondly, releasement is rooted in a "prior": it must be a steadfast abiding in the origin of man's nature, that is, in regioning, which is the origin both of man's nature and of the determinateness of the thing. Hence, truth can emerge in man: "man is he who is made use of for the nature of truth" (CC, 84-85). Through this exploration of releasement, Heidegger finally comes to the "nature of thinking," which is "in-dwelling releasement to that-which-regions."

Thinking is "the essentially human relation to that-which-regions" (CC, 87).

Heidegger now proposes a name for this sort of "thinking and so of knowing" (CC, 87). This is a one-word fragment of Heraclitus, 'αγχιβασίη, interpreted as "moving-into-nearness." This word for knowing, Heidegger pointedly remarks, "could rather . . . be the name for our walk today along this country path" (CC, 89). The advent of night, rather than any human deed, exemplifies "knowing," for night "nears" the distances of the stars in the heavens: "night neighbors the stars," "She binds together without seam or edge or thread." This "gathering together in the nearness of a distance," the emerging appearance of the starry night sky, suddenly stands forth as the goal of Heidegger's mental "walk" along a "country path," or trace of thinking.

What emerges from this conversation is a characterization of "recollective thinking." But in the course of the conversation, something more is achieved implicitly. The slow and meditative uncovering of names which guides thinking exemplifies the sort of naming appropriate to recollective thinking. These are the names which, to repeat Heidegger's words, "are owed to a naming in which the namable, the name and the named occur altogether." The name "releasement" has not emerged as the result of any willed designation of an object. It has emerged because the thinker has abided in "the region of the word," where his task is "only to listen to the answer proper to the word." What *Being and Time* calls "putting into words" (of discourse) here becomes "a retelling of the answer heard."[30] It is on this theme that the conversation closes, with a question whose answer, broken into phrases, is distributed among all the participants, indicating that it comes from "regioning" rather than from any single will: "Then wonder can open what is locked? By way of waiting . . . if this is released . . . and human nature remains *appropriated* to that . . . from whence we are called" (CC, 90). When man hears this call, that is, when he steadfastly and composedly abides in the originary appropriation of his nature to that-which-regions, he can then in language expropriate this hearing, that is, he can in manifesting it in words at once bring it forth and conceal it (the joint disclosure and concealment which is truth). The poetic word is, especially clearly, the enduring location of appropriation-expropriation, and in it we can trace the grant of Being with its epochal transformations in history.[31] When philosophy is properly conducted, or rather, when philosophy yields to recollective thinking, a similar power is disclosed in the word. At the end of "The Way to Language," Heidegger quotes Humboldt's assertion that *"time —* by a growing development of ideas, increased capacity for sustained thinking, and a more penetrating sensibility — will often introduce into language what it did not possess before" (WL, 136). The resulting transformation of significance in existing words and syntax "is a lasting fruit of a people's *literature*, and within literature especially of *poetry* and *philosophy*."

290

Hence, "all reflective thinking is poetic, and all poetry in turn is a kind of thinking" (WL, 136).

For Heidegger, the literary sign shows forth human being's grasp of its own existence in the world. The sign is not to be understood simply as "present-at-hand" (as in Jakobson); nor even as an "object" within transcendental-horizonal, representational thinking, even when this object has the capacity to represent symbolic intuitions by analogy or metaphor. The literary sign is to be grasped neither as self-subsisting thing nor on the model of self-consciousness. Again, "Poetry is the saga of the unconcealment of what *is*." It will not be enough for criticism to unpack the immanent structure of the literary sign, conceived as a special variant of a functional model of communication. Nor will it be enough to explicate the systemic coherence of the poem, even when this is taken tacitly as correspondent to some objective substantive or moral reality. A Heideggerian criticism will try to grasp the literary sign as constituted by showing forth what *is*. Such a showing is possible only for human existence within a world. That world is legitimately an object for criticism, because criticism's own signs must show forth the poem's signs as an interpretation. Interpretation is here structural *and historical*, because it is a composed and steadfast abiding in the original appropriation of human nature to regioning.

In the literary sign especially we encounter the indexical foundation of language. In the index, the sign has an existential connection with what it signifies. Through Heidegger, we approach a full understanding of what "existential" can and must mean here, and in particular we discover the connection between the "existential" and the "historical." In this discovery lies the possibility of overcoming the presumed opposition of philological to formalist criticism, an overcoming that is neither eclectic nor a blurred "synthesis."

University of Iowa

NOTES

1 I use and cite the revised trans. of the 3rd ed. by Thomas Goddard Bergin and Max Harold Fisch (Ithaca, New York: Cornell University Press, 1968). For the three stages of language, see pp. 127-53 (paragraphs 400-55). Additional references cited in text as: NS.

2 Ed. Charles Bally and Albert Sechehaye with Albert Riedlinger, trans. Wade Baskin (New York: McGraw-Hill, 1966). Additional references cited as: GL.

3 See Martin Heidegger, *The End of Philosophy*, trans. Joan Stambaugh (New York: Harper & Row, 1973), pp. 19-26.

4 In *Philosophical Writings*, ed. Justus Buchler (New York: Dover, 1955), pp. 98-119. Additional references cited as: LS.

5   "Closing Statement: Linguistics and Poetics," in *Style in Language*, ed. Thomas A. Sebeok (Cambridge, Mass.: The MIT Press, 1966), pp. 350-77. The diagram occurs on p. 353. Additional references cited as: CS.

6   Strictly, the pronoun is an indexical symbol. See Jakobson, "Shifters, Verbal Categories, and the Russian Verb," in *Selected Writings. II. Words and Language* (The Hague: Mouton, 1971), 131-32. For the interpretation of all pronouns in terms of the subject and non-subject of the utterance, see Emile Benveniste, "Relationships of Person in the Verb," *Problems in General Linguistics*, trans. Mary Elizabeth Meek (Coral Gables, Florida: Univ. of Miami Press, 1971), pp. 195-204.

7   See Victor Shklovsky, "Art as Technique," in *Russian Formalist Criticism*, trans. Lee T. Lemon and Marion J. Reis (Lincoln, Nebraska: Univ. of Nebraska Press, 1965). Additional references cited as: AT. For Richards, see *Principles of Literary Criticism* (1925; rpt. New York: Harcourt, Brace and World, n.d.), pp. 202 ff.

8   Actually, Saussure used the terms "syntagmatic" and "associative" (GL, 122-27). His followers later proposed the parallel term "paradigmatic," thus exemplifying Saussure's notion of "motivation."

9   In Jakobson's analyses of poems, the exhibition of patterns of features frequently gets quite out of hand, because it is not controlled by any notion of meaning. See the objections to Jakobson and Claude Lévi-Strauss' reading of Baudelaire's *Les Chats* in Michael Riffaterre, "Describing Poetic Structure: Two Approaches to Baudelaire's *Les Chats*," *Yale French Studies*, No. 36-7 (1966), esp. pp. 200-13.

10   See Georg Lukacs, "Reification and the Consciousness of the Proletariat," in *History and Class Consciousness: Studies in Marxist Dialectics*, trans. Rodney Livingstone (Cambridge, Mass.: The MIT Press, 1972), p. 137.

11   See Riffaterre, p. 201 of the article cited in n. 9. See also Michael Shapiro, "Two Paralogisms of Poetics," forthcoming, *Poétique*.

12   See his essay "Thematics," trans. in *Russian Formalist Criticism* (cited, n. 7 above), pp. 61-95.

13   Trans. George G. Grabowicz (Evanston, Ill.: Northwestern Univ. Press, 1973).

14   See especially "The Heresy of Paraphrase," in *The Well Wrought Urn: Studies in the Structure of Poetry* (1947; rpt. New York: Harcourt, Brace and World, n.d.). Additional references cited as: HP.

15   (1954; rpt. New York: Farrar, Straus and Co., 1964). Additional references cited as: VI.

16   Benveniste makes a similar point in an attempt to qualify Saussure's principle of the arbitrariness of the linguistic signifier. See "The Nature of the Linguistic Sign," pp. 43-48 of *Problems in General Linguistics*, n. 6 above.

17   The combination of substantive, referential meaning with an awareness of language's systemic autonomy as a "spiritual" product has here a decidedly

Kantian flavor. Kant transformed the perceptual object of classical empiricism into an object of *experience* constituted within categories granted by transcendental consciousness. In Kant, this process is not discursive, but Wimsatt's terms apply essentially the same structure to language. On Kant, see Heidegger, *What Is a Thing?*, trans. W. B. Barton, Jr., and Vera Deutsch (Chicago: Henry Regnery Co., 1967). There is a clear spectrum from the Russian formalist view that the poem transforms language from an instrument of knowing to an object of perception (see the references to Shklovsky in n. 7 above); to Brooks's more complicated view that the poem does not "communicate" a theme but "communicates an experience" (see p. 75 of *The Well Wrought Urn*, n. 14 above; and see Kant's argument that the beautiful pleases universally apart from a concept, that is, remains a singular representation, like an experience, but is communicable, like conceptual universals: *Critique of Judgement*, trans. James Creed Meredith, Sec. I, Book I, Second Moment); and finally, to Wimsatt's full characterization of the constitutive structure of language.

18 In Greek, "mesothesis" names the number which is a proportional mean between two other numbers; for example, 2:4::4:8, "4" being the mesothesis. Coleridge (and Wimsatt) here brush against a topic — the relation of analogy to metaphor — which is of great importance, but would carry us too far afield. I would argue that a fully Heideggerian theory would see metaphor as deriving from collapsed analogy, rather than from comparison with the sign of comparison ("like" or "as") omitted. For an extensive bibliography on analogy, see James F. Anderson, *Reflections on the Analogy of Being* (The Hague: Martinus Nijhoff, 1967). See also Ralph McInerny, *Studies in Analogy* (The Hague: Martinus Nijhoff, 1968), and — richly suggestive in relation to Heidegger — the historical survey in Hampus Lyttkens, *The Analogy Between God and the World* (Uppsala: Almqvist and Wiksells Boktryckeri AB, 1952).

19 Ed. George Watson (London: Dent Everyman's Library, 1956), pp. 149 ff. Additional references cited as: BL.

20 The terms in which I analyze Coleridge depend heavily on Heidegger, *The End of Philosophy*, trans. Joan Stambaugh (New York: Harper & Row, 1973), esp. pp. 32-54.

21 *Critique of Judgement*, trans. Meredith, Article 59, "Beauty as the symbol of morality."

22 Trans. John Macquarrie and Edward Robinson (New York: Harper & Row, 1962). Additional references cited as: BT.

23 "Concept" here means the appearance of the object in a transcendentally determined "experience."

24 For such an interpretation — a subtle misemphasis, in my view — see Ingarden, *The Literary Work of Art*, n. 13 above, p. 281, n. 7.

25 Trans. Albert Hofstadter, in *Philosophies of Art and Beauty*, ed. Albert Hofstadter and Richard Kuhns (New York: The Modern Library, 1964). Additional references cited as: OW.

26 "Letter on Humanism," trans. Edgar Lohner in *Philosophy in the Twentieth*

Century, ed. William Barrett and Henry D. Aiken, III (New York: Random House, 1962), 298. Additional references cited as: LH.

27 Trans. Peter D. Hertz in *On the Way to Language* (New York: Harper & Row, 1971). Additional references cited as: WL.

28 Included in WL, n. 27; see esp. p. 18.

29 Trans. of *Gelassenheit* by John M. Anderson and E. Hans Freund (New York: Harper & Row, 1969). Additional references cited as: CC.

30. Heidegger makes the same point in "The Way to Language," in WL, n. 27 above, p. 123: "But speaking is at the same time also listening. . . . Speaking is of itself a listening. Speaking is listening to the language which we speak."

31 See *The End of Philosophy*, n. 20 above, pp. xiii-xiv.

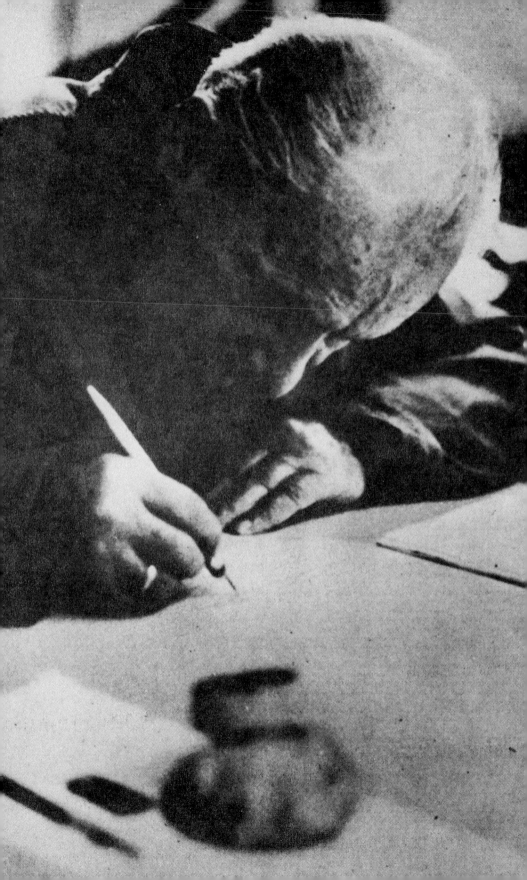

Attuned to Being:
Heideggerian Music in Technological Society

Gerry Stahl

The hopes and frustrations of technology are revealed in the most advanced works of art. This implication of the Heideggerian standpoint contradicts the popular notion that art steers clear of science.

These days, however, where art skirts the realm of industrial technique, it falls prey to the same commercial interests which rule there and which it may have hoped to slip by. Despite itself, the hapless work functions as a commodity to meet the demand for a holiday from commodities. Unfortunately, it necessarily fails to satisfy this real need for long.

The partial truth of conventional understanding is that twentieth century art, when it still packs a punch, registers a protest against the present character of technological society. Paradoxically, perhaps, the work of art must embody, no matter how subtly, the state of technology in order to criticize its contemporary social form.

I. *Music and social Being*

The art and philosophy of a culture capture more than just the most developed consciousness of a people. Particularly in their structural forms — as well as in their emphases, selection, and transformation of material — cultural artifacts reproduce essential elements of the social context, bringing out the prevailing suppositions and conditioning forces and displaying them prominently. According to Martin Heidegger, the work of art is characterized by its ability to present in an obtrusive fashion its own Being, which it shares with the less dramatic beings around it. Our world, which provides the material of art, is, quite clearly, technological, both in terms of its Heideggerian Being and its Marxian productive powers.

Because art is both dependent and autonomous, expressive of its world yet relieved of immediate practical restrictions, developments in creative realms can anticipate the possible future realization of social and technical potentials which are today suppressed. However, no one can foresee concretely how altered forms of the production process, which Karl Marx showed to be basic to our plight, would manifest themselves throughout society, transforming all interpersonal relations. It is only possible to indicate which repressive forces must be abolished. Artistic anticipation must, accordingly, take the form of critical negations of the past, thereby transcending the economic fetters on existing technology.

Heidegger looks to art and to philosophical reflections on art for glimpses of a new interpretation of reality. However, he does not recognize that the social change necessary to alter perceptions takes place primarily through reorganization of the forces of material production and social reproduction. His hopes for the future are laced with conservatism and formulated in messianic anachronisms, based as they are on receptivity to a New Word which must spontaneously call to us from deep within our linguistic institutions. He cannot, therefore, recognize the necessity of a social movement for economic restructuring as a precondition of essential change.

Although he has failed to take into account crucial political relations, Heidegger has broken much ground in the task of unearthing a philosophical alternative to forms of thought which correspond to capitalist production. It is therefore important to study as well as to criticize Heidegger's writings; to appropriate but also to transcend his position. Particularly necessary, considering Heidegger's central weakness, is a merging of his insights into art and interpretation with Marx's critical theory of capitalist society.[1]

A critical perspective on Heidegger's thought can be reached through an analysis of electronic music's questioning of aural Being as seen in relation to the social context. Electronic music, emerging primarily out of influences from the Schoenberg/Berg/Webern school in the 1950's, adopted a strikingly Heideggerian attitude toward sound. In this it contrasted sharply with classical and especially romantic music, to say nothing of pop. Thus, electronic music provides a particularly appropriate phenomenon for developing Heidegger's categories, which he himself had never applied to music. The relationship of art to technology will, of course, play a decisive role in the discussion of electronic music.

The correspondence between developments in electronic music and in existential philosophy is not accidental. The importance of the social setting against which both rebelled is, however, inadequately recognized by Heidegger's theory. His philosophy, carried to both sides of the front in World War II, has for years exerted a telling influence on the arts and social sciences, in theological circles, and among intellectuals generally; it revived interest in existentialism, hermeneutics, ontology, and speculative philosophy. Yet, despite the centrality of its abstract concepts of history and context, it fails to comprehend its own social, historical, and political posture.[2] Correspondingly, Heidegger's aesthetic theory is formulated in ahistoric terms and applied to everything from a Greek temple to Paul Klee's watercolors.

Because it has to be concrete, an aesthetics of electronic music can provide a corrective to Heidegger's inadequate self-understanding and his lack of historical specificity. The formal elements and social function of electronic works are essentially conditioned by the struggle against the co-opting of the musician and the corresponding fetishizing of sounds. The specific workings of the commodity form of economic value (which accounts for co-optation and fetishism), not merely vague technological characteristics, penetrate to the core of each piece of music, of any philosophy, and of every being produced in our society.

Analysis of music is, of course, a risky business. In matters of music, discussion can no more substitute for attentive listening than Heidegger's books can replace the experience of Being. Words may only suggest what the ear must know and judge. Heidegger does, nevertheless, make room for prose. His own reflections on art are necessary in relating, for instance, van Gogh's painting to the ontological character of the shoe as dependable tool and to the revelatory nature of art as the setting-into-work of truth. Similarly, a philosophy of electronic music can conceptualize the new experience of sound and noise as well as explore the relationship of music to the culture industry and to advanced technology.

Theory is particularly important in the case of electronic music; accordingly, the leading composers are important theoreticians as well.[3] In this field there exists what Heidegger might call a "hermeneutic gap" between an advanced composition and its bewildered audience. Analytic writings are needed to fill the role of Hermes, god of interpretation, providing the orientation and concepts which facilitate understanding. Where no common tradition ties a work of art to its perceiver, as with a poem in a forgotten tongue or the ritual of a strange culture, the work cannot speak for itself. In the case of electronic music, the historical ties to familiar forms are part of few people's experience. Prose must join the music in helping an audience bridge the chasm.

The difficulty electronic music presents to most ears requires a training for the future, rather than the retrieval of past traditions which Heideggerian themes stress. To be sure, electronic music wishes to recapture, for instance, the strivings of medieval music which led to the major and minor keys, long since become second nature. It does this through a critique of the traditional system of pitches and scales. The liberation of sound and the new schemes developed to exploit it only make sense in reference to so-called classical music up to Arnold Schoenberg. However, the goal of this critical recapitulation is to move beyond both past and present by confronting them from a future-directed perspective.

The critical thrust of electronic music has a political form different from music commonly taken to be progressive social protest. The difference corresponds to the contrast between the aesthetic implications of Heidegger's meta-ontology, or history of Being, and those of an orthodoxy which traces its philosophical roots to liberalism or to Lenin. Where protest songs speak out against injustices within one musical tradition or another, electronic music seeks to transform the language of music itself. Carrying out its project through electronic means, this experimental music re-forms technological practice and re-thinks — in aesthetic, acoustic terms — the technological mentality which Heidegger considers so central. Electronic music aims at a new mode of auditory existence.

Where there has been a social movement against the status quo, its music has had an explicit political force. This is not only true for the marching songs of revolutionaries or the propagandistic lyrics which follow upon the seizure of power. Recent American music, too, has a lively history of protest. The slave and his oppressed descendants sang out against their troubled lives in the rural blues. Jazz then incorporated the bustle of industrial life and the syncopated clank of machinery into a continuing series of improvisational styles which relentlessly rejected accepted patterns of performance. In the 1960's, protest folk songs articulated an alternative politics in a native idiom. For teenagers, rock and roll came to symbolize their side of a generation gap; as they grew into the drug sub-culture, rock moved as far out as was still profitable.

If there is no alternative social base, straight-forward methods of simple anarchism cannot succeed. Not the simple abolition of the present state, but its specific negation, its transformation into a qualitatively different organization, is required. In music as in politics one must start with what exists, criticize its faults, and set about eliminating the sources. The necessity of this procedure is due in part to our inability to imagine anything too different from what we already know. Our situatedness opens our possibilities by establishing their limits, although it is also true that we alter our situation, and hence its limitations, when we actualize what was latent.

A materialistic respect for the importance of situatedness unites

300

Heidegger and Marx in opposition to the German Idealism out of which both developed as well as against most competing social thought. Where Marx concretized the given situation, which embodies the preconditions for change, in terms of the technology of production and its social organization, Heidegger, particularly in his early work, focuses on how people understandingly exist in the context of all contexts: the world.

II. *Sound out of context*

Heidegger's *Being and Time* is an extended reflection upon the consequence of the fact that human existence is a matter of being in a meaningful context. According to its theory of interpretation, "hermeneutics," raw reality cannot be experienced as such. Even perception requires a context of interpretation. Disavowing a limited perspective, whether in politics or in art, involves establishing a broader understanding, not rejecting all structure. It is not just human frailty, naive habit, or social conditioning which causes us to impose categories and to stress certain aspects above others. The nature of comprehension specifies its own requirements.

To be effective, the refusal to support all that the silent majority condones necessitates the avowal of a more sophisticated politics. Analogously, a musician who balks at the impositions of commercial interests must develop a new music — a more authentic music, to echo Heidegger's jargon. What is minimally called for is a context of one sort or another in which interpretation can take place with intersubjective validity. A deed must, that is, be perceived as situated within the political arena or it will remain politically meaningless, unperceived. In the auditory domain, the same holds true. Sounds are never heard indeterminately, but always with a more or less distinct character, as belonging within some category, however vaguely defined.

Heidegger puts it this way in *Being and Time:*

> What we "first" hear is never sounds or complexes of tones, but the creaking wagon, the motorcycle. One hears the column on the march, the north wind, the woodpecker tapping, the fire crackling. It requires a very artificial and complicated frame of mind to "hear" a "pure sound."[4]

Perception is always already interpretation. The sophisticated concert-goer hears certain played instruments, particular pitch intervals, or specific harmonic relationships. Outside the music hall sounds join images in giving meaningful content to our situatedness in the world. Sound which strikes the ear but is not perceived as the sound of something or as a definite kind of sound is noise. Noise is the refuse of existential understanding.

Music, which thrives on the sensuous character of sound, today rejects the objective references of sounds. It has become increasingly non-representational, abstract. Discarding traditional frameworks of meaning, electronic music borders on noise. This marks the culmination of an historical tendency. Music probably had its origins in mimesis, the imitation of natural sounds, in bodily rhythms, and in holy evocations. Early Western music exploited verbal texts, especially familiar Biblical verse, to facilitate perception, interpretation, and memory, for speech is the most immediately meaningful sound. Later, instrumental music relied upon characteristic sounds of the instruments to facilitate comprehension. To a large extent, what are still perceived in instrumental music are the performer (in nuances of interpretation) and the composer (in structural and emotive intention).

Serious contemporary music has been forced to reject all props to listening. They have outlived their usefulness historically. The names of composers, conductors, and performers have become trademarks which distract from whatever may be behind the names, inhibiting the auditory experience itself. Rebellion against the commercial context has raised the question of just what music is.

Those who wonder if the abstract works which result are still music should recall the many different roles music has historically filled. Music took part in religious ritual long before the ballad served purposes of communication and moral instruction. Folk songs, nursery rhymes, and popular ditties are often structurally related to instrumental dance music, though they serve other functions. Mood music and contemplative compositions meet still different needs. Electronic music introduces further variety and choice. It has, in fact, irrevocably broadened the definition of music. This requires that electronic music not be forced to conform to the old criteria.

Just because instrumental music was not as directly tied to the human body as singing did not mean that either one or the other was not music. Rather, the extended possibilities of the instrument probably high-lighted for the first time the emotive power of the more personal vocal performance. Similarly, anyone who has been involved with electronic music will relate afterwards differently to instrumental and choral productions. More advanced technologies always put their forerunners in a new perspective.

The process of abstraction from structures imposed on music as a result of its social origins clarifies the essential elements of sound. No longer restricted to the pitch and interval ranges of the human voice, the rhythm and meter of dance, or the practicalities of live performance, the new music takes on qualities strange enough to present old sounds as strikingly fresh experiences — provided, of course, that the barriers to listening are overcome in the individual, the culture industry, and the composition in a way which does not reduce all to familiarity.

302

The clearest examples of abstract music have been in the realms of chance music and electronic music. Music composed with the use of probabilistic procedures, mathematical schemes, or computerized algorithms shows no trace of human intention. Sounds produced by electronic components rather than by conventional instruments can be kept connotation-free. The abstractness of this music, which carries no suggestion of subjects and objects that could have made such sounds, registers as undifferentiated noise in the ears of those who can't imagine how to relate to it. Such music must develop its own contexts, its own tradition.

Having suppressed the references of individual sounds to extra-acoustic objects, electronic music rejected the ties of musical styles to particular audiences: ages, classes, ethnic groups, and nations. This development corresponded historically to a repulsion against nationalism, particularly in Germany. The non-referential sound eliminated local color, except for purposes of commentary and critique. Abstract and international, electronic music found itself without an audience. In order to keep inwardness and intellectualization from exceeding healthy limits without foregoing the progress made to date, electronic musicians are forced to develop a broader audience by means of their music.

The difficulty at the heart of all contemporary art is particularly extreme here: isolated at elite schools and in scattered studios, the musician has no broad cultural tradition from which to draw material, no critical response to lend him direction, and no responsive audience with which to engage in dialogue. Where culture is annihilated under the pressure of the commodity motive, even those select few who manage to survive find themselves homeless. Paul Klee remarked, when he was part of the Bauhaus movement, that without a social base modern art lacked ultimate power: *"Uns trägt kein Volk"* (1924).

Although Marx disavowed any direct relation between economics and epochs of great art, he could well have pointed out art's social a priori. Even if art no longer can be founded on a general cultural base as in pre-industrial times, community remains essential. Schoenberg's Vienna, Stravinsky's Paris, and Stockhausen's Darmstadt Summer Institute formed preconditions for the music which emerged from these centers. Especially if the romantic ideology of individualism is to be rejected and art is to reveal social Being, intense interaction is necessary, both among artists and with an audience. In our day, the economics of commodity relations systematically destroys community, making art impossible yet all the more urgent.

Audiences must discover their way through the strange terrain of electronic music; they need to learn to hear whatever is at work in structures of abstract, unsituated sound. Fortunately there is an historical continuity, however tenuous, between instrumental and electronic music so that it is partly a matter of time for the so-called cultural gap to be crossed. However, the existence of qualitative differences requires that the new music be perceived in terms which it alone can teach. Heidegger's theory of understanding suggests an approach to this task, for hermeneutics becomes significant in cases of problematized understanding, of disrupted contexts.

III. *The situation of understanding*

The circularity in having to hear how to hear is an instance of the paradoxical character of all understanding. This "hermeneutic circle" need not be a vicious one according to Heidegger. He resolves it through an analysis of the moment of anticipation which belongs to interpretation:

> Whenever something is interpreted as something, the interpretation will be founded essentially upon pro-jecting, fore-sight and pre-conception. An interpretation is never a presuppositionless apprehending of something presented to us. (BT, 191-92)

In perceiving a sound, we perceive it *as* something, as the sound of a certain object, instrument, or process, or as a certain kind of sound. To do this, we must have already intended to perceive such a sound, we must be open to the possibility of such a sound, and we must have the concepts for distinguishing such a sound. Of course, our anticipations need not be exact. It suffices that we be open to a range of possibilities which includes the actual sound.

To perceive the surprising, it seems, we must await it; to discover the unknown, we must know what we seek; to comprehend the innovative, we must subsume it under already available categories. Plato's recognition of such circularity led him to the theory that all learning must be remembrance, that we literally did know everything that could be known, although most of us have forgotten almost all of it. Subsequent variations on this theory of knowing attribute preknowledge to racial memory, the subconscious, or world-spirit. The Kantian conclusion, still exerting its influence through Structuralism, is that we are forever limited to knowing that which we are genetically equipped to know. Such consequences are deeply conservative. They imply that human existence — which includes social structures — can never change essentially.

Heidegger recognizes the hermeneutic circle and its full implications without falling victim to it. In fact, his entire career can be viewed as a struggle to break free of the circle by spiraling around it incessantly. Heidegger neither mythologizes the fact that knowledge has its prerequisites, nor does he absolutize it. Either approach would abolish history, especially the history of meanings. Rather, he locates a social and historical base of preunderstanding.

However, Heidegger never analyzes the historical or social character of this base in his early discussions. At this point, the ambiguity of Heidegger's work is particularly clear. While brilliantly uncovering crucial relationships, Heidegger consistently refrains from exploring the all-important specifics for fear of lacking profundity. He exposes the ontological cover-up by which Being has successively been obscured since Plato, but he fails to finger the culprit, to point to social forces which carried out the deed and political interests which oppose its reversal.

The attempt to uncover forgotten Being ends in political impotence. Similarly, in the theory of understanding, insight into the possibility of transcending the given is over-powered by respect for the role of tradition. The progressive potential is ignored in the context of the conservatism of Heidegger's personal associates, his self-understanding, and his social background. None of this is, however, necessary, as the application of the basic principles in the concrete, socially-situated realm of electronic music should show.

Heidegger grasps the hermeneutic paradox by means of an analysis of socially-given everyday understanding. The anticipatory projection, foresight, and preconception which we usually bring to understanding are those which "one" generally holds. Understanding is normally based on conventional wisdom. Such common preunderstanding may get us through the daily routine, but it has its limitations, as Heidegger points out at length.

In *Being and Time* understanding according to what "one" already knows proves insufficient for allowing me to comprehend my own death and thus to deal knowingly with the possibilities corresponding to my own finite temporality. Later essays of Heidegger underline the inadequacy of technological rationality to respond properly to the dangers faced by an epoch which is pervaded by this calculative mentality. Heidegger strives throughout to transcend these restrictions.

The problem with conventional wisdom is that it obscures so very much in the act of making superficial understanding possible. The half-truth character of knowledge gained through the socially prevalent categories and attitudes applies to the appreciation of music as much as to political acuity and existential self-reflection. Without going into the role of the mass media, art, and folk traditions in molding the languages in which we interpret — and hence perceive — sights and sounds, our institutions, and ourselves, Heidegger makes the general point:

> Within the totality of its complexly interrelated meanings, the spoken language preserves a certain understanding of the disclosed world and simultaneously an understanding of the being-there-together of other people and an understanding of one's own contextuality. The understanding already deposited in the spoken

language concerns the disclosedness of beings which has at any time been achieved and passed down as much as it concerns the understanding of Being then and the available possibilities and horizons for fresh interpretation and conceptual articulation. (BT, 211)

Common understanding provides the starting point for any possible transcendence of its limited perspective. No exterior vantage-point of superior knowledge is possible: the walls of convention must be crashed from within when they oppress.

If the established word discloses, it also closes. The phenomenon, frozen in speech, loses its substance even as one gains a handle on it. In second-hand knowledge, one may be caught up in interpreting verbal symbols and fail to understand that which is supposedly communicated. In fact, one scarcely knows how much one has experienced of the reality behind the words. Hearing words becomes believing already interpreted facts. The disk-jockey approves of a hit; the press analyzes a politician's speech; advertizing proclaims eternal youth. It is impossible for me to be critical of more than an insignificant fraction of what floods into my ears. Worse yet, my personal experience does not go untouched by all this. Even listening to music, even seeing a politician's actions, even reflecting on myself, the available categories and approaches have all come handed down to me.

Conventional wisdom rules with an authority and reach that puts the most unquestioned monarch to shame. In politics it makes a farce of democracy, in life-styles it insures conformity. The popular in music is not simply a statistical tendency among autonomous personal tastes, but a self-perpetuating system of interpretation. As long as "one" recognizes melodies in harmonic keys but finds dissonances incomprehensible, popular music will either limit itself to the well-established or find that no one "likes" it. Within the domain of art, the requirement of familiarity stands in obvious opposition to the creativity which is also expected. This contradition is sharpened by the fact that the artist's own understanding must begin with traditional conceptions and manners of perceiving, although he longs to open eyes and ears.

For Heidegger, public understanding, the system of commonly held meaning-structures, is simply a given. To comprehend interests manipulating or exploiting the public requires social theory. Heidegger's phenomenology of the individual cannot analyze powerful social forces, even though it breaks with the Cartesian tradition by viewing the individual in terms of his physical and social context. Thus *Being and Time*, published in 1927, explains the obedience of the individual to the public subjectivistically, in terms of the individual's *Angst*: I fear for my own existence.

To escape my *Angst*, I turn to the public realm which, according to Heidegger, is divorced from my ownmost, personal existence. Here the concern is exclusively with things in the world or with how one — everyone — feels, thinks, and acts. I can forget my fearful, mortal sense by becoming caught up in a world in which self-reflection is quite impossible. A revised version of *Being and Time* could today refer to the child who lives on Sesame Street, the housewife whose concerns stem from the soap opera, or the sports fan who can only think of the next game. With television one's public world has become clearly visual and aural.

It is characteristic of Heidegger's short-coming that he set out to analyze the structure of human existence without noting that modern life is structured around wage earning, that temporality has been redefined in terms of labor time, that relations to objects are determined by property relations, that needs are met through social production, and that existence is now characterized by alienation. Even in his analysis of society — of being-together and of the public realm — Heidegger fails to see that the commodity form of economic value defines the social Being of working people, of exchanged products, and of cultural artifacts in a society long based on capital investment and accumulation.

In the mid-1930's, when the power of supra-personal forces could scarcely be ignored in Germany, Heidegger carried out a reversal of emphasis, situating the origin of preunderstanding in a movement of autonomous Being, rather than in the individual fearful human being. This movement takes place within linguistic — or prelinguistic — media, whose developments are not to be comprehended in social, let alone psychological terms.

The determination of the way in which all beings are perceived, Being, is given to us historically and preserved within language, broadly understood. Especially in Heidegger's late writings, "Being" refers to the most general level of the form of presence of all beings: as creations of God in medieval times or as calculable material for manipulation in our technological era, for instance. Again, with no theory of society, Heidegger has no categories for comprehending the historical changes in Being. He can at most catalogue the various forms of Being and, perhaps, discover hints of a possible future form.

Nevertheless, the history of Being suggested by Heidegger may aid in understanding the situation of music. For Heidegger, the development of Western thought has meant the progressive obfuscation of Being. This is the story behind the present dictatorship of the public, which hides the essence of human Being. In a sense, the nature of sound has also become successively obscured since the Greeks, as the perception of it has become increasingly indirect.

The origin of music in experiential time and bodily rhythms was first neglected in the numerological interpretation developed by the pre-Socratic school of Pythagoras, which then proved determinant of Plato's thinking about music. The classical period in music developed extraordinary mastery over sound, controlling it for such intellectual purposes as the elaboration of conceptual relationships as emobided, for example, in counterpoint technique and thematic variation. Romantic music adapted this skill over its object to the subjectivistic task of titilating human emotions and "painting" beautiful pictures.

Auditory experience became subservient to visual or emotive ends and thereby lost its original character. Recent commercial music combines the least aural aspects of folk, classical, and romantic styles. Sound as such has long since been forgotten in the scurry to control and exploit it. This is certainly one component of what Heidegger conceives as the pervasive oblivion of Being. Following its own historical course, but not accidentally, music, too, adheres to the general tendency.

The historical and social context of music in our century, particularly since World War II, poses a dilemma for composer, performer, and music-lover. In order for music to be intersubjectively comprehensible, it must be expressed in a language which veils sound under layers of extra-musical meaning. Music which rebelliously thrusts unknown realms of sound at its audience inevitably meets with resistance, fear, and incomprehension.

The dilemma has widened the gap between popular and serious music, whose separation originally had a class base but is now even more fundamental. Not that either extreme can escape the contradiction. Even easy-listening music must inhabit the auditory realm with some semblance of creativity, and that means at least rattling the bars of convention. At the other end of the continuum, the most relentlessly avant-garde composers still need enough of a foothold on familiar ground to communicate among themselves and with an audience, however homogeneous and emancipated. Between the extremes, performances of rock and jazz take their considered stands at various points, and classical pieces are buffeted about according to the understandings of their arrangers, conductors, sponsors, and audiences.

IV. Ontological interrogations of technological sound

Heidegger recommends a way of living within the contradictions and tensions which correspond to the forgetfulness of Being. Even in *Being and Time*, where the circularity of understanding is not historically comprehended, a way out is indicated:

> In the circle is hidden a positive possibility of the most primordial kind of knowing. To be sure, we genuinely take hold of this possibility only when, in our interpretation, we have understood that our first, last and constant task is never to allow our pro-ject, fore-sight and pre-conception to be presented to us by

308

fancies and popular conceptions, but rather to make the scientific theme secure by working out these pre-liminary structures in terms of the things themselves. (BT, 195)

The battle cry of Husserlian phenomenology, "To the things themselves," takes on a broader significance, proclaiming a method for everyday knowledge as well as philosophy.

In later reflections on the question of uncovering buried Being, Heidegger proposes to "let Being be" and to remain "open to Being." The obscuring of Being is found to be a consequence of man's drive for control, the preponderance of subjective will. Rather than imposing our wishes upon the objects being interpreted — perceived or created — we should garner the categories of understanding from the material itself.

The general historical development of will has its exact counterpart in music. Wagnerian opera, which represents a pinnacle of subjectivism not so different from the will-full politics of its fascist admirers, strove to induce definite responses with each thematic stimulus. The listener revels in his responses more than he listens.

The complete rejection of such will in music would be an arrangement in which sounds existed which had no relation to human intentions. The ideal would be an auditory environment in which composer, performer, and audience would no longer perform their traditional functions, but would all be "tourists," in John Cage's provocative metaphor. Travelling together through strange sonic terrain, they would have to comprehend the foreign language without a guide's assistance.

This straightforward approach, largely adopted by an American school of experimental composers inspired by Cage, corresponds to certain pronouncements of late Heidegger. The difficulty with the acoustic processes and events which they let happen is that the sounds which result are too likely to be understood with the chauvinism of a condescending tourist, by whose standards the natives are dirty and dull. Visits to such irrelevant auditory experience may provide occasional larks, but they scarcely transform the normal routine. For a "happening," whether of sounds or of Being, to be appropriately perceived, the proper attitude is already required. Anticipation is, however, originally and usually based on common understanding, as Heidegger early showed.

Electronic music, a European movement in which Karlheinz Stockhausen, Iannis Xenaxis, and Pierre Boulez can be singled out as important composers and theoreticians, incorporates the proposals of early as well as late Heidegger into the project of opening ears to aural Being. In fact, each of these three representatives has referred to his music as a new form of Being-in-the-world, implicitly citing the outlook of *Being and Time*. A more profound, if less conscious, relation to Heidegger can be seen in their practice of getting at the sounds themselves through critical transformation of the prevailing categories which all too often silence the sounds.

During the last two decades, electronic music has come into its own out of developments in classical music up to Schoenberg, Stravinsky, Webern, and Varése. From the most sophisticated perspective of Western music, electronic composers have systematically criticized the categories which define their heritage. These recent composers accept the challenges which Cage also enunciated, but they relate them to an historical context of interpretation. Their understanding of the tradition which Cage simply rejects allows them to go beyond its limitations through reflection. Reflection is here not exclusively intellectual, but primarily musical and historical, although it has its conscious moment. Electronic technology transforms sound and provides the material precondition for a music which is contemporary in the strict sense of the term.

The electronic transformation of everyday sounds, common musical elements, and background tonal webs has an educative effect. It reawakens the ear from an overly literal, visual world. It e-ducates by leading-out what was implicit but went unnoticed.

Electronic music has an experimental *élan* about it, not just because we are in a transitional period and electronics defines a new medium, but because these works lead the listener on an exploratory path through the universe of sound around him. Intimations of warfare, space-age movement, and motoric rhythm in electronic pieces are only the most obvious instances of this. Electronic technology gives us our world, particularly its noisy acoustic dimension; Stockhausen, always one to draw the radical conclusion, stresses that electronic music should sound electronic.

Two reasons for electronic music's experimental quality can be given in terms of its social context. Recent composers reject the props to listening exploited by commercial music, arrangements of romantic music, movie sound-tracks, television backgrounds, and advertising jingles. They are thereby forced to search for new approaches less manipulative of their material and their audience. Techniques suggested by the electronic instruments are tried out, judged by the ear, varied, explored. Encouragement of the unanticipated becomes the paradoxical goal. The listener, too, must remain open to the unknown, struggle with a work's meaning, and draw conclusions.

Secondly, the use of generalized technical equipment for synthesizing sound structures creates its own world of possibilities, circumscribed by the use of one or more loudspeakers. This largely unexplored realm calls for new emphases and for divergences from practices appropriate to instrumental music. Traditional instruments were developed with the triadic chord in mind and expressive interpretation as a primary goal. Now, with synthesis by means of scientifically standardized

310

circuits, the elements into which the technician can analyze all acoustic phenomena assume a major role.

Theory of sound emerges in the practice of electronic music with thematic prominence. Because everything must be built up from scratch — from abstract temporal orderings, that is — certain effects unrealizable with an orchestra can be achieved more easily than can simple harmonies. Previously unimaginable sonorities and the whole range of temporal intervals are readily available. Through careful splicing of tape or with the aid of electronic control, the most intricate rhythms can be produced.

One useful formal approach to an electronic composition is to select a potential of the medium and to explore it systematically, cycling through the various possibilities under a series of conditions, much as Husserl used to vary the thing-itself in imagination. The parameters of permutation can, as in several works by Stockhausen, mediate between polar extremes of some compositional factor such as interpretational determinacy or timbral complexity. The piece produced by such a more or less autonomous system could be considered an experiment or investigation. Both the formal structure and the sensuous experience resulting are derived from the acoustic material and the choice of system for articulating it. The ring of objectivity is likely to be present, for emotional manipulation has been fairly thoroughly excluded.

The compositional form which results from such an investigatory approach, assuming no traditional form is inadvertently imposed, is that of interrogation or "dialogue," a favorite term in Heidegger's vocabulary. From this orientation, the history of electronic music appears as a series of question-and-answer interchanges between the human ear and physical sound, where both participants essentially belong to the technological age. The work as magnum opus dissolves into an event within a continuing social process. This change in artistic form agrees with developments in social production and political relations: individual objects, machines, personalities, and institutions merge into all-encompassing processes.

V. Revelation's musical form

The processual character of the larger compositional form reflects back on the elements in terms of an emphasis on acoustic patterns. Aspects formerly taken for granted or left to the composer's instinct and intuition are now subjected to systematic inquiry. Melody is frequently eliminated in order to focus attention on the background: general feel, rhythmic support, textural richness, the incidental or the accidental, silence and noise. The technical frame on which melody was formerly draped is now unveiled.

Such shifts in focus imply an altered relation to musical form, not just new forms. Whereas classical concerns with form had to be translated into techniques, technical interests now tend to determine form. The unity of an electronic work and its mode of elaboration must meet dual criteria: they must be appropriate to the technical equipment and procedures while also resulting in a musically aesthetic piece. Form follows.

In his day Bach was admired as a craftsman. The contrapuntal intricacies which now earn him an exalted position as compositional genius were then primarily means for producing lively, graceful, coherent music. Subsequently, a stage of self-reflection transformed music; the craft became an art; supporting structure assumed thematic priority. The past was thereby subjected to reinterpretation.

Now electronic music takes a further step, exploring the universe within a single note rather than always stressing relationships between notes, as in previous harmonic construction. The atom of traditional music is split. This is a move beyond modernity. It departs from the mechanical *niveau* of form and function.

The new openness to aural Being establishes a context in which every category of music is reinterpreted along with the central notion of form. The new unity which coherently relates the categories redefines, for instance, the relation of form to content, process to event, composition to performance, work to perceiver. That the individual sound is now built up a parameter at a time, carefully put together, literally com-posed, means not only that the momentary event and the process in which it occurs must each be interesting in its own right. It also means that together they must be so intimately related that the process is nothing but the formation or de-construction of the individual sound, the event but a moment in the working of the work.

Criteria and means of performance must be redefined. The complexities of intonation which come naturally to the skilled performer cannot be duplicated electronically, nor is the spontaneity or inspiration of a live performance likely to be matched in the more conceptual new medium. Conversely, acoustic automata could spare the instrumentalist repetitive motions and rote procedures where they no longer serve a creative function. Particularly serialized compositions in the Schoenberg style (where a system of values for each parameter of a note is defined and the values are realized in turn) or stochastic works (in which values are selected by strictly random procedures) are often most sensibly accomplished electronically or with the aid of a computer. The concept underlying a piece, its form of expression, and the manner of its performance are intimately related.

For form to follow the music's experimental character implies experimenting with forms, for here more than elsewhere form and content must be one. To demand that all works adhere to one pattern would be to imitate the mass media, rendering rebellion harmless by freezing one potential into law and advertising it as the avant-garde, which all who wish to be timely must obey. An avant-garde which measures up to its promise is united only in its rejection of the commercially codified; it seeks alternatives everywhere. Each of Stockhausen's pieces, for instance, pursues a different idea: rhythmic permutation, timbral variety, spatial movement, changing essential parameters: total system, human improvisation, pure chance, degrees of determination; vocal, orchestral, electronic, mixed sources. Each idea could become a school, but he prefers to use each as a base for further innovation.

As a work of art, each composition must be able to stand on its own, although some may be inherently more significant and others will appeal more to certain tastes. Differing directions within the avant-garde are interrelated primarily by mutual recognition throughout the art world. They do not fall behind the discoveries of one another. Each successful piece responds to the historical state of the musical materials. Its lesson for future composing is fundamentally critical, not dogmatic.

The work of art plays an integral role in society by participating in the questioning of Being. The experimental work provides a locus for the revelation of truth. This is, in fact, the sole reason for Heidegger's interest in art. As Heidegger puts it, the origin of the work of art is the setting-into-work of the truth of Being. The character of our world in this age of automated production, computerized information processing, and mass-media communications is, indeed, screamed at us by the finest electronic compositions, wrestling the nature of technology out of the silence of its concealment behind scientist and technocratic ideologies.

Less creative attempts, which manipulate or ignore musical technology according to commodity considerations, only conceal their own basis of existence. Heidegger fails to see the essential antagonisms of modern art toward such forms of entertainment. He consistently trivializes the political implications operative in artistic critiques of commercial culture and the commercialized tradition.

To obscure Being is, however, a politically reactionary act. The impetus behind subjectively imposing structures on given materials despite their inherent characteristics has always been the drive for control: over the environment, one's self, and one's neighbors. The manipulative techniques of pop music serve to maintain existing power relations throughout society. Their removal would clear the way for democratic alternatives in the production, distribution, and consumption of culture.

VI. *Composed noise as ideology critique*

The labelling of forbidden sounds as "noise" is one mechanism whereby the boundaries of the acceptable are reinforced. Noise is sound which cannot be comprehended either because it is too complex, too unusual, or too fearful. It extends beyond our limits of tolerance. To say that these limits are maintained in order to ward off existential *Angst* is to simplify the mechanisms, which are more essentially social than individual:

they serve the interest of social stability, at whatever cost to the individual.

The incomprehensibility which defines noise is peculiar to the auditory domain. Through linguistic training, we expect sound to be meaningful. But language is conventional, compared to visual and tactile objects, thus requiring more strain at interpretation. Accordingly, there are differences between the experiences of non-representation in visual and in musical art, between the corresponding senses of artistic illusion, and between the respective possibilities of mediating representational with non-representational images and sounds. Listening to electronic music is the best way to observe these contrasts.

Contrary to Heidegger's view, electronic music teaches that meaning in sounds — including speech — is not so spontaneously "given" as in sights and touches. Language is a product of social, i.e. human, traditions, not of autonomous self-appropriation. In the visual or tactile dimension things may appear somewhat differently. Common sense philosophers who beat their breasts and stub their toes to prove the existence of the real world suggest that the materiality of what is seen and felt is not the result of subjective convention. However, even here the form and significance of, for instance, this printed page comes from a complex system of social institutions: its message has its place in cultural production, and its physical manifestation was produced by wage-labor to be sold. The Being of this particular being is scarcely independent of the actions and relations of humans.

The new music reveals the conventional character of traditional sounds and compositional devices; it calls for a more creative, less certain approach to aural understanding. Electronic music, which hopes to re-educate our ears on the basis of what they already recognize, deals extensively with noise. The ability to mediate between tonal purity and noise is as important to today's composer as doing the same with sound and silence.

Stockhausen sees the limitations as technical difficulties. He credits Anton Webern, who is famed for thoroughly integrating silence into his works to stress individual sounds, with going as far as instrumental music can in organizing the parameters of sound. However, the exclusion of noise from music has its historical and social as well as technical sources. The continued resistance of popular music and its public to anything approaching noise, even the dissonances of twelve-tone works, confirms this.

Chaos in sound is disturbing; we must either struggle to discover meaning or flip off the switch. The Renaissance craft of ordering tonal compositions has sufficiently refined itself and educated us to the point where we can enjoy a complex orchestral symphony without a twitch. The techniques of control over the organization of sound, originally promoted by the royalty, long preserved in the conservatory, and now categorized but scarcely comprehended, are, unfortunately, today used by rote — for non-musical motives.

Laziness reigns over producer and consumer, who are, after all, only out to make and spend money. Maintaining the status quo requires that only select reflexes be trained, that nothing demanding be ventured, that the unknown be kept out of knowledge's reach. With all else hidden, order, balance, and clarity appear to reign naturally in the kingdom of sound, as on earth.

Mastery over the musical material has been transformed into the pretense that there is no noise. The vulnerability of such an illusion in a world of machinery, advertising, chatter, and television makes the gullible victim that much more defensive when ruling dissonance out of the definition of music. Only those who intuitively rebel against sweet commercialism, consciously break the bonds of convention, and forcefully overcome the dominant alchemy of sound can move freely between harmony and noise, demonstrating that freedom from the fear of noise is possible on the basis of a new and renewed approach to aural Being. Electronic music makes a science of the struggle to come to terms with noise.

Rebellion against accepted forms took place throughout musical history, often leaving shocked, indignant, offended audiences behind. In America, blues, jazz, rock, and avant-garde music have known this tendency. The history of American music appreciation could, no doubt, be written in terms of the taming of criticism through the popularizing of its spokesmen.

Co-optation works through such strong mechanisms that no individual can withstand them. The contrast of the popular hits of any rebellious performer or group to their most original works reveals this enormous power. The paradoxes which confront the musician who strives to be both critical and popular leave unintelligible most of what he has to offer. The price he must pay to offer anything is to have his music systematically misunderstood. Electronic music is, of course, likewise threatened.

If our culture permitted us to pronounce only vowels, insisting that consonants offended the ear, were irritating and unnatural, then it would be necessary to overthrow convention for the sake of communication. Such a situation would be more than just vaguely analogous to commercial music's relation to noise. The soothing vowel sounds of sweet melody may be capable of expressing in stereotypical manner certain non-disruptive emotions, but they scarcely encourage thoughtful creativity, let alone justifiable rebellion.

It is no more accidental that we are taught in school and church to sing with the vowel-dominated syllables do, re, mi than that the gruff curses of the working-class are suppressed in favor of the tones of romance so dear to aristocracies and their supporting institutions. Curt four-letter words, culminating in hard consonants, articulate too much of the anger which stems from exploitation — both material and spiritual. Popular music today continues the teaching of harmony and restraint, at most permitting a cathartic release of violent feelings.

While it may be that the ever-popular love song has always spoken more of the nightingale's melodic warbling than of crude physical urges, it is also true that the recent mass character of culture has ultimately failed to change this. The spread of culture from the leisure class to the leisure time of all has scarcely democratized the values and interests incorporated. They have only been further imposed on those who have less to gain from the social arrangement which mass culture buttresses. Abhorrence of noise, an anachronism in industrial society, remains with us as a social phobia indicative of our subservience to economic shackles.

In a technical sense, noise is pure sound. White noise consists of the whole spectrum of possible pitches simultaneously sounding, and that excludes all melodic or harmonic relations. Scientifically speaking, noise is unorganized sound, that is, strictly random changes in air pressure. Consonants, dissonant chords, and over-loaded timbres approach this in their relative lack of sustained acoustical structure. They are primarily recognized by the shifts and changing patterns of emphasis, pitch, and overtones.

VII. *Controlled receptivity*

Noise is sound so complex that auditory understanding cannot handle it. Accordingly, compositional control over noise must be more sophisticated than that over pure pitches, clear melodies, and harmonic chords. Electronic music, which is determined to eliminate the subjective willfulness inherent in the suppression of all noise, requires increased control over its materials. The mastery of noise through control grants electronic music the critical distance lacking in the earlier "noise music" of the Italian Futurists, who ended up glorifying precisely those social phenomena which must be criticized.

Theodor W. Adorno, an agile dialectician, examined the contradiction in which extreme control is necessary for the Heideggerian goal of letting sound "be." Writing at almost the same time as Heidegger, Adorno, who taught philosophy and sociology at Frankfurt, reinterpreted many of Heidegger's insights within the context of a non-orthodox Marxist social theory. A leading musicologist who had studied in Schoenberg's school, Adorno brought the philosophical issues to bear on music at the time that electronic music was being born.

Although Adorno's social critique of pop music opened a dimension scarcely suggested by Heidegger, his discussion of control in the following passage reveals strong affinities to Heidegger's position:

If art truly wishes to renounce the domination of nature, if it stands for a time in which men no longer exert domination by means of spirit, then it can only achieve this through the power of the domination of nature. Only a music which is master of itself would also be master of the freedom from every constraint, even from its own. This follows the analogy that only in a rationally organized society would the necessity of oppression by organization disappear along with want. . . . But the domination of material, as a reflection of the composer's ear, must advance itself self-critically, until it no longer finds itself confronted with heterogeneous material. It must evolve into the form of reaction of the sort of compositional ear which at the same time passively appropriates the tendency of the material. The consequence of artistic technique as truthful domination is always simultaneously also its opposite, the development of the subjective sensibility into a receptivity toward the impulse of that which is not itself subject.[5]

In numerous analyses, which are historically concrete in ways which Heidegger's are not at all, Adorno focuses on the interplay between the historically- and socially-situated composer and his material, which is historically- and socially-given. For Adorno, sound is not to be analyzed into simplistic elements, as an ahistorical science of acoustics would do. If sound can be manipulated in terms of amplitude and frequency or duration and spatial location, that is itself partially a result of our scientific age. Further, it is a consequence of the history of Western music, including, not least of all, developments within electronic music and its precursor, serialized music.

Through the evolution of musical traditions, knowledge of sound increased. More and more pitches became intelligible: the octave, fifth, fourth, the eight-note tonal scale, Schoenberg's twelve tones, unpitched abstract sounds. Simple repetition gave way to increasingly complex rhythms, syncopation, and polyrhythm. From natural and vocal sources, mechanical instruments were developed, and then were transformed electronically. The production of sound has always adapted general productive techniques to its own uses; composers have responded to technology by seeking out its unknown resources.

With the advent of the electronic construction of sound, a radically new stage in the relation of music to technology has been reached. The historical dialectic now comes under the kind of conscious, creative control that Marx envisioned for the relation of productive forces to social relations but which Heidegger judged impossible for the ontological difference between Being and beings. In music, at least, the composer can determine the character of the materials of his utopia to whatever degree of precision he desires.

Available acoustic material has varied with each age. For Adorno, musical material must be conceived as that with which a composer works. This is, however, nothing but the objectified and critically reflected level of the technical means of production which the composer finds at his disposal. The language in which composers expressed themselves was scarcely something over which they could freely dispense. Classical forms like the sonata were, in their day, more givens than freely elected modes of presentation.

If the traditional forms have been rejected as too confining by electronic composers, then new categories must be developed. The articulation of sounds by creator and by perceiver requires this. The new material, on the other hand, calls for categories appropriate to it. Since, however, the material is not static, but, as evolved, still open-ended, it will itself be transformed through the compositional and interpretational process. Truth to material implies more than just the skillful manipulation of already available materials.

The secret of composition, says Adorno, is the power to transform the material in the process of progressive adequation. Where it achieves this, electronic music provides a model of an openness to Being which forswears the imposition of will in favor of an appropriation which lets Being be what it historically could be. Here, more than in any of Heidegger's own writings, it becomes clear how much fine-tuning attunement requires.

The example of electronic music also demonstrates the possibility of an active process of bringing about a new epoch of Being. Although Heidegger insists that we must wait for destiny to descend mystically, his own theory of interpretation, with its potential for transforming common understanding, provides a foundation for a more active approach.

Adorno develops that foundation through a dialectical mediation of passivity and activism, openness and domination. A difficult unity of control and receptivity is required. Understanding, which must start within limits, can be led beyond them — by the lure of what is to be understood and by means of what is already understood. History, which conditions both interpretation and that which is interpreted, provides a medium for bringing about change on the basis of those past changes which have given us the present.

It is part of electronic music's dialectical character that it transcends fear of noise through human control and dispenses with subjective control through fearlessness; that it surpasses subjectivism with mathematical means and returns thereby to human perception; that it replaces the performer with technology in order to free humanity from the machine. If Greek music symbolized an urgent and progressive mastery

318

over the elements, electronic music demonstrates that such control is no longer an issue. The domination still at work in popular music is that over large segments of society, not over an alien cosmos. Electronic music shows that a new, unexploitative relationship to sound is now technically feasible, indicating that the artificial preservation of a monopoly by the old attitudes of control only serves socially repressive ends.

The kind of control which fosters receptivity is an historical product of technological progress, that is, of the development of willful control to its logical conclusion. Heidegger believes that technology must play itself out and reach its end, which is coterminus with the elaboration of its origin, before a new epoch of Being can begin. Less idealistically, Marx interprets the Hegelian doctrine in terms of the bourgeois industrial revolution providing the technical precondition for truly socialized production.

Marx is not being sarcastic when he calls the wage-laborer "free"; the emancipation from traditional feudal social positions is a necessary stage in the elimination of domination even if it involves subjugation to the dictates of capital. Marx lauds the bourgeois era for its systematic universalizing of human powers and of productive processes. With the liquidation of feudal relations, society is potentially flexible enough to allocate its resources where needs arise. The only problem now is that production is used to maximize capital rather than to respond to need. Electronic music actualizes the potential within the realm of sound, producing universally without the natural limitations of traditional instruments or the social restrictions to accepted styles.

To the extent that electronic music points the way for everyday, productive life, it is implicitly revolutionary. The confrontation of instrumental with electronic music redefines the realm of the distinctively human for the present age. It thereby argues for relieving human activity of all that has become inhumanly repetitive. Harnessing the technology of automation to the requirements of control, electronic music suggests possibilities for the realm of labor, the manipulation of nature par excellence. The automation of controlled processes could establish a new form of harmony between worker, work, product, and consumer. Technology in such a context would bear little resemblance to the nineteenth-century factory. Alienation is not a result of technology per se; this is the message of technological music. It is not for nought that electronic music so frequently sounds like a protest against alienation in technological society.

Technology's concrete, capitalist "form of appearance" (Marx) or ontological "form of presence" (Heidegger) must be transformed. Within the categories which define the social fabric, the creatively human must be effectively distinguished from the repetitively mechanical. Ideally, a new structure could thereby coalesce in which people are no longer mere adjuncts to machinery or receptacles for commodities. New economic ties

319

would be a first prerequisite for such different relations among beings. In its contrast to industrial applications, the thoughtful and appropriate adaptation of electronics to musical endeavors, free of over-powering profit constraints, suggests that technology elsewhere can also foster Marx's goal of a humanized nature and a naturalized humanity or Heidegger's vision of a unity of the mortal and the holy, nature and the heavens.

However, art can never effect social change by itself. Those art forms which could instill revolutionary consciousness cannot, by their nature, become widely accepted until material transformations are at least well under way. But to those few individuals who have both the intellectual energy and the economic autonomy necessary, works of art can speak as witnesses of objective potential.

The problem of reaching a wide enough audience has yet to be solved. All that has been shown is that neither pandering to the habits of the public nor ignoring them, neither accepting given techniques nor ignoring half-concealed potentials, can succeed. Art must relate to the historical context of its desired audience and appropriately interpret the truth of its own medium.

VIII. *Hymns for tomorrow*

Within the tradition of rock music, Jimi Hendrix's rendition of "The Star-Spangled Banner,"[6] performed at the Woodstock concert, goes a long way toward this goal. Unlike most protest songs, this piece does not rely on lyrics; no imported rhetoric, revolutionary slogans, or faddish symbols were necessary. The explosion of notes into the screams of napalm spiraling downward toward its victims forced social and musical questions upon the listeners in subculture America of 1969: What are we doing in Vietnam? Where has our beloved national anthem gone? How can a man with a skinny guitar produce such complex, sliding, noisy, vibrating sounds? You call that music?

The interpretation's critical sytle establishes a distance, which is carried over to political allegiances. By simply exploring the anthem with its historical connotations, Hendrix's guitar makes it clear that American involvement in Vietnam was no accident. The reasons are already present in the song as part of America's heritage. Hendrix is merely the mediator, interpreting an historical text in a manner suited to a contemporary audience.

The interpretation is appropriate musically as well as politically. In translating from piano to electric guitar, Hendrix does not press the simple, most ordinary elements into the handy mold of established guitar techniques and ignore what was originally unique and significant, the way much adaptation and improvisation proceeds. He uses the occasion to explore the qualities peculiar to his own instrument. He constantly moves

320

from the clear, melodic notes of the piano original to the distortion, vibration, noise, and feed-back characteristic of the electric guitar. Rather than suppressing these effects, he encourages them to develop to the point at which they completely annihilate the pitched tones. Yet they are never uncontrolled. They unfold in precise patterns of rhythmic complexity and tonal variety.

The most traditional music is here transformed into a vibrant electronic composition. The rhythm and intensity which often serve an ideological function in hard rock, making thought impossible under the guise of excluding parents and other outsiders, functions critically instead. The violence which melody struggles to confine and conceal is now released. The listener, grasped through his familiar childhood music and shaken by elements of adolescent rock, is confronted with the difficult reality of maturity.

Hendrix was not an electronic music composer, although he experimented extensively with electronic modifications of his guitar and succeeded in creating powerful sonorities in his music. His strength was in his interpretational skill; his fingers had absorbed something from every socially critical tradition. Recent releases of early recordings show that he was musically more advanced than his popular recordings indicate; the worst contradictions of commercial music caught him in a grip in which he could not survive. Yet, he revealed a dynamic in rock which is still being both discovered and co-opted — a tendency toward what is at work in the electronic music tradition, with the difference that it would have to be more spontaneously expressive and would seek to attract a larger following. Hendrix may have proven the incompatibility of these strivings in our world.

Stockhausen's *Hymnen*[7] shows how an electronic composer has dealt with the same material as Hendrix chose for Woodstock. In this piece, Stockhausen composes sounds with varying degrees of disorder and noise. The requirements of intelligibility thereby assert themselves forcefully and freshly, rather than being imposed in their traditional, petrified form of harmonic, melodic, rhythmic laws.

Over a period of two hours, *Hymnen* moves from the static of short-wave radio distortion and a jumble of international broadcasts to a utopian world-wide cultural peace by means of electronic control and transformation. The work uses splicing and synthesizing techniques to handle and imitate national music, characteristic sounds, and various noises from around the world. Not only are the musical qualities of familiar national anthems presented with unaccustomed force, but the flavor of their local performance is also clearly articulated. References to "The Star-Spangled Banner" conjure up the exaggerated pomp and pompous chauvinism of American sports events, political rallies, and elementary school assemblies.

Within the symphonic structure of the whole, snatches of

immediately recognizable anthems function in place of melodic theme, while they shift register, intensity, and timbre from point to point. Pitch sequences are taken from original scores and used to determine relative amplitudes or durations instead. Purely electronic passages, found material, poetic vocal structures, silences, and the controlled noise of wind, waves, crowds, and breathing are interwoven in a manner reminiscent of Webern's instrumental compositions.

Perhaps most intriguing in Stockhausen's transformation of "The Star-Spangled Banner" is his use of well-known music as raw material for electronic creation. Rather than selecting pure sine-waves at given frequencies, adding overtone structures, and arranging them in temporal sequences, Stockhausen works from complex but more or less recognizable acoustic sources, adjusting their pitch and volume according to need.

The manipulation of familiar material seems to provide a natural way of appealing to a broad audience and introducing a twentieth-century sensibility. Unfortunately, electronic compositions, following the lead of Schoenberg and Webern, tend to use German and French verse or to cite musical sources which are esoteric by American standards. They suggest, however, analogous compositional procedures which would analyze idiomatic language and popular tunes, appealing to those excluded from the elite of consumers and re-presenting to the senses the flavor of our aural life. Further, the reflection of conventional sounds in an electronic context audibly demonstrates the awesome power of technological media to restructure perception for their own purposes.

Here, as in general, the electronic means of production permit totally new ways of working with sound, different conceptions of music, and a fresh perspective on tradition. Inhabiting the auditory realm, electronic music has broad implications. It encourages an origin-al way of creatively dwelling in the world, of existentially understanding contemporary Being, and of receptively anticipating a new epoch. When perceived as situated in industrial society, electronic music, like Heideggerian philosophy, evokes a radically different form of technology without enunciating its necessarily post-capitalist character or proposing a strategy for realizing the appropriate material context.

NOTES

1   I have argued for the relevance of this task in "The Jargon of Authenticity: An Introduction to a Marxist Critique of Heidegger," *boundary 2,* 3 (Winter 1975). The general problematic, which is pursued in the present article in terms of a specific phenomenon, was discussed with reference to the original texts of Marx and Heidegger in my Ph.D. dissertation, "Marxian Hermeneutics and Heideggerian Social Theory: Interpreting and Transforming Our World," Northwestern University 1975.

2   Explicit social analyses of Heidegger and of music lead too far afield for this essay. I rely largely on the work of Theodor W. Adorno. His reflections on Heidegger's position can be found in *The Jargon of Authenticity* (Evanston: Northwestern University Press, 1973) and in *Negative Dialectics* (New York: Seabury, 1973). Adorno's critique of American popular music is most accessible in "The Culture Industry: Enlightenment as Mass Deception," *Dialectic of Enlightenment* (New York: Seabury, 1972) and "Perennial Fashion — Jazz," *Prisms* (London: Spearman, 1967).

3   Examples of rigorous theoretical considerations abound in Stockhausen's *Texte* (in German), Xenaxis' *Formalized Music*, Boulez' *Boulez on Music Today*, and the articles by Stockhausen and others in issues of *Die Reihe* (in English) and *Perspectives of New Music*. Naturally, each of these composers stresses his own concerns, and views history through them. An objective, unsituated, empirical study of the movement I label electronic music would be far less interesting than these engaged intellectual struggles with the musical material, even if such a study were feasible. My own analysis is consciously informed by Heideggerian and Marxian conceptualizations and is directed toward the present American situation. It hopes to carry social force precisely by being a personal statement. While aimed at expressing my perception of actual electronic works, it makes no claim to being an empirical survey limited to what has already been realized. I take such an "unscientific" approach to be consonant with hermeneutic and materialistic principles.

4   Martin Heidegger, *Being and Time*, trans. John Macquarrie and Edward Robinson (New York: Harper & Row, 1962), p. 207. The quoted discussions all take place in the chapter on "Being-in as such." Further references will be incorporated in the text in parentheses as: BT. I take *Being and Time* as definitive of Heidegger's early (1927) position; his 1935 lecture on "The Origin of the Work of Art," translated in *Philosophies of Art and Beauty*, ed. Hofstadter and Kuhns (New York: Modern Library, 1964), as his basic statement on aesthetic themes; and the 1962 lecture, "Time and Being," in *On Time and Being* (New York: Harper & Row, 1972), as his final summary.

5   Theodor W. Adorno, "Vers une musique informelle" in *Quasi una Fantasia* (Frankfurt: Suhrkamp, 1963), p. 432. This article and another in the same volume, "Musik und neue Musik," demonstrate that Adorno was far more open to electronic music than is generally thought. It now seems that the rigor of Adorno's aesthetic arguments and his personal contact with Stockhausen and Boulez stimulated progress in electronic music more than it was stunted by Adorno's controversial criticism of composers who leaped upon the Schoenberg or Webern bandwagon without retaining the creative sophistication of the masters.

6   For some reason this song was never promoted. It was released on the expensive *Woodstock* concert album and gained a certain popularity then. It was quietly rereleased in 1973 on a two-record album of "Soundtrack Recordings from the Film *Jimi Hendrix*" (Reprise Records). A different rendition of "The Star-Spangled Banner" was recorded five months before Woodstock for the movie *Rainbow Bridge* and released in 1971 as part of the sound track to that movie (again by Reprise).

7   *Hymnen* is available as a two-record album import on the prestigious Deutsche Grammophon Gesellschaft label with Stockhausen's liner notes in

three languages. Some people take all this as a sign of class character; the extent to which it is a result of the present record industry rather than of the music itself must, however, be questioned. Other works by Stockhausen, such as *Stimmung* (vocally produced music, whose title could be translated as "attunement") and *Mantra* (electronically modified piano music based on a twelve-tone series with an Indian influence) are more popular in America and may provide a less frustrating introduction to Stockhausen. It should be remembered that as sound his compositions are far more intricate than the theories which inspire them. For clear examples of electronic manipulation of given sounds, listen to *Gesang der Jünglinge* and *Beethoven Opus 1970*, which transform human voices and well-known passages from Beethoven, respectively. These works are all on the DGG label, but can often be found in university and public library record collections.

CONTRIBUTORS

Stanley Corngold is an associate professor of German at Princeton. He has published a translation of Kafka's *The Metamorphosis*, a study of that work called *The Commentators' Despair*, and other essays on Kafka, as well as on Rousseau, Thomas Mann, Musil, Kosinski, and Tarn.

Frances C. Ferguson is an assistant professor of English at The John Hopkins University in Baltimore. Her work deals primarily with the Romantic period; her book *Wordsworth: Language as Counter-Spirit* will appear later this year.

Michael Gelven is an associate professor of philosophy at Northern Illinois University. While on a Fulbright Fellowship he studied at the University of Freiburg in Breisgau, where he wrote his dissertation on the fundamental ontology of Martin Heidegger. He has published two books, *A Commentary on Heidegger's "Being and Time"* and *Winter, Friendship and Guilt: the Sources of Self-Inquiry*. Having completed his third book, *Eros and Tragedy*, he is now working on a book on dialectic.

Marjorie Grene, the well-known philosopher, is the author of a number of important pioneering critical studies of existentialism and phenomenology. She is now teaching at the University of California at Davis. Her recent books include *Spinoza, Sartre*, and *The Understanding of Nature: Essays in the Philosophy of Biology*.

Karsten Harries is a professor of philosophy at Yale University. The present essay is part of an ongoing attempt to determine the essence of the modern, especially of modern art and poetry. He has also published "Das befreite Nichts," in *Durchblicke. Martin Heidegger zum 80. Geburtstag*, and "Hegel on the Future of Art," in *The Review of Metaphysics*.

Albert Hofstadter is the author of *Agony and Epitaph: Man, his Art, and his Poetry* and *Truth and Art* and co-editor of *Philosophies of Art and Beauty*. His widely used translation, with an introduction, of several of Heidegger's seminal essays concerning literature and the arts appeared in 1971 as *Poetry, Language, Thought*. His recent study "Ownness and Identity: Re-Thinking Hegel" in *The Review of Metaphysics* (June 1975) will be of particular interest to readers of "Enownment." Mr. Hofstadter is now a professor of humanities at the University of California, Santa Cruz.

David Couzens Hoy is an associate professor of philosophy at Barnard College, Columbia University. In addition to articles dealing with Kant, Hegel, and Heidegger, he has written a book, *The Critical Circle*, on hermeneutical philosophy and literary criticism.

David Farrell Krell has translated Martin Heidegger's *Early Greek Thinking* with Frank A. Capuzzi. He is also translating Heidegger's two-volume study of Nietzsche. He is currently pursuing post-doctoral studies at Albert-Ludwigs-Universität-im-Breisgau.

Donald G. Marshall is an associate professor at the University of Iowa, where he teaches courses in critical theory. He is currently interested in Heidegger, Marxism, theory of narrative, and the problems of literary history and literature's historical context.

Richard E. Palmer, author of *Hermeneutics*, is presently at work on a book that relates philosophical hermeneutics to the development of a postmodern interpretive self-awareness. He is a professor of comparative literature and philosophy at MacMurray College in Illinois.

Joseph Riddel is a professor of English at UCLA. He has published studies on the poetry and poetics of Wallace Stevens, William Carlos Williams, and C. Day Lewis, and more than thirty essays in major periodicals. He currently holds a Guggenheim Fellowship for the study of American poetics from Poe to postmodernism.

Alvin H. Rosenfeld is director of Jewish Studies and professor of English at Indiana University. He is a contributing editor of *The American Poetry Review,* editor of *Collected Poems of John Wheelwright,* and co-editor of *Confronting the Holocaust: The Impact of Elie Wiesel.* He is author of a forthcoming large-scale study of Holocaust literature.

Reiner Schürmann is an associate professor of philosophy at the Graduate Faculty of the New School for Social Research in New York. His recent books include *Meister Eckhart: Mystic and Philosopher* and *Les Origines.* He has published numerous articles on phenomenology, Eastern and medieval Western mysticism, the theory of symbols, Meister Eckhart, and Heidegger in European and American journals.

Armand Schwerner has published several volumes of poetry: *The Tablets I-XV, The Tablets XVI-XVIII,* and *The Bacchae Sonnets.*

William V. Spanos is a professor of English and comparative literature at SUNY-Binghamton and co-editor of *boundary 2.* His article is a part of his forthcoming book on hermeneutics.

Gerry Stahl explored the Heideggerian tradition in Heidelberg and twentieth-century Marxist thought in Frankfurt. His interest in postmodern music was sparked by Adorno's social aesthetics. He currently works as a computer systems-programmer/analyst at Temple University.

Acknowledgements

The editors wish to thank Marjorie Grene for allowing us to reprint her translation of Heidegger's "Die Zeit des Weltbildes."

Many of the photographs of Heidegger used throughout this issue are reprinted, by permission of Rowohlt Taschenbuch Verlag GmbH and Professor Walter Biemel, from *Martin Heidegger* by Walter Biemel, copyright Rowohlt Taschenbuch Verlag GmbH, Reinbek bei Hamburg, 1963. The editors extend a special thanks to Martin Heidegger for allowing us to reprint a number of the original photographs of his early life and to Professor Biemel and David Farrell Krell for gathering these.

The photograph of Matisse's "The Shark and the Gull" (page 514) was taken by Louis Comtois.

The photographs of the Temple of Aphaia (500-490 B.C.) on the island of Aegina, appearing on the cover and the credits pages, were taken by William V. Spanos.

Publication of this issue was made possible in part by a grant from the Coordinating Council of Literary Magazines, through funds received from the New York State Council on the Arts.